T0152233

As a professional illustrator, I spend almost every day drawing. I always bring my sketchbook along wherever I go because you never know when you'll be presented with the opportunity to draw something new. Just like with any skill, the more you practice, the more you'll improve your abilities.

Please use this book as a reference whenever you're wondering how to draw a particular image. Keep it nearby whenever you draw. I've also included several "challenges" to help develop your skills along the way. Now grab a pencil and let's get started!

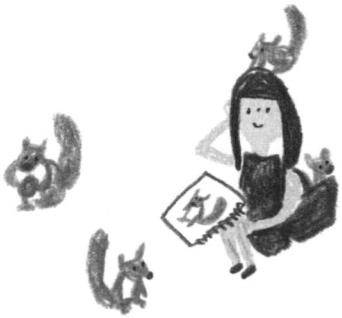

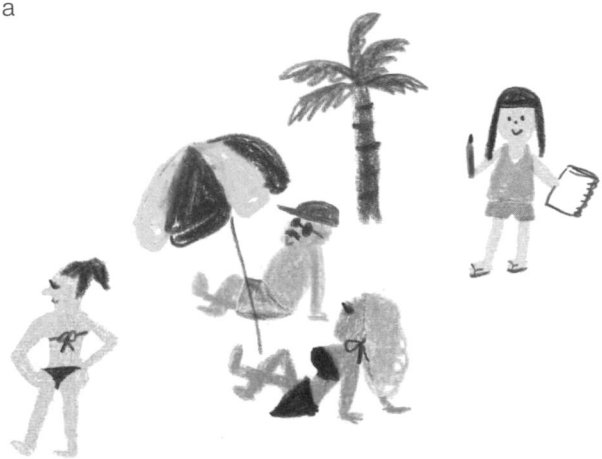

# Contents


**INTRODUCTION 4**

**GETTING STARTED 8**

Materials 8

Warm Up: Practice Drawing Lines 12

Warm Up: Practice Drawing Shapes 13

How to Use This Book 14

**ANIMALS 15**

Terrestrial Animals 16

Aquatic Animals & Fish 31

Birds 42

Bugs & Insects 48

Dinosaurs 54

*Challenge #1: Draw a Zoo 60*

Unidentified Mysterious Animals 62

**PEOPLE 65**

Faces 66

Expressions 68

Actions 69

People by Age & Gender 70

Clothing 84

Occupations 88

Famous Faces 94

**PLANTS 97**

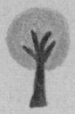

Trees 98

Shrubs 102

Flowers 105

Other Unique Plants 112

**FOODS 113**

Fruits 114

Vegetables 118

Main Dishes 126

Snacks 136

Drinks 141

*Challenge #2: Draw Bottles 141*

Packaged Foods 142

*Challenge #3: Draw Food Packaging 143*

*Challenge #4: Make a Food Journal 144*

# HOW TO DRAW ALMOST EVERYTHING

**Quarto.com**

© 2013 miyatachika

Original Japanese edition published by SEIBUNDO SHINKOSHA PUBLISHING CO., LTD
English language licensed by World Book Media LLC, USA via Tuttle-Mori Agency, Inc., Tokyo, Japan.
English translation and production by World Book Media LLC
Email: info@worldbookmedia.com

First published in the United States of America in 2016 by
Quarry Books, an imprint of
Quarto Publishing Group USA Inc.
100 Cummings Center
Suite 265-D
Beverly, Massachusetts 01915-6101
Telephone: (978) 282-9590
Fax: (978) 283-2742
Quarto.com

All rights reserved. No part of this book may be reproduced in any form without written permission of the copyright owners. All images in this book have been reproduced with the knowledge and prior consent of the artists concerned, and no responsibility is accepted by producer, publisher, or printer for any infringement of copyright or otherwise, arising from the contents of this publication. Every effort has been made to ensure that credits accurately comply with information supplied. We apologize for any inaccuracies that may have occurred and will resolve inaccurate or missing information in a subsequent reprinting of the book.

Quarry Books titles are also available at discount for retail, wholesale, promotional, and bulk purchase. For details, contact the Special Sales Manager by email at specialsales@quarto.com or by mail at The Quarto Group, Attn: Special Sales Manager, 100 Cummings Center, Suite 265-D, Beverly, MA 01915-6101. USA.

30 29 28 27 26 25

ISBN: 978-1-63159-140-2

Translator: Ai Toyoda
English Language Editor: Lindsay Fair

Printed in China

# HOW TO DRAW ALMOST EVERYTHING

## AN ILLUSTRATED SOURCEBOOK

CHIKA MIYATA

QUARRY

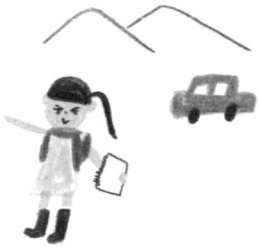

# Introduction

I was inspired to create this book after a friend confided that she could not draw as well as she wished whenever her kids asked her to draw pictures for them. Like my friend, many people get confused and frustrated when they draw. Maybe they're not sure where to start, or maybe they doubt their abilities.

To help my friend and others like her, I have developed a simple technique that breaks down every illustration into basic steps. Once you get started, you'll see how fun drawing can be. In fact, I feel that this book teaches you to enjoy drawing more, rather than how to draw better.

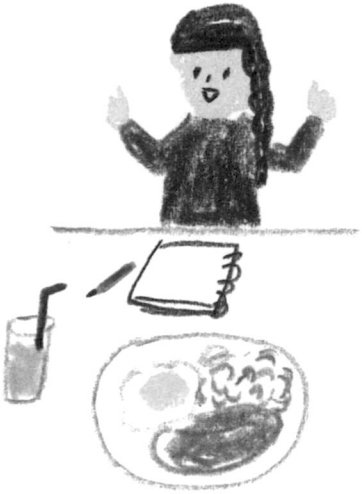

**AROUND THE HOUSE 145**

Entryway 146

Kitchen 147

Living Room 152

Bedroom 154

Study 155

Bathroom 156

Patio 159

Home Maintenance 160

*Challenge #5: Draw Windows and Doors 160*

**ARCHITECTURE AND SITES 161**

Around the Neighborhood 162

*Challenge #6: Draw a Street Map 167*

Famous Sites in Japan 168

Famous Sites Around the World 171

**VEHICLES 177**

On the Road 178

On the Tracks 192

In the Air 195

*Challenge #7: Draw Vehicles and Landscapes 198*

On the Water 200

Other Vehicles 205

**SEASONS 209**

Everyday Events 210

*Challenge #8: Illustrate Your Date Book 211*

Holidays & Seasonal Events 212

Weather 215

Chinese Zodiac 218

Astrological Signs 219

*Challenge #9: Draw Scenes from Your Favorite Movies 220*

*Challenge #10: Animal Alphabet 221*

**AUTHOR'S NOTE 222**

**ABOUT THE AUTHOR 223**

## Materials

This guide introduces the various drawing materials used in this book. Choosing the correct drawing instrument is important because it influences the syle of your drawing, but not to worry...there are so many options available today. I recommend that you experiment with different materials in order to find your favorites.

### Materials Key

*Look for these icons on the first page of each chapter. They indicate which drawing material was used for each category of illustrations. Use the suggested material to replicate the illustration in the book, or experiment with your favorite drawing supplies.*

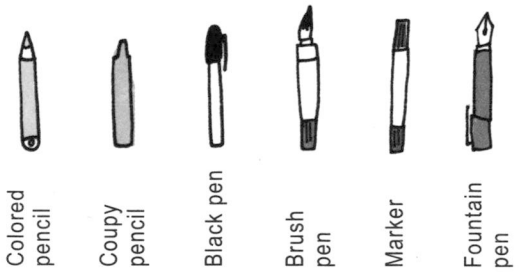

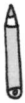

## Colored Pencils

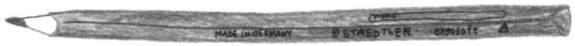

Staedtler Ergosoft: Hard lead. Good for small details.

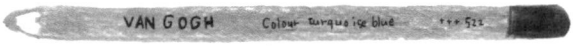

Royal Talens Van Gogh: Beautiful color.

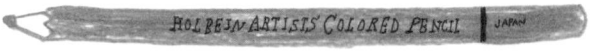

Holbein Artists': Wide range of colors available. Can be used with Holbein Meltz to create watercolor effect.

Faber-Castell Polychromos: My favorite black colored pencil.

## Coupy Pencils

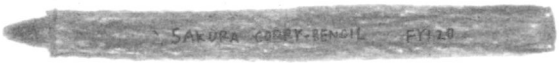

Sakura Coupy Pencil: Woodless colored pencil with the brilliance and texture of a crayon.

## Black Pens

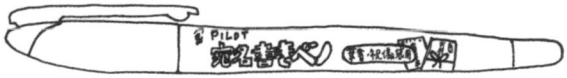


Pilot Envelope Address Writing Gel Ink: Oil-based pen that dries fast and produces dark, shiny lines.

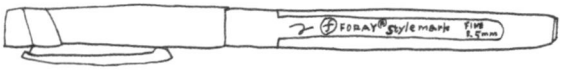


FORAY Stylemark 0.5 mm: Quick-drying pen that resists smearing. Great for lefties!

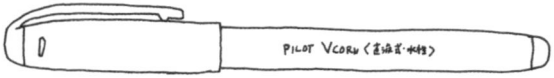


Pilot V CORN: Liquid ink rollerball pen with cone-shaped tip.

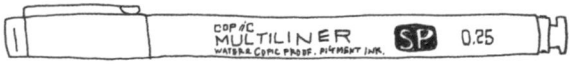


Copic Multiliner SP 0.25: Produces a thin line perfect for small details.

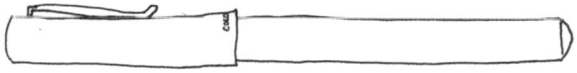

Itoya Paper Skater: Super smooth ink flow makes drawing easy.

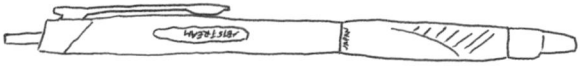

Uni Jetstream Standard: Offers a flexible, smooth feel.

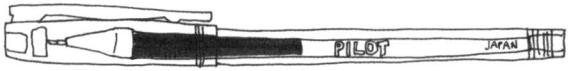


Pilot Hi-Tec-C: Gel pen with a comfortable grip.

## Markers

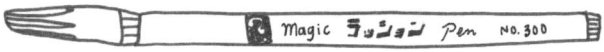


Teranishi Magic Ink: Fine-tipped permanent marker that does not bleed. Excellent for drawing details.

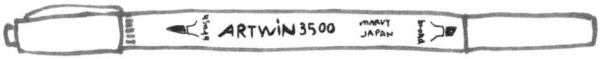


Marvy Uchida Artwin 3500: Dual-tipped water-based marker.

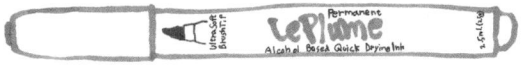


Marvy Uchida Le Plume Permanent: Features a soft, brushlike tip. Good for coloring large areas.

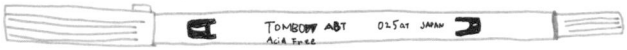


Tombow ABT Brush Pen: Dual-tipped marker with fine point and brush-style tips.

## Brush Pens

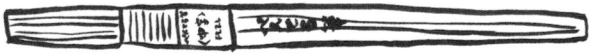

Pentel Medium Tip: Nylon brush tip good for thick, bold sketches.

## Fountain Pens

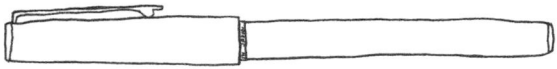

Sailor Young Profit Medium Nib: Reasonably priced fountain pen with a simple design.

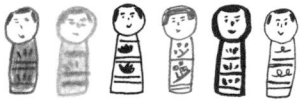

## Warm Up: Practice Drawing Lines

Draw different styles of lines, such as squiggly lines, wavy lines, and jagged lines. Use lines to express movement or mood within your drawings.

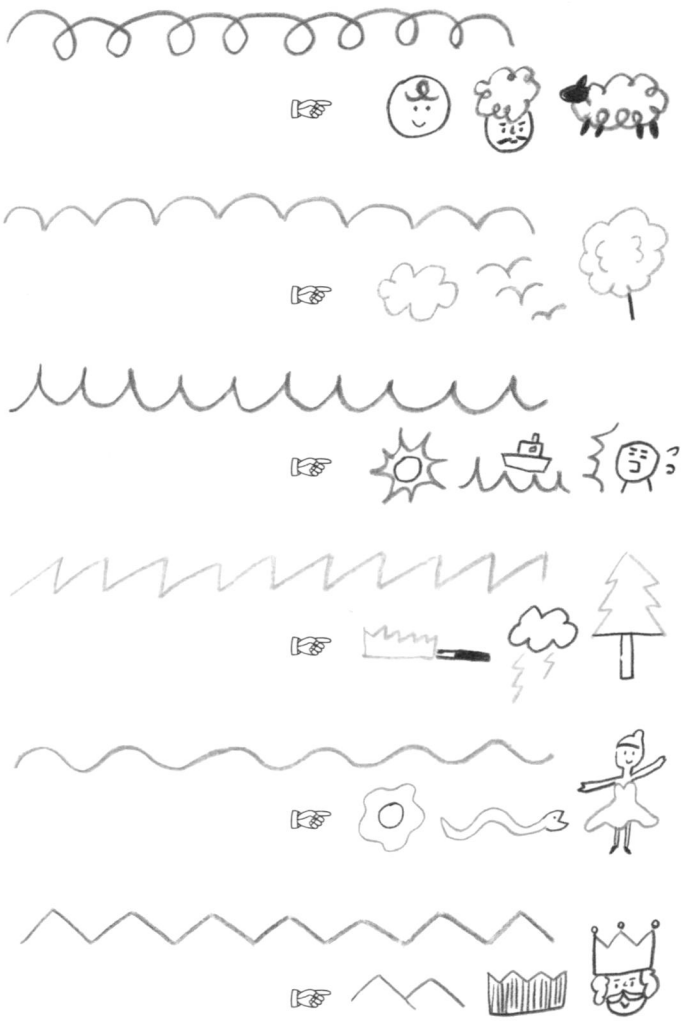

## Warm Up: Practice Drawing Shapes

Most illustrations start out with a basic shape, such as a circle, triangle, or square. Add lines and other details to transform a basic shape into a finished object.

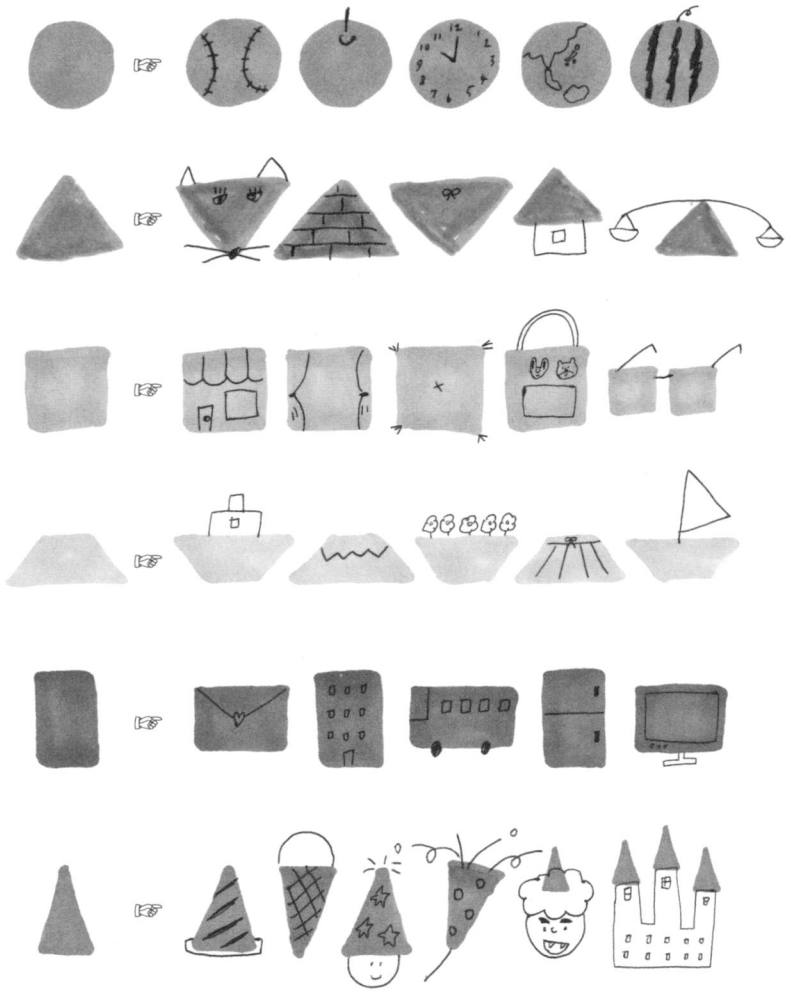

# How to Use This Book

## The Drawing Process

Most of the entries in this book include step-by-step illustrations that show the drawing process from start to finish. Some of the more advanced entries, or those which are variations of other entries, are not broken down into individual steps. Simply trace the image to practice drawing these entries.

Step-by-step illustration

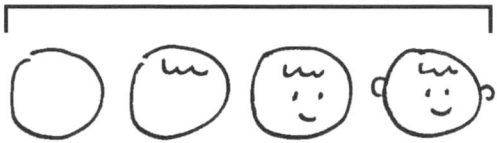

Start Finish

Variation

Advanced variation

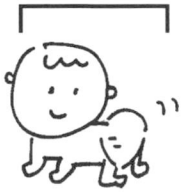

# Animals


Terrestrial Animals

Aquatic Animals & Fish

Birds

Bugs & Insects

Dinosaurs

Unidentified Mysterious Animals

# Terrestrial Animals

*Adding details like fur texture and pattern will help make your animal drawings more realistic.*

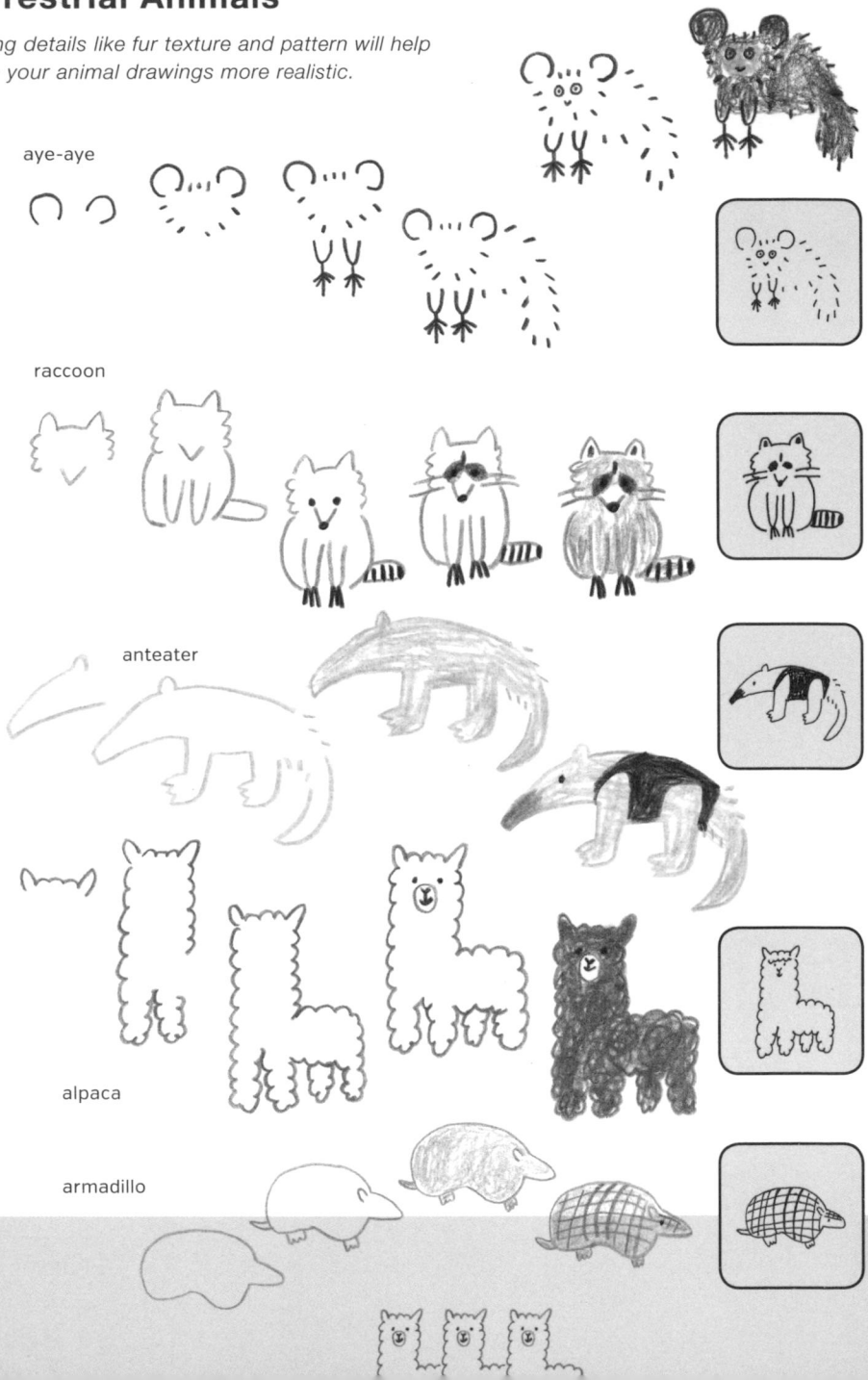

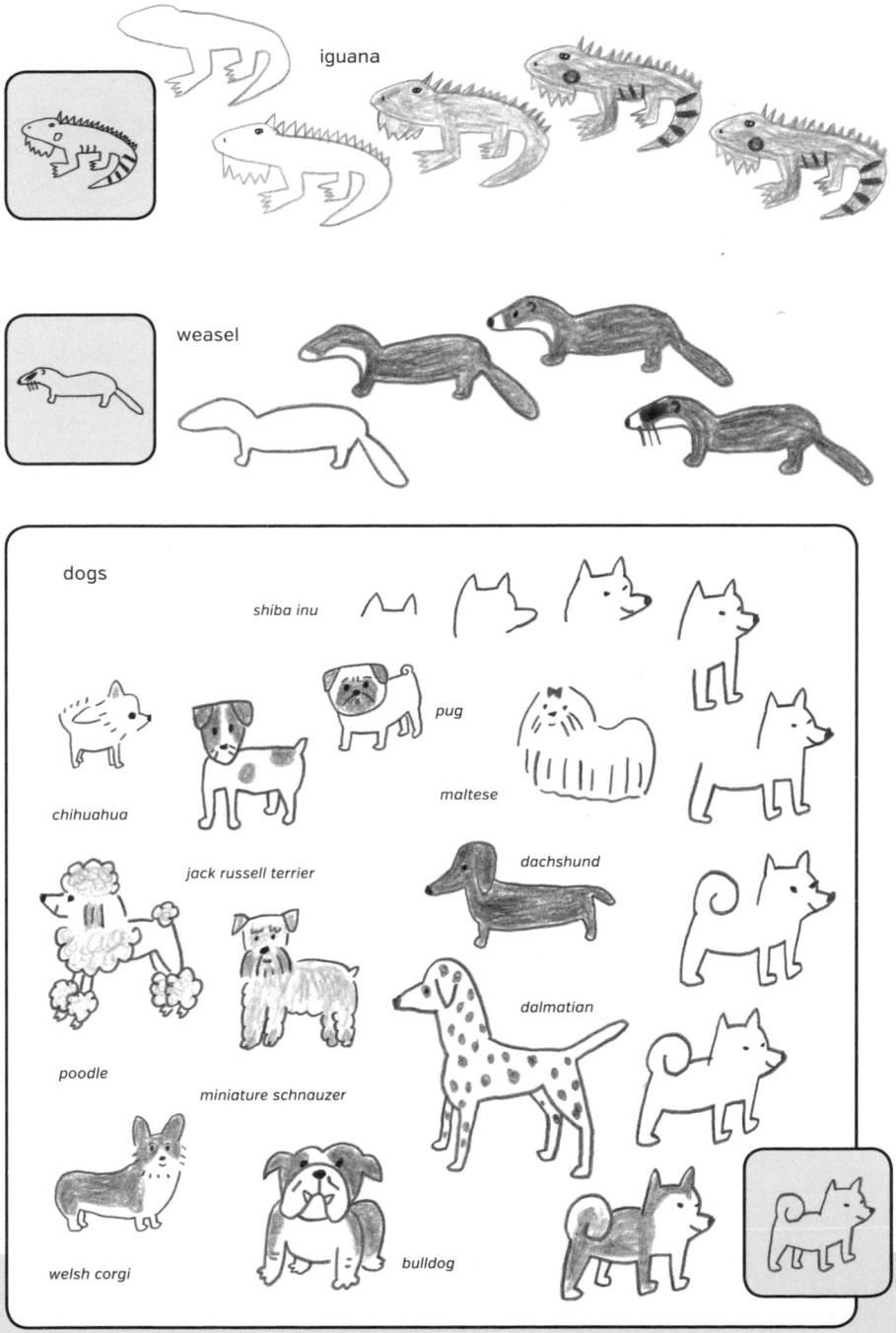
iguana
weasel
dogs
shiba inu
pug
chihuahua
maltese
jack russell terrier
dachshund
poodle
dalmatian
miniature schnauzer
welsh corgi
bulldog

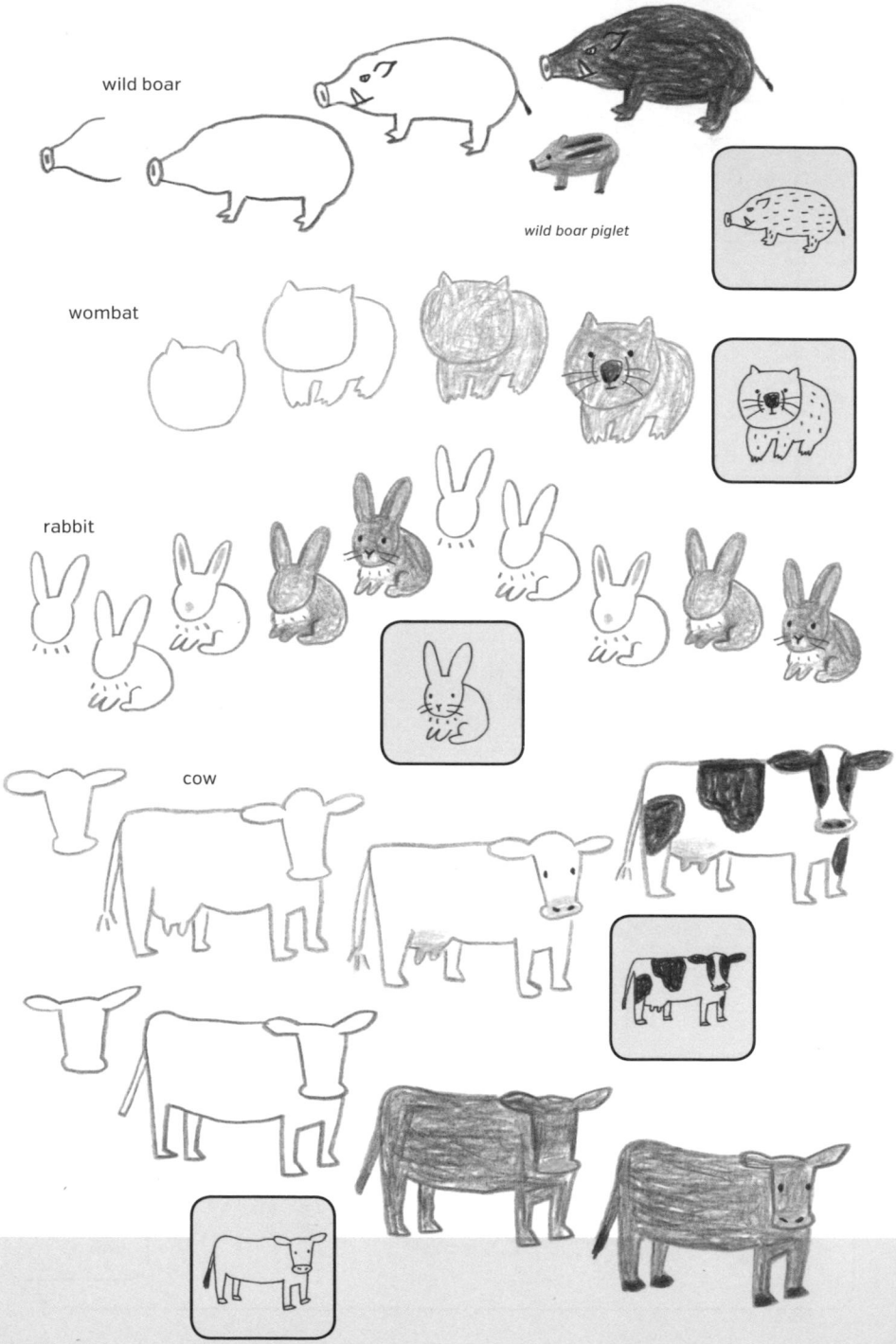
wild boar
wild boar piglet
wombat
rabbit
cow

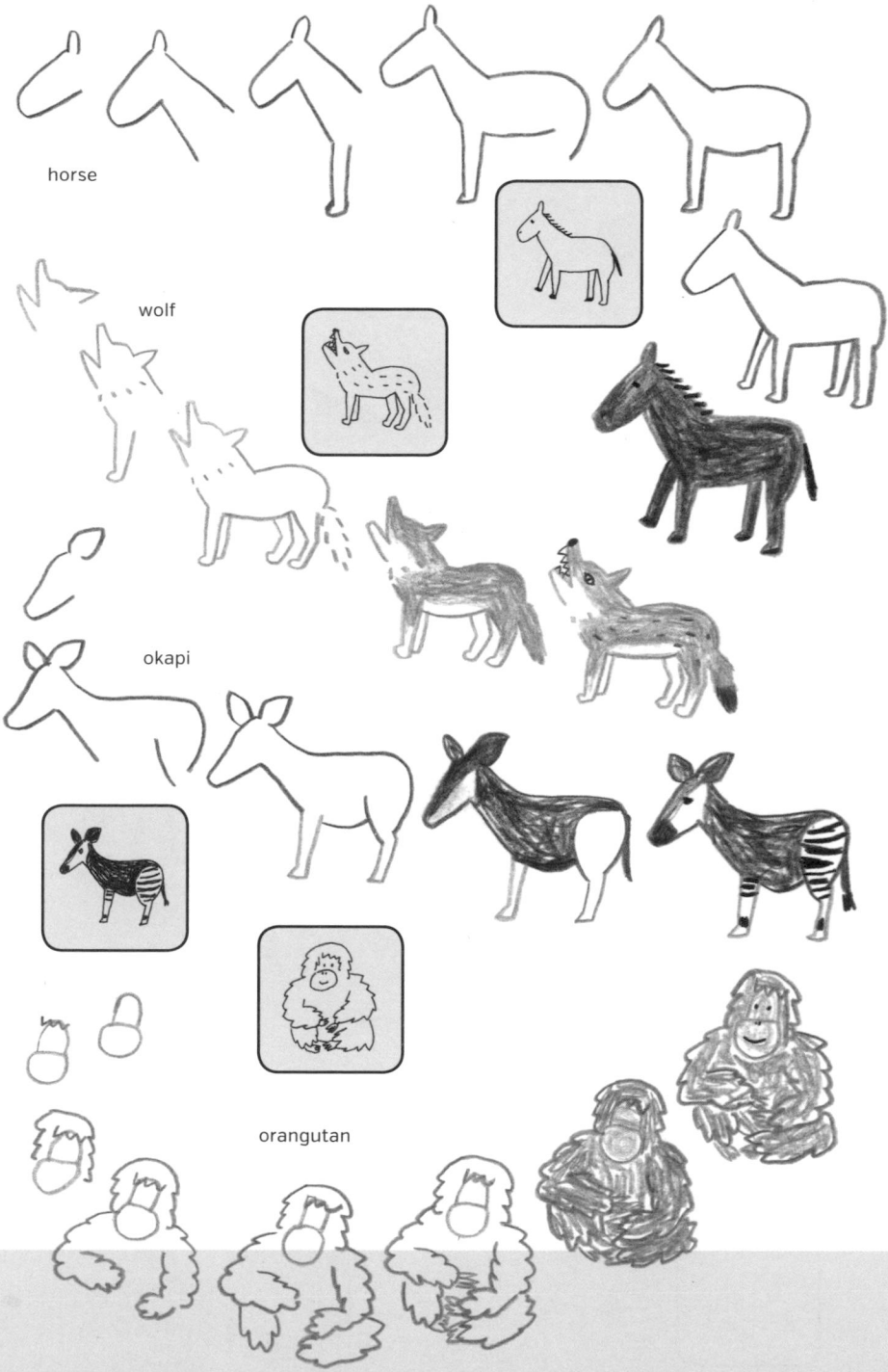
horse
wolf
okapi
orangutan

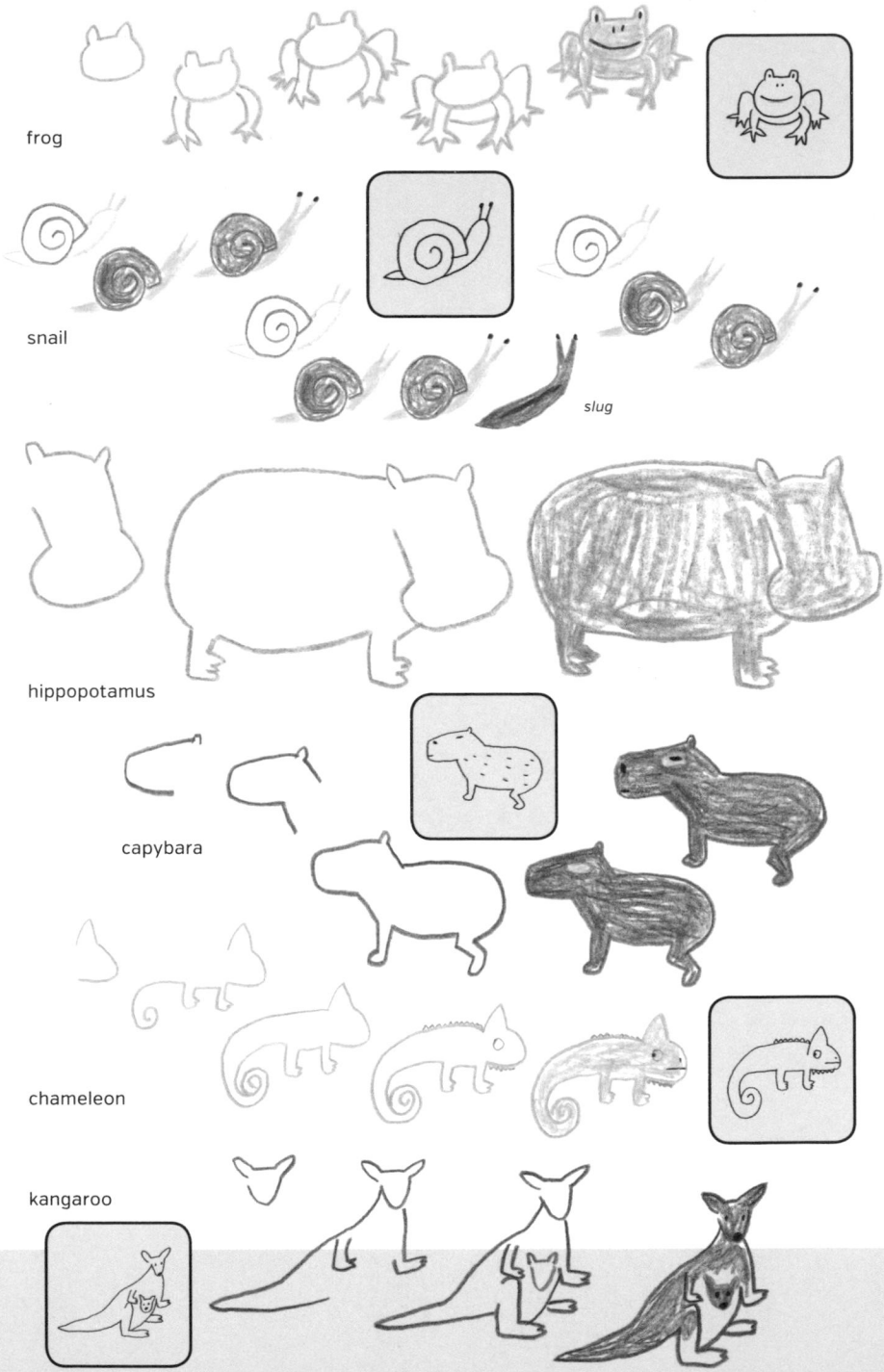
frog
snail
slug
hippopotamus
capybara
chameleon
kangaroo

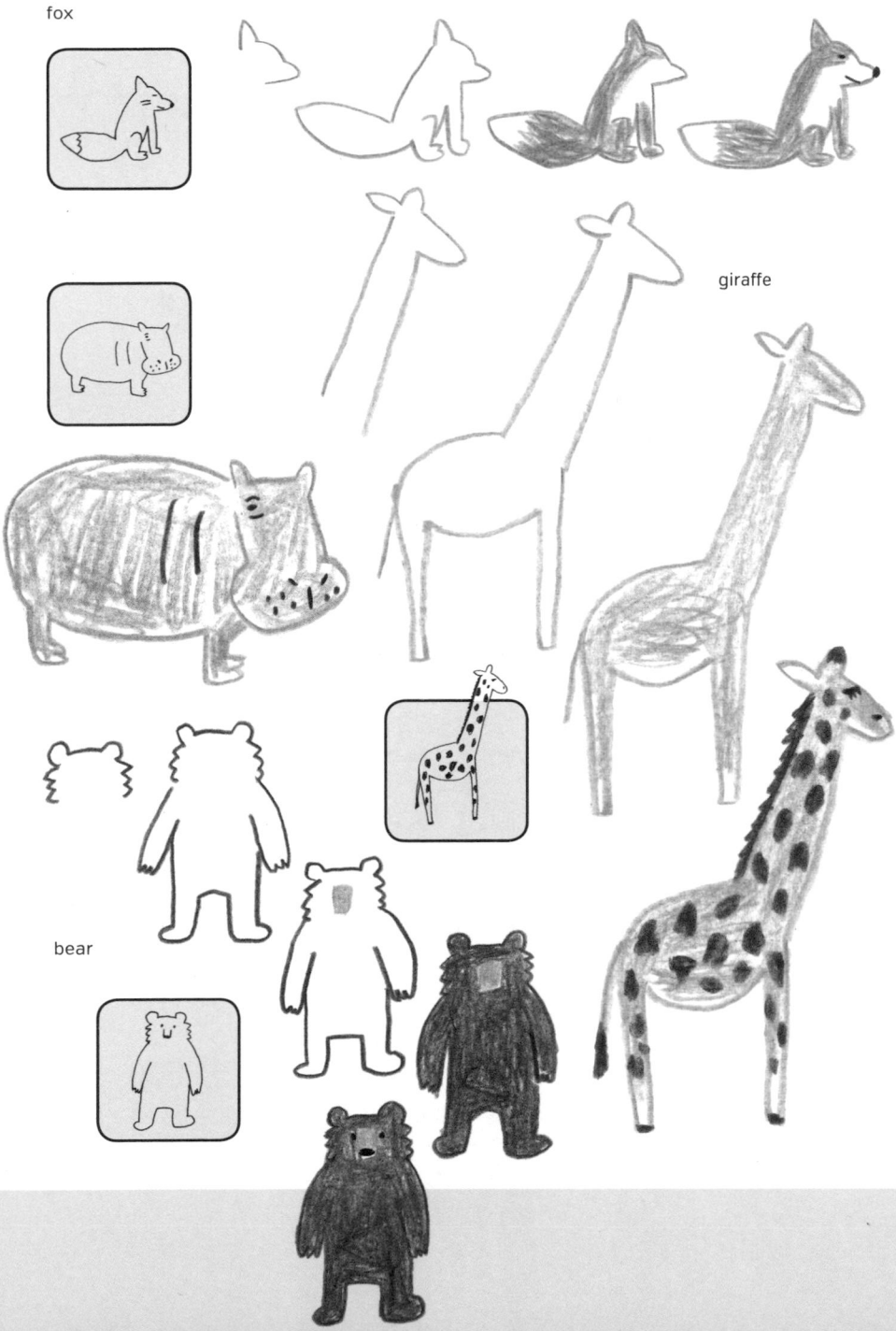
fox
giraffe
bear

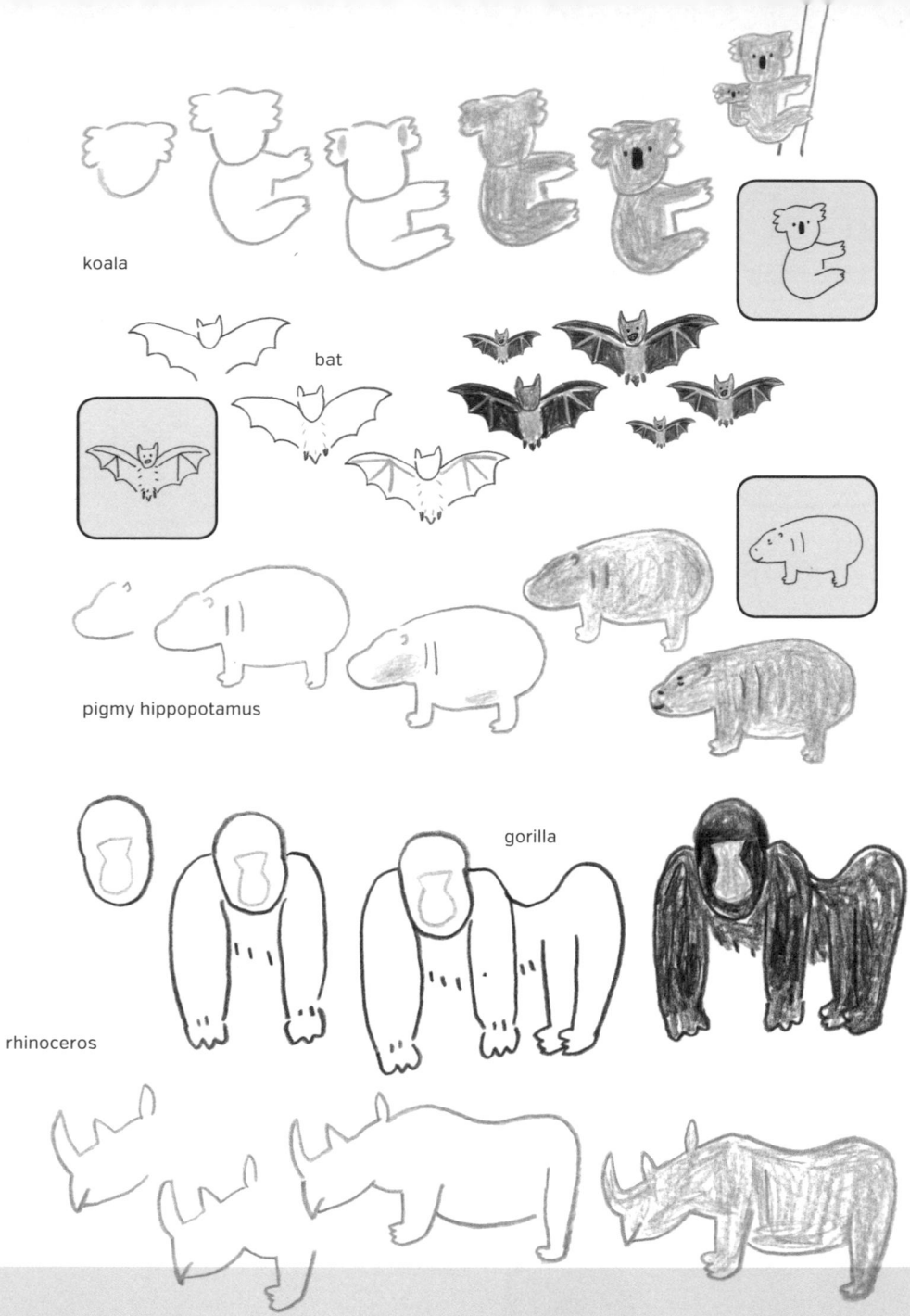
koala
bat
pigmy hippopotamus
gorilla
rhinoceros

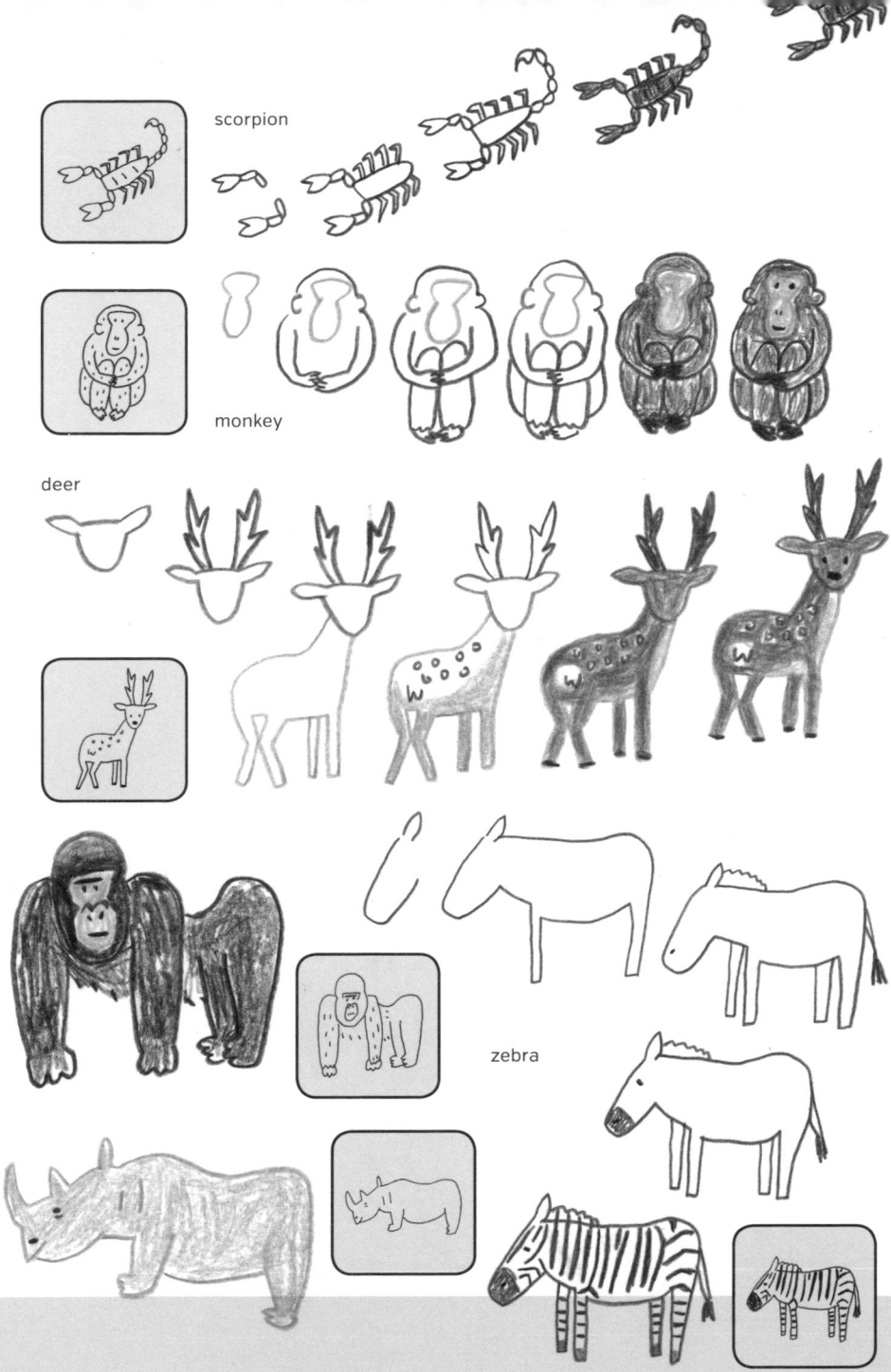
scorpion
monkey
deer
zebra

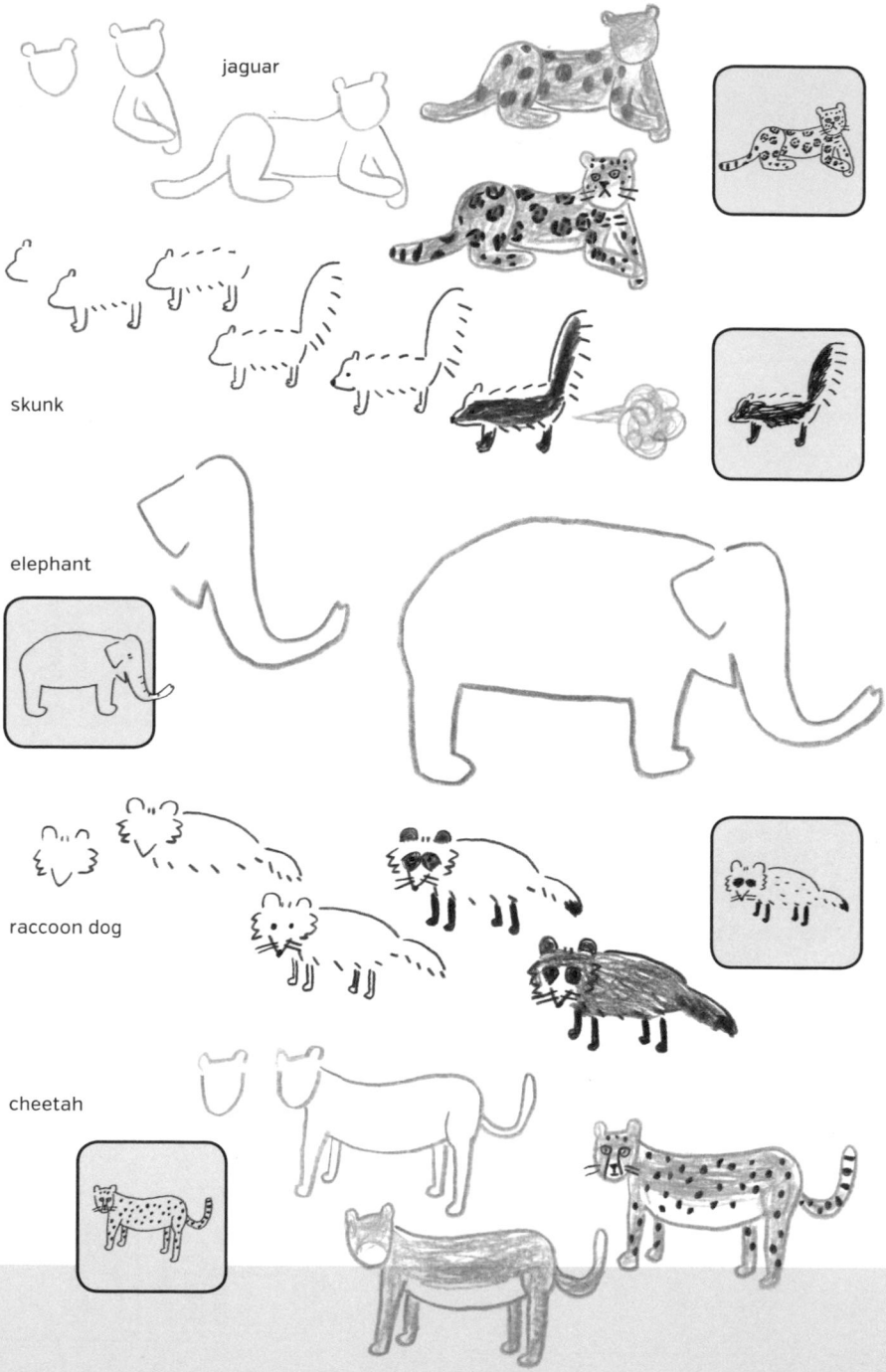
jaguar
skunk
elephant
raccoon dog
cheetah

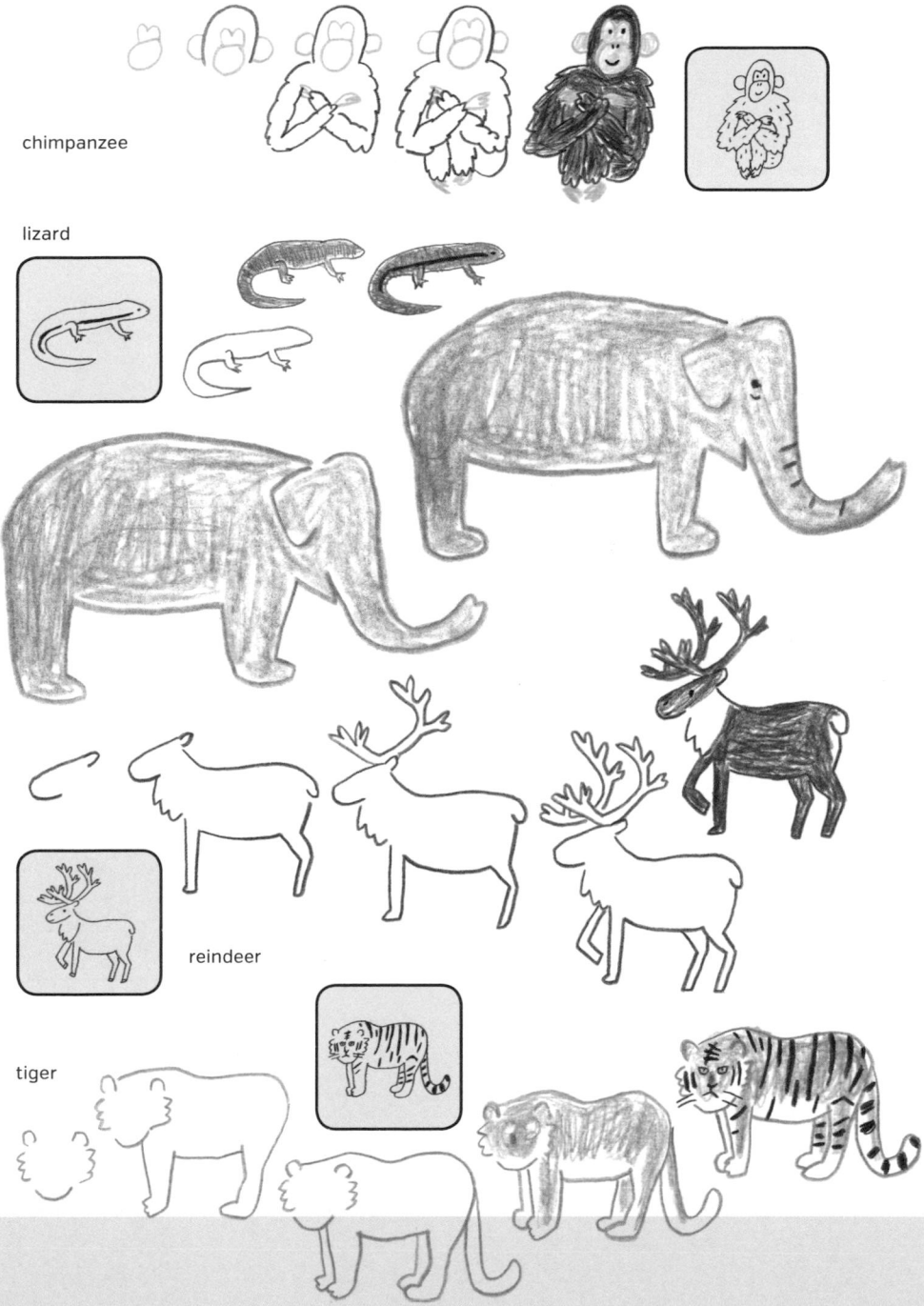
chimpanzee
lizard
reindeer
tiger

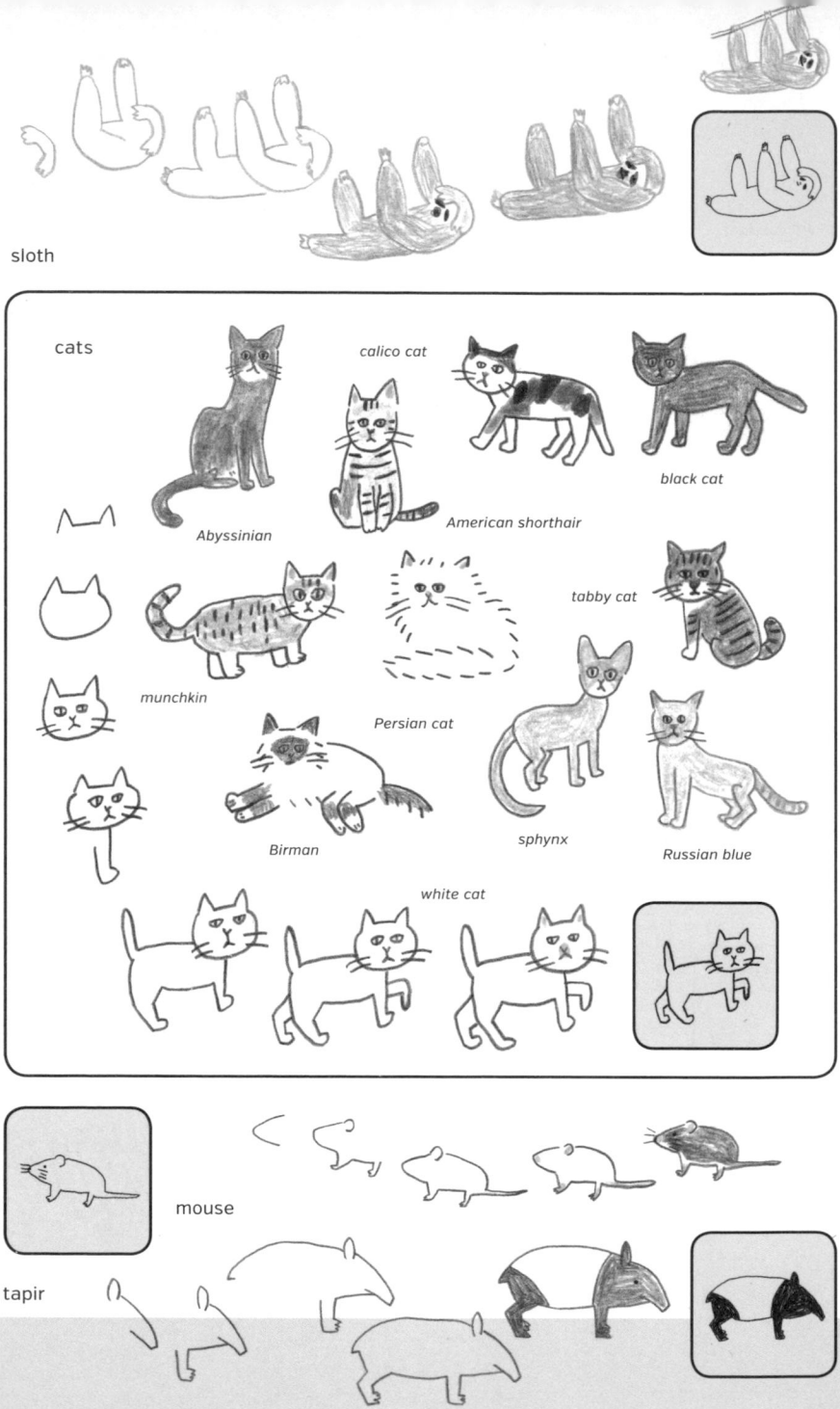
sloth
cats
calico cat
black cat
Abyssinian
American shorthair
tabby cat
munchkin
Persian cat
Birman
sphynx
Russian blue
white cat
mouse
tapir

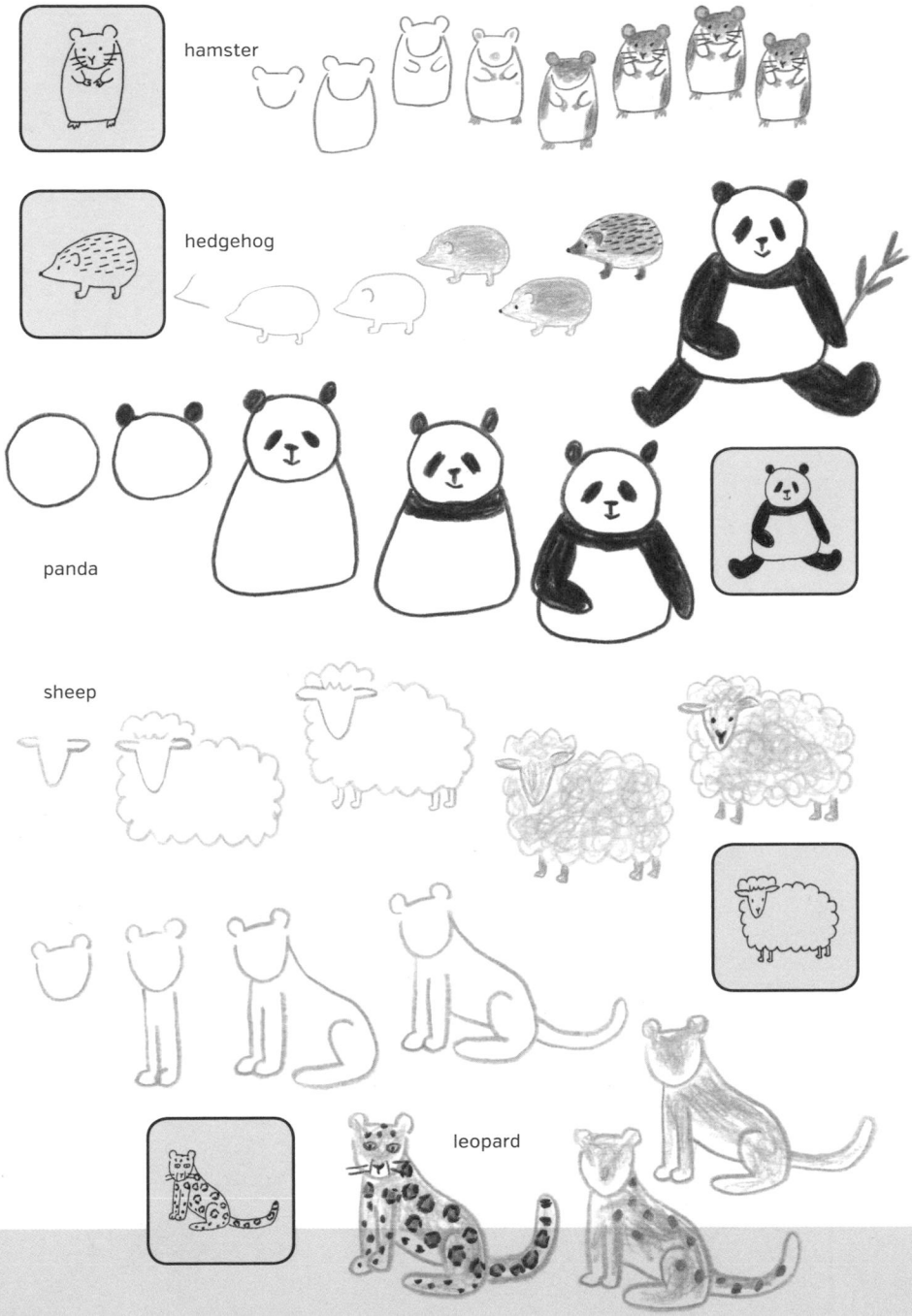
hamster
hedgehog
panda
sheep
leopard

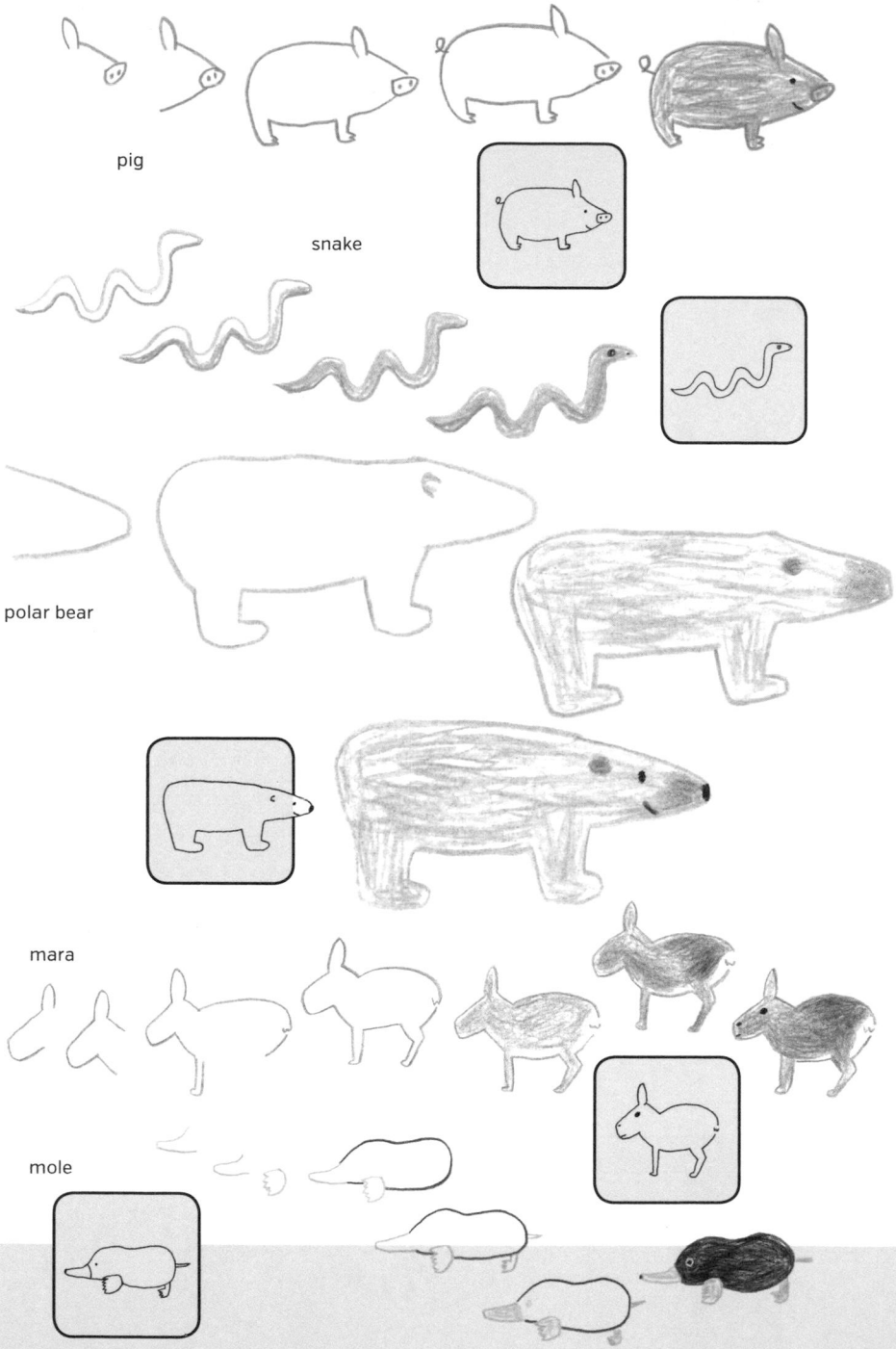
pig
snake
polar bear
mara
mole

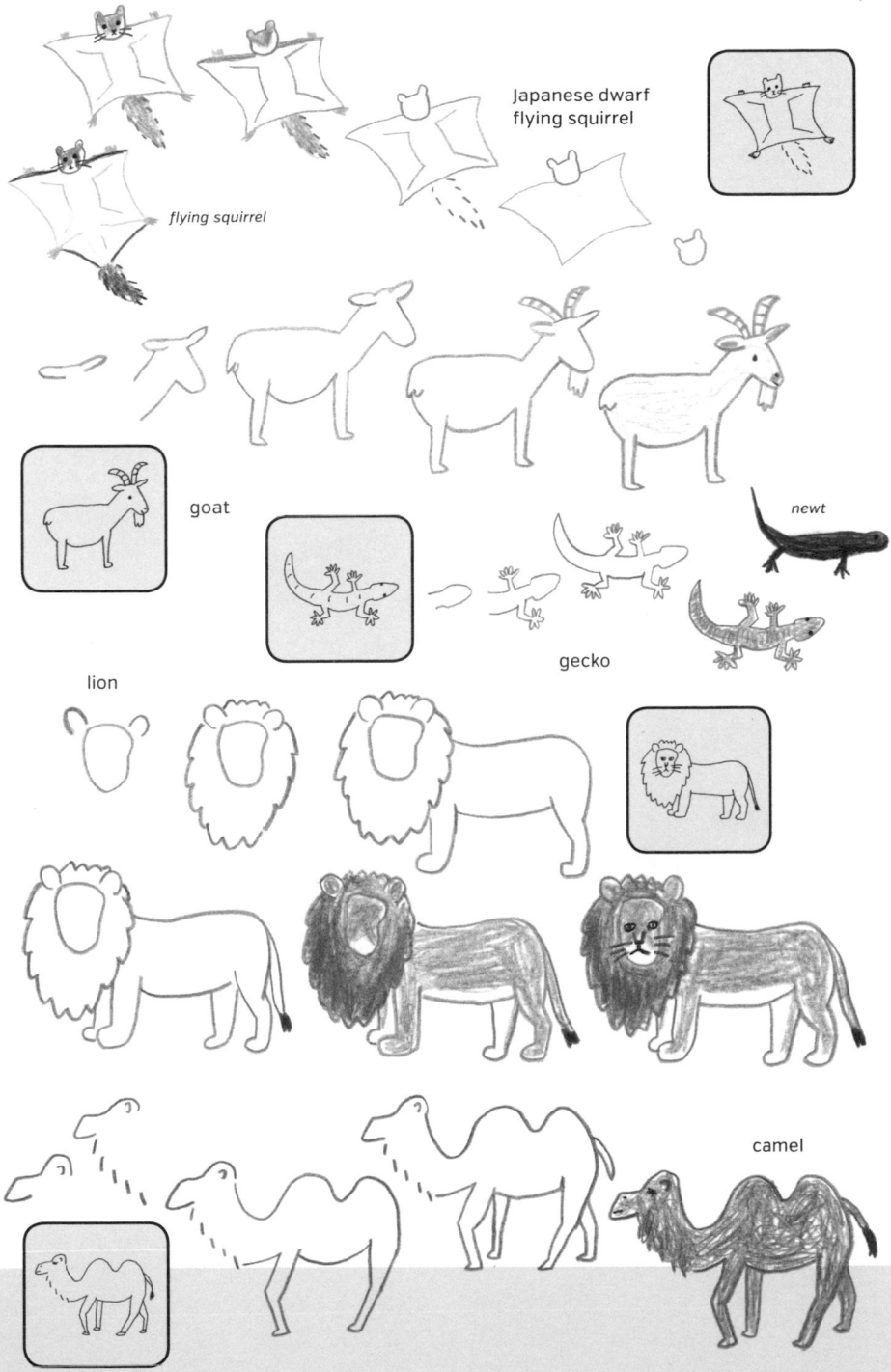
Japanese dwarf
flying squirrel
flying squirrel
goat
newt
gecko
lion
camel

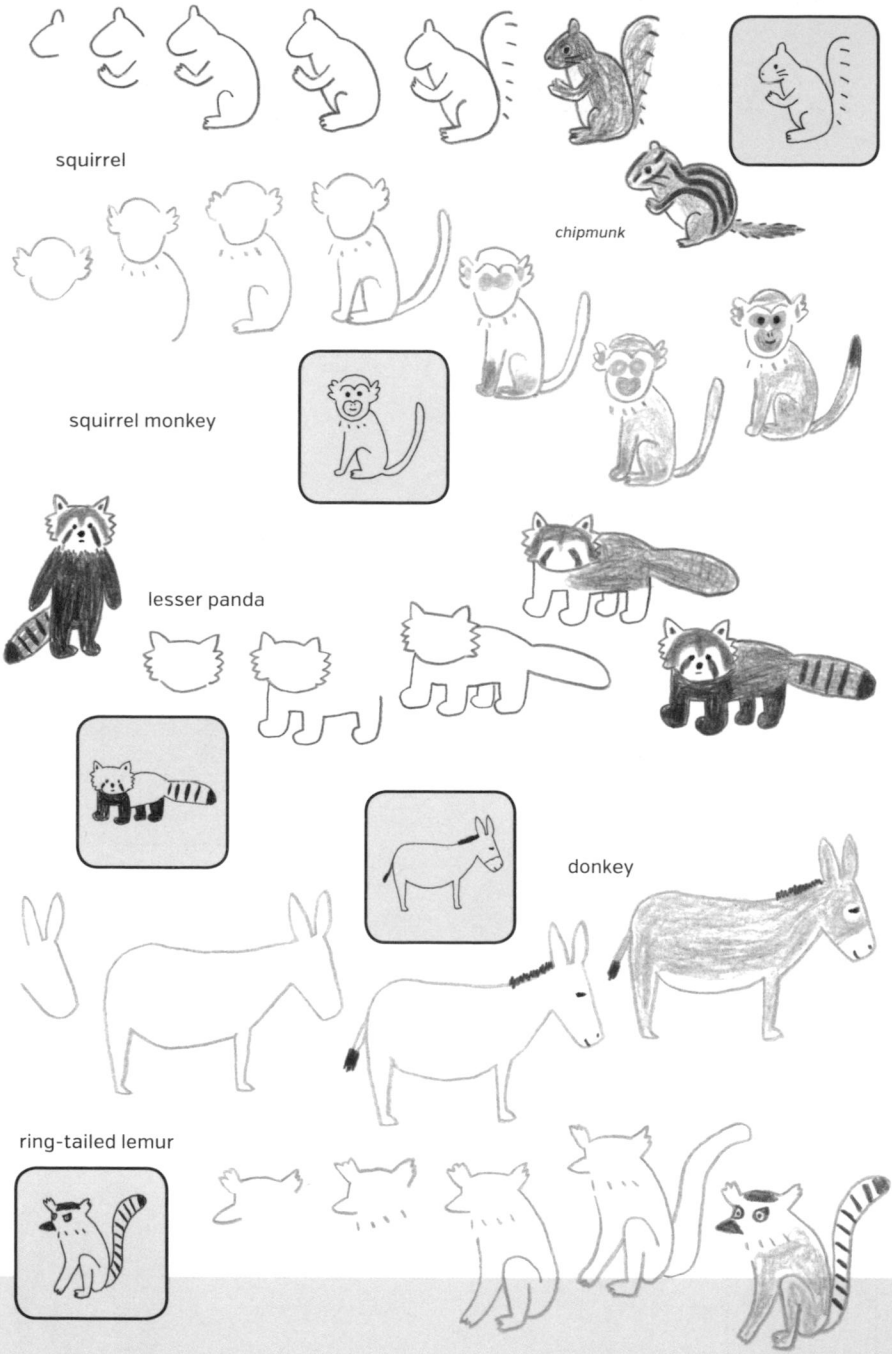
squirrel
chipmunk
squirrel monkey
lesser panda
donkey
ring-tailed lemur

# Aquatic Animals & Fish

*Use a felt-tipped pen to lend your drawings an underwater impression.*

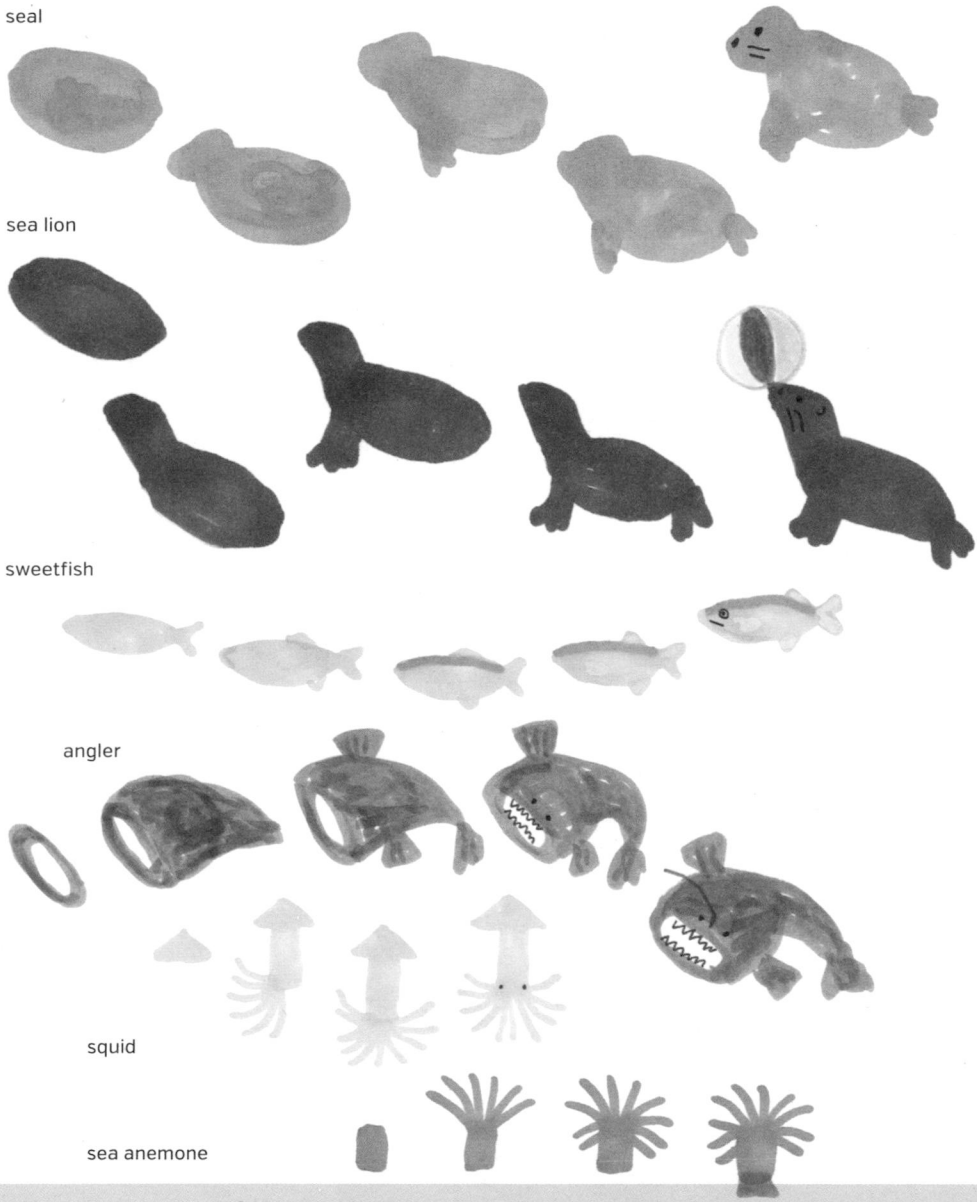

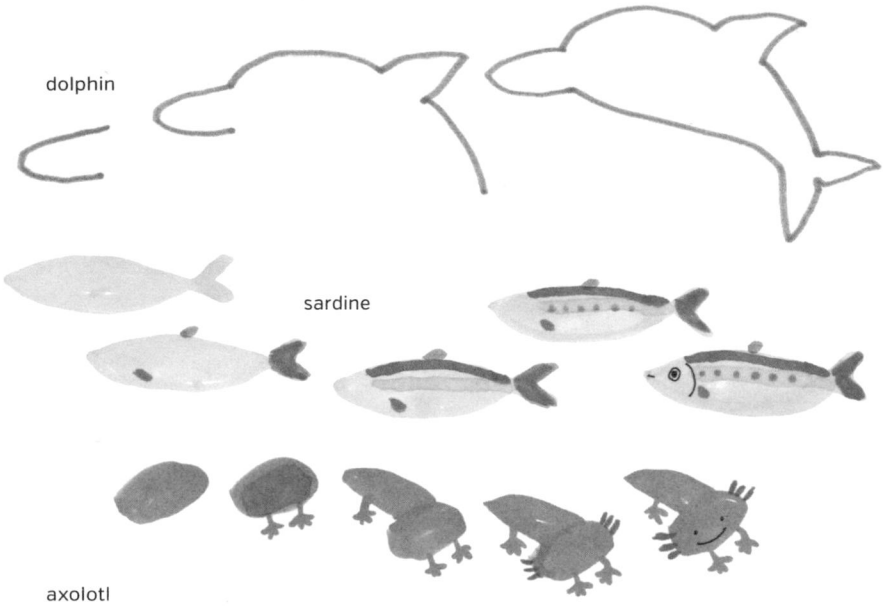
dolphin
sardine
axolotl

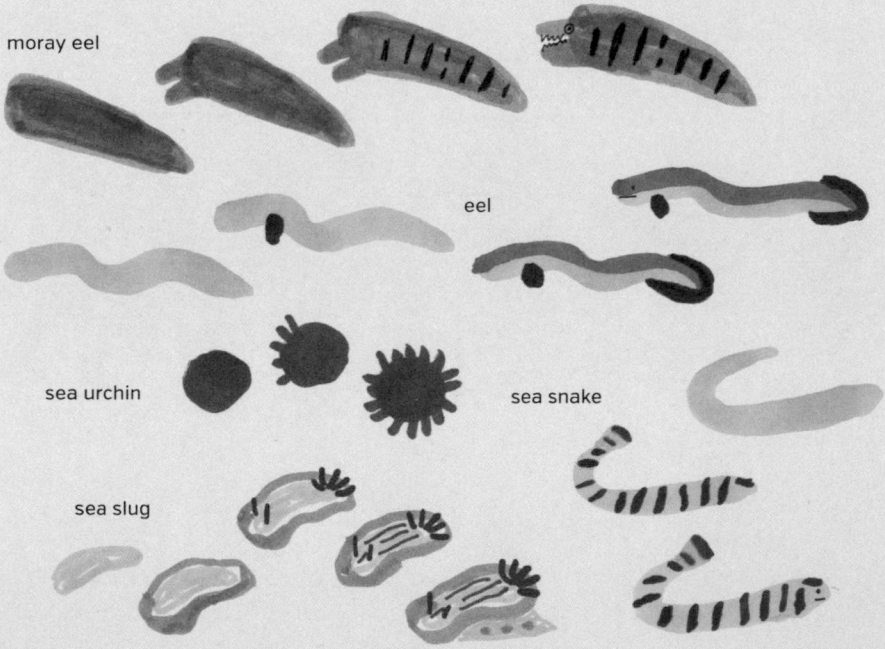
moray eel
eel
sea urchin
sea snake
sea slug

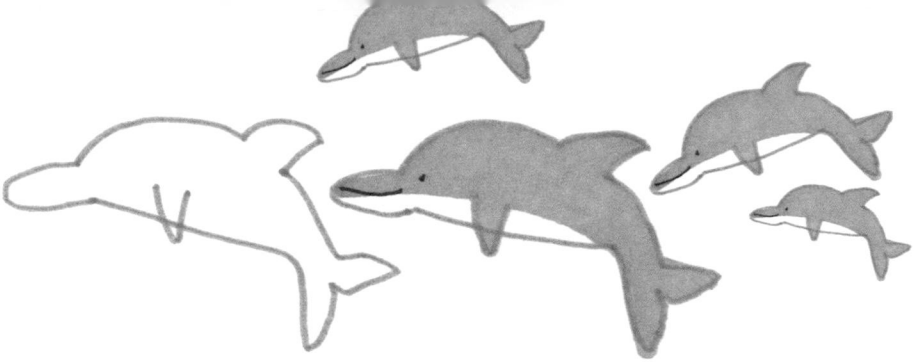

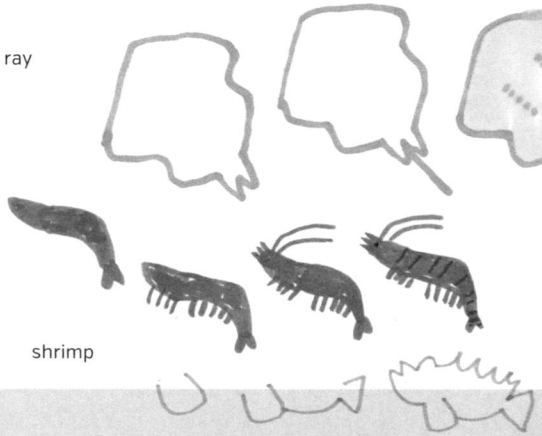
ray
shrimp

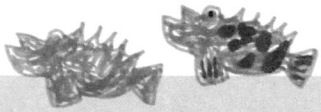
demon stinger

shellfish

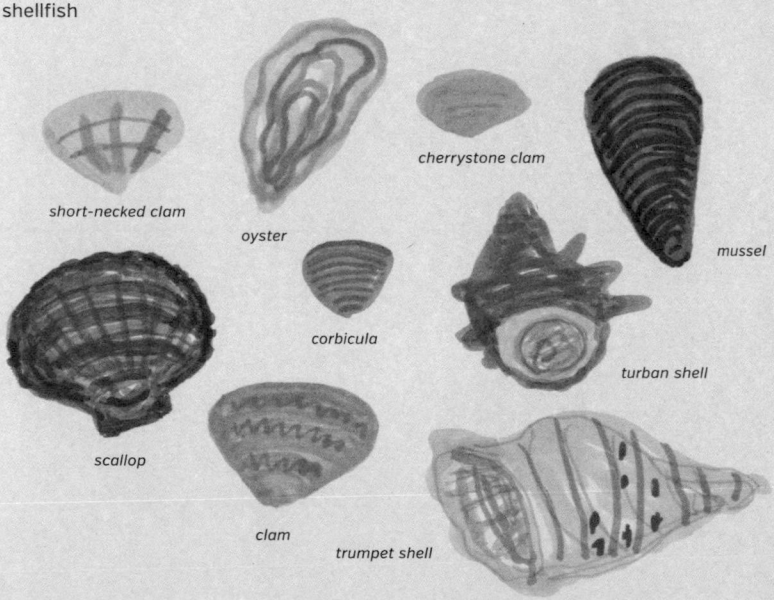
short-necked clam
oyster
cherrystone clam
mussel
corbicula
turban shell
scallop
clam
trumpet shell

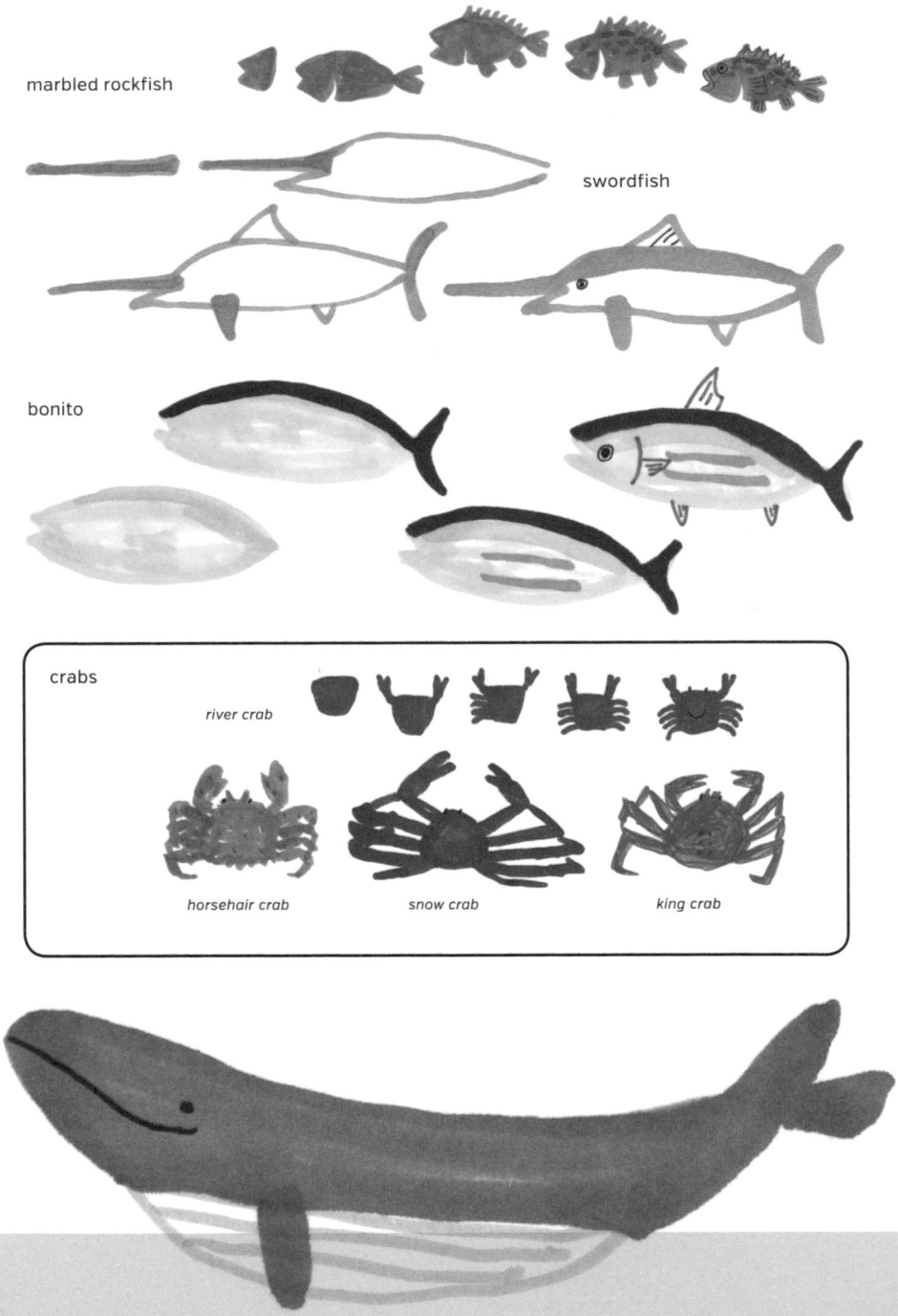
marbled rockfish
swordfish
bonito
crabs
river crab
horsehair crab
snow crab
king crab

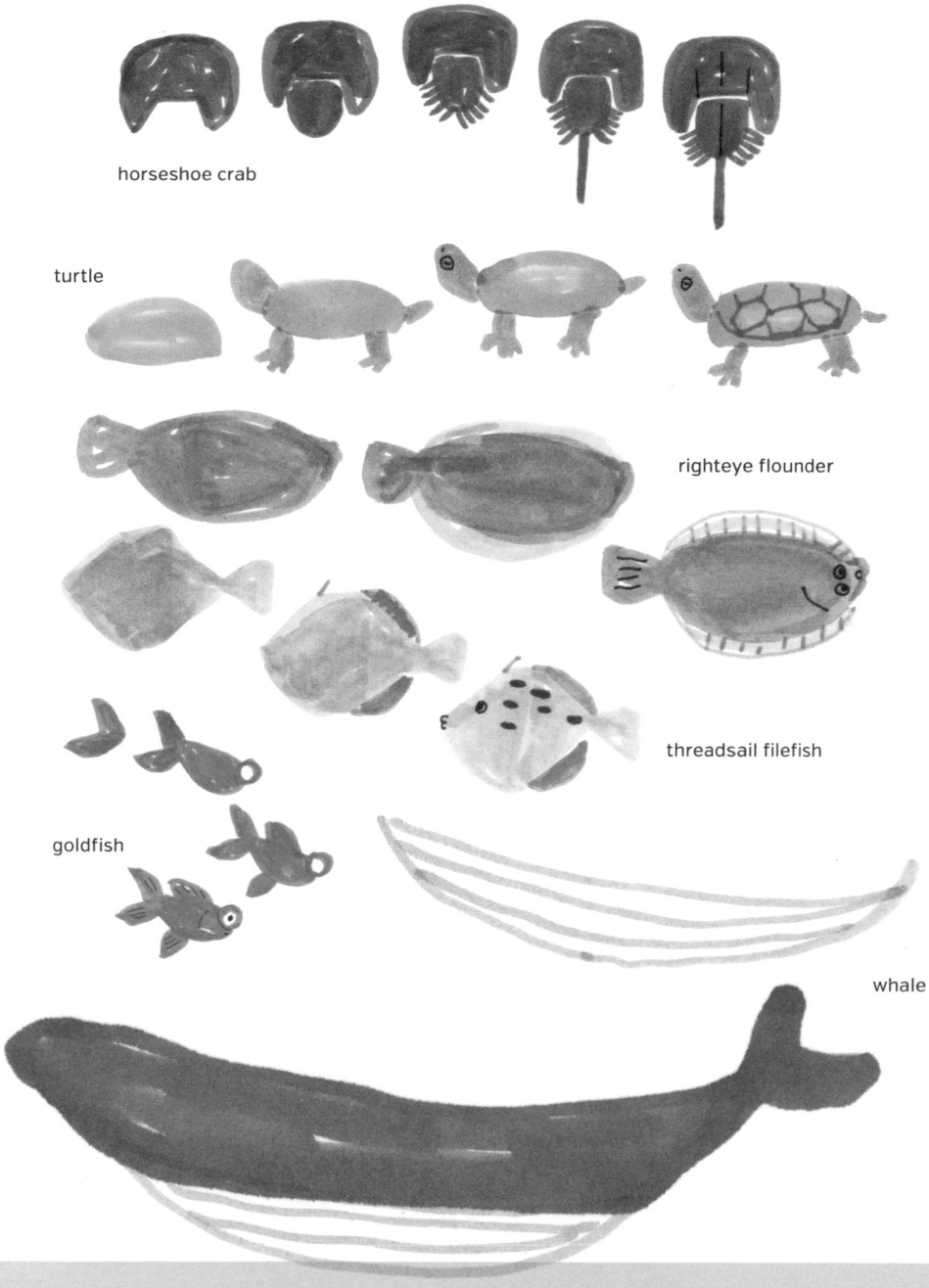
horseshoe crab
turtle
righteye flounder
threadsail filefish
goldfish
whale

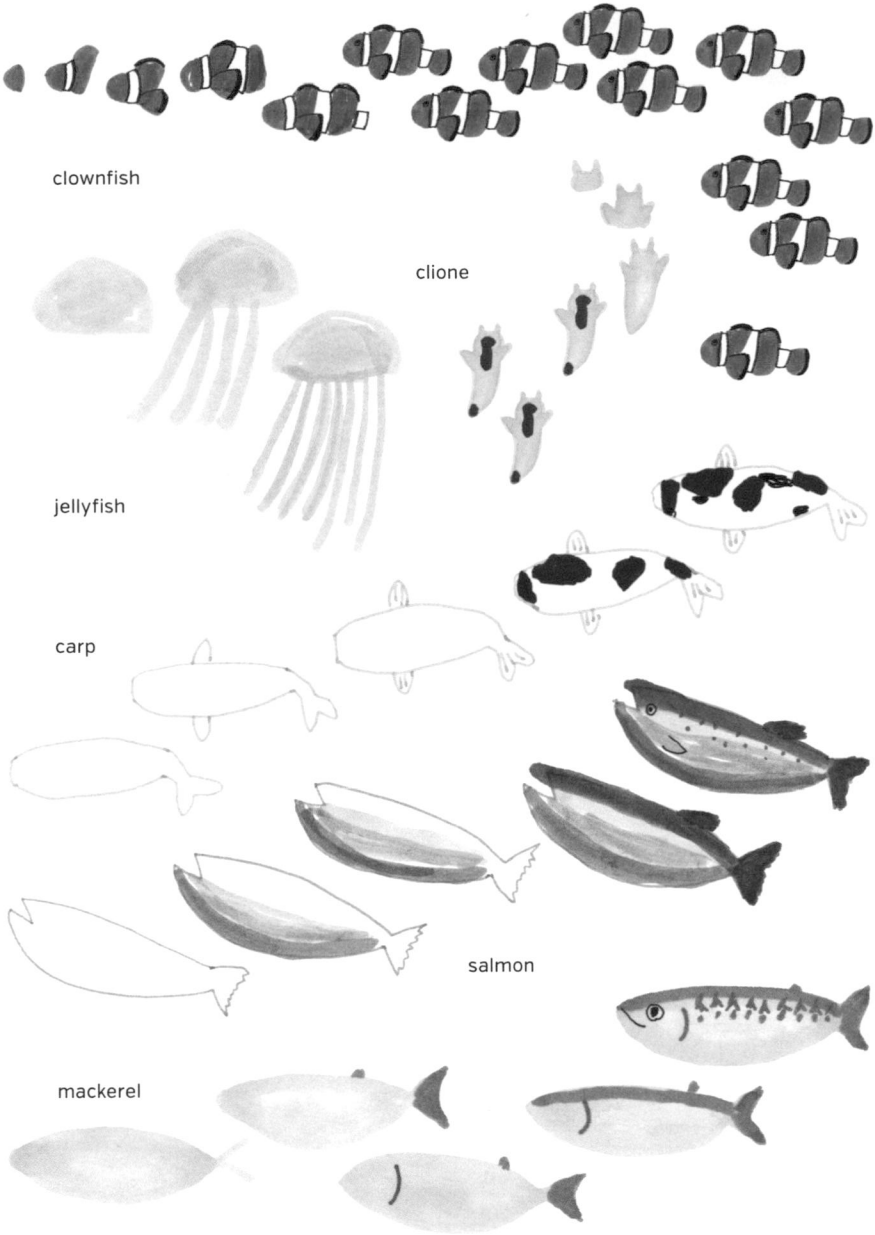
clownfish
clione
jellyfish
carp
salmon
mackerel

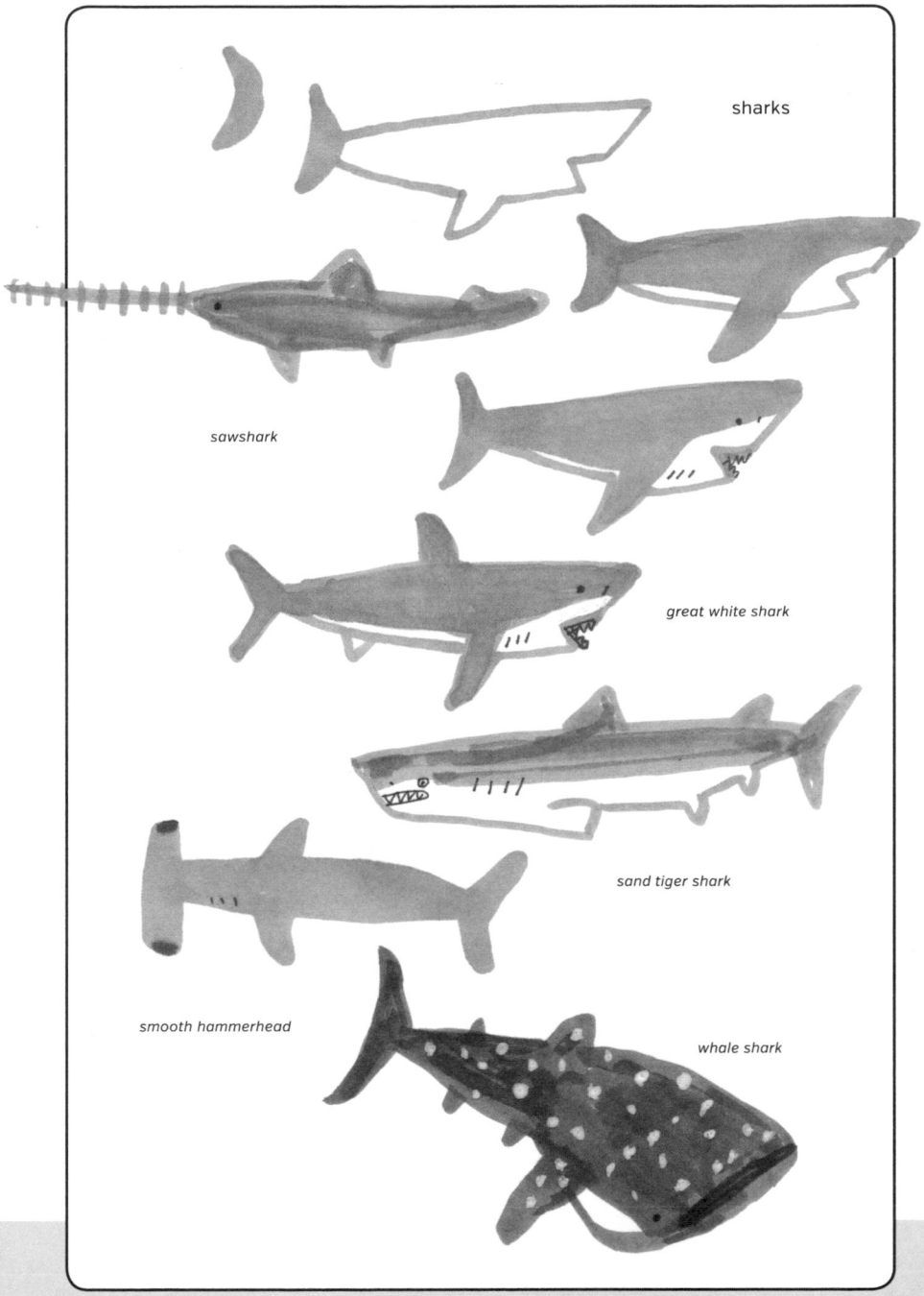
sharks
sawshark
great white shark
sand tiger shark
smooth hammerhead
whale shark

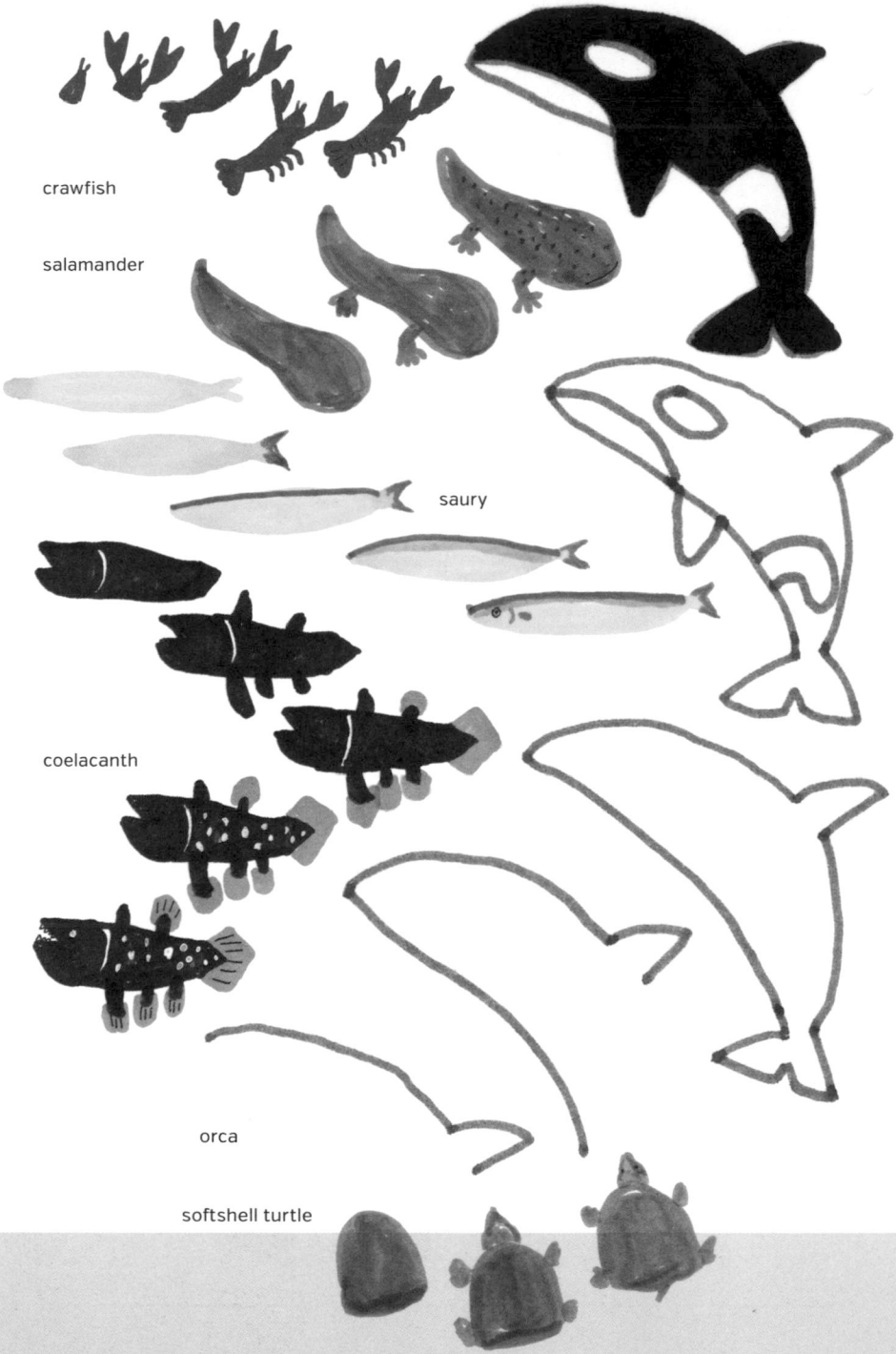
crawfish
salamander
saury
coelacanth
orca
softshell turtle

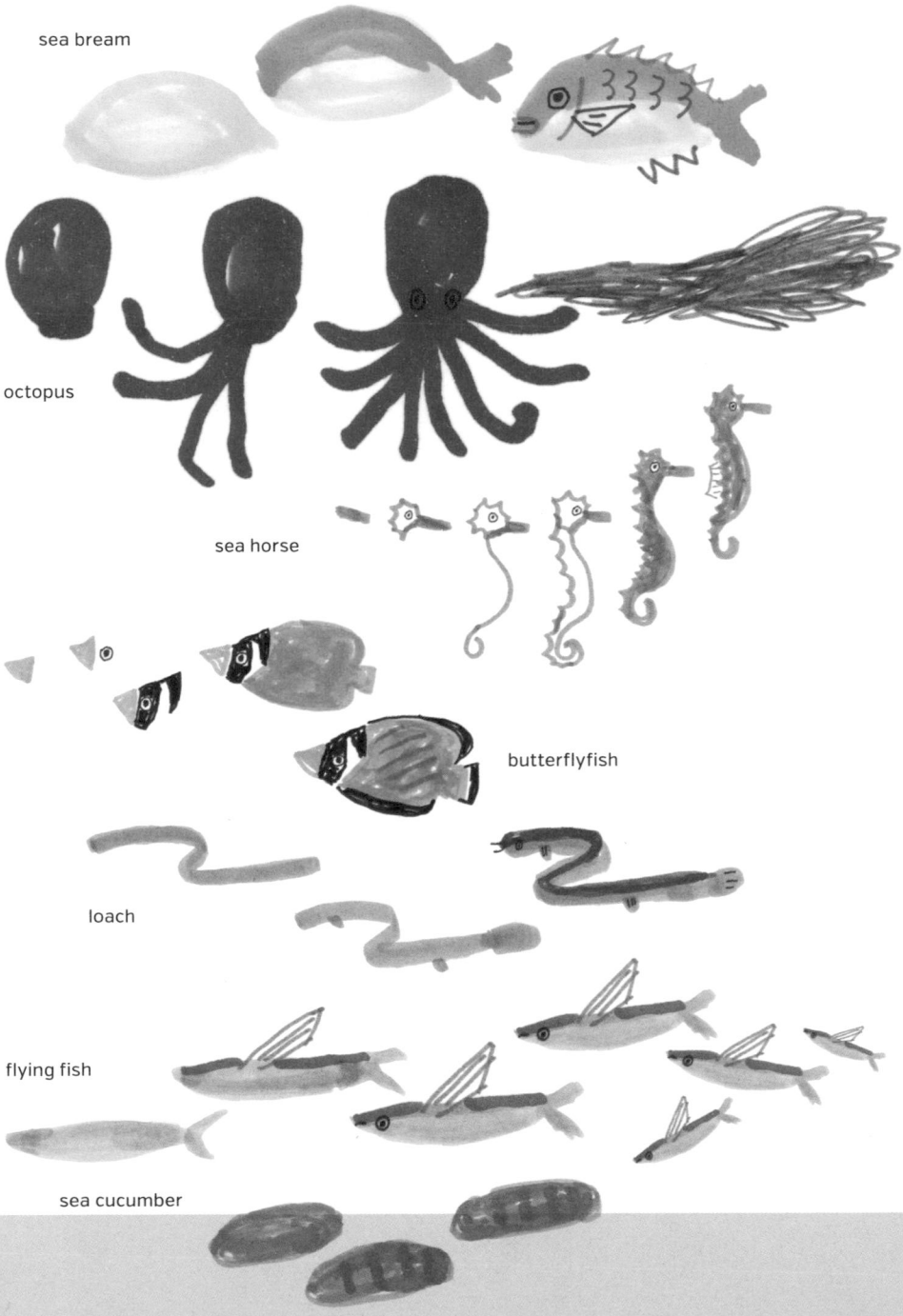
sea bream
octopus
sea horse
butterflyfish
loach
flying fish
sea cucumber

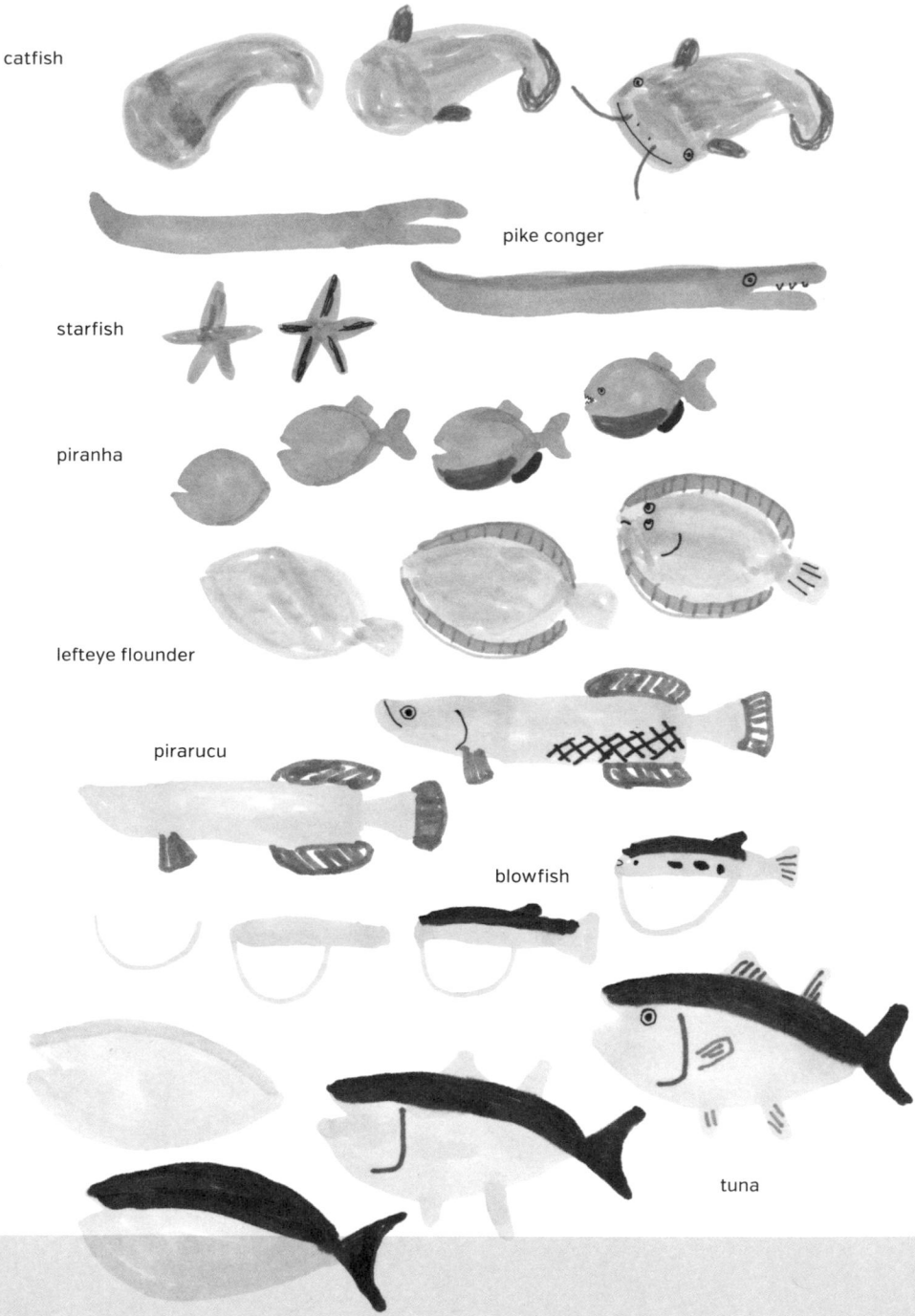
catfish
pike conger
starfish
piranha
lefteye flounder
pirarucu
blowfish
tuna

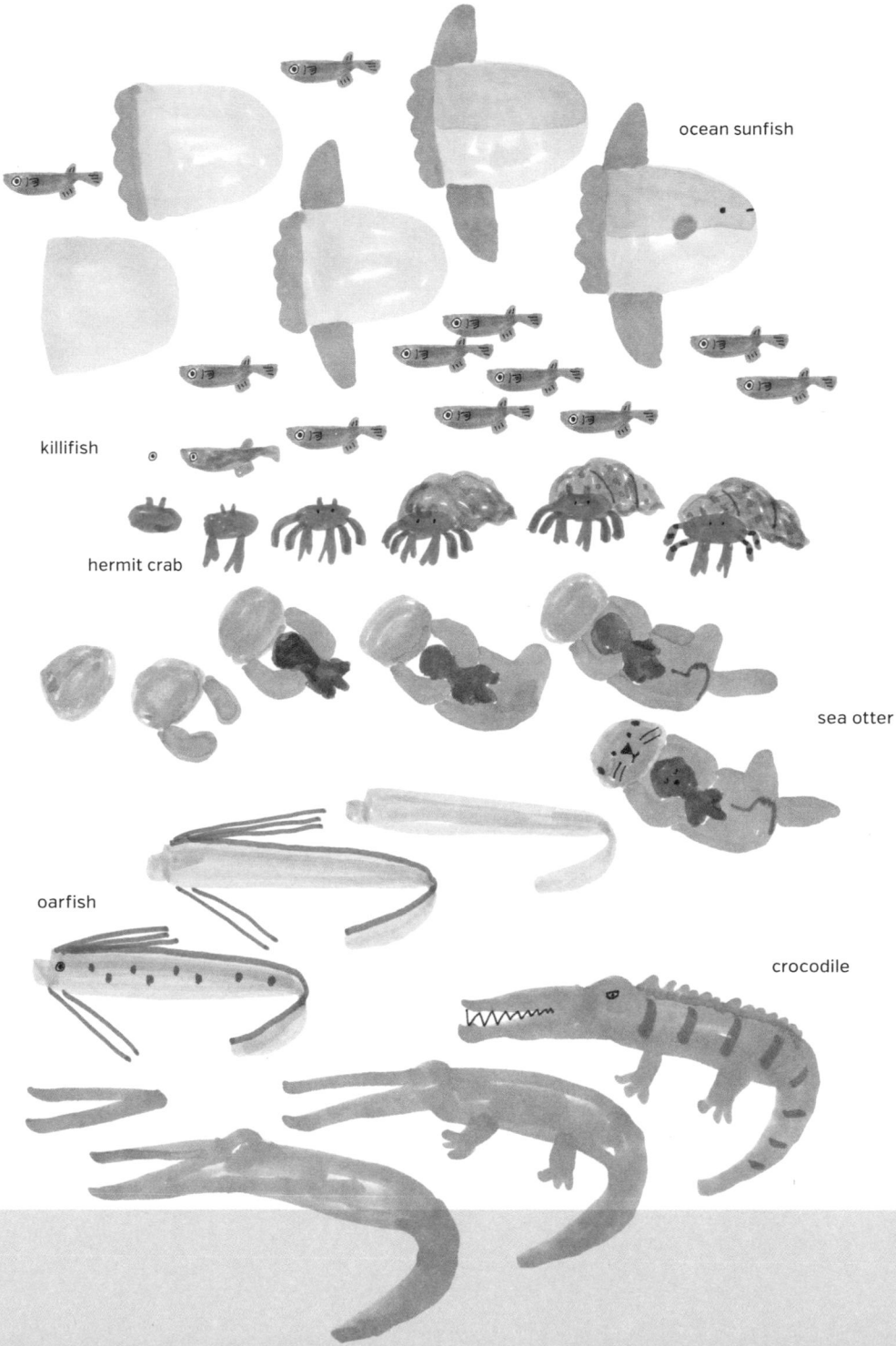
ocean sunfish
killifish
hermit crab
sea otter
oarfish
crocodile

# Birds

*Details such as feather pattern and length and thickness of the legs will help make your bird drawings more accurate.*

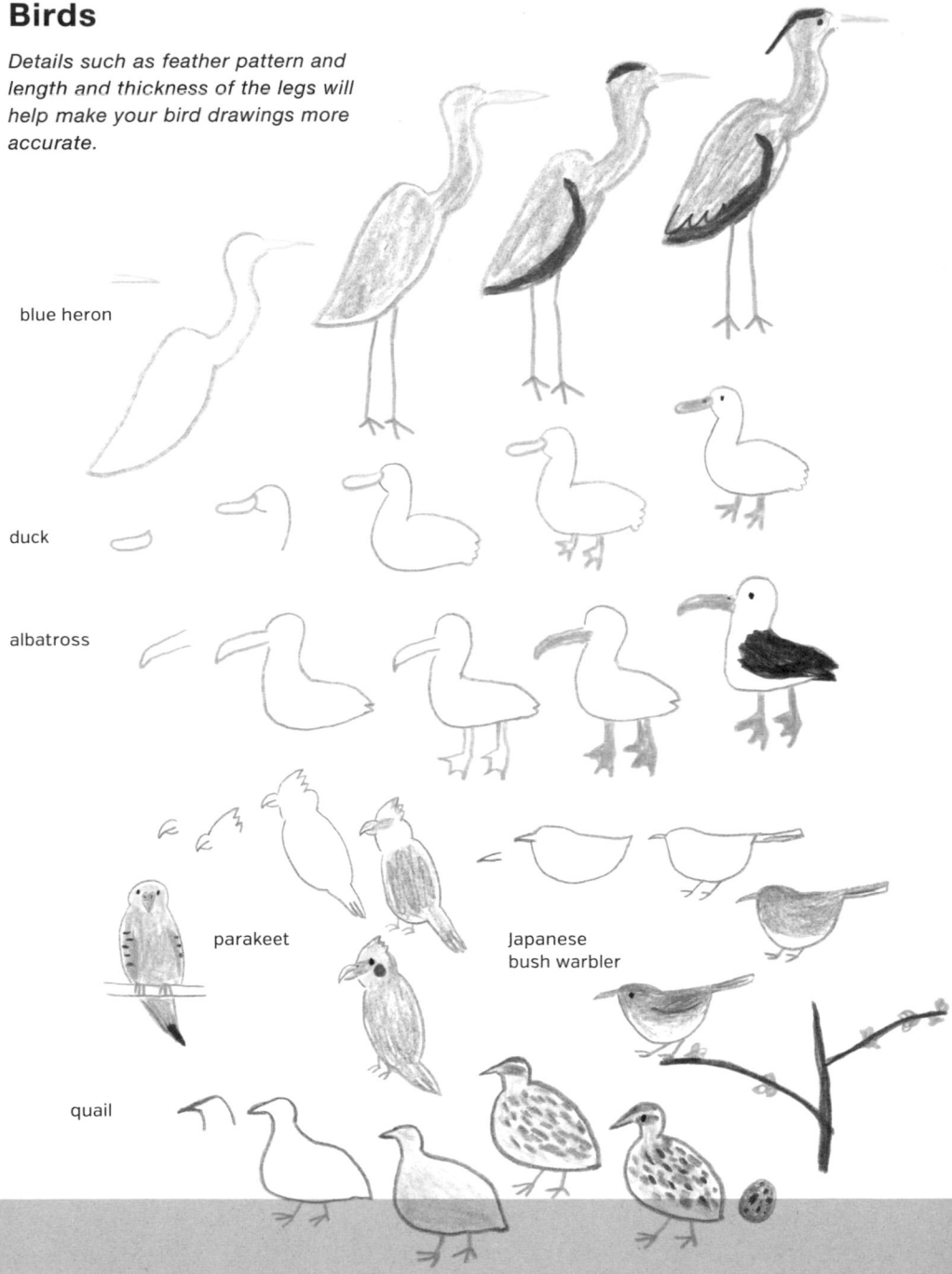

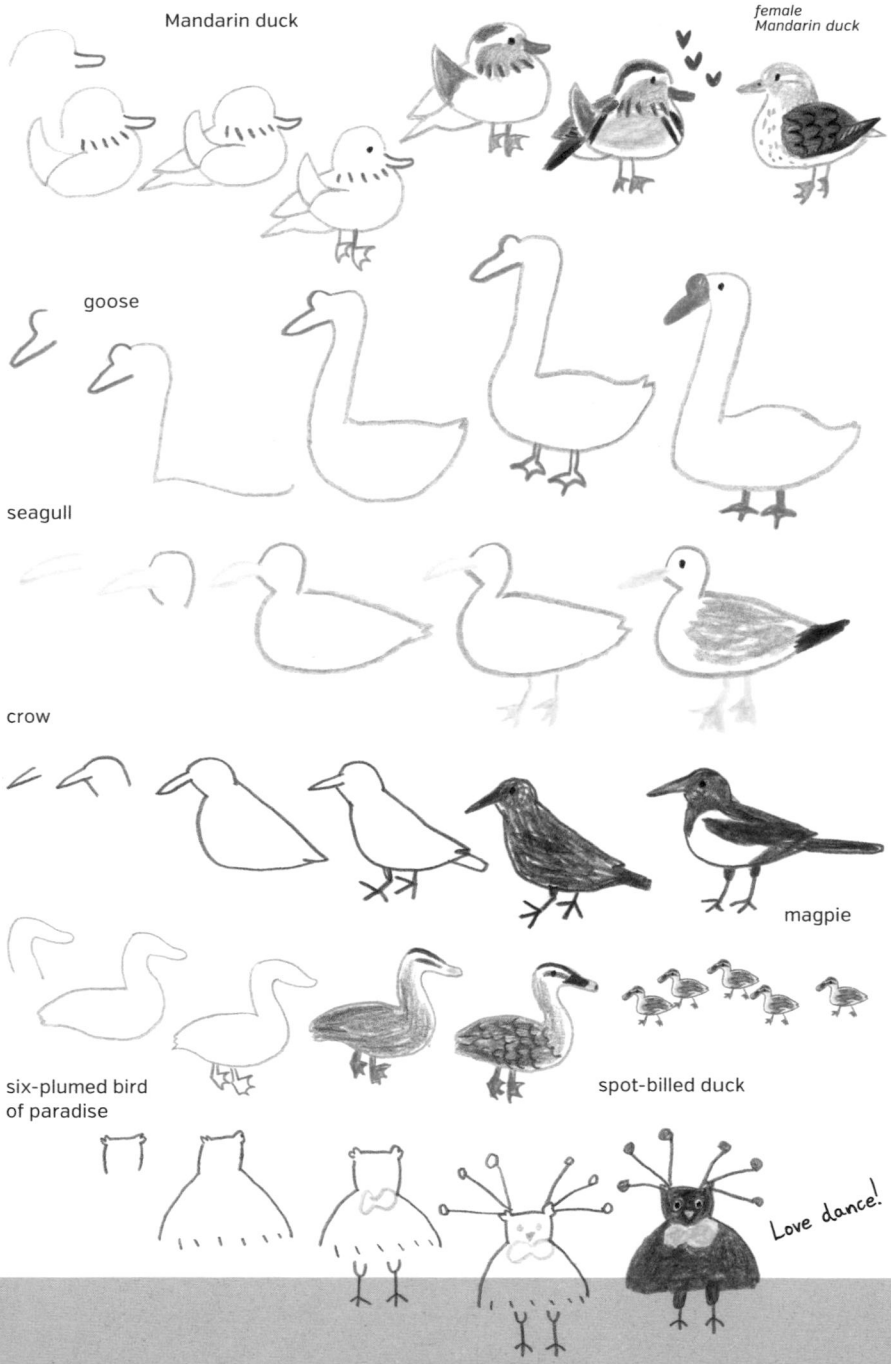
Mandarin duck
female
Mandarin duck
goose
seagull
crow
magpie
six-plumed bird
of paradise
spot-billed duck
Love dance!

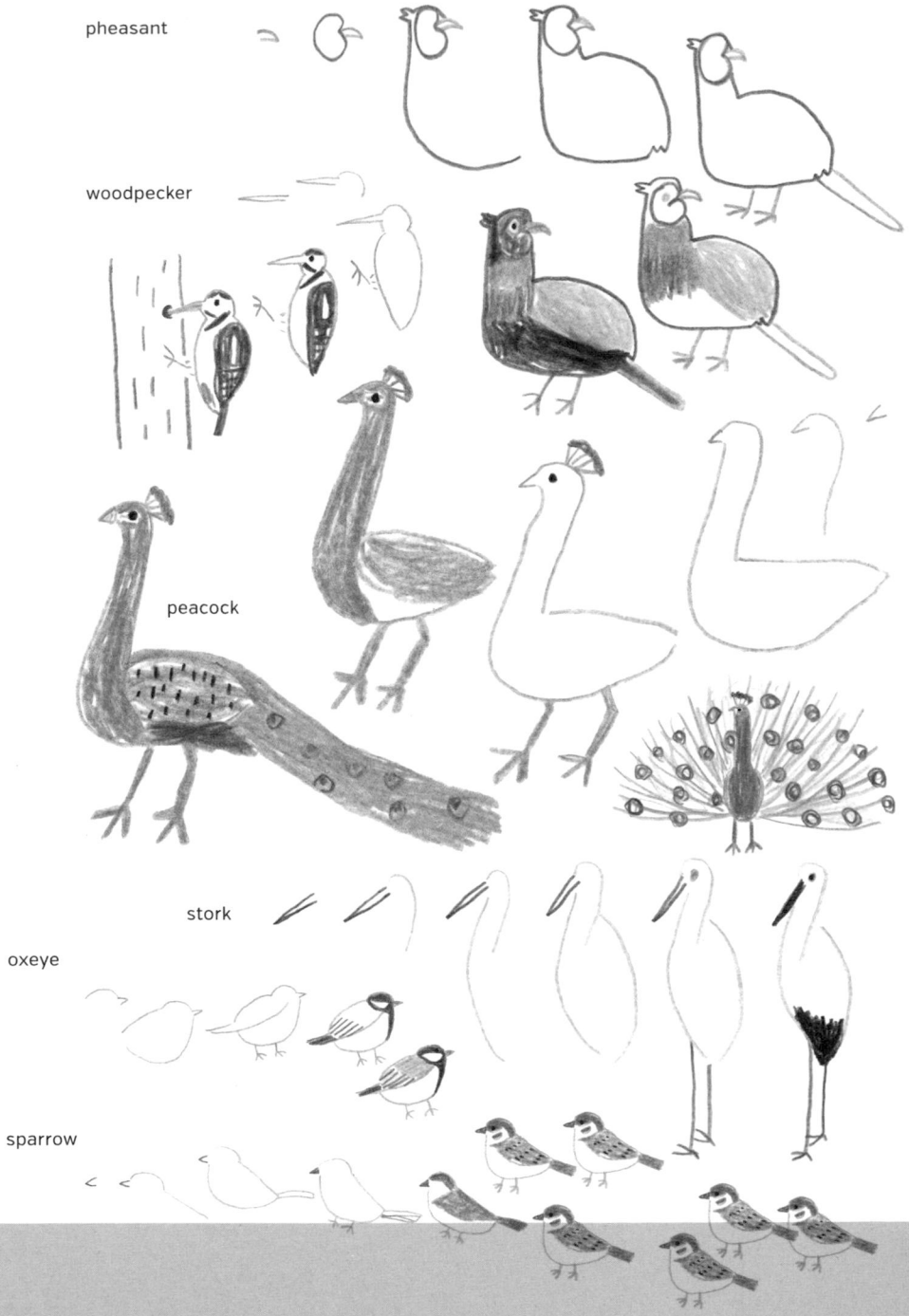
pheasant
woodpecker
peacock
stork
oxeye
sparrow

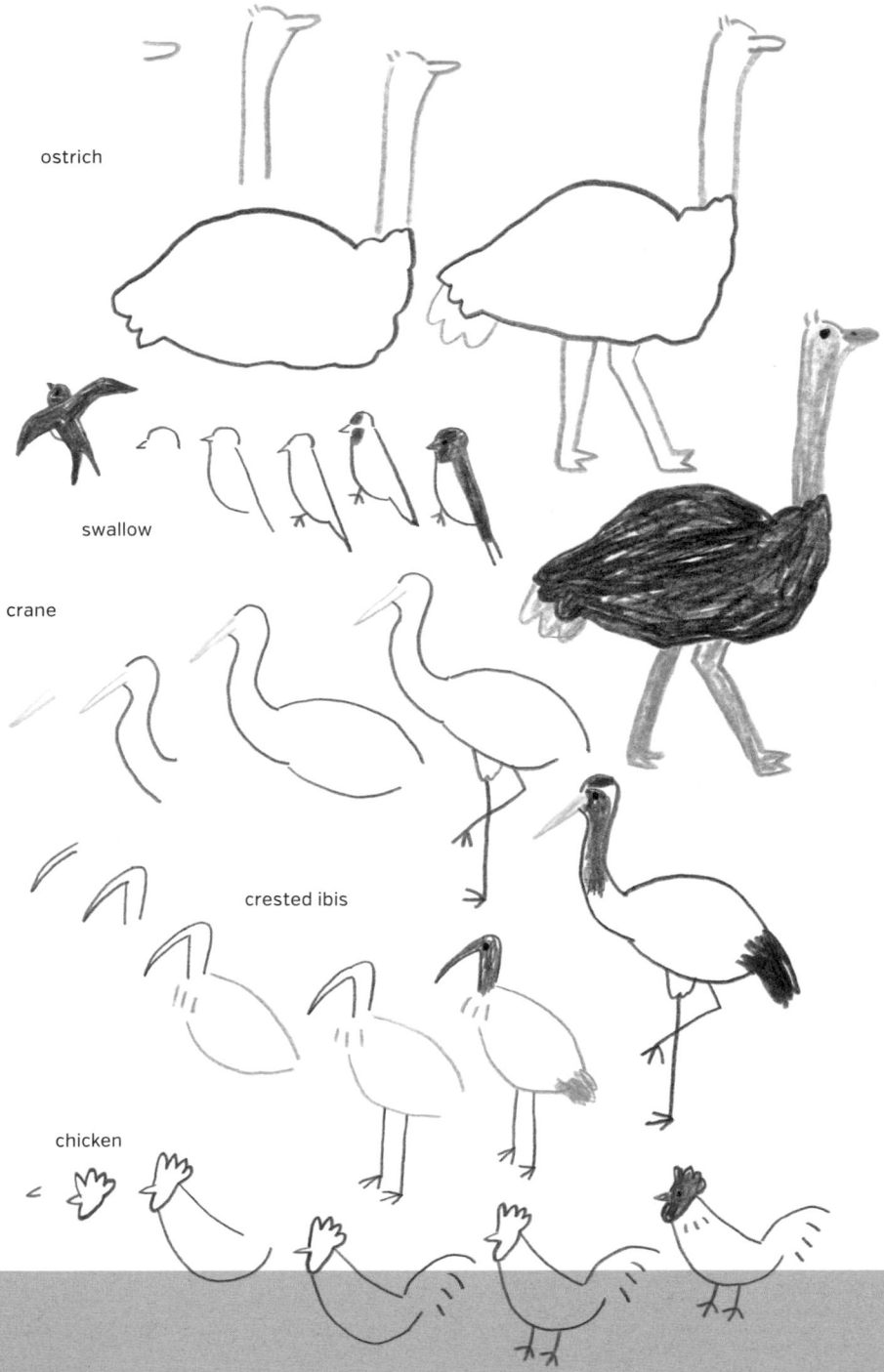
ostrich
swallow
crane
crested ibis
chicken

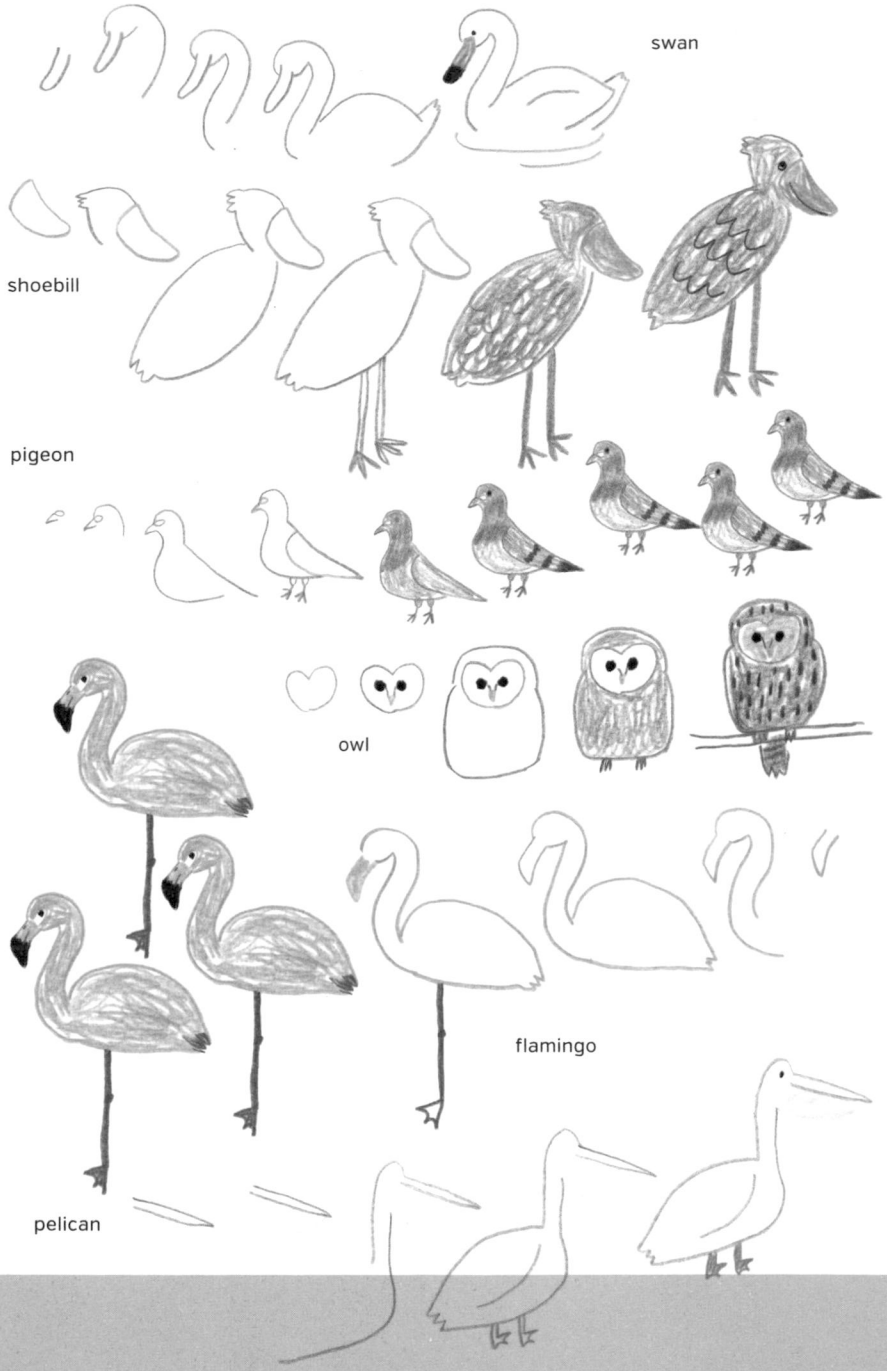
swan
shoebill
pigeon
owl
flamingo
pelican

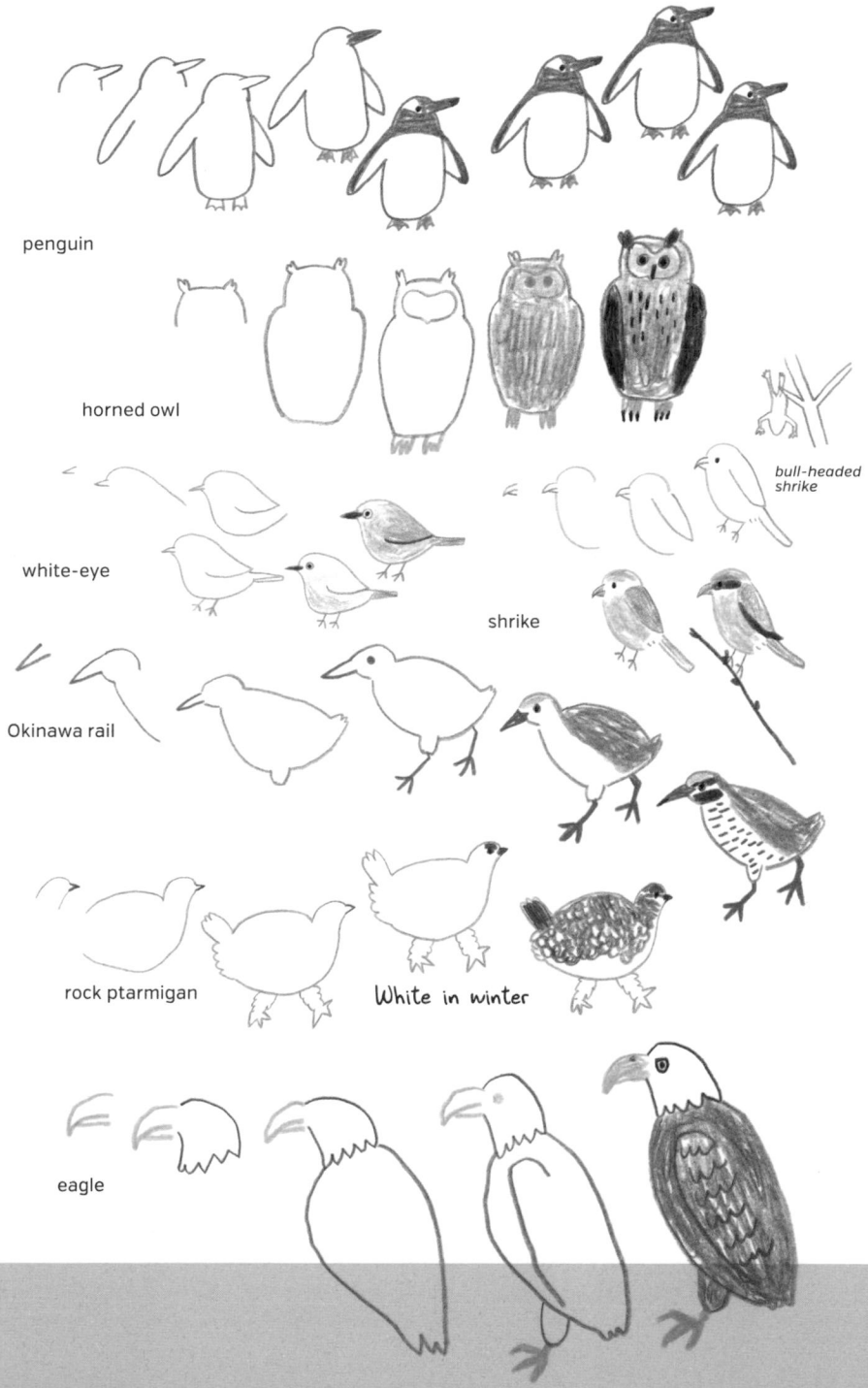
penguin
horned owl
bull-headed shrike
white-eye
shrike
Okinawa rail
rock ptarmigan
White in winter
eagle

# Bugs & Insects

*Details such as the shape of the head and the length of the antennae will help differentiate between similar insects.*

aphid

water strider

ant

locust

green caterpillar

mosquito

moth

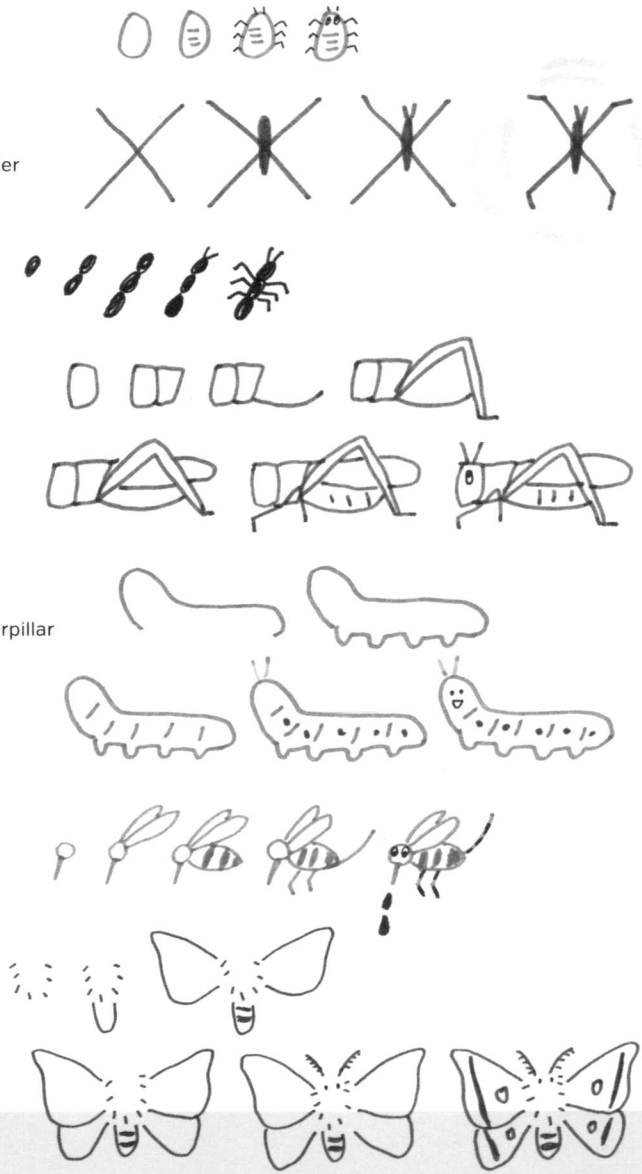

scarab beetle

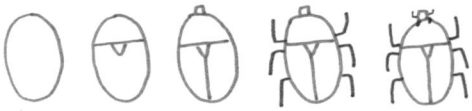

beetles

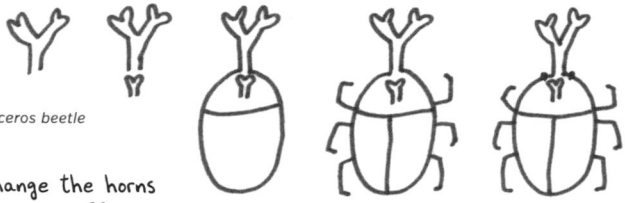

*rhinoceros beetle*

Change the horns to draw different types of beetles:

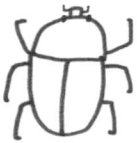

*female beetle*

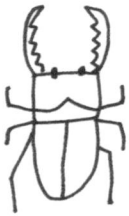

*stag beetle*

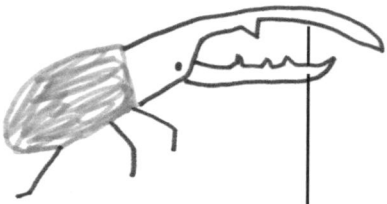

*Hercules beetle*

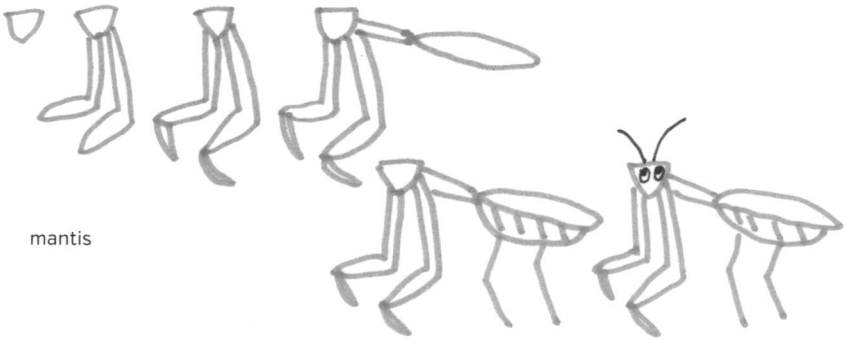

mantis

longicorn

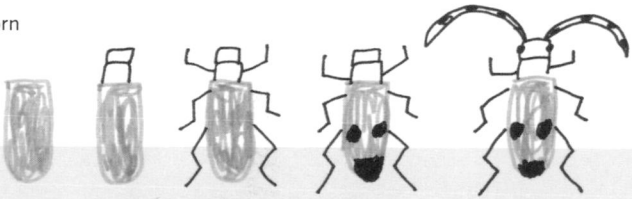

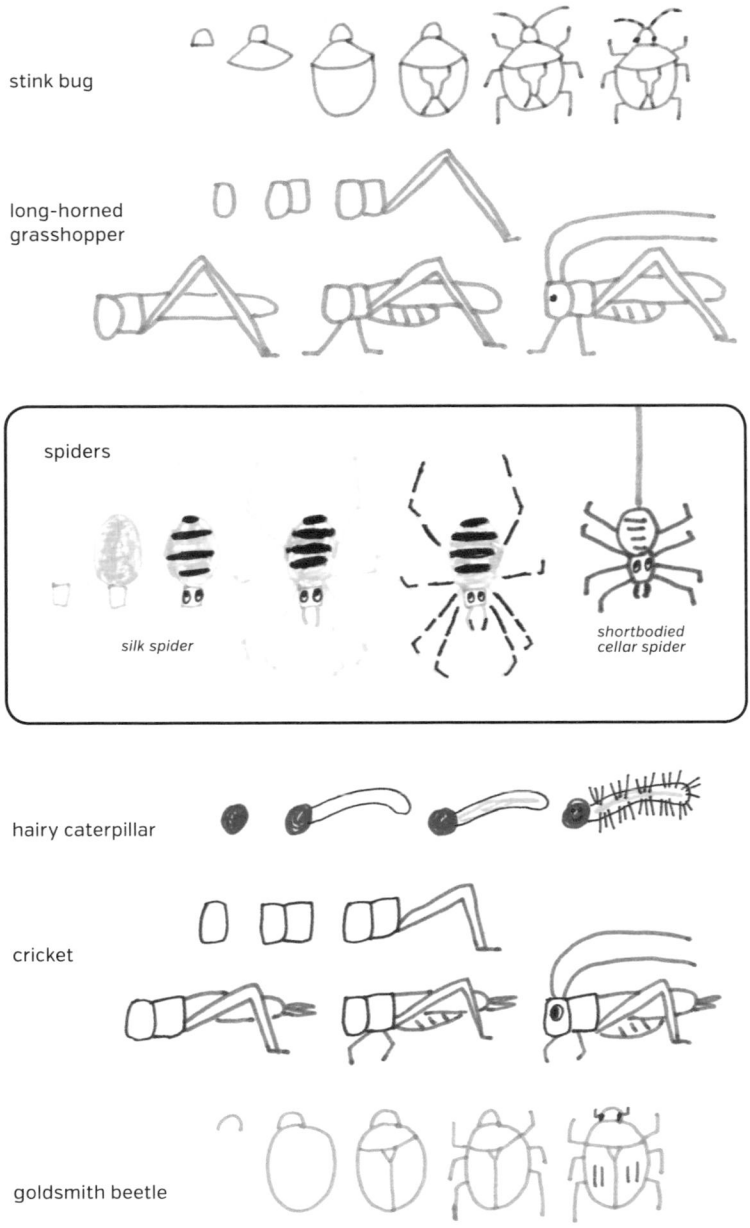
stink bug
long-horned grasshopper
spiders
silk spider
shortbodied cellar spider
hairy caterpillar
cricket
goldsmith beetle

cockroach

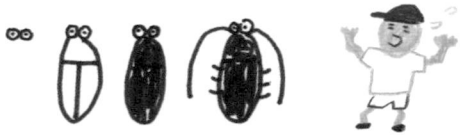

Oriental long-headed locust

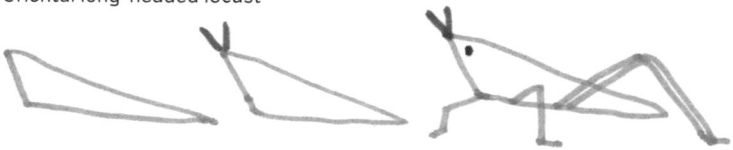

bell cricket

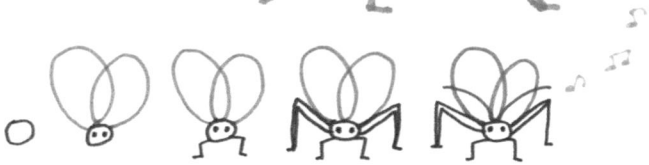

skipper

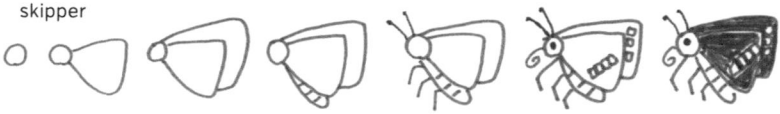

cicada

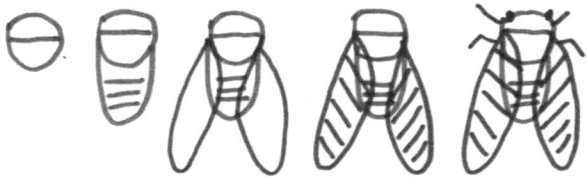

tarantula

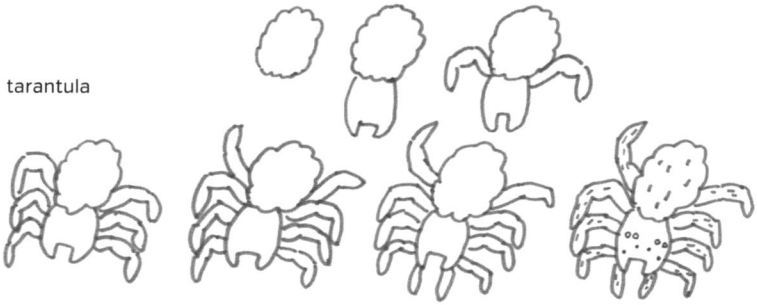

pill bug

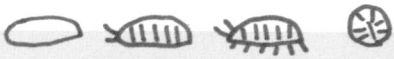

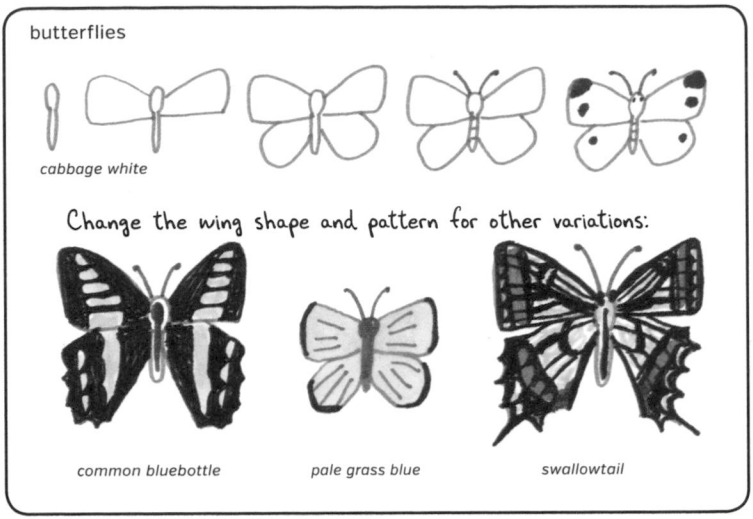
butterflies
cabbage white
Change the wing shape and pattern for other variations:
common bluebottle
pale grass blue
swallowtail

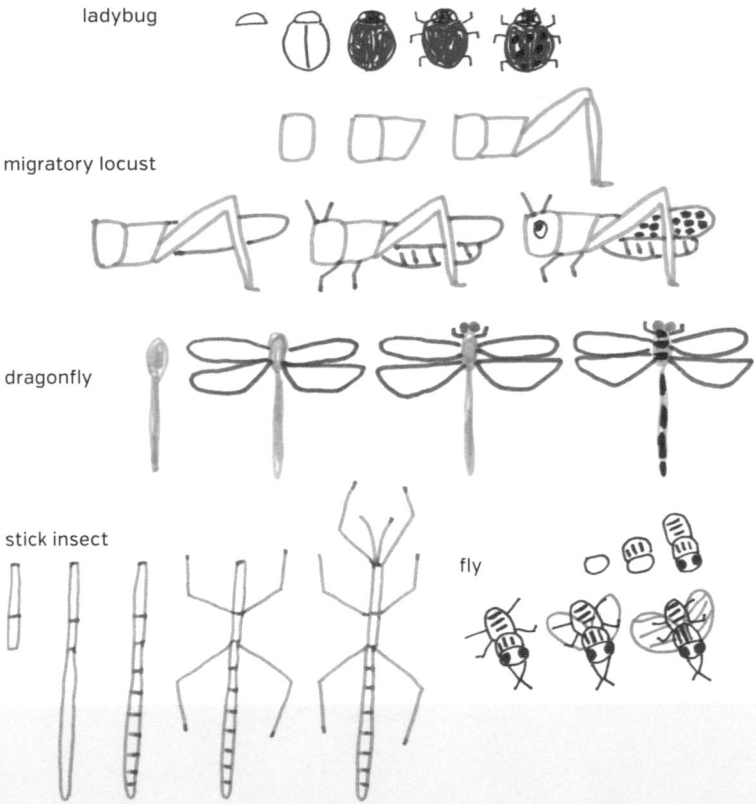
ladybug
migratory locust
dragonfly
stick insect
fly

bees

*honey bee*

*honeycomb*

*bee pupa*

*large carpenter bee*

*wasp*

*bumblebee*

*queen bee*

dung beetle

firefly

earthworm

centipede

# Dinosaurs

*To recreate these dinosaur illustrations, draw bold outlines, then have fun adding color.*

archaeopteryx

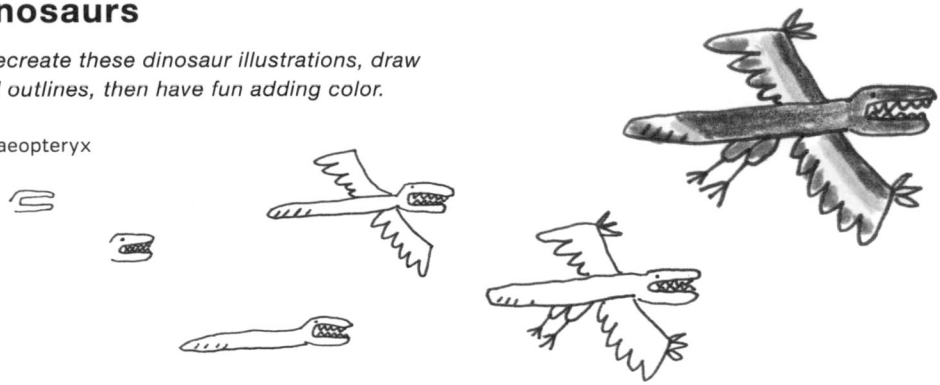

argentinosaurus

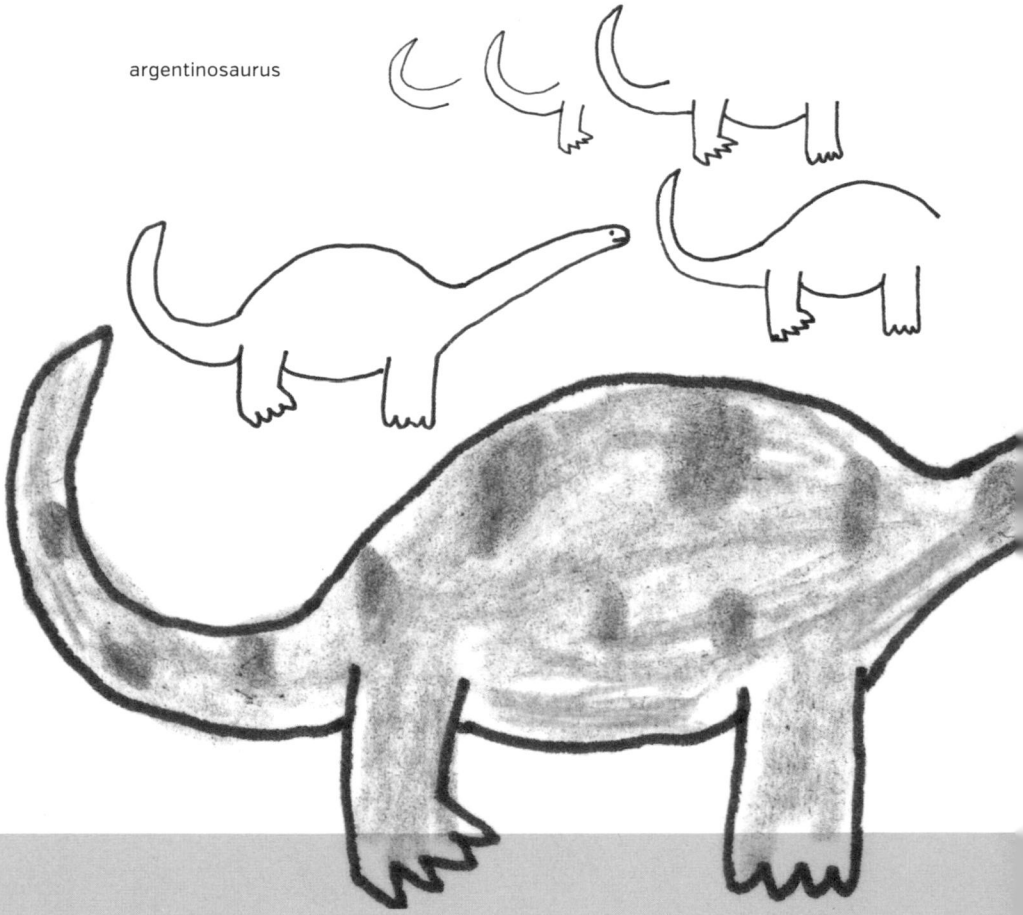

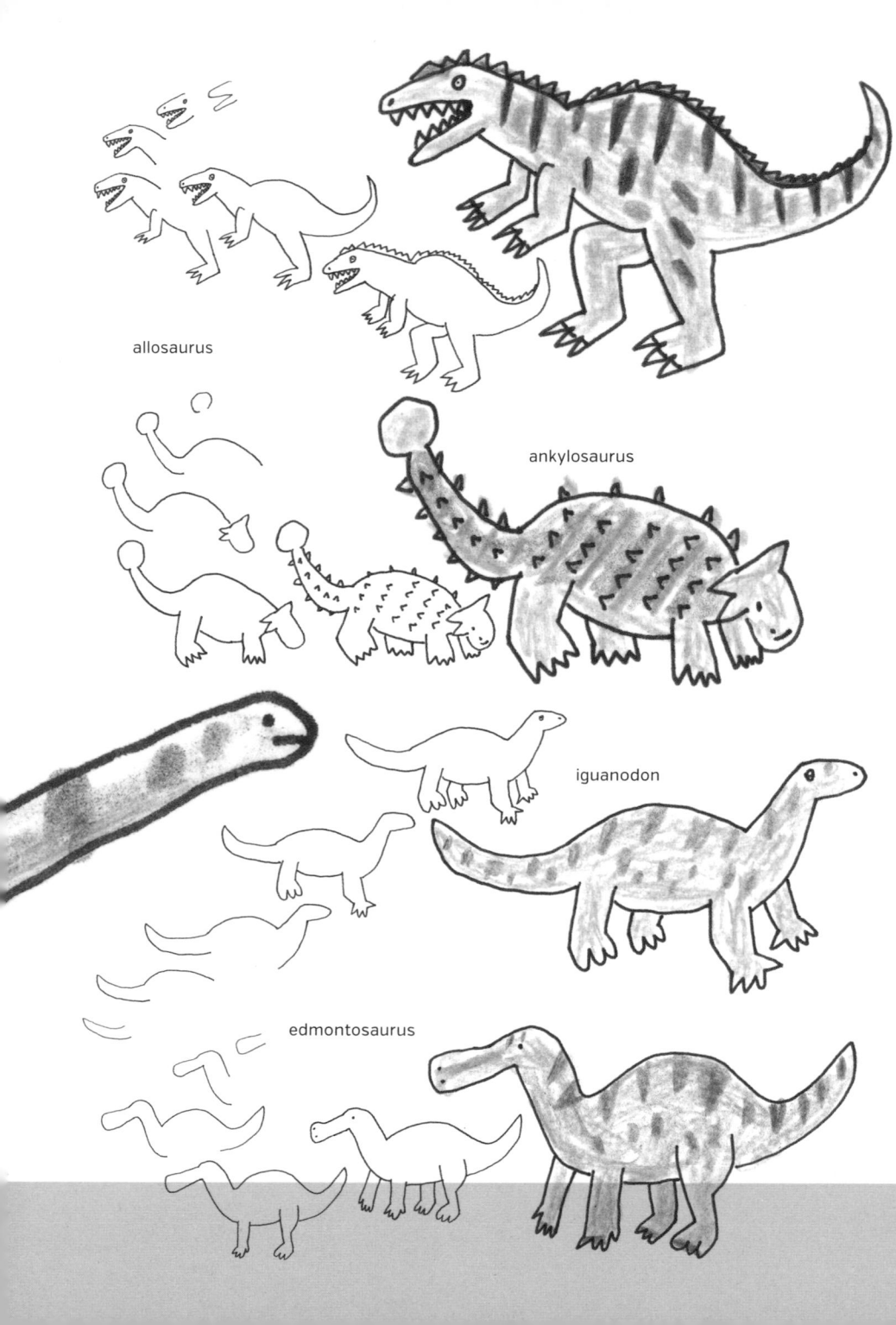
allosaurus
ankylosaurus
iguanodon
edmontosaurus

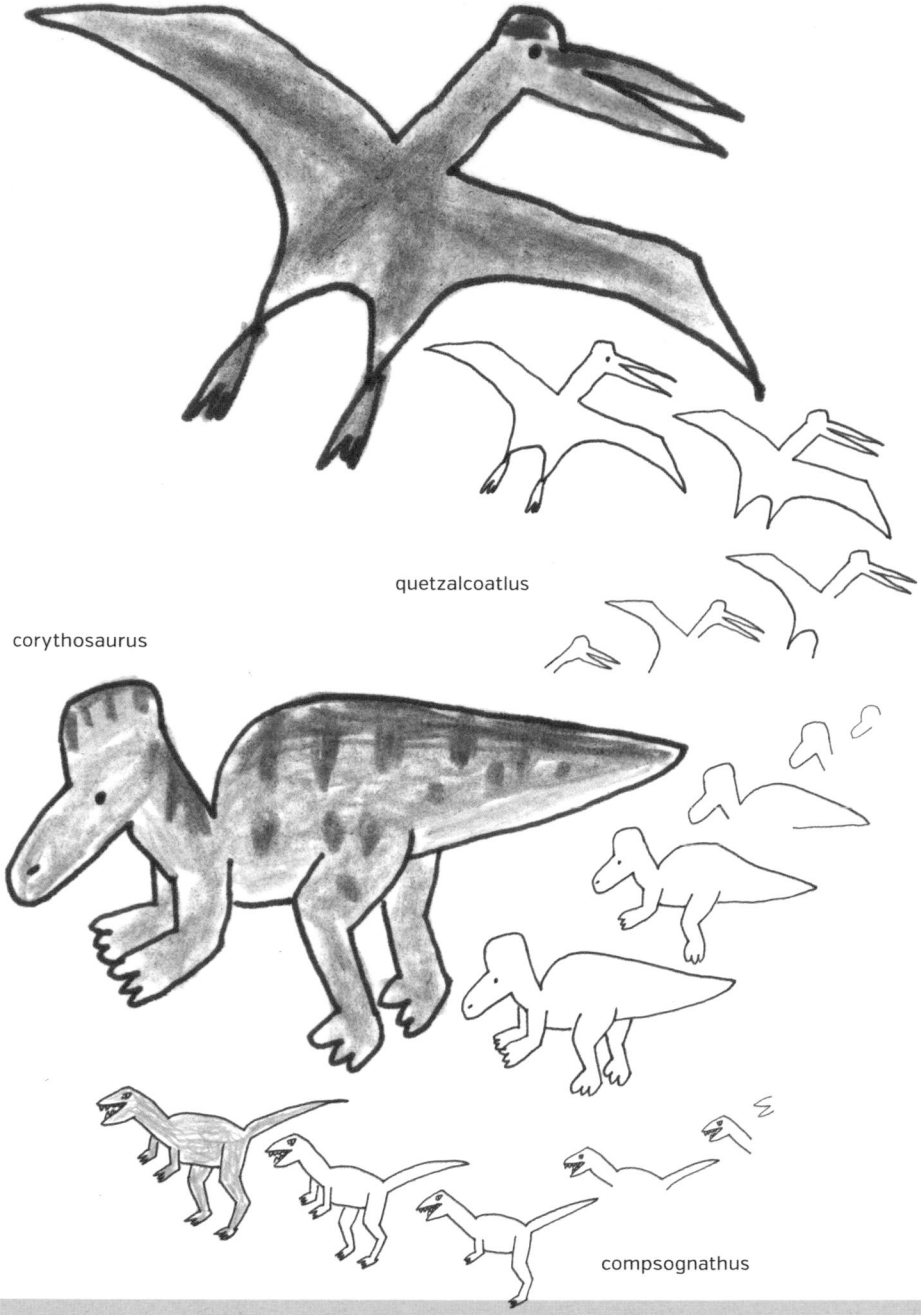
quetzalcoatlus
corythosaurus
compsognathus

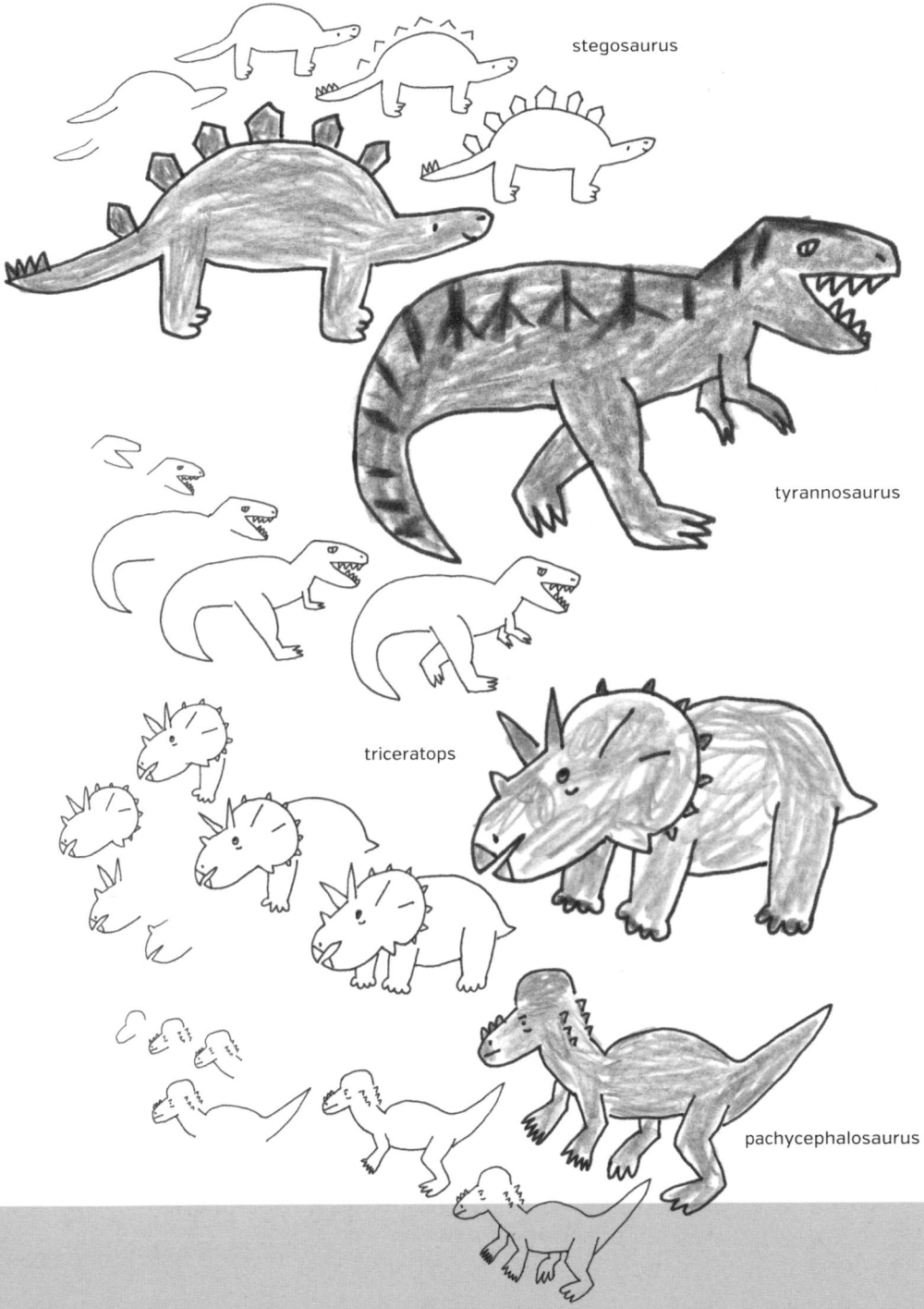
stegosaurus
tyrannosaurus
triceratops
pachycephalosaurus

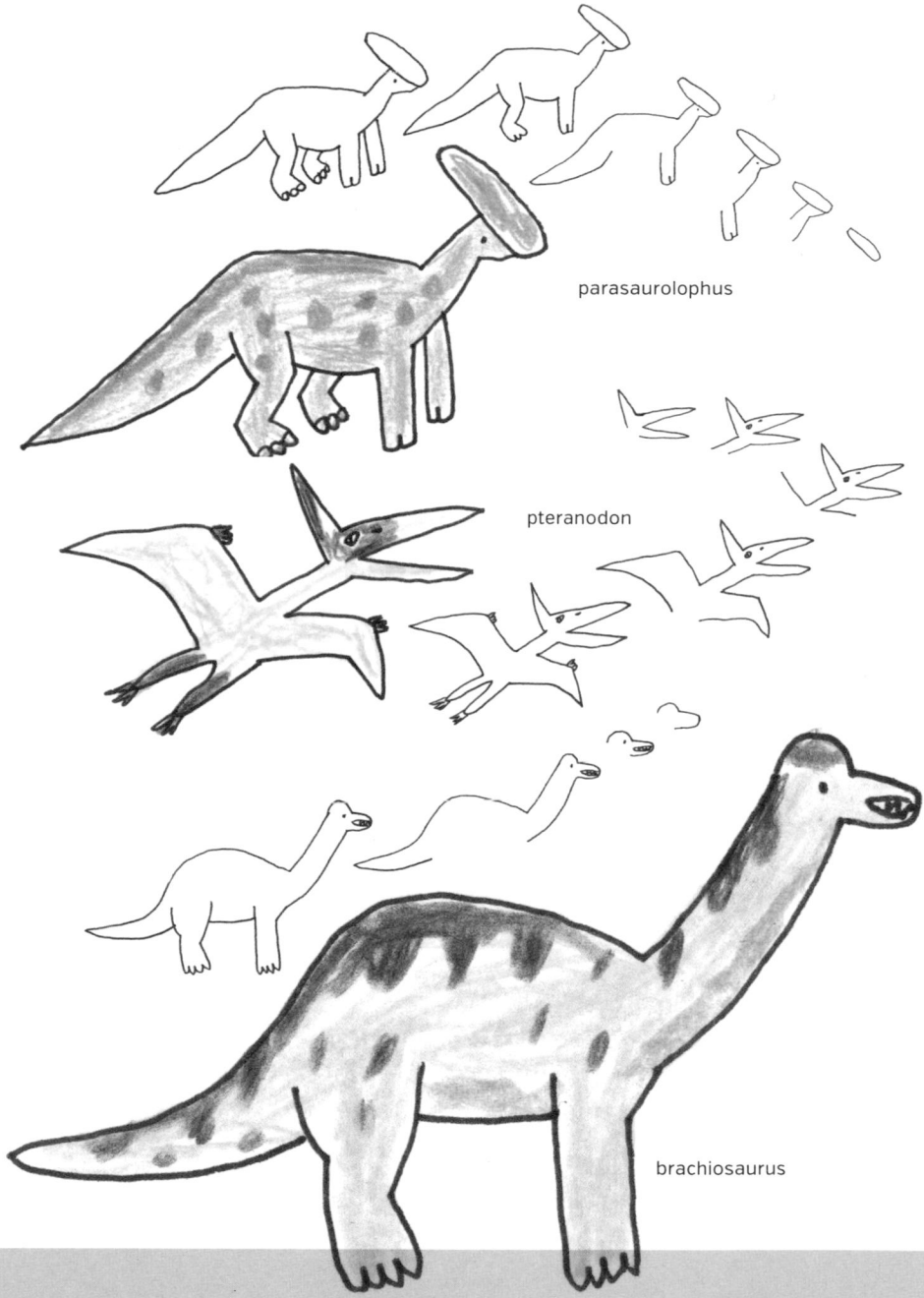
parasaurolophus
pteranodon
brachiosaurus

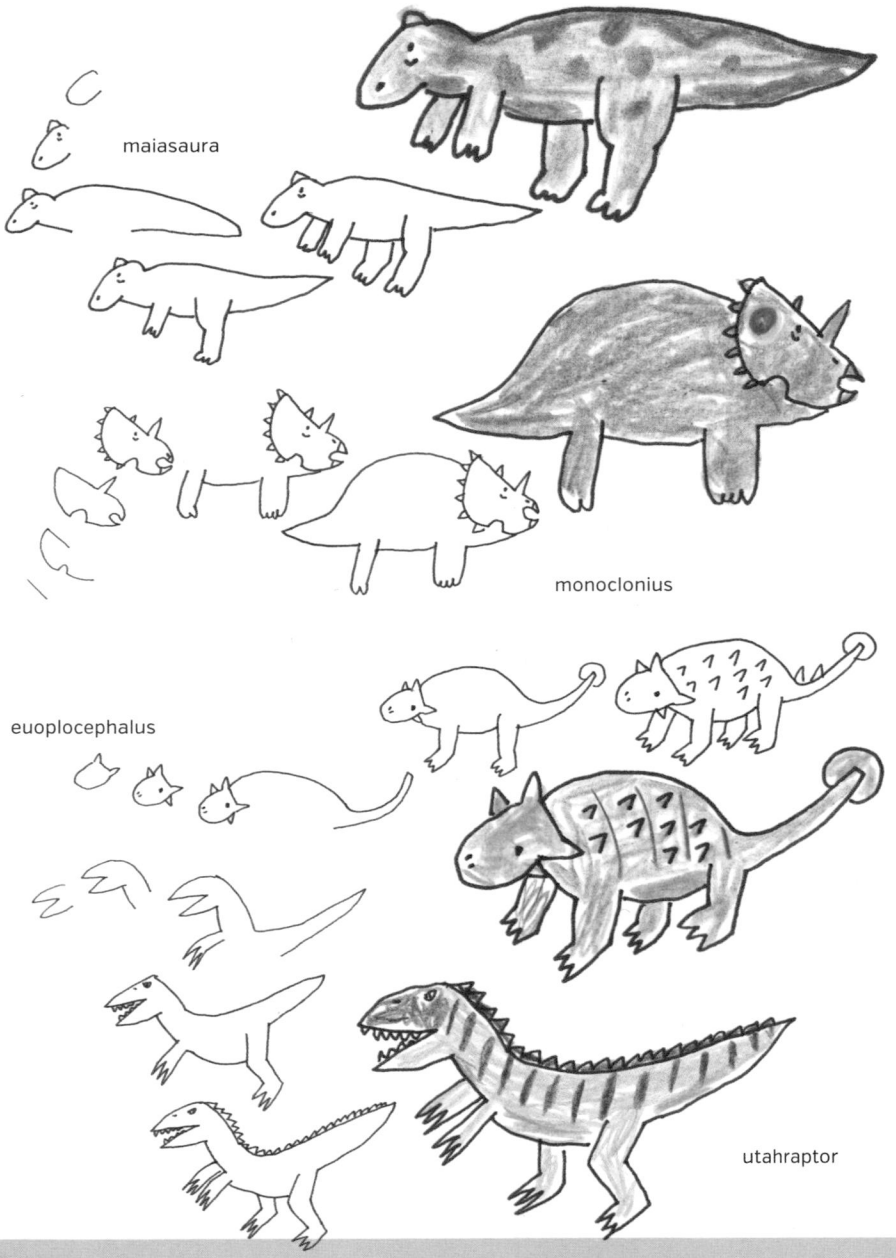
maiasaura
monoclonius
euoplocephalus
utahraptor

## CHALLENGE #1:
## Draw a Zoo

Once you've perfected drawing animals, put your new skills to work by drawing a zoo scene. This challenge will provide you with an opportunity to practice drawing animals in action as they sleep, eat, and climb. Use a variety of art supplies for the different components of the drawing, including the animals, fences, and landscape, to create a 3-D look.

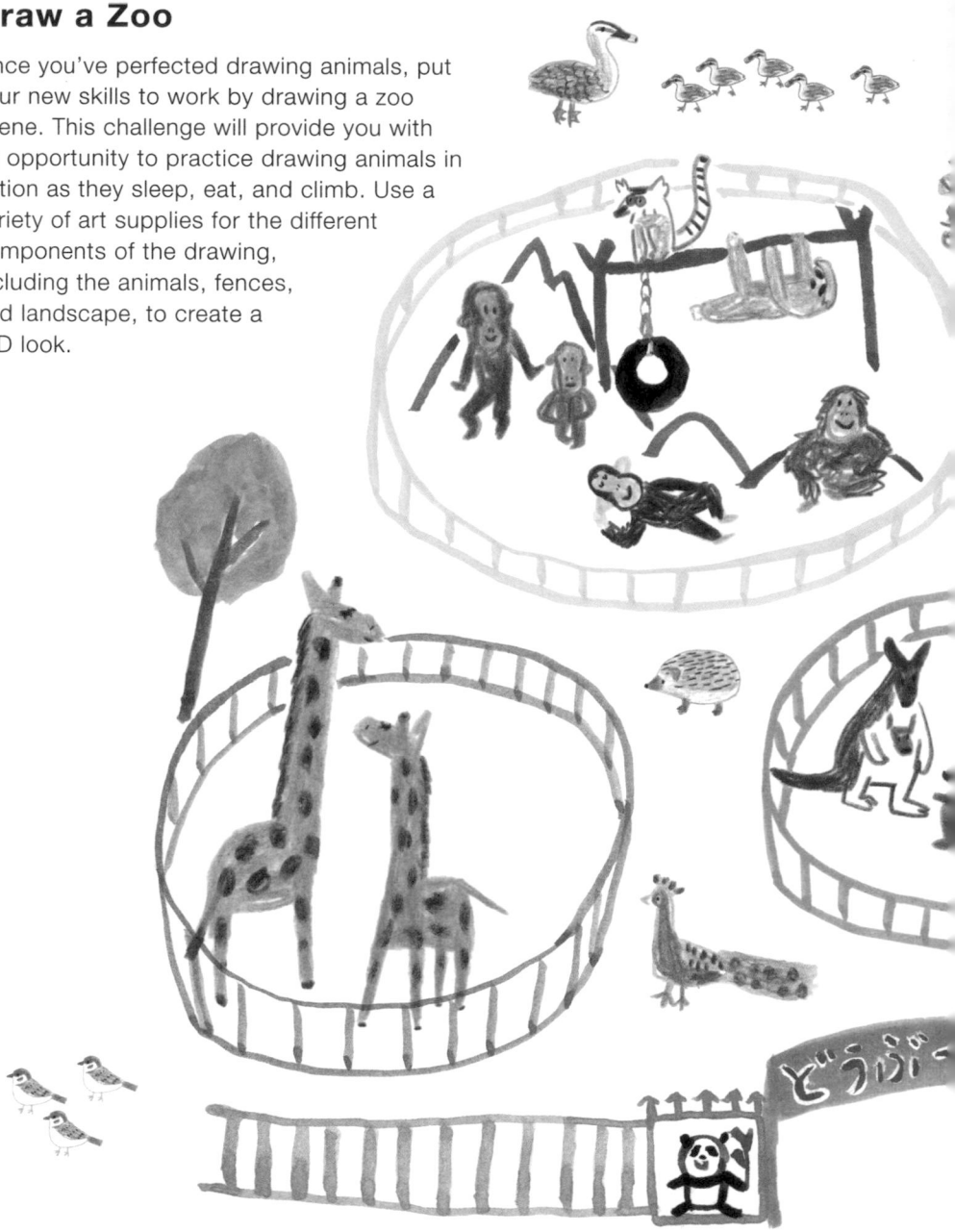

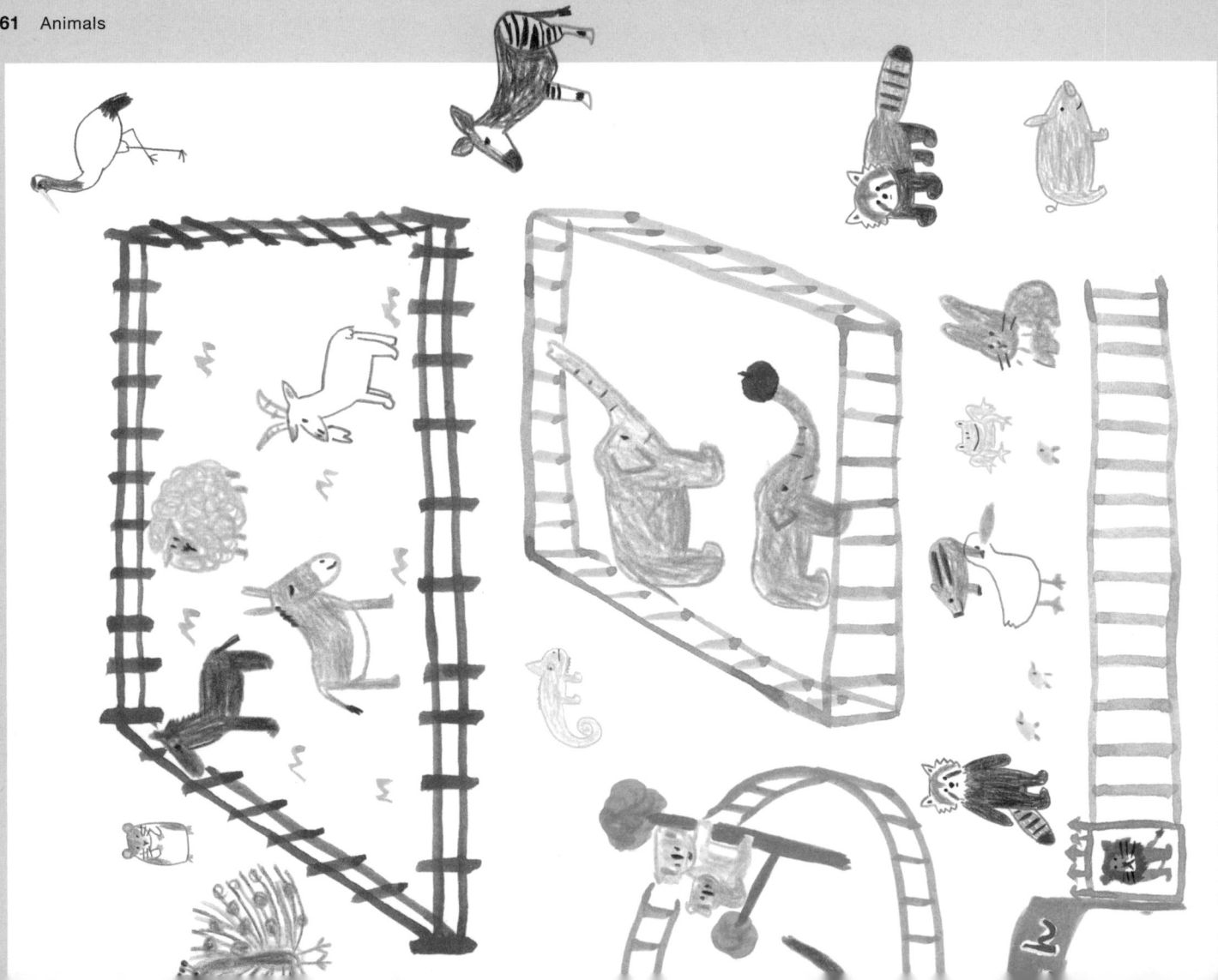

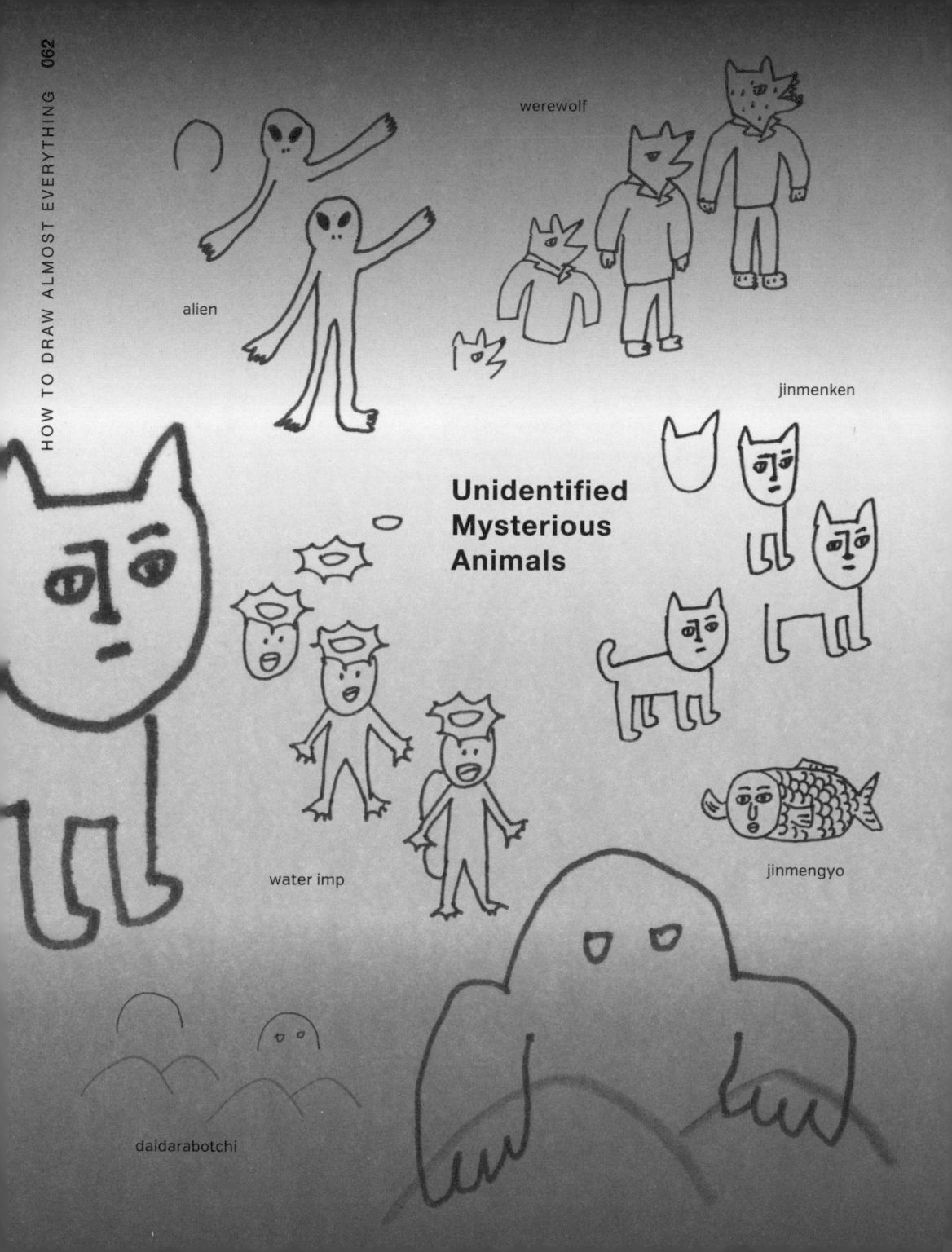


# Unidentified Mysterious Animals

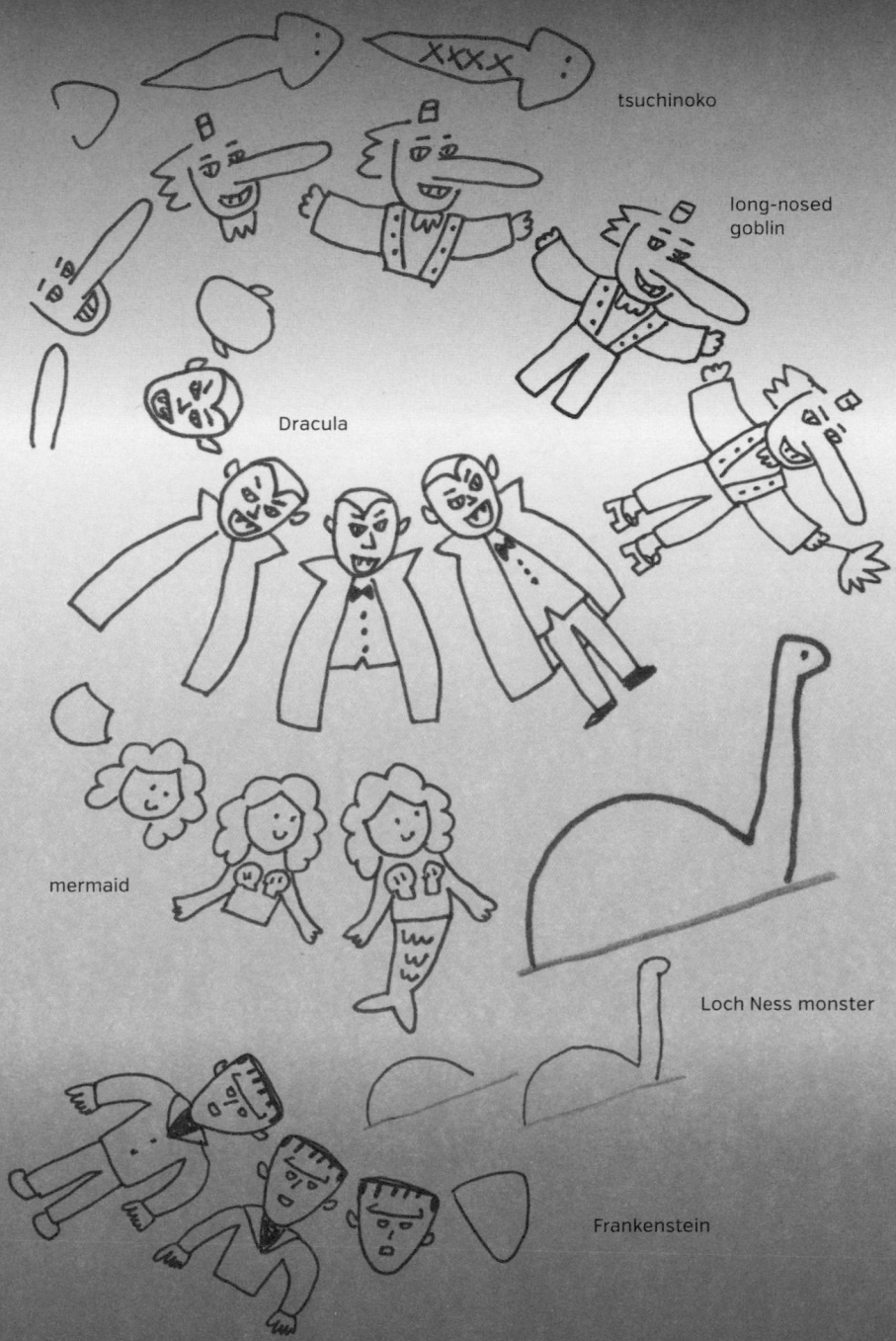
tsuchinoko
long-nosed goblin
Dracula
mermaid
Loch Ness monster
Frankenstein

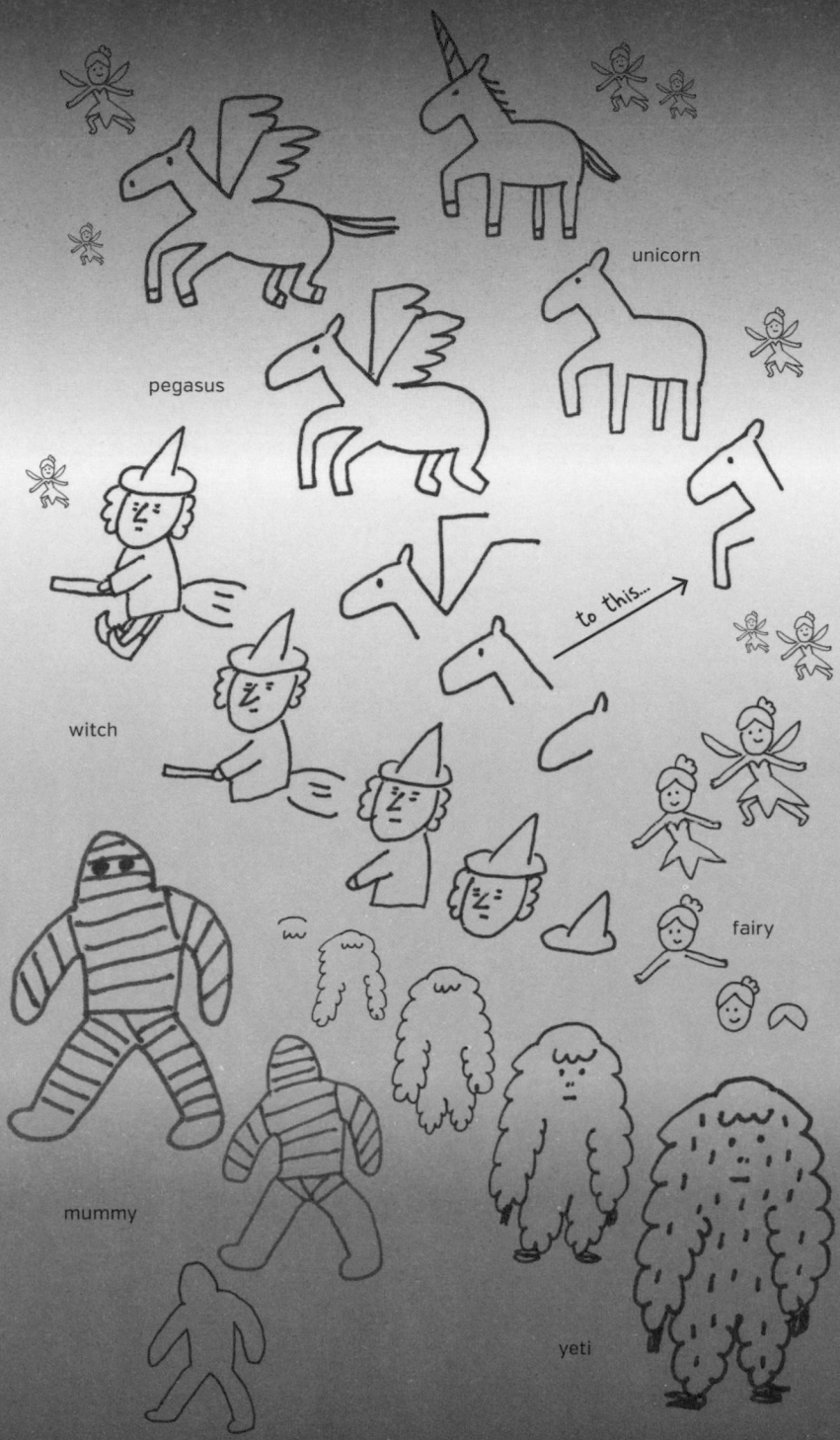
unicorn
pegasus
to this...
witch
fairy
mummy
yeti

# People

- Faces
- Expressions
- Actions
- People by Age & Gender
- Clothing
- Occupations
- Famous Faces

## Faces

*Just changing one component of the face will give a person a completely different look.*

Use simple lines

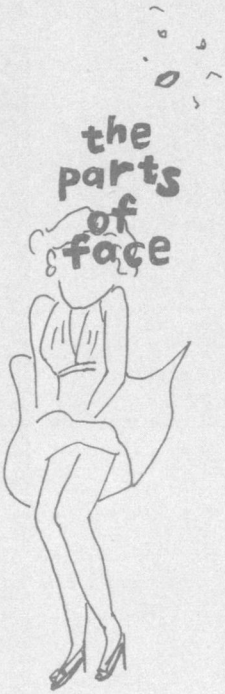


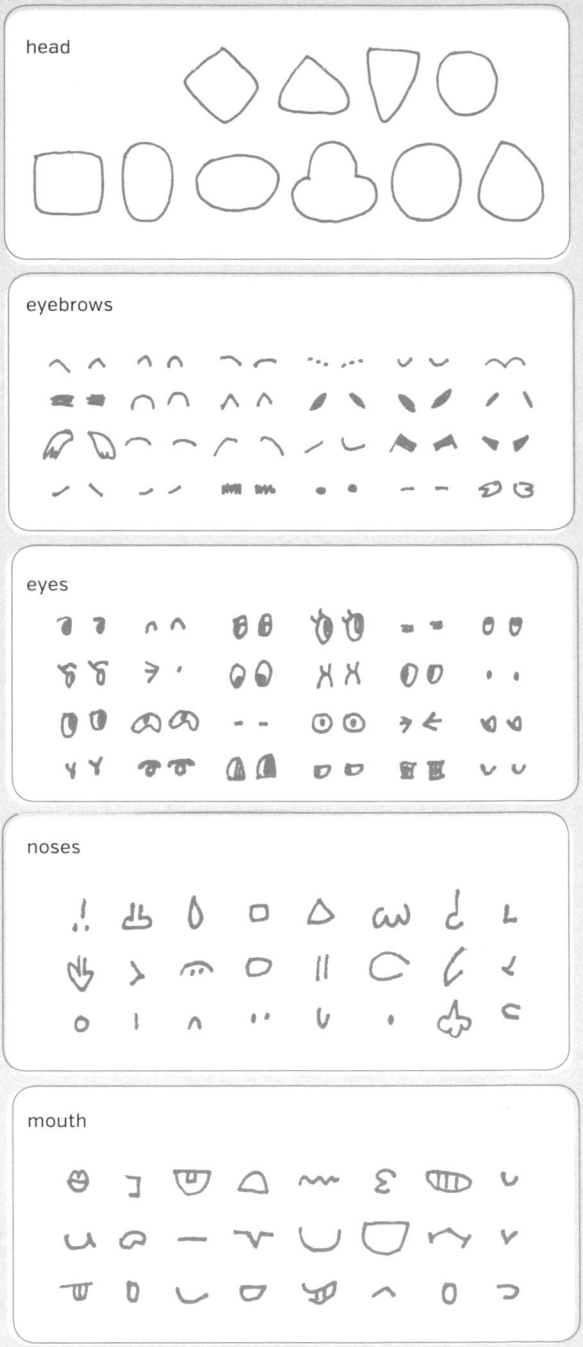

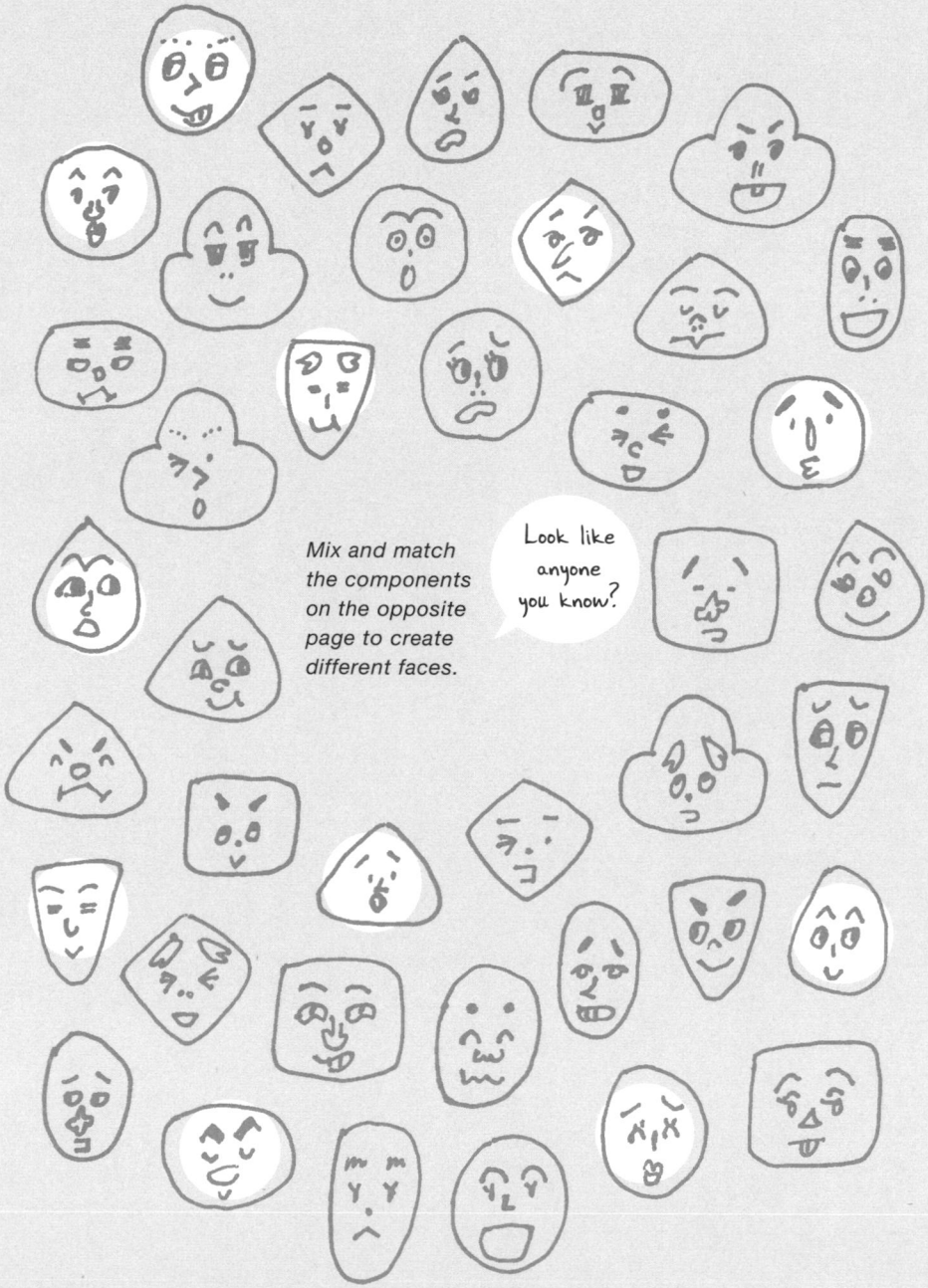


*Mix and match the components on the opposite page to create different faces.*

# Expressions

*You can draw so many different emotions using just a few quick lines.*

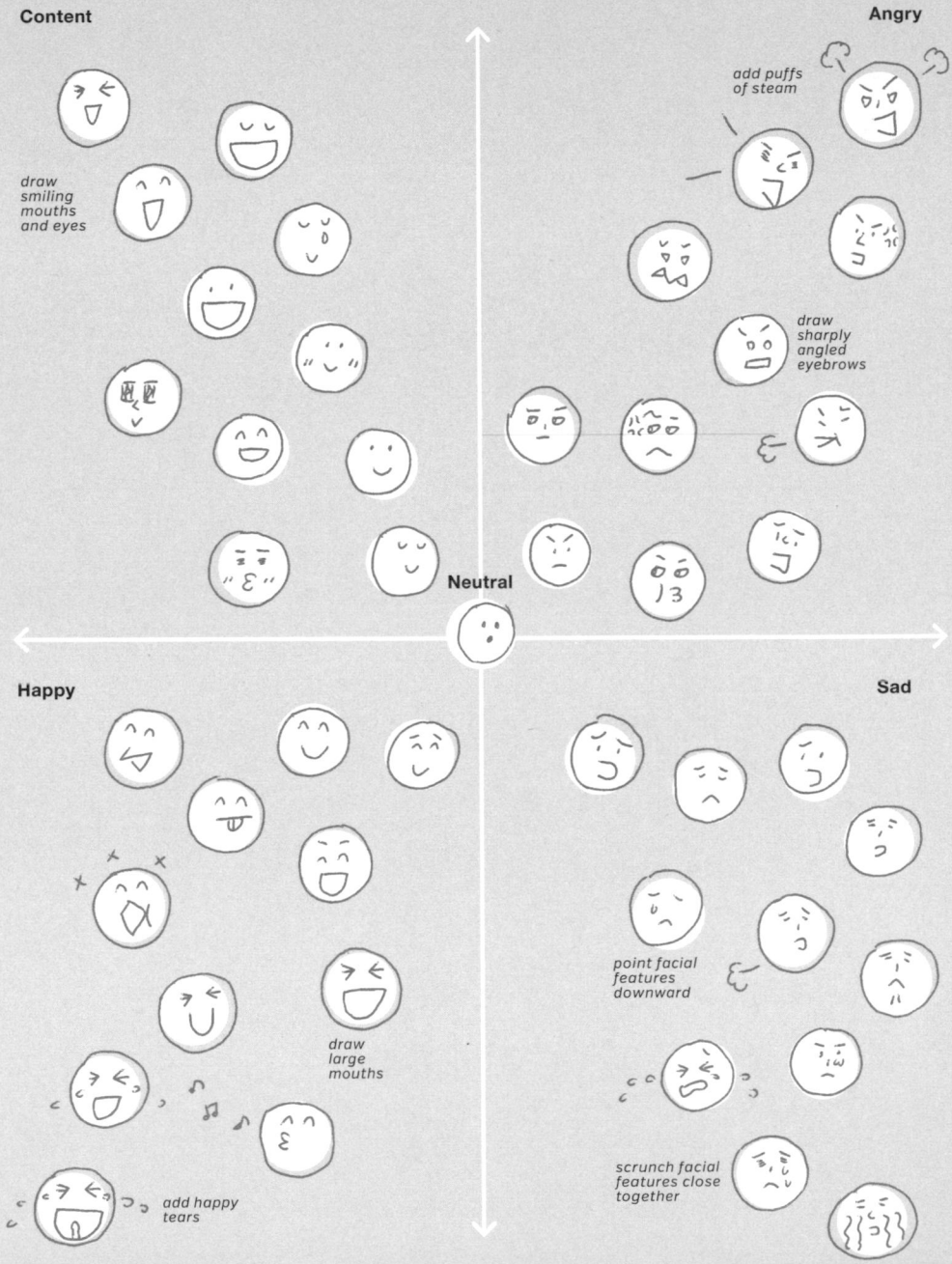

# Actions

*Add arms and legs to illustrate various movements.*

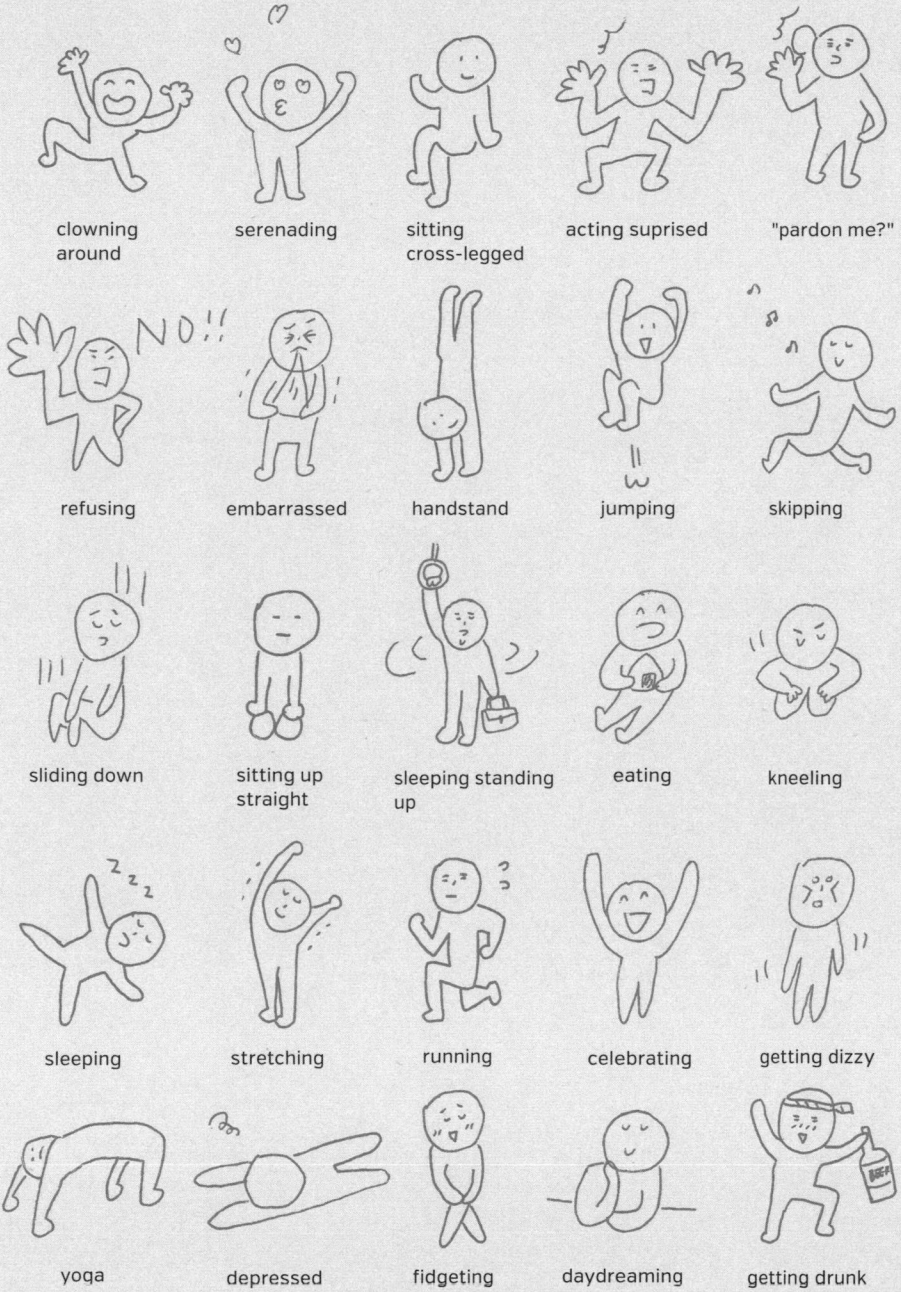


clowning around | serenading | sitting cross-legged | acting suprised | "pardon me?"

refusing | embarrassed | handstand | jumping | skipping

sliding down | sitting up straight | sleeping standing up | eating | kneeling

sleeping | stretching | running | celebrating | getting dizzy

yoga | depressed | fidgeting | daydreaming | getting drunk

# People by Age and Gender: Babies

*When drawing a baby, make both the head and body rounded. Add extra hair and ribbon for a baby girl.*

head

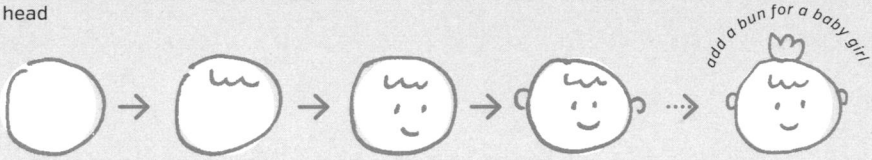


body

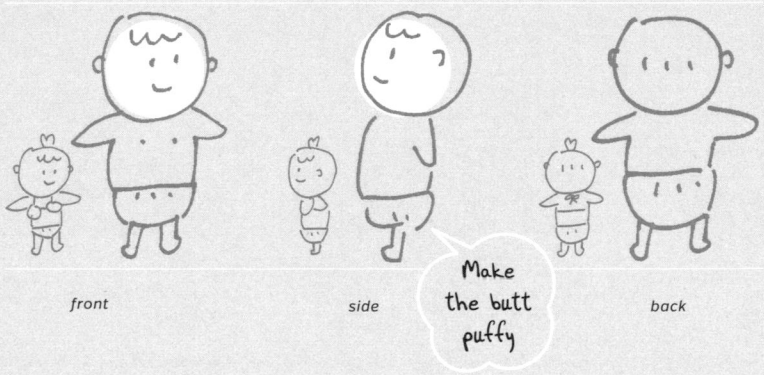


hair

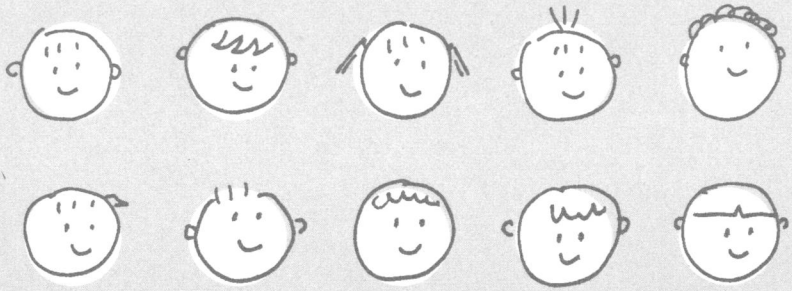

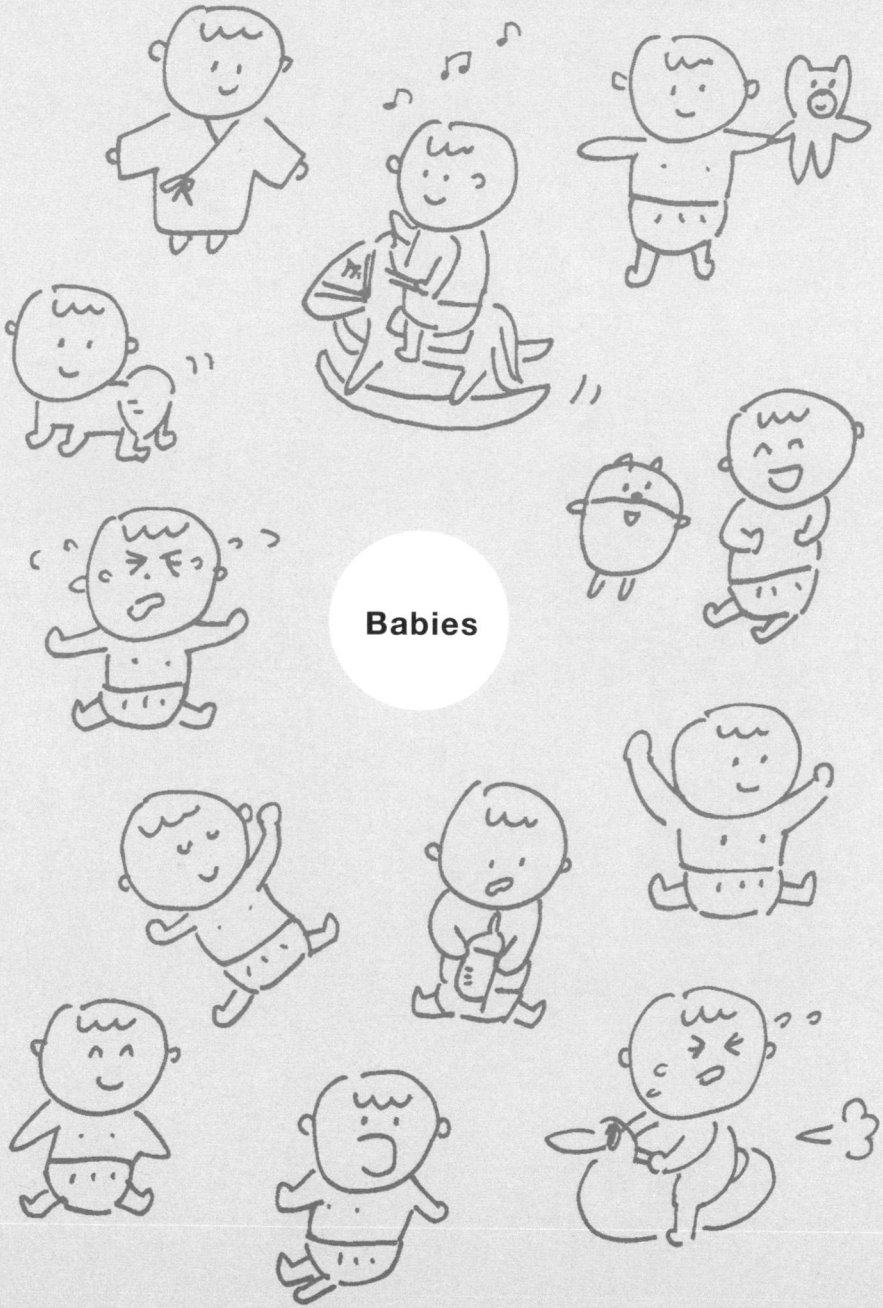
Babies

# People by Age and Gender: Boys

*As boys grow up, their faces change from round to oval. You can also indicate age by changing the proportion of the head and body.*

head

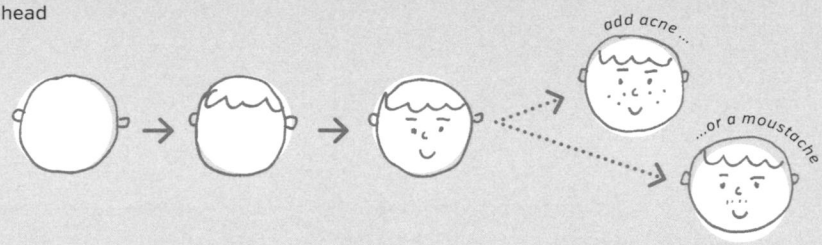


body

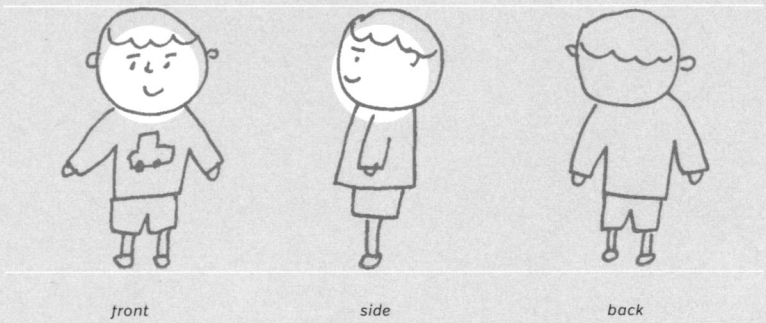


hair

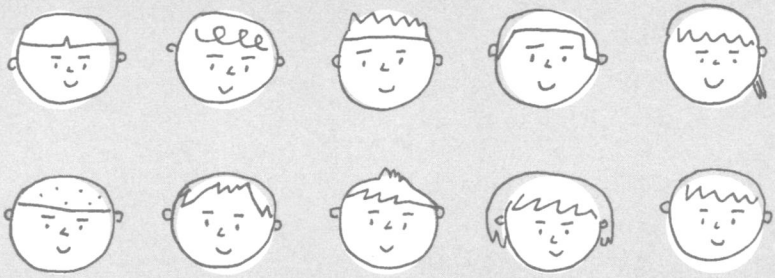

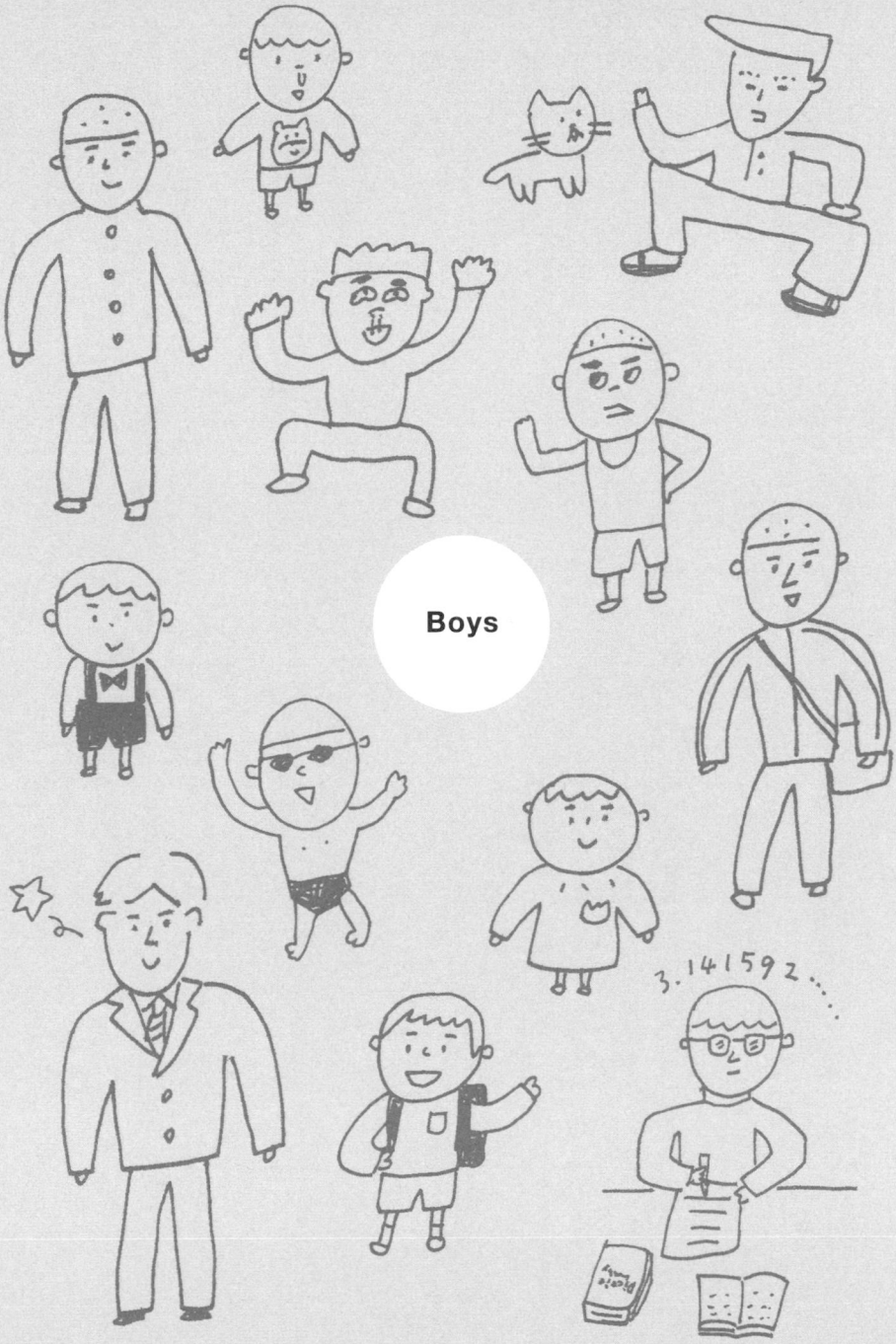
Boys
3.141592……

# People by Age and Gender: Girls

*Express a girl's individuality by changing her hairstyle or her clothes. Just like when drawing boys, adjust the proportion of the head and body to indicate age.*

head

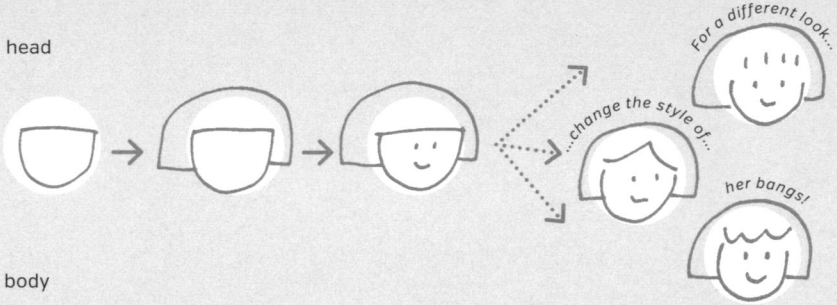


body

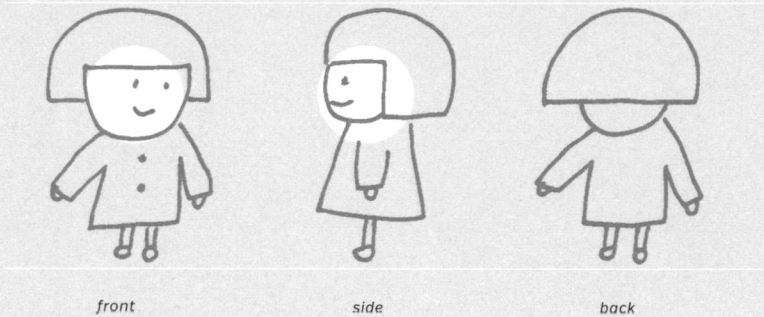


hair

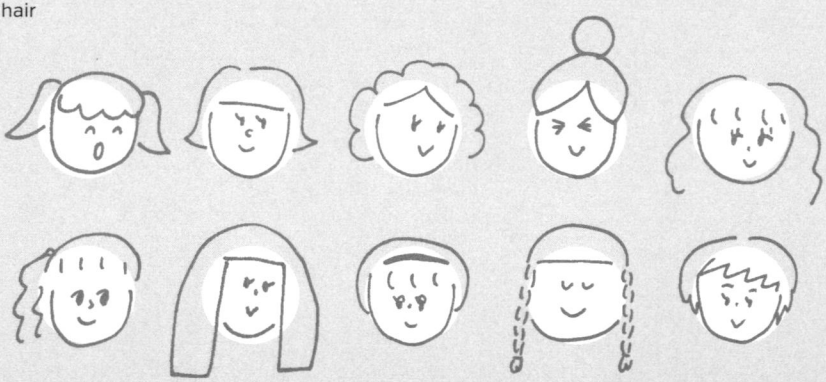

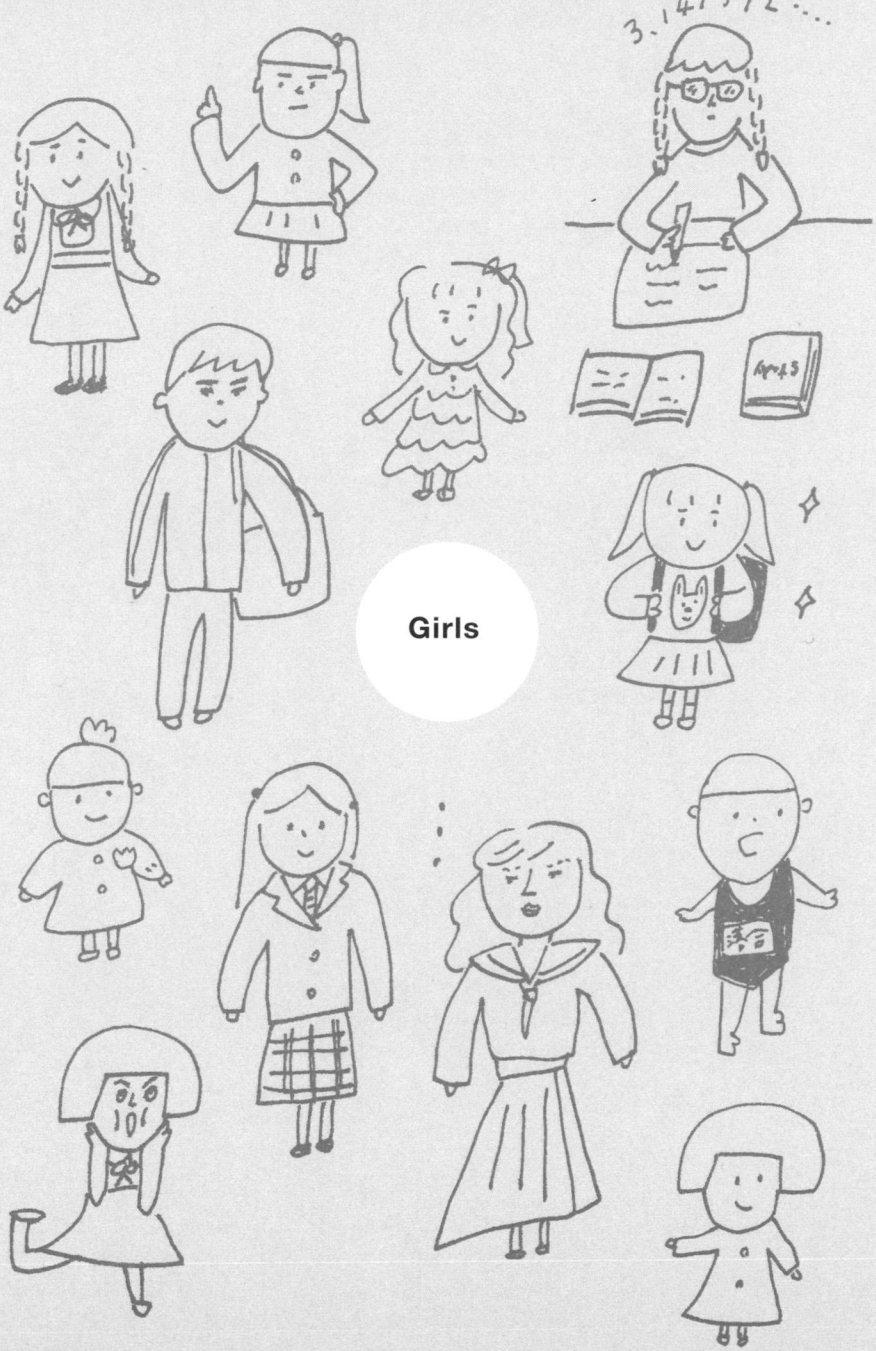


## Girls

# People by Age and Gender: Men

*Consider body type—draw wide shoulders for an athletic body or narrow shoulders for a slim body.*

head

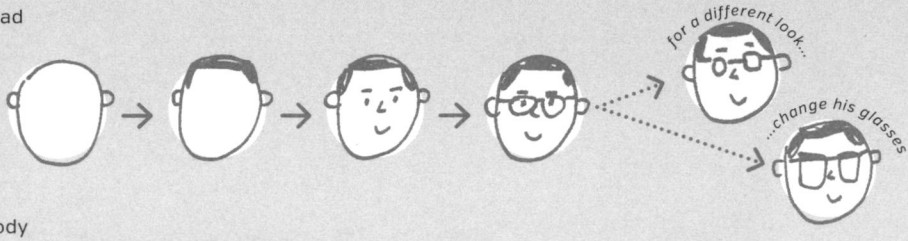


body

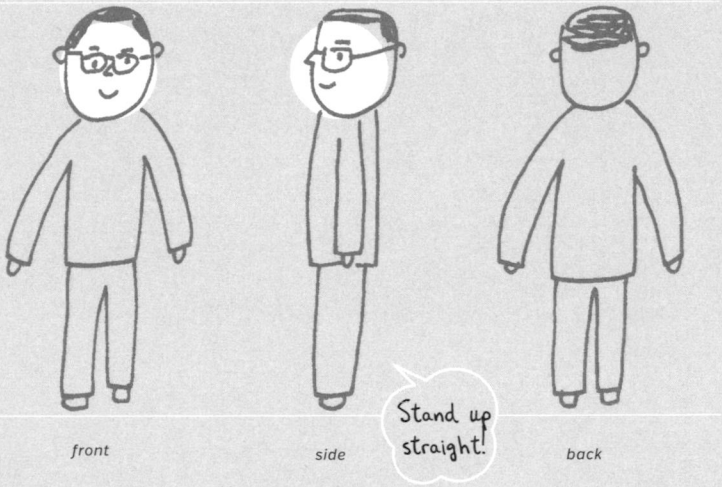


hair

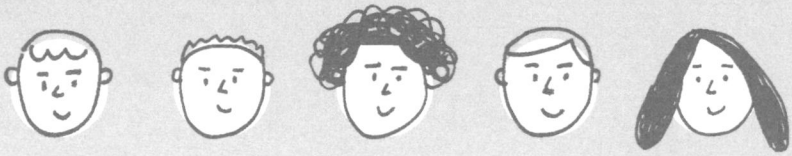

facial hair

# Men

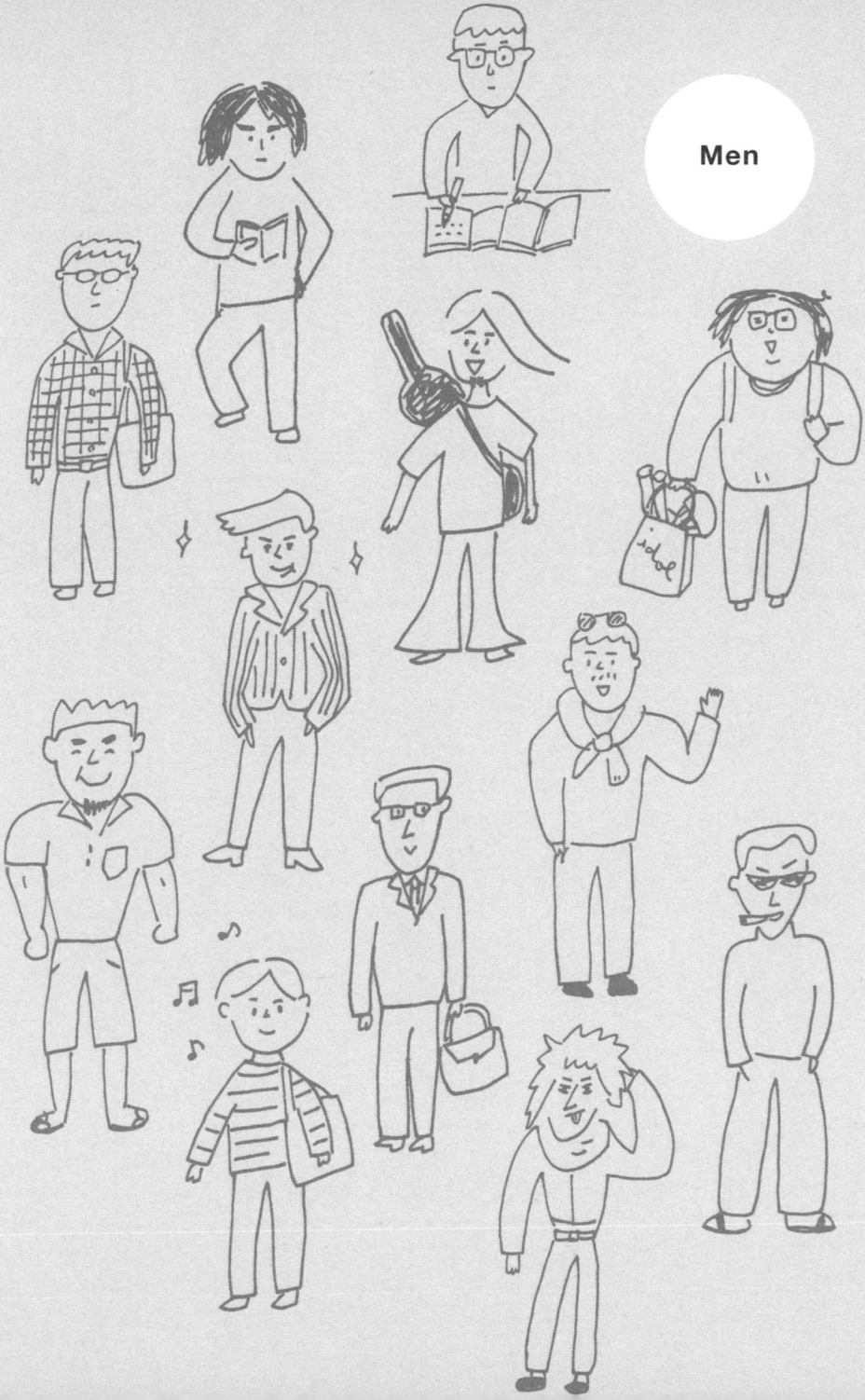

# People by Age and Gender: Women

*Create different impressions by altering a woman's hairstyle, eyelashes, and eyebrows.*

head

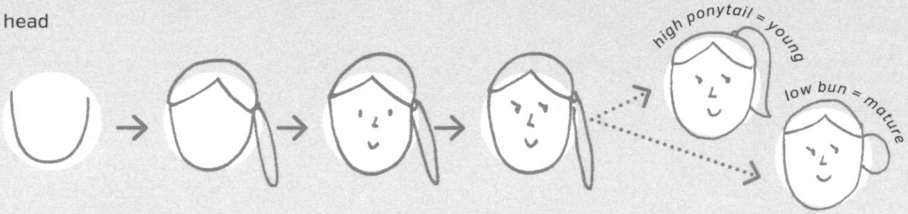


body

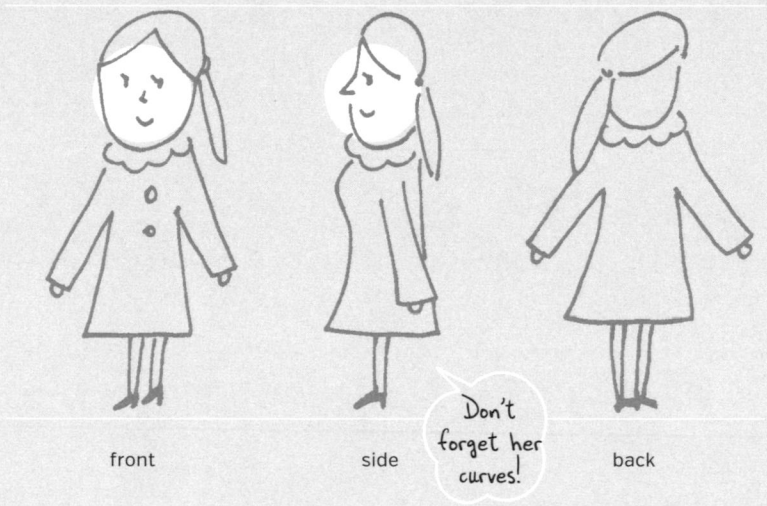


hair

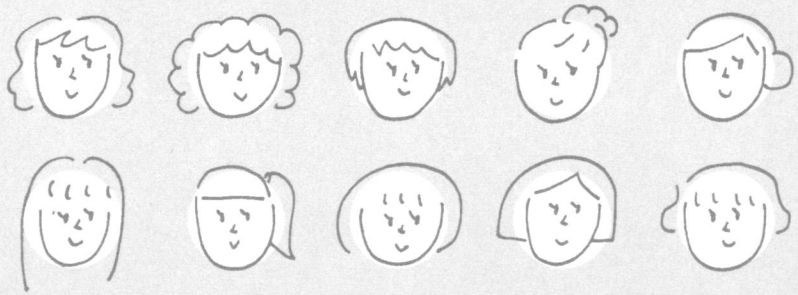

## Women

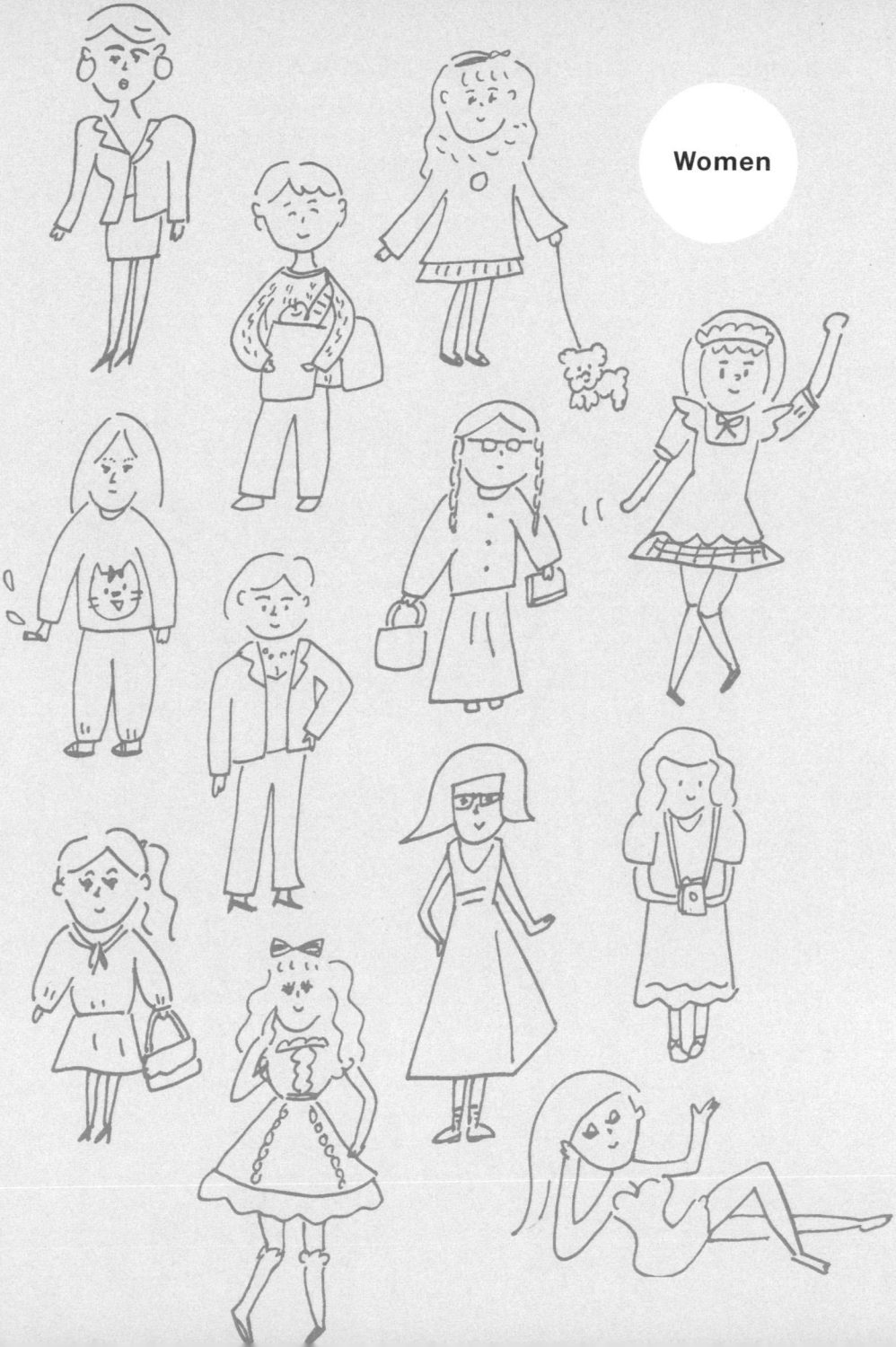

# People by Age and Gender: Elderly Men

*Use laugh lines, crows feet, and bushy eyebrows to express age within the face. When drawing an elderly man's body, consider his posture and include details such as hunched shoulders.*

head

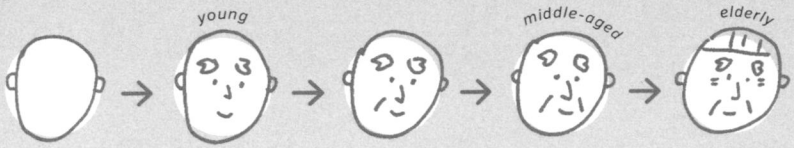


body

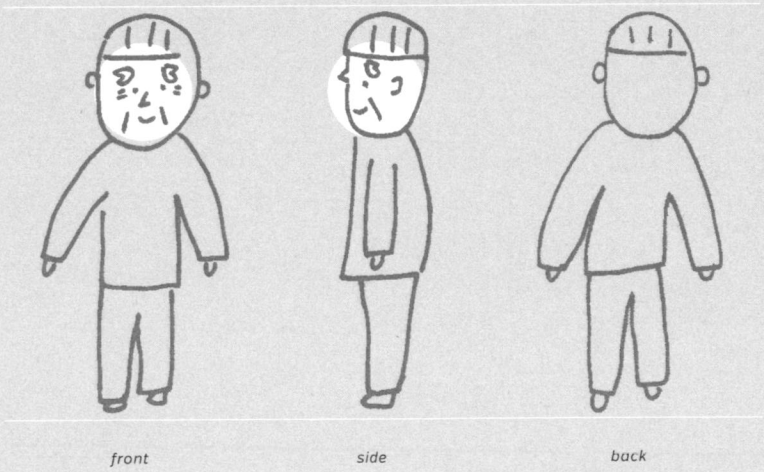


hair

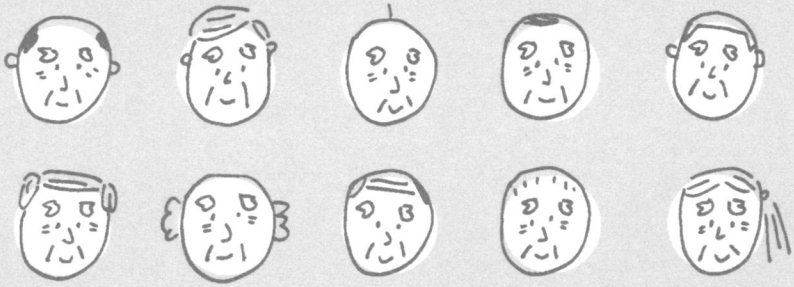

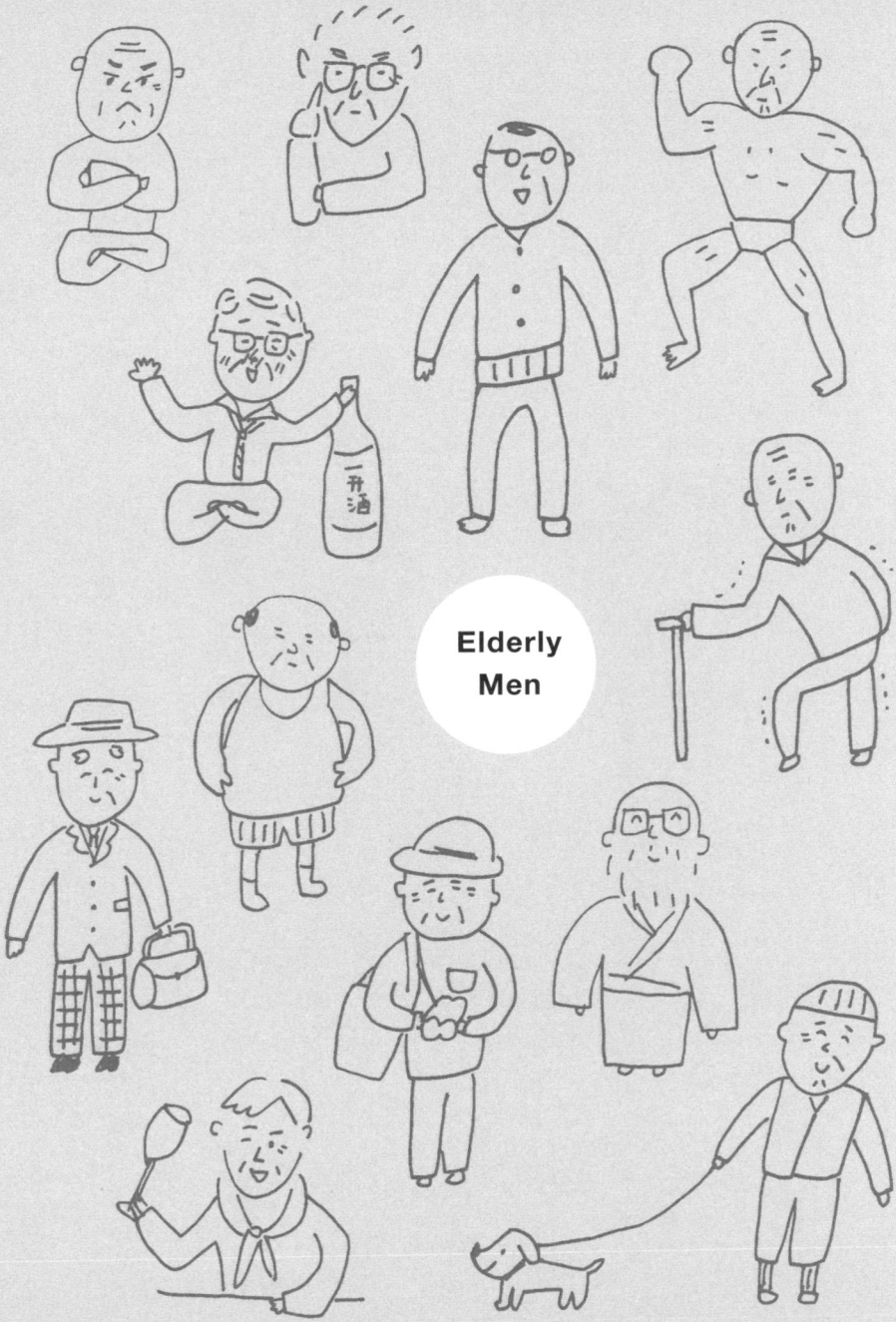


# Elderly Men

# People by Age and Gender: Elderly Women

*Older women often wear their hair short or pulled back in a low bun. Don't forget to add deep laugh lines around her mouth.*

head

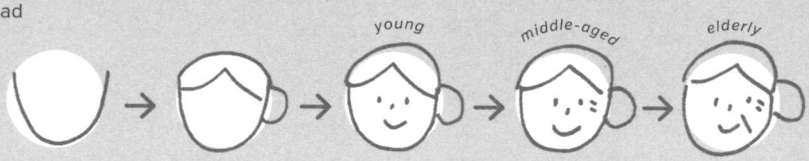


body

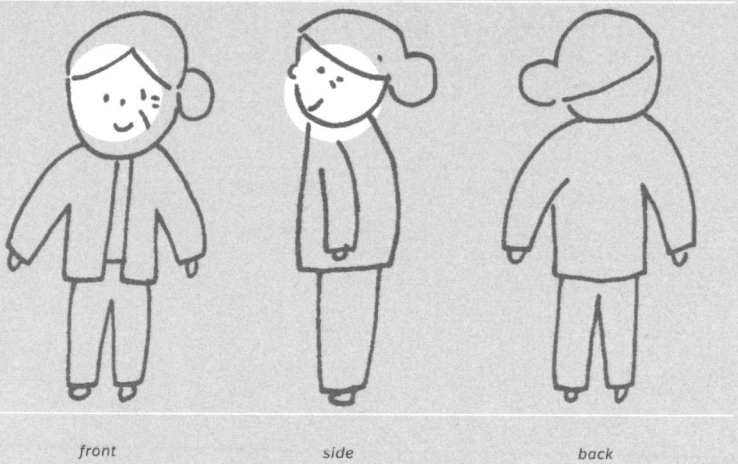


hair

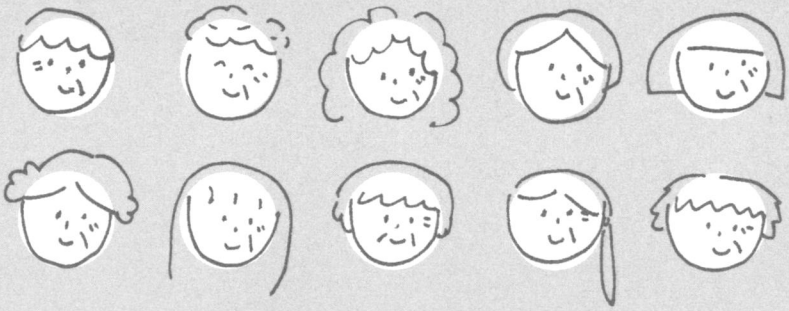

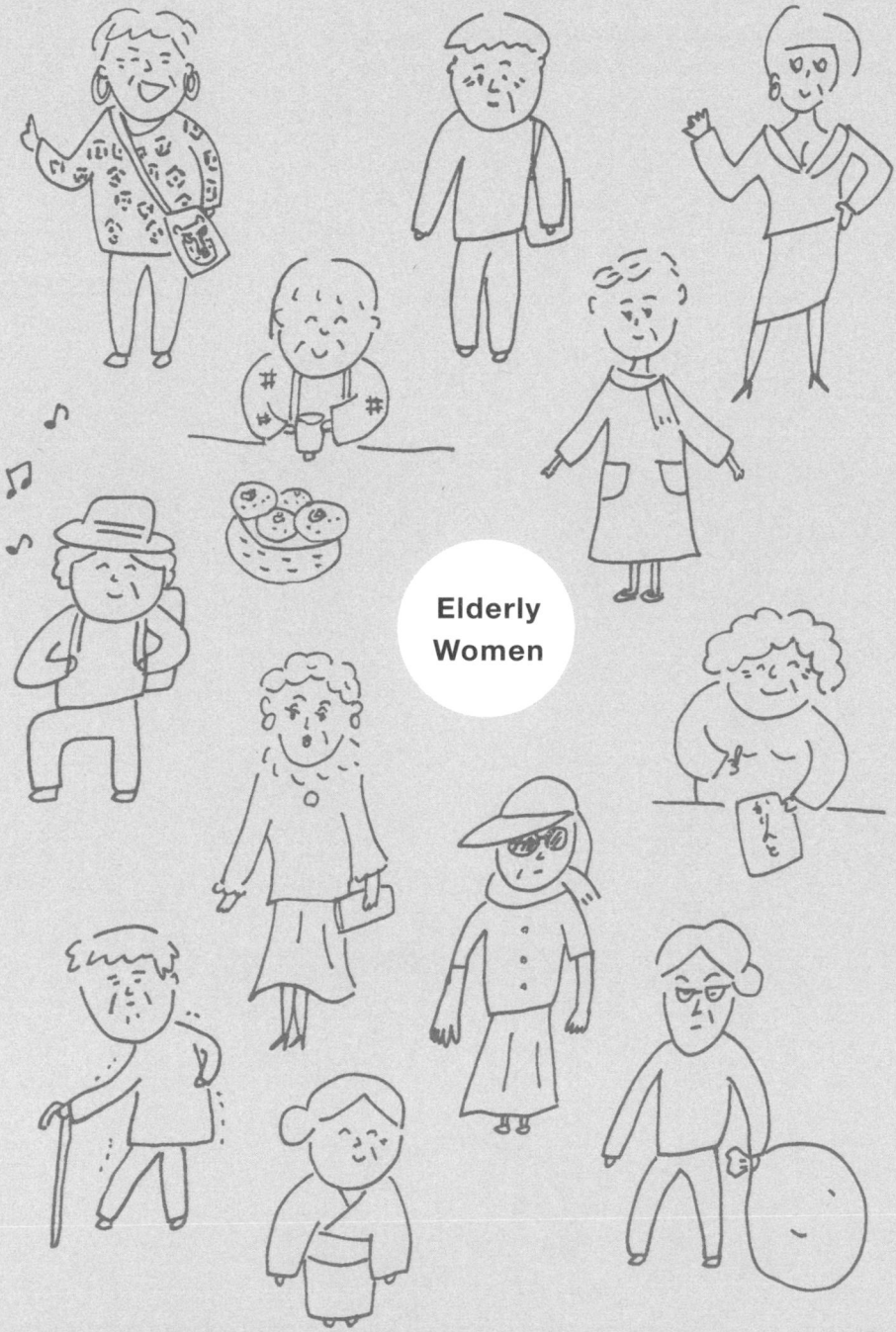
Elderly
Women

# Clothing

*Clothing provides an excellent opportunity to include details about a person's age, gender, and personality.*

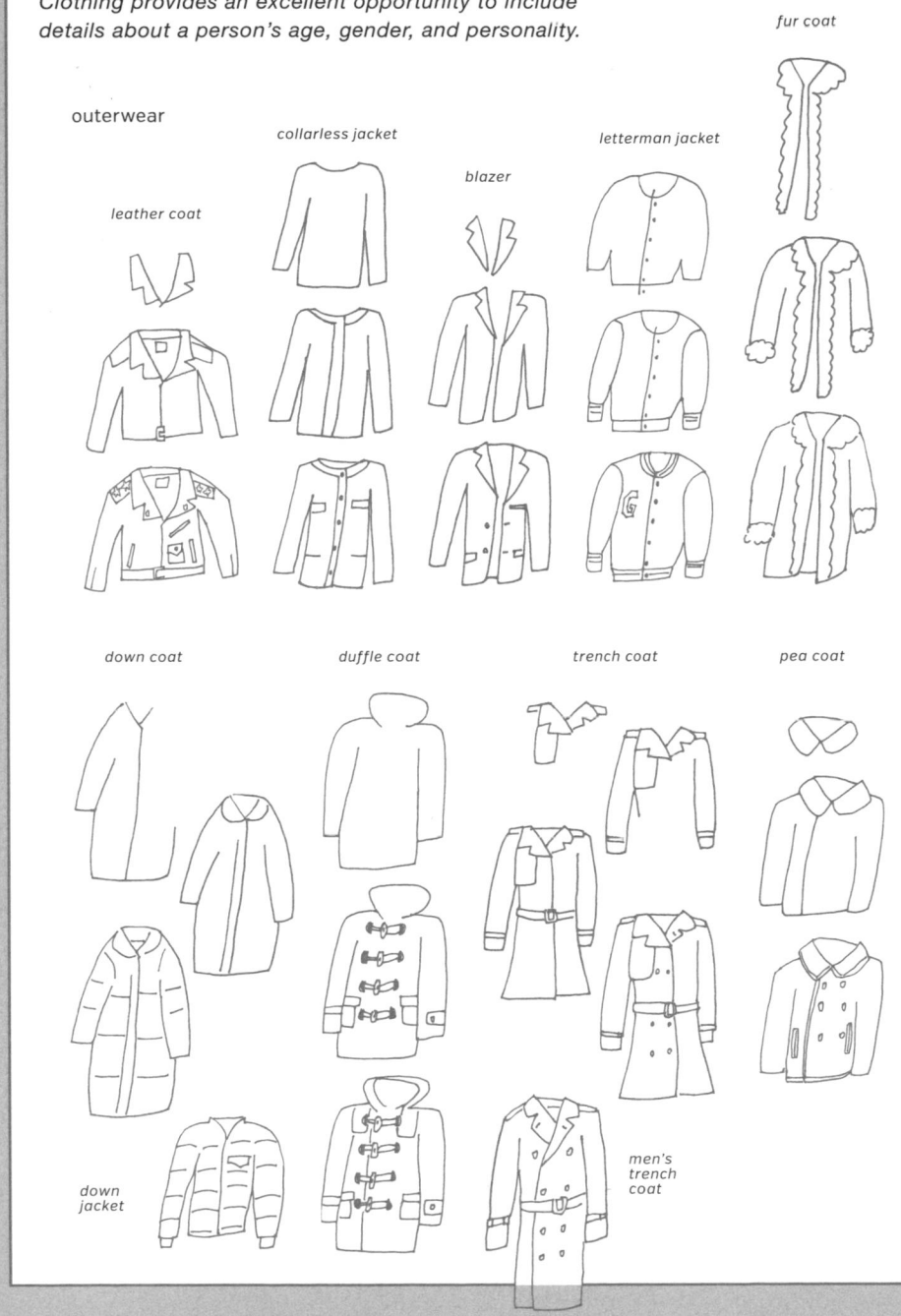

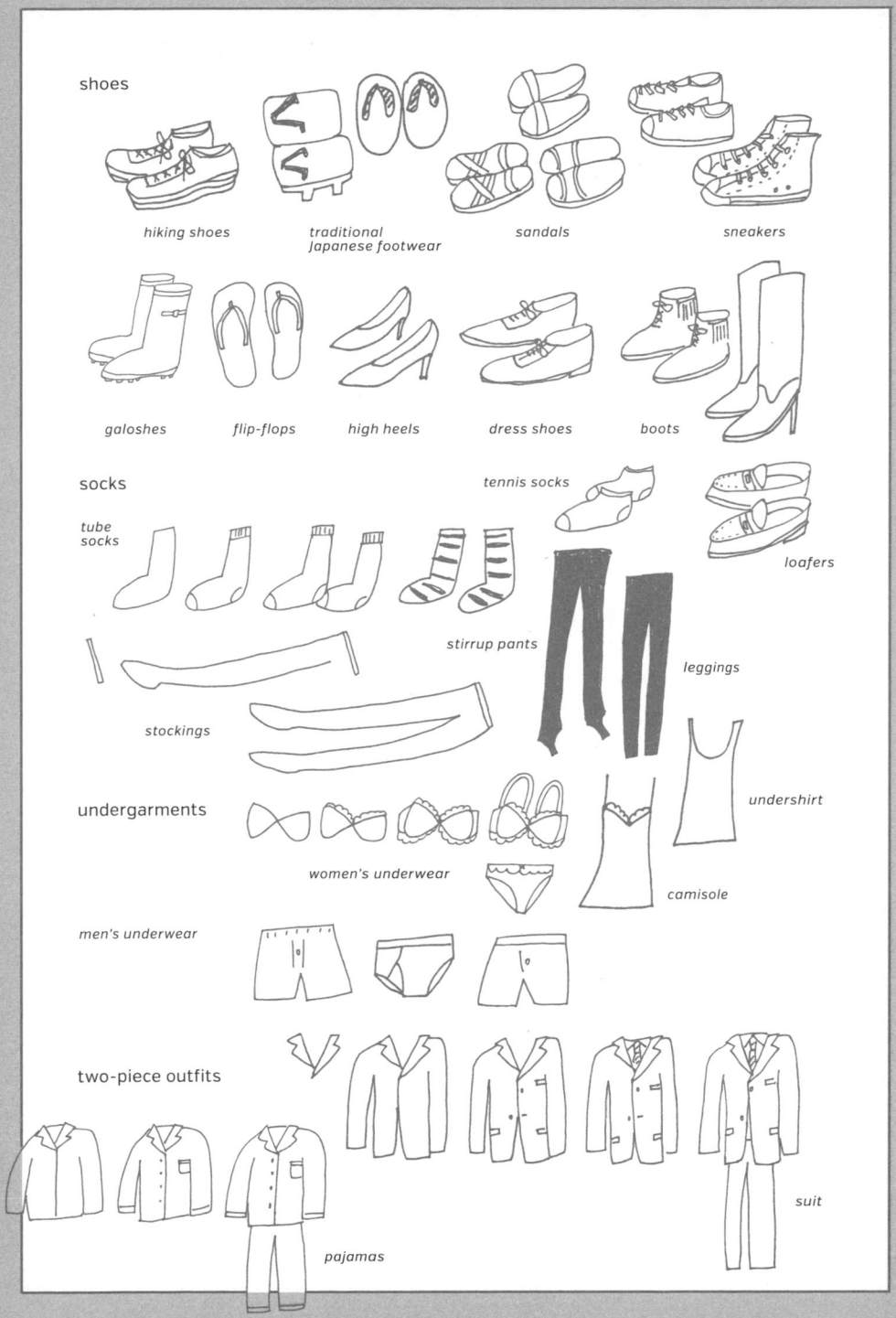
shoes
hiking shoes
traditional Japanese footwear
sandals
sneakers
galoshes
flip-flops
high heels
dress shoes
boots
socks
tennis socks
tube socks
loafers
stirrup pants
leggings
stockings
undershirt
undergarments
women's underwear
camisole
men's underwear
two-piece outfits
suit
pajamas

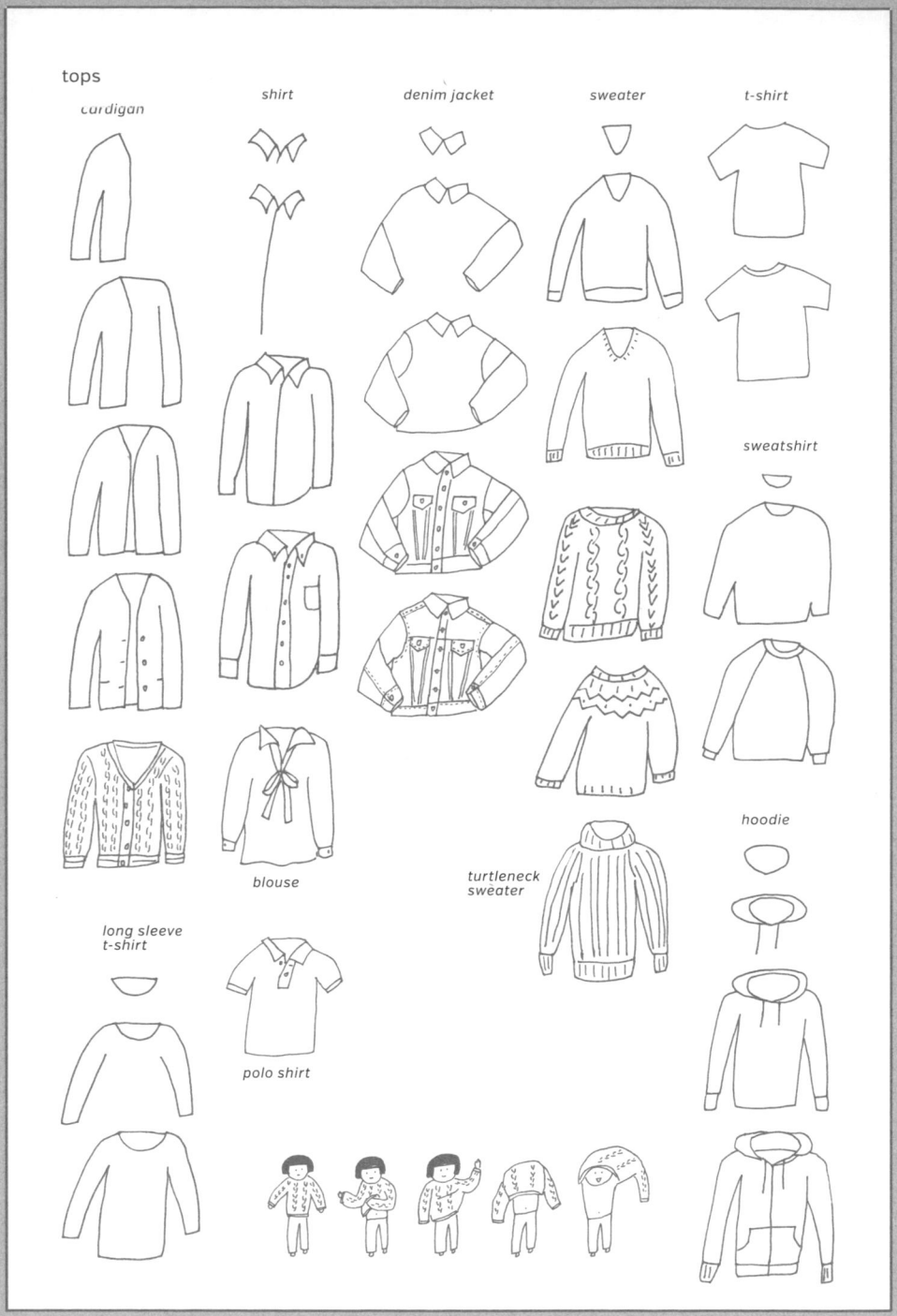
tops
cardigan
shirt
denim jacket
sweater
t-shirt
sweatshirt
blouse
turtleneck sweater
hoodie
long sleeve t-shirt
polo shirt

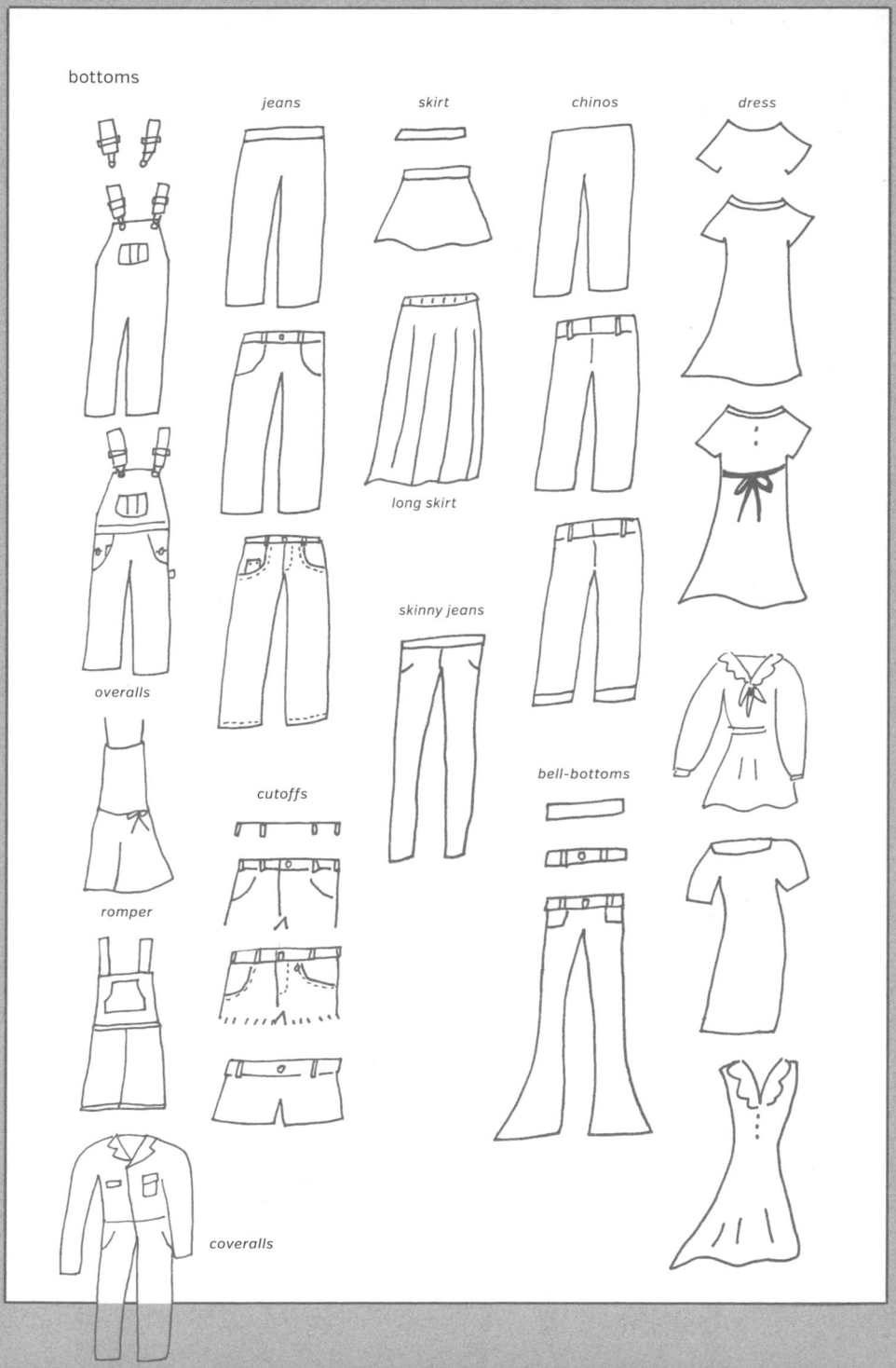
bottoms
jeans
skirt
chinos
dress
long skirt
skinny jeans
overalls
cutoffs
bell-bottoms
romper
coveralls

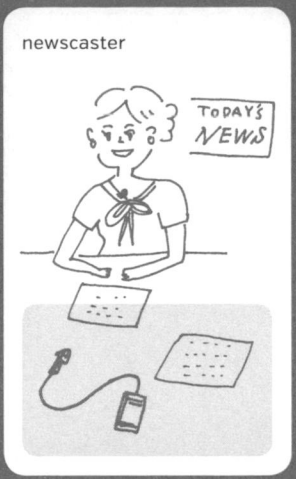


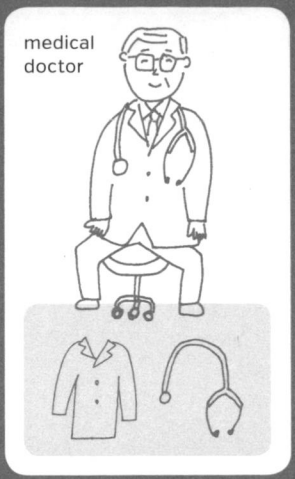


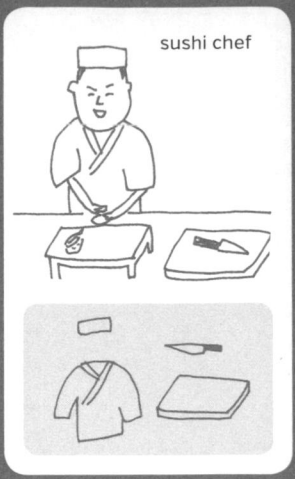


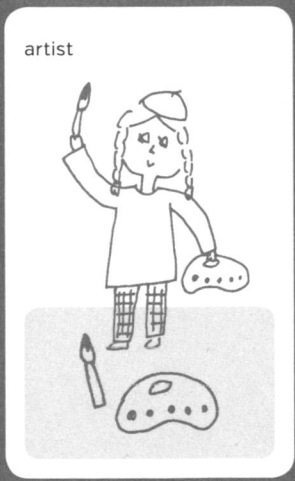


Remember to add detail!

## Occupations

*For realistic looking drawings, add detailed outfits and props related to the occupation.*

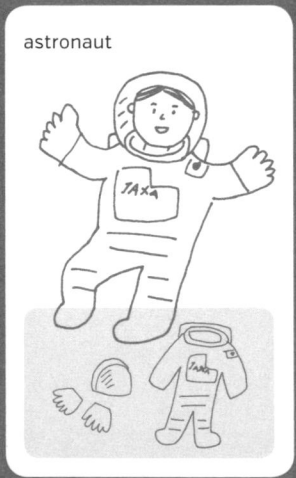


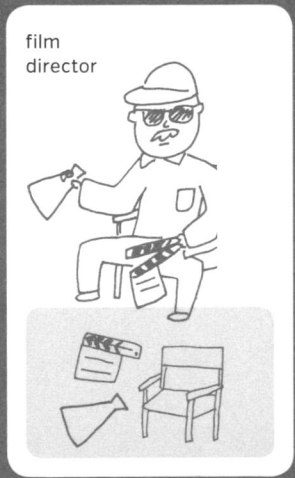


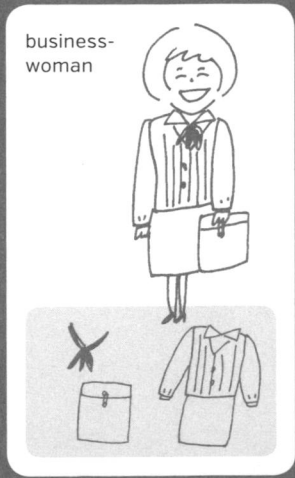

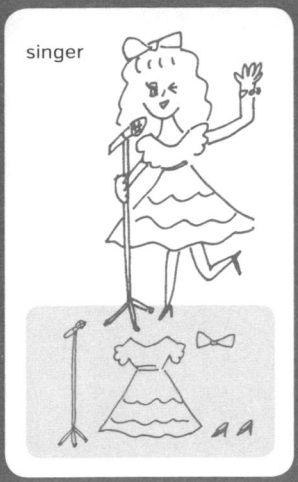
singer

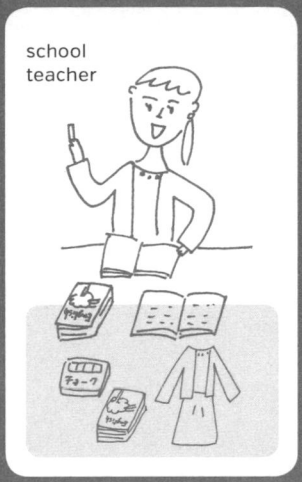
school
teacher

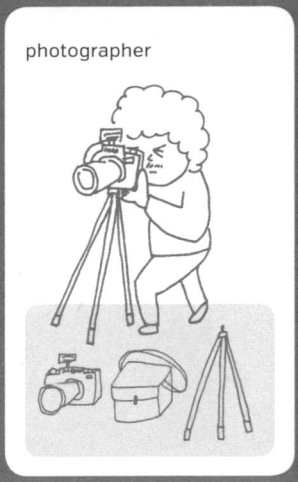
photographer

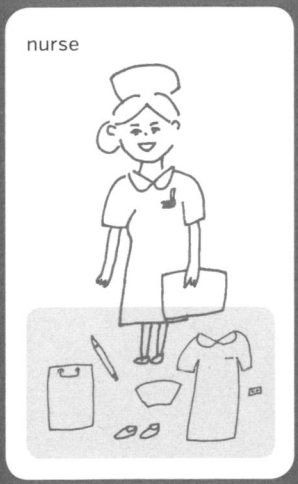
nurse

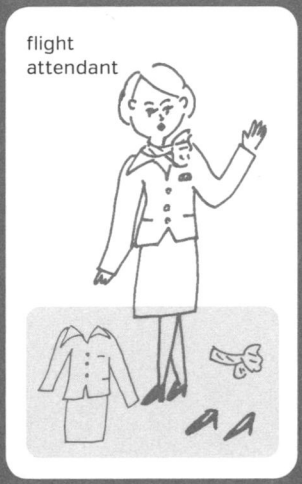
flight
attendant

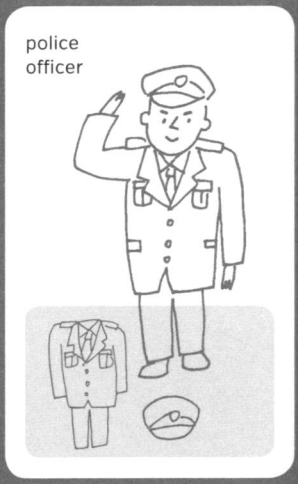
police
officer

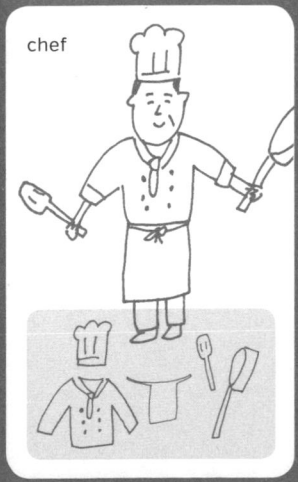
chef

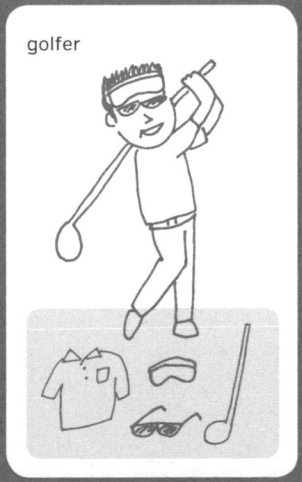
golfer

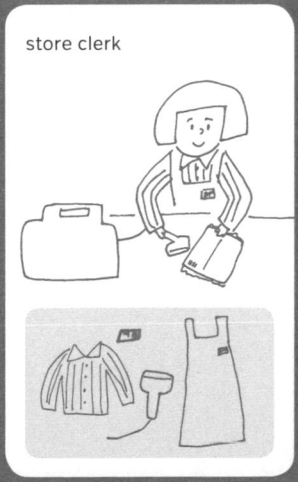
store clerk

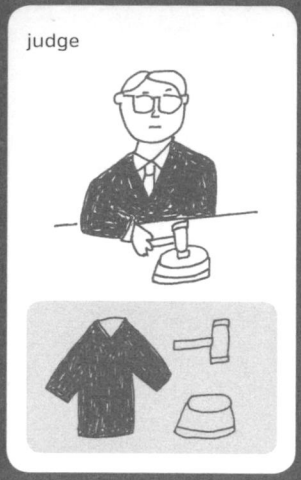
judge

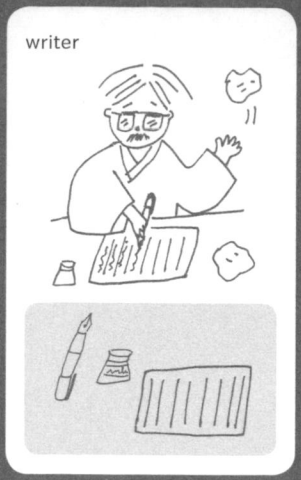
writer

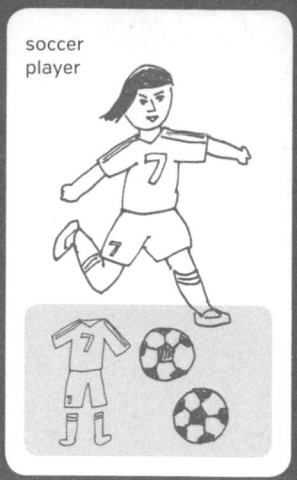
soccer
player

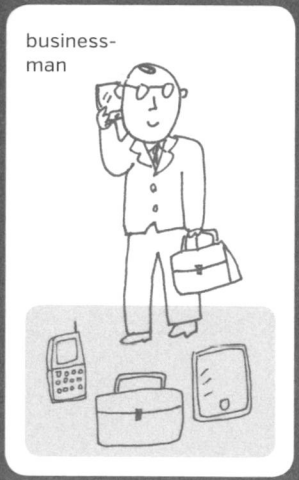
business-
man

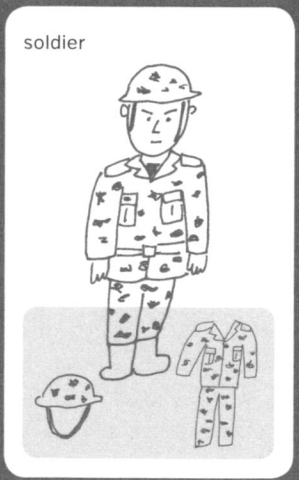
soldier

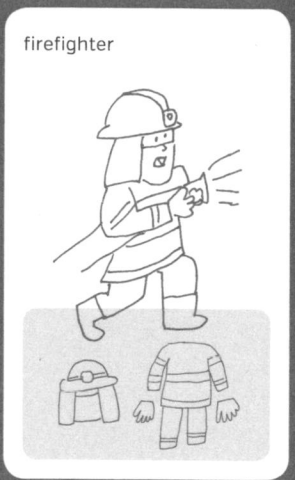
firefighter

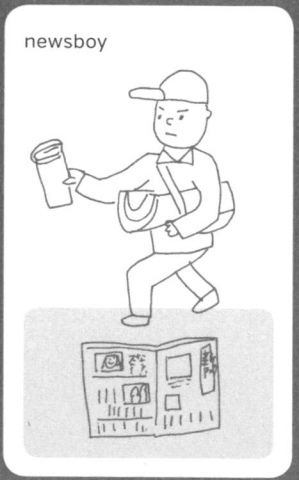
newsboy

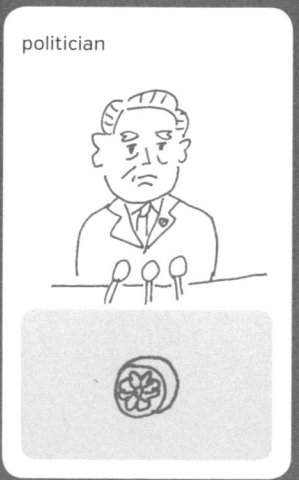
politician

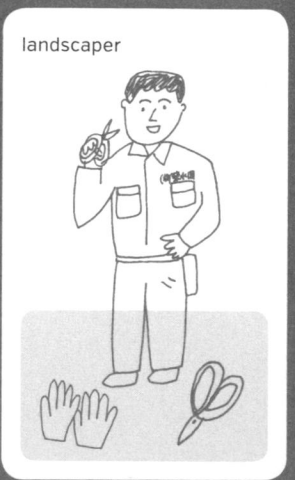
landscaper

carpenter

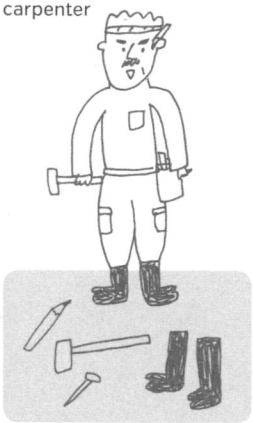

taxi driver

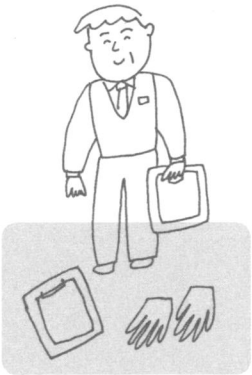

home delivery driver

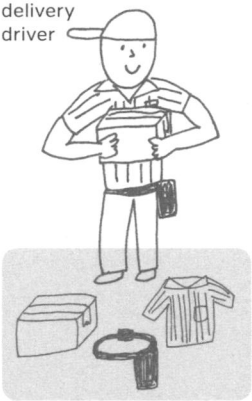

chef

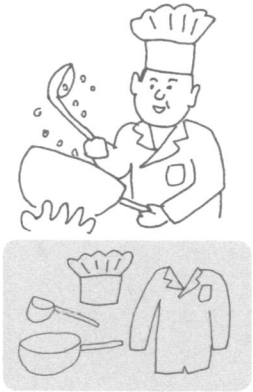

designer

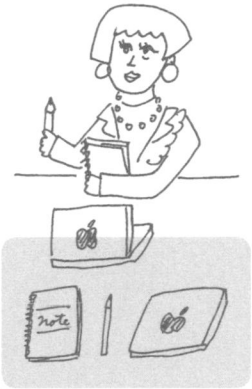


tennis player

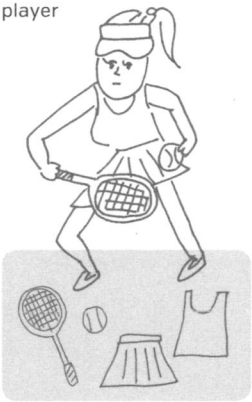

train conductor

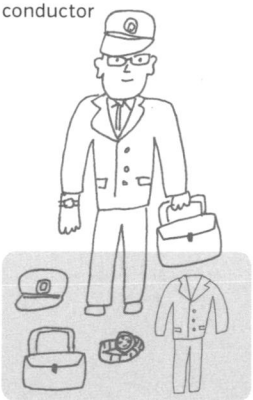

farmer

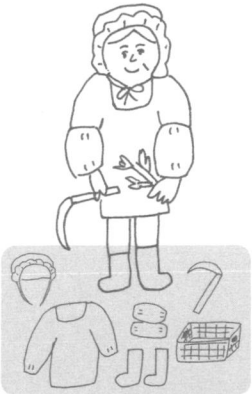

pilot

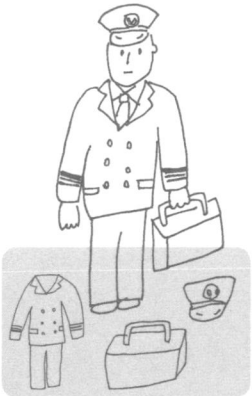

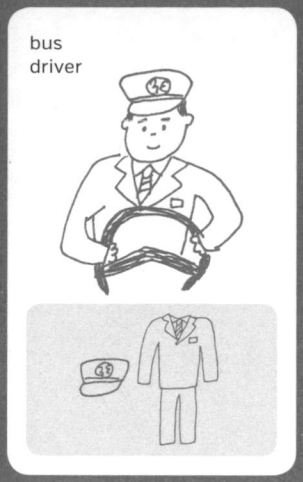
bus
driver

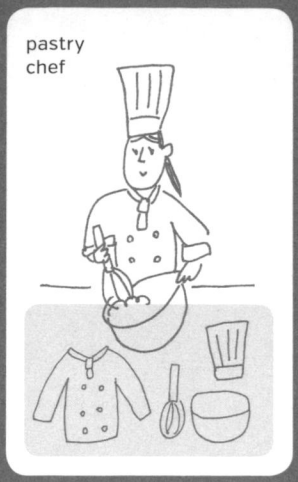
pastry
chef

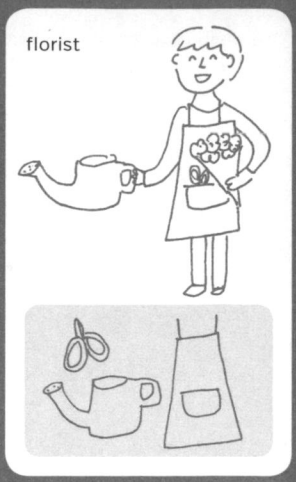
florist

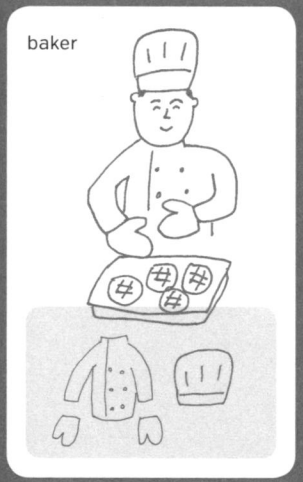
baker

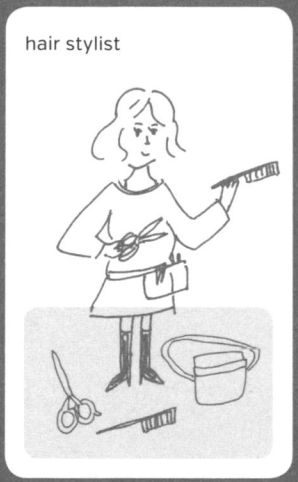
hair stylist

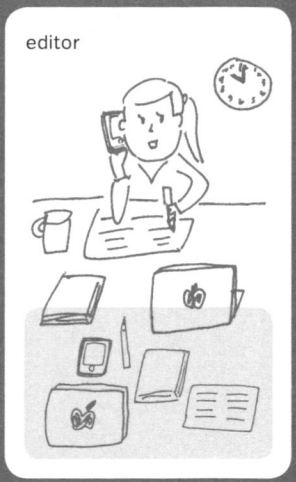
editor

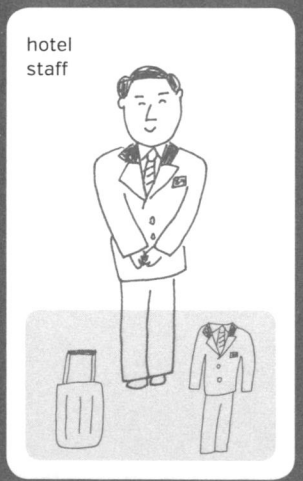
hotel
staff

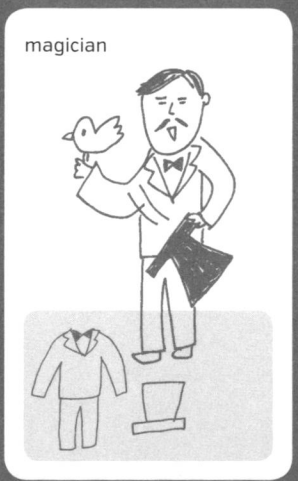
magician

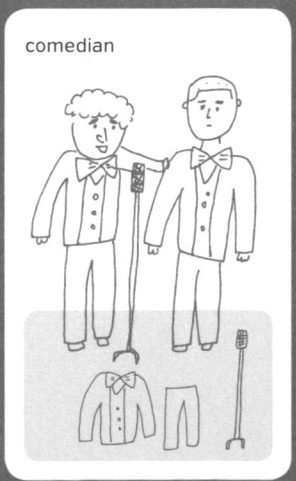
comedian

model

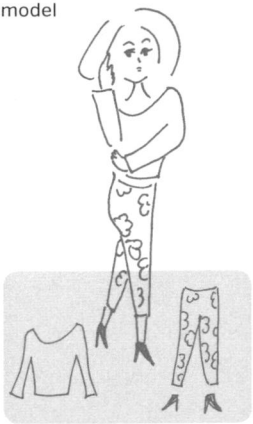

green grocer

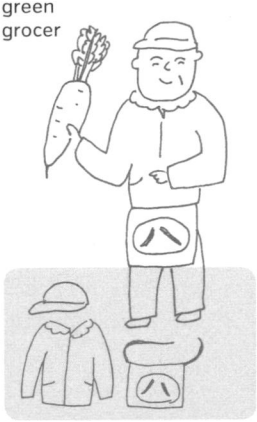

baseball player

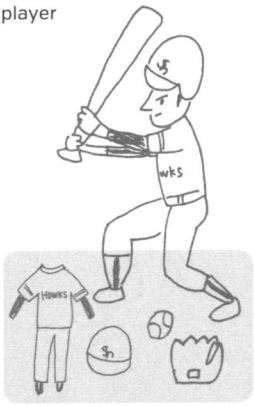


kindergarten teacher

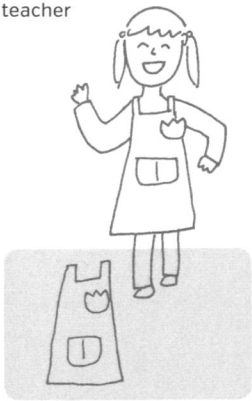

traditional storyteller

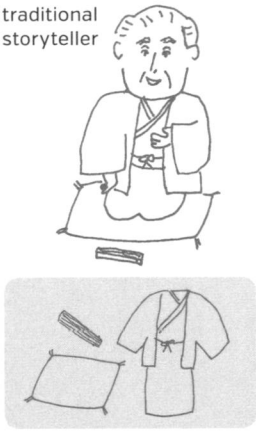

sumo wrestler

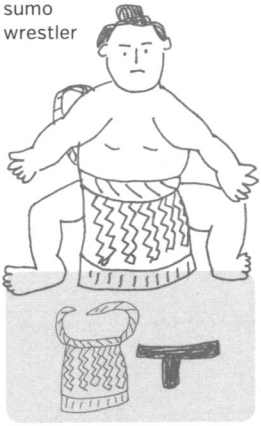

fisherman

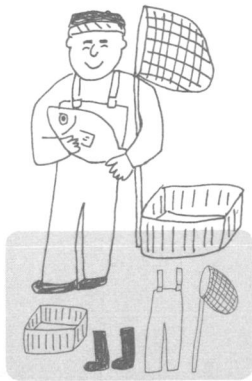

forestry worker

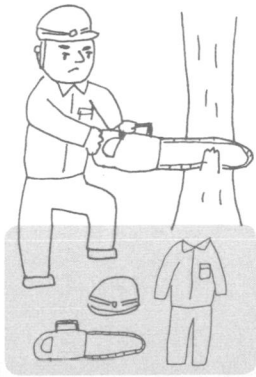

racecar driver

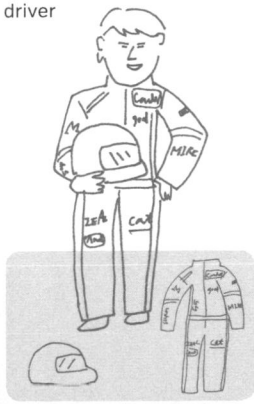

# Famous Faces

*Capture the most memorable characteristics by concentrating on the hairstyles, expressions, and outfits worn by these famous figures in history.*

Musicians

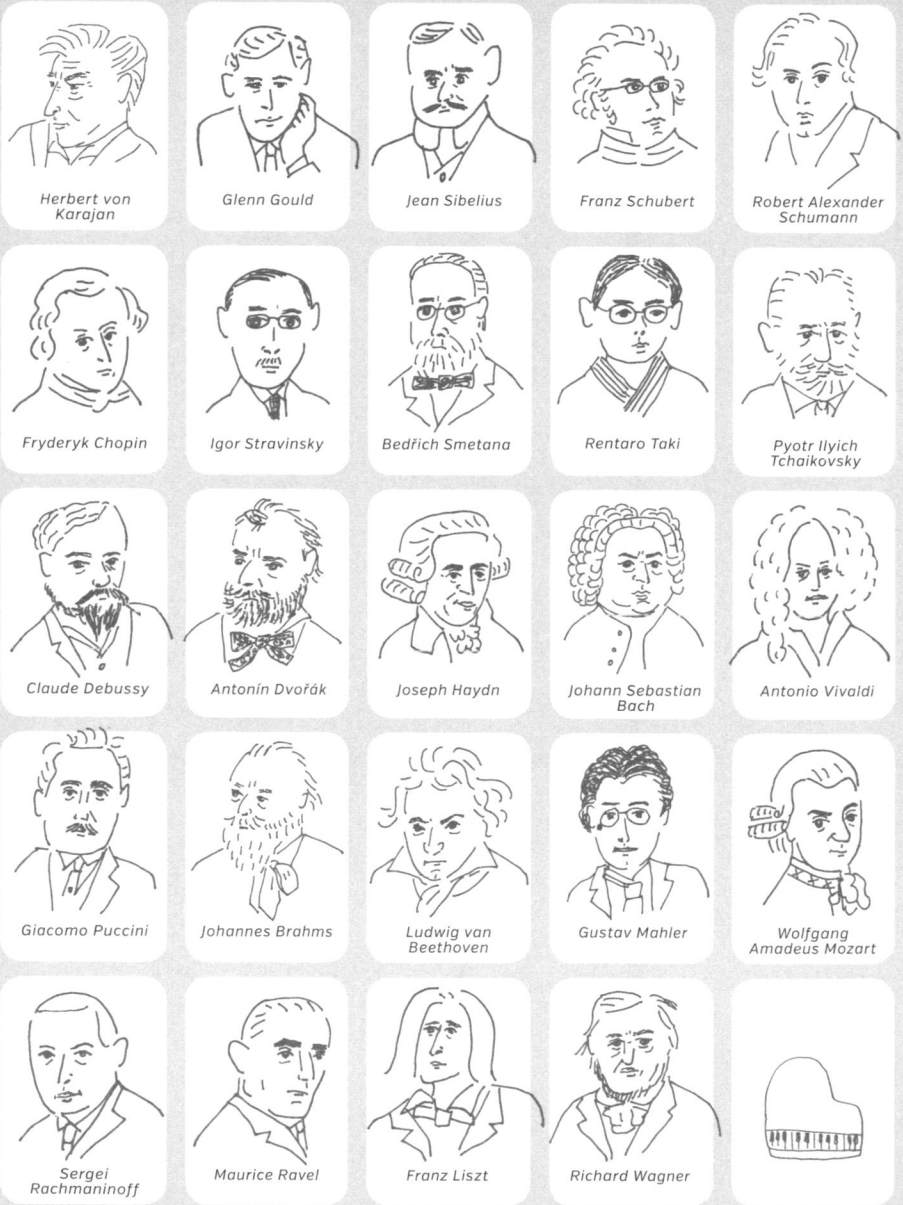

Artists

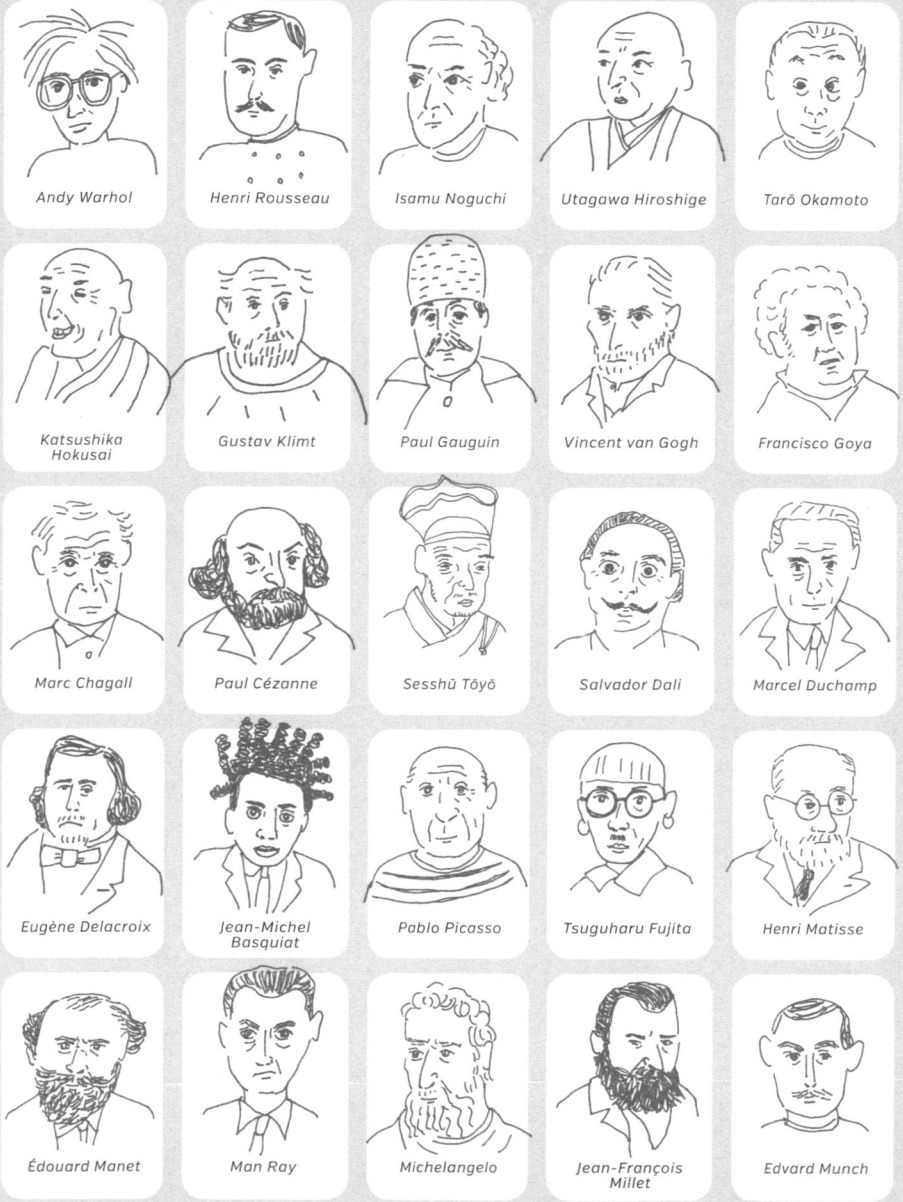
Andy Warhol
Henri Rousseau
Isamu Noguchi
Utagawa Hiroshige
Tarō Okamoto
Katsushika Hokusai
Gustav Klimt
Paul Gauguin
Vincent van Gogh
Francisco Goya
Marc Chagall
Paul Cézanne
Sesshū Tōyō
Salvador Dali
Marcel Duchamp
Eugène Delacroix
Jean-Michel Basquiat
Pablo Picasso
Tsuguharu Fujita
Henri Matisse
Édouard Manet
Man Ray
Michelangelo
Jean-François Millet
Edvard Munch

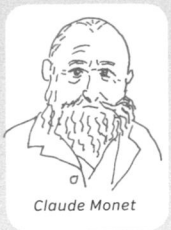
Claude Monet

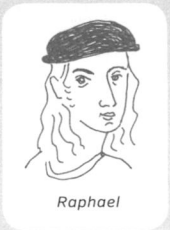
Raphael

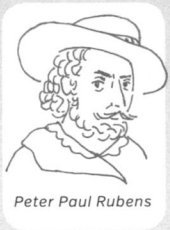
Peter Paul Rubens

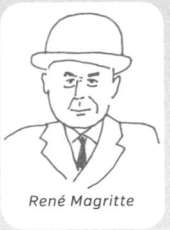
René Magritte

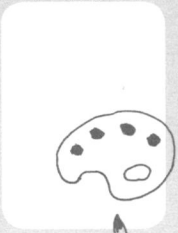

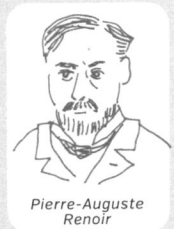
Pierre-Auguste Renoir

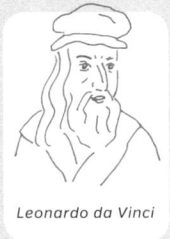
Leonardo da Vinci

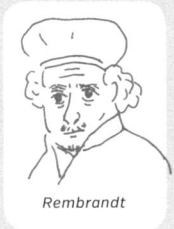
Rembrandt

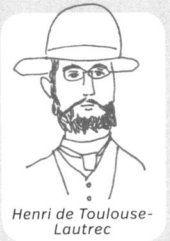
Henri de Toulouse-Lautrec

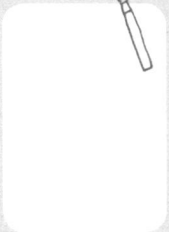

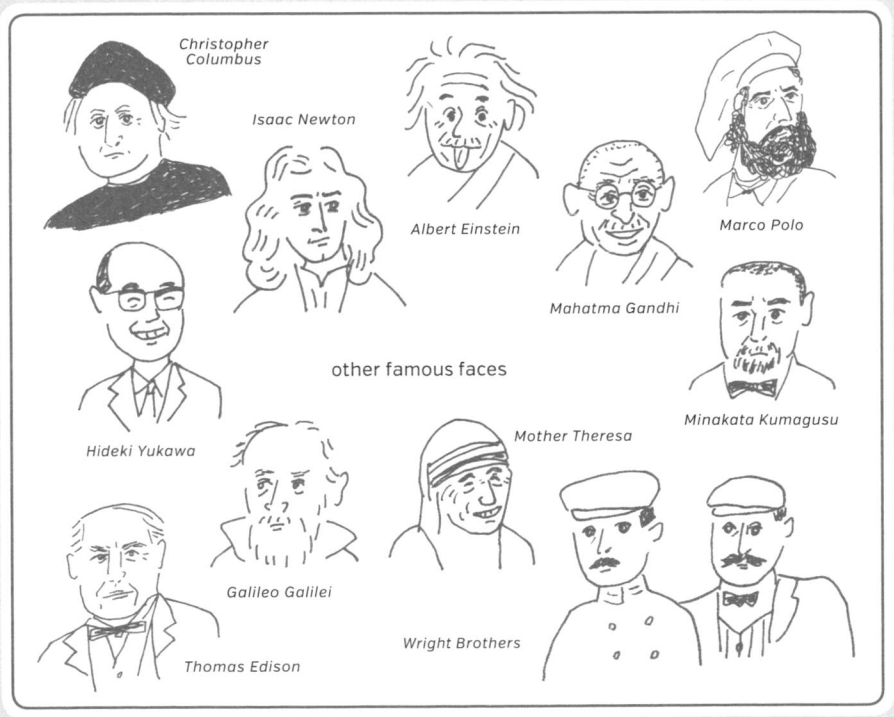

# Plants

- Trees
- Shrubs
- Flowers
- Other Unique Plants

# Trees

*Pay attention to the color and shape of both the leaves and trunk, as these details will make the tree species identifiable.*

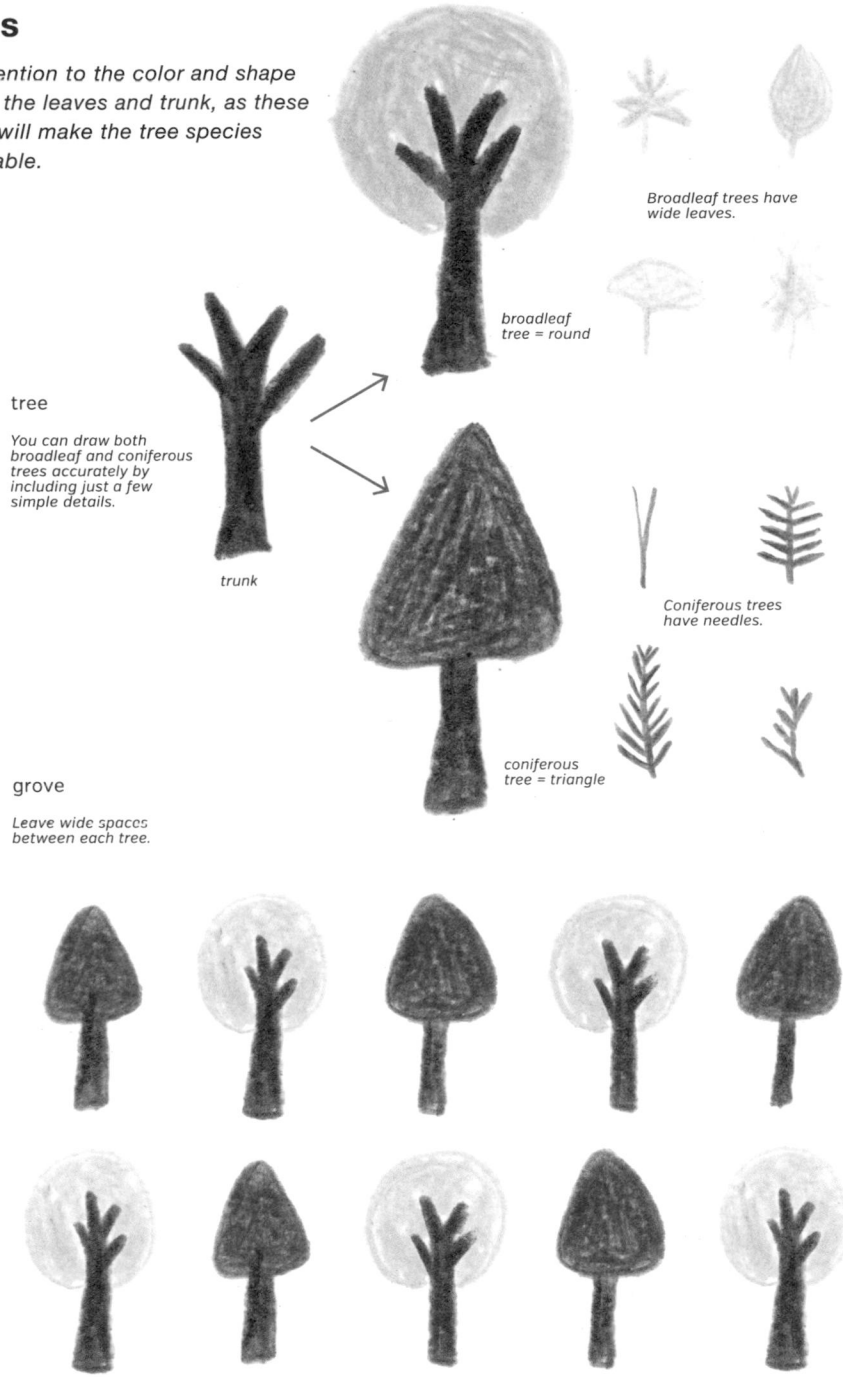

## woods

*Draw thick leaves and position the trees close together.*

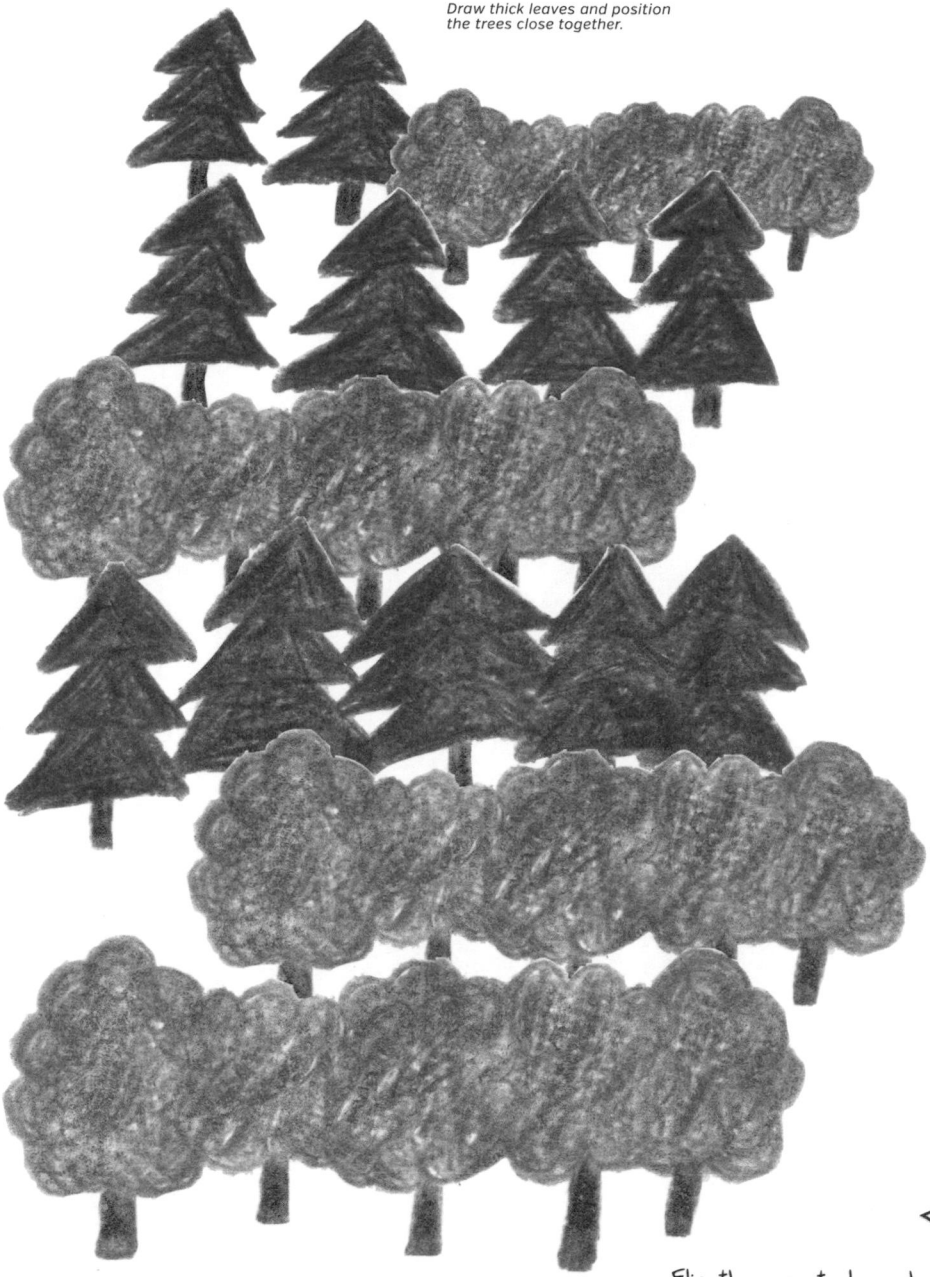

Flip the page to learn how to draw various trees

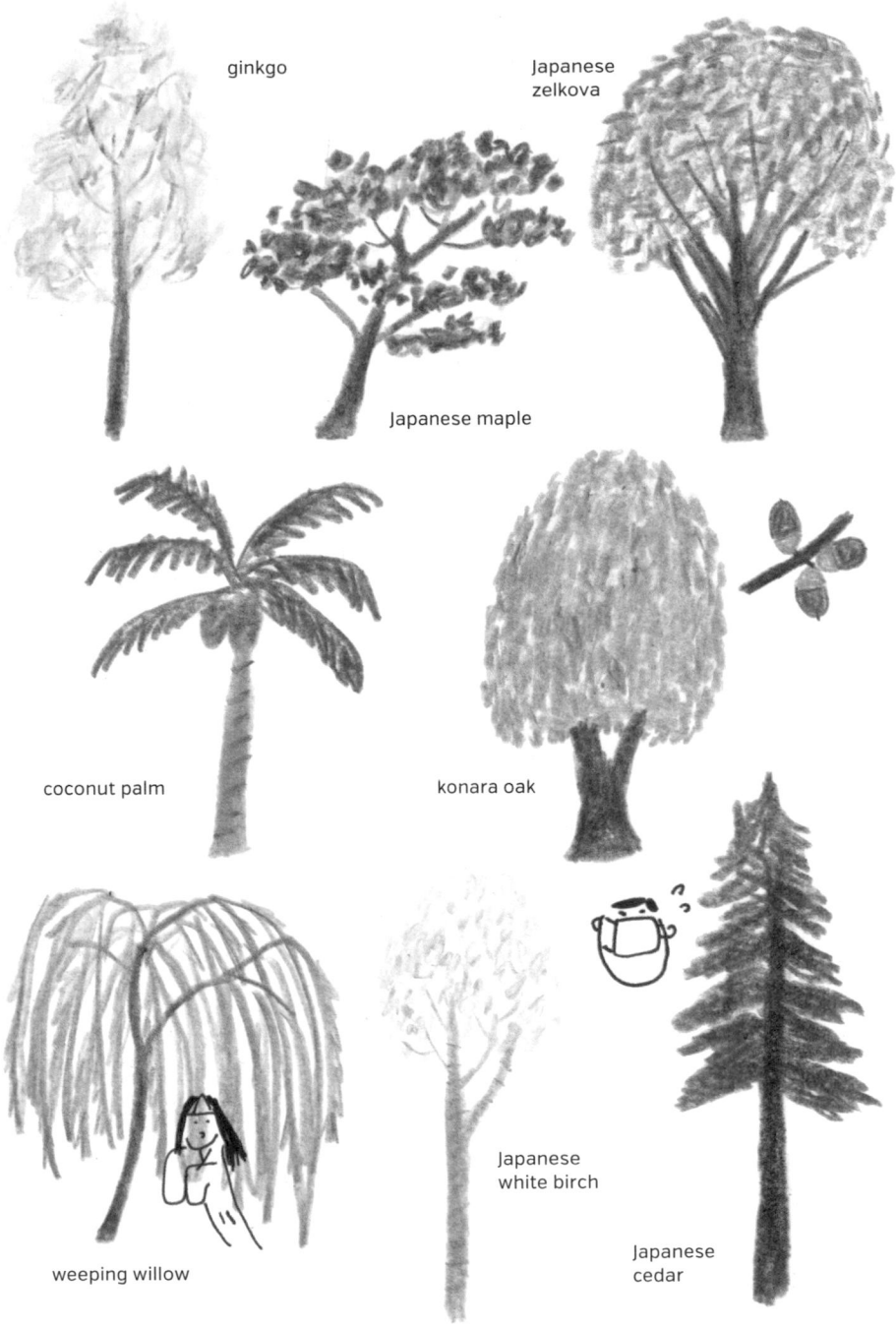
ginkgo
Japanese zelkova
Japanese maple
coconut palm
konara oak
weeping willow
Japanese white birch
Japanese cedar

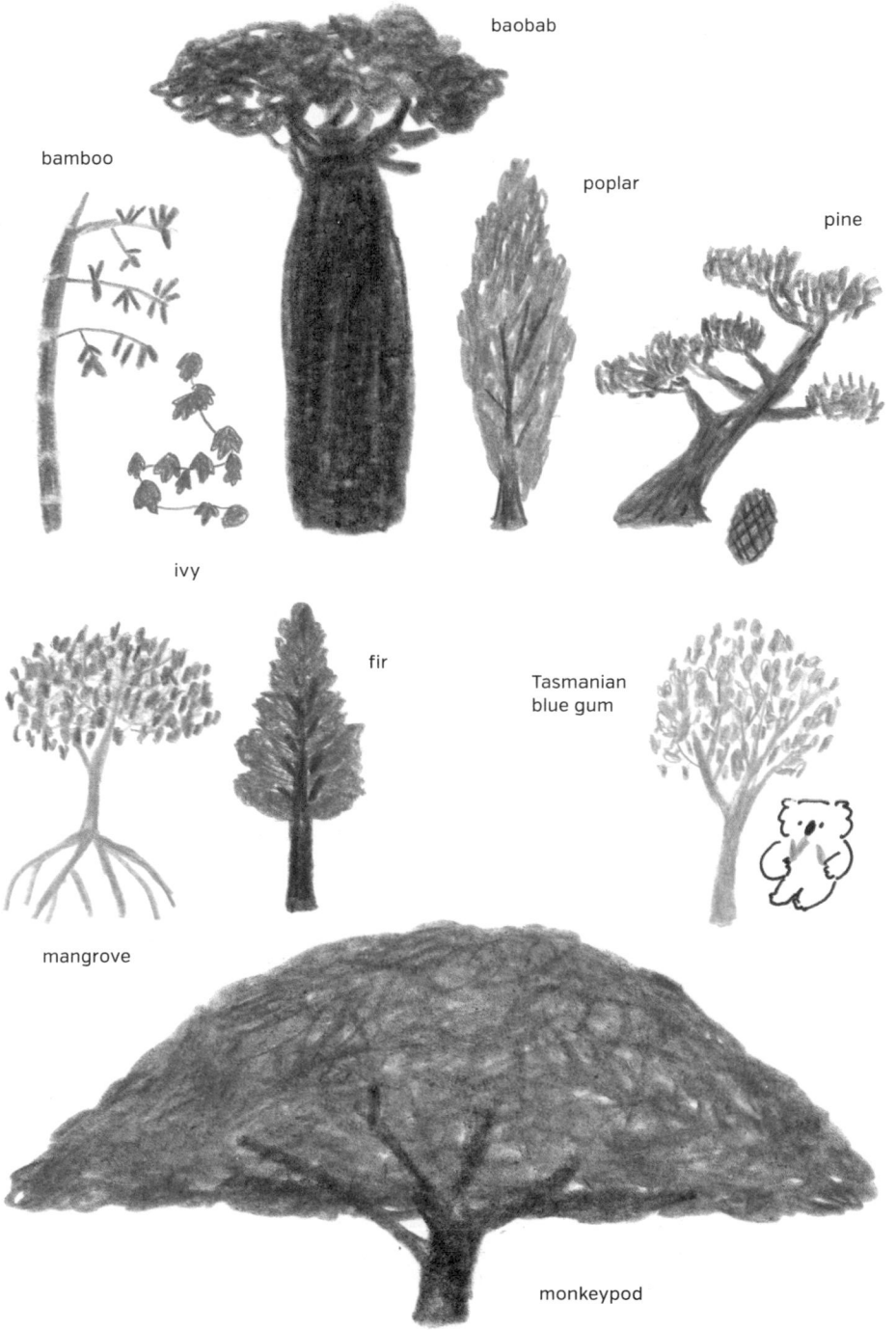
baobab
bamboo
poplar
pine
ivy
fir
Tasmanian
blue gum
mangrove
monkeypod

## Shrubs

*Draw the petals as accurately as possible since many shrubs have similarly shaped flowers.*

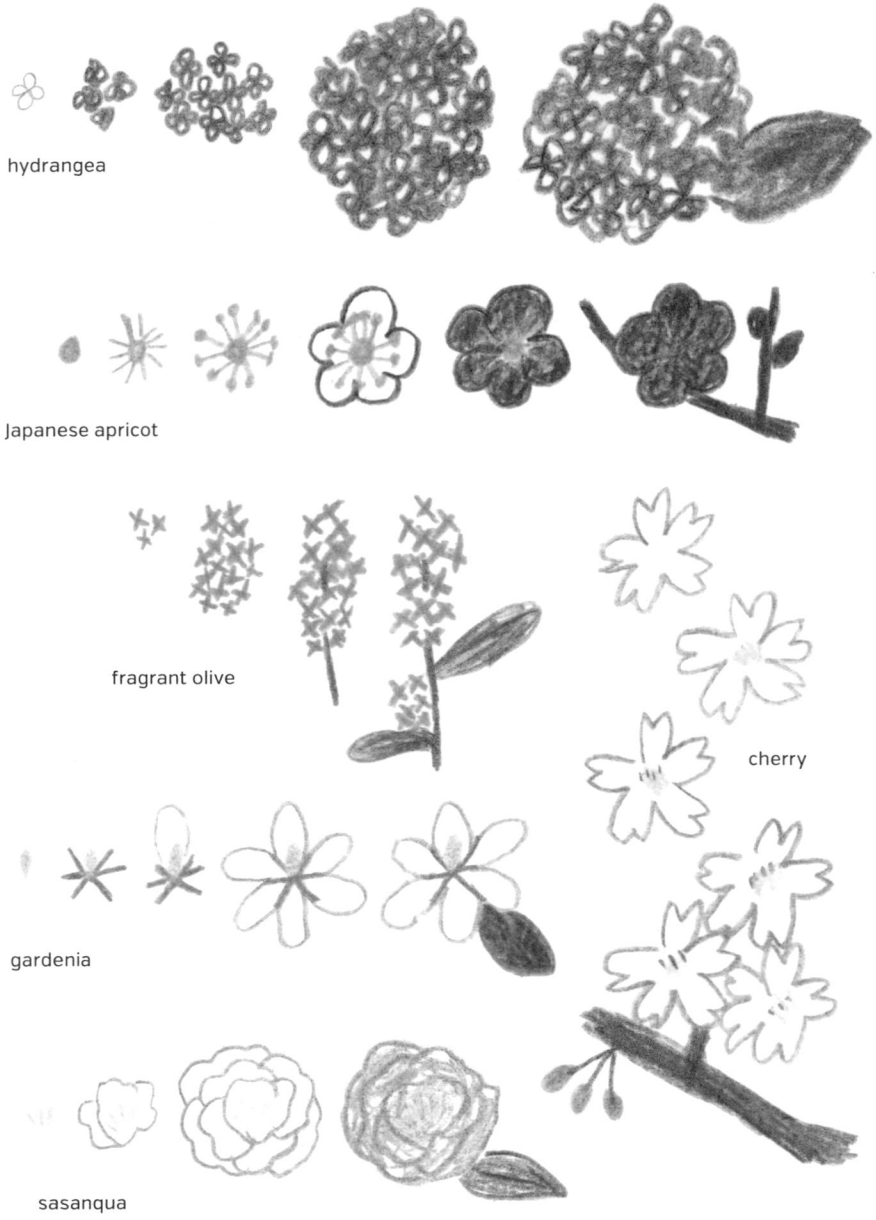

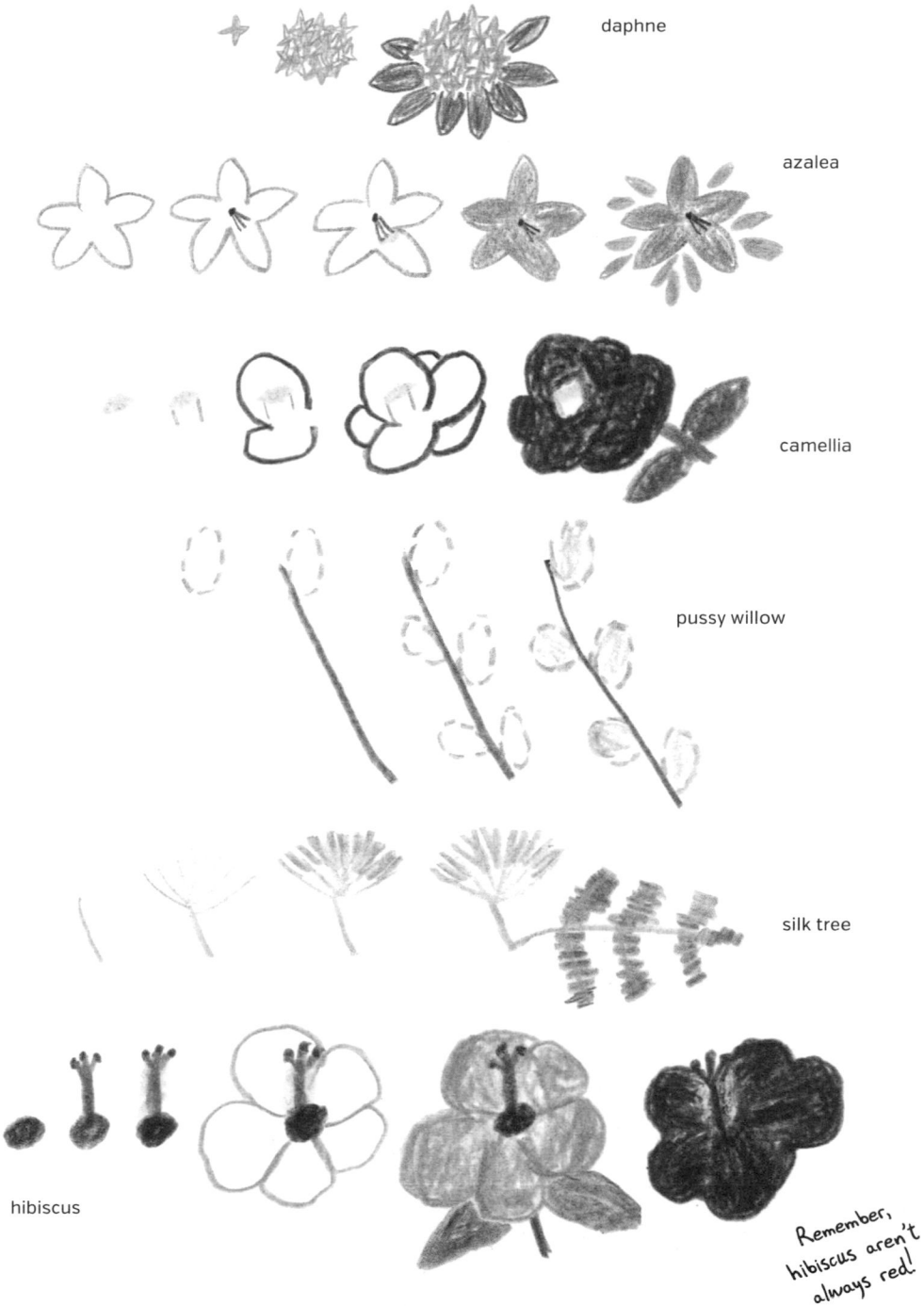
daphne
azalea
camellia
pussy willow
silk tree
hibiscus
Remember, hibiscus aren't always red!

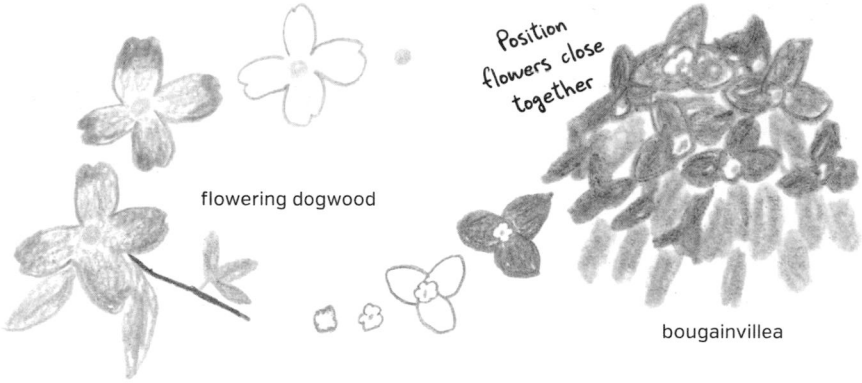
Position flowers close together
flowering dogwood
bougainvillea

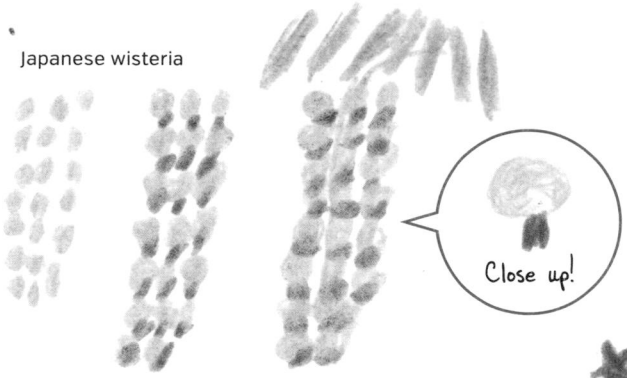
Japanese wisteria
Close up!

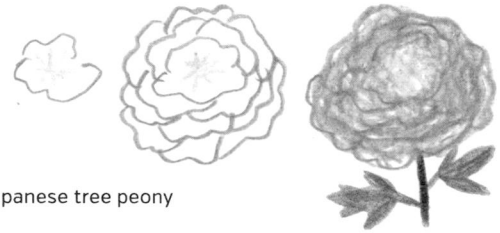
Japanese tree peony

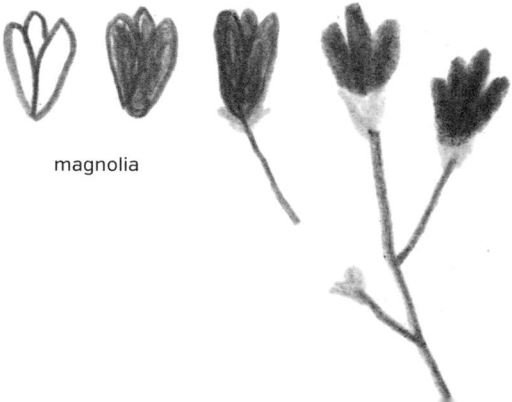
magnolia

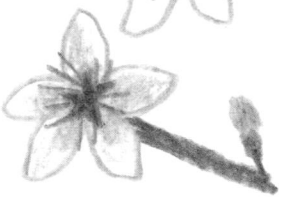
peach

# Flowers

*Although a flower's colorful petals may catch your eye, don't forget to pay attention to the shape of the leaves—each flower has unique foliage.*

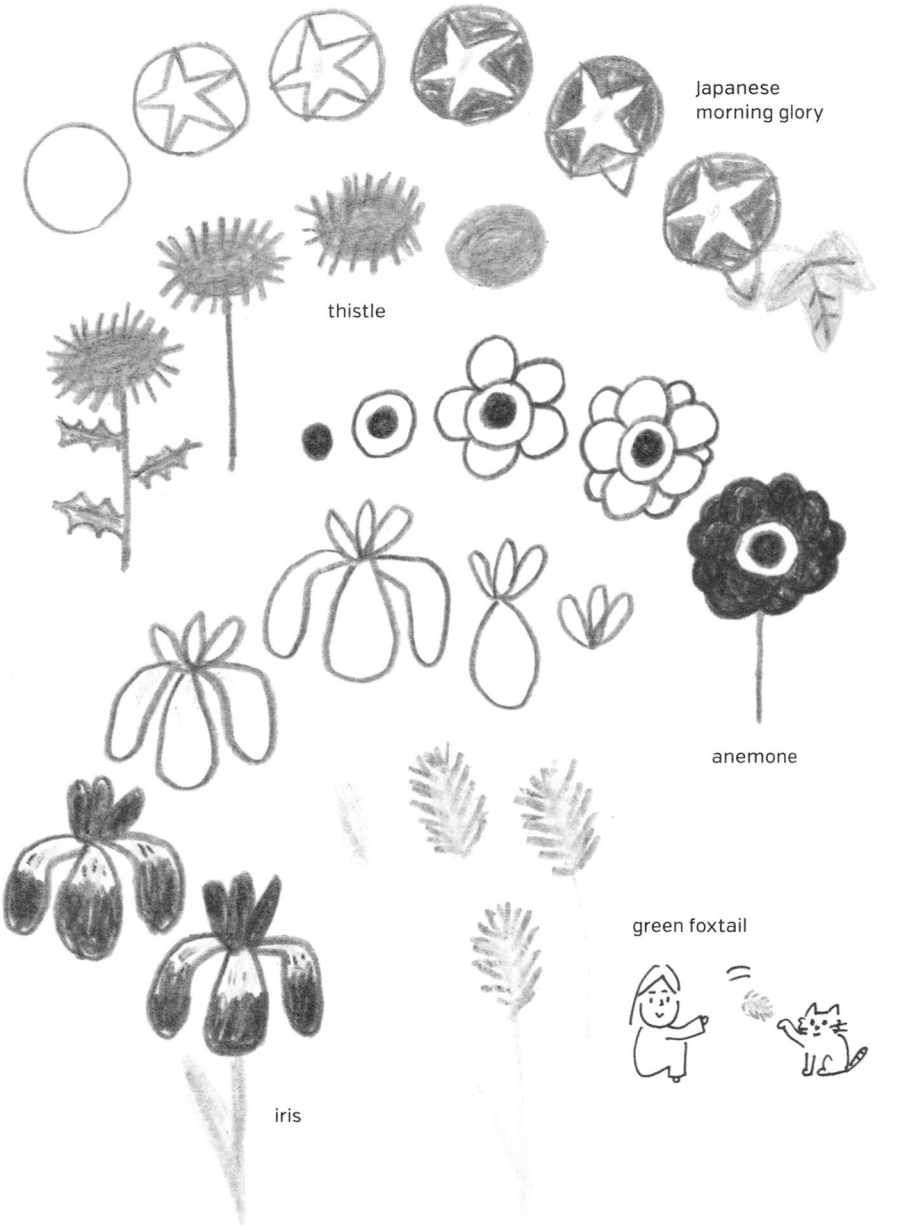

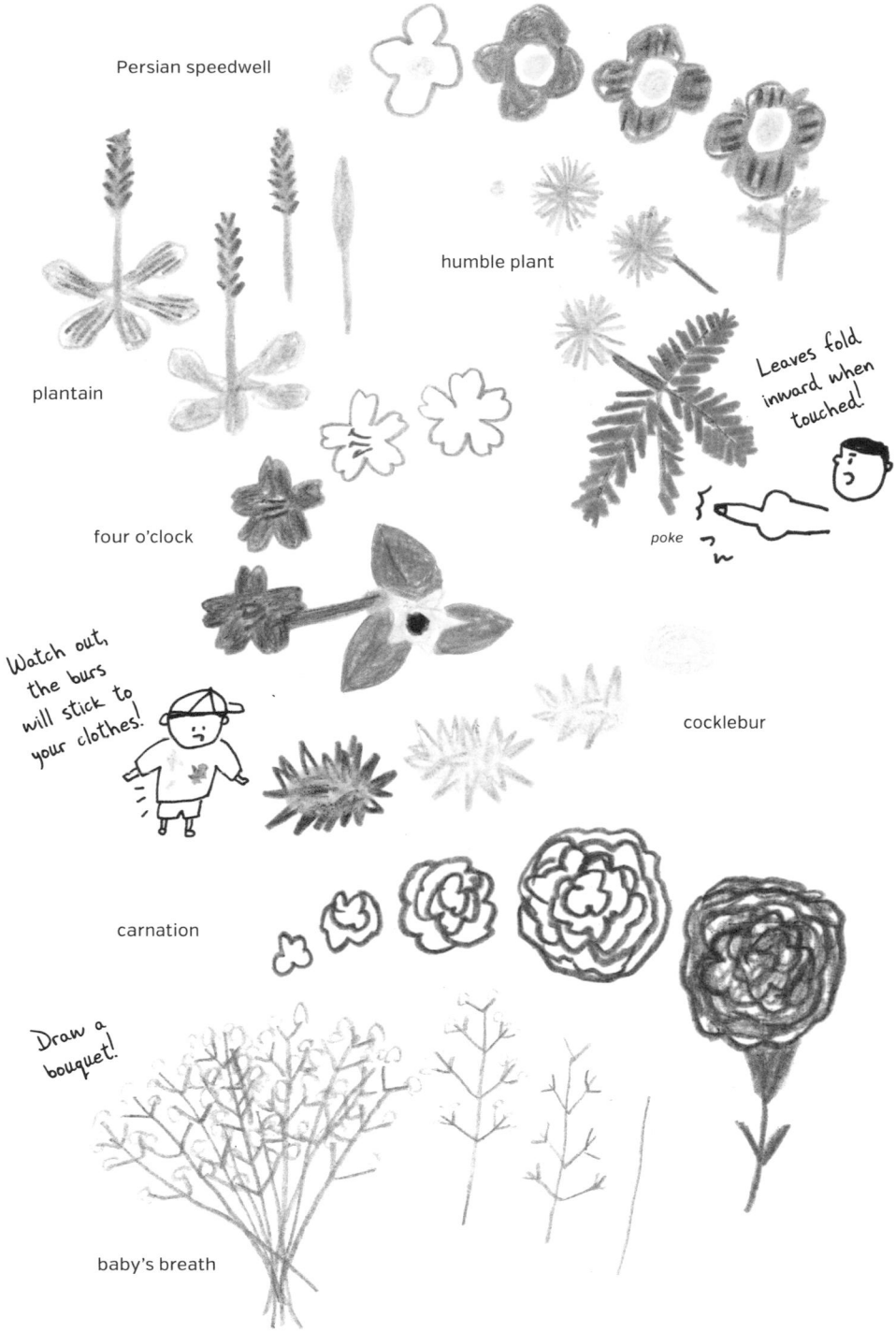
Persian speedwell
humble plant
plantain
Leaves fold inward when touched!
poke
four o'clock
Watch out, the burs will stick to your clothes!
cocklebur
carnation
Draw a bouquet!
baby's breath

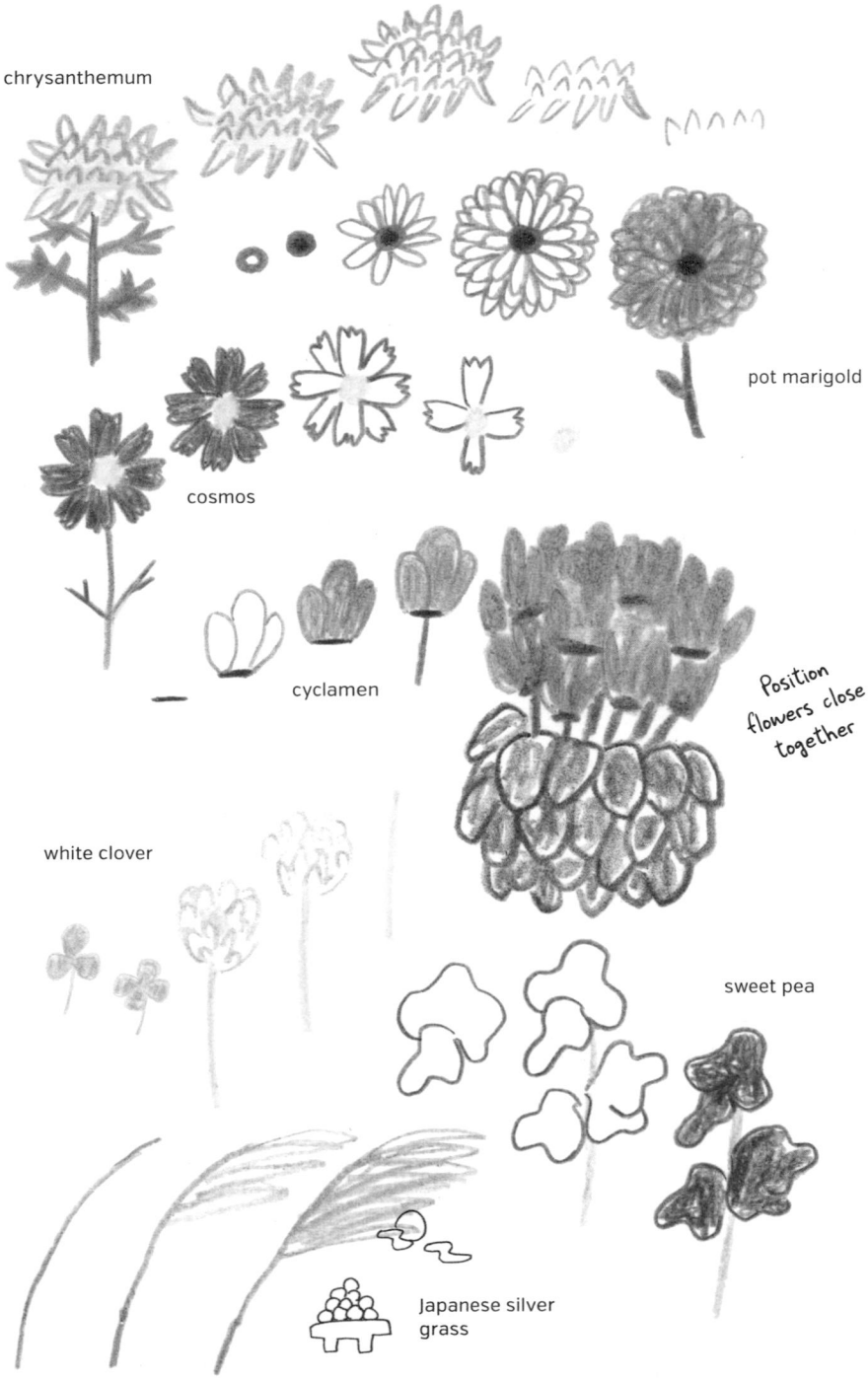
chrysanthemum
pot marigold
cosmos
cyclamen
Position flowers close together
white clover
sweet pea
Japanese silver grass

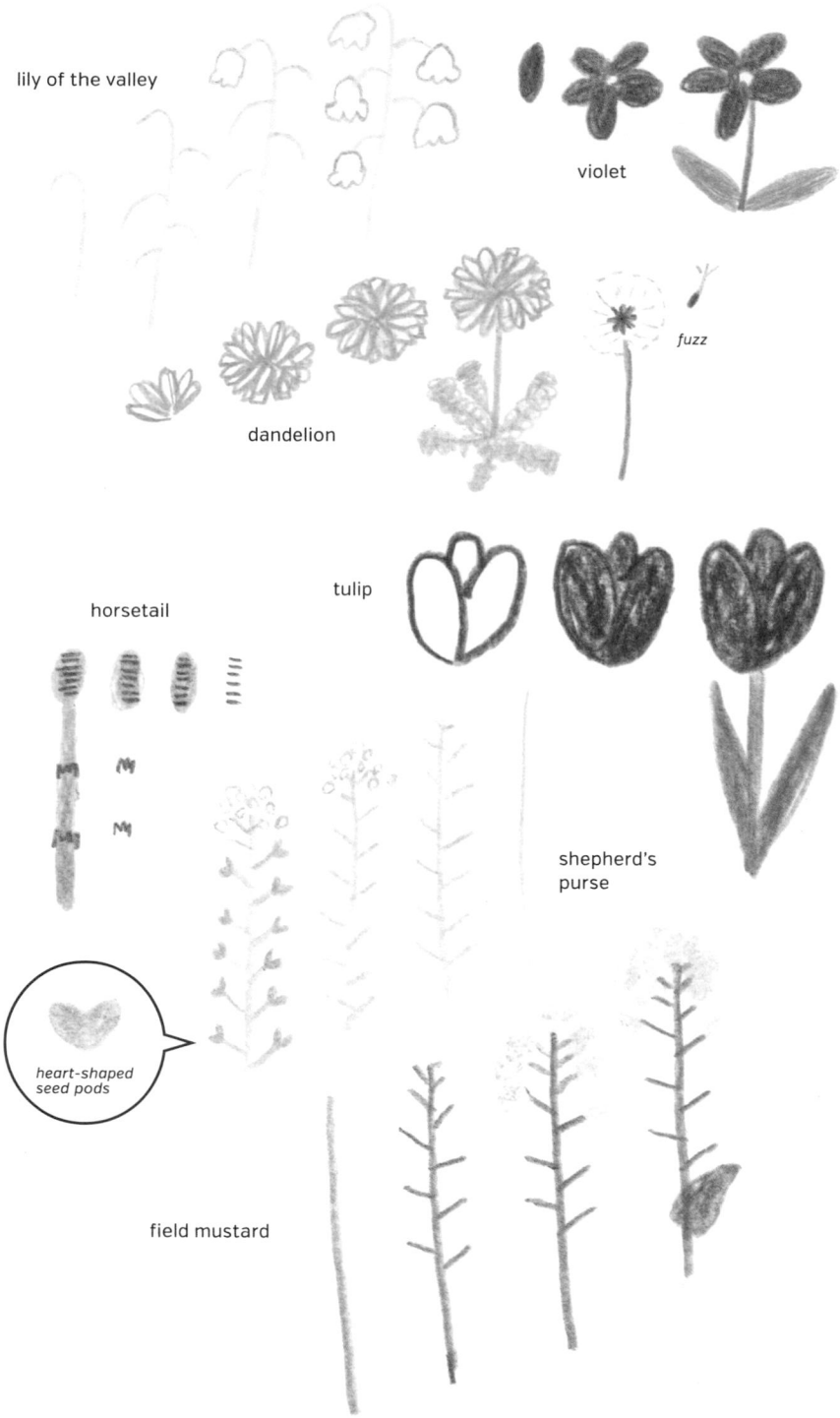
lily of the valley
violet
fuzz
dandelion
tulip
horsetail
shepherd's purse
heart-shaped seed pods
field mustard

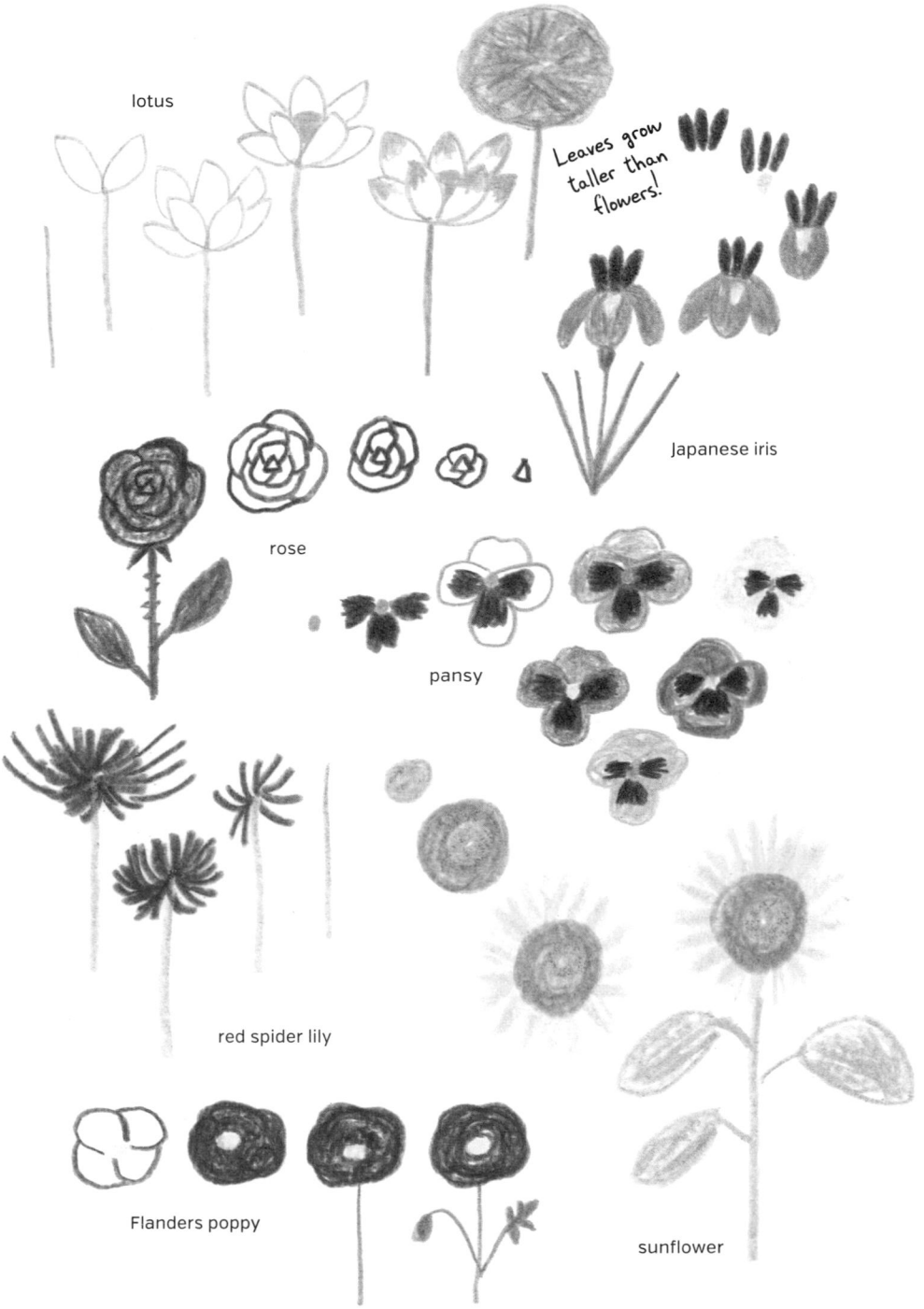
lotus
Leaves grow taller than flowers!
Japanese iris
rose
pansy
red spider lily
Flanders poppy
sunflower

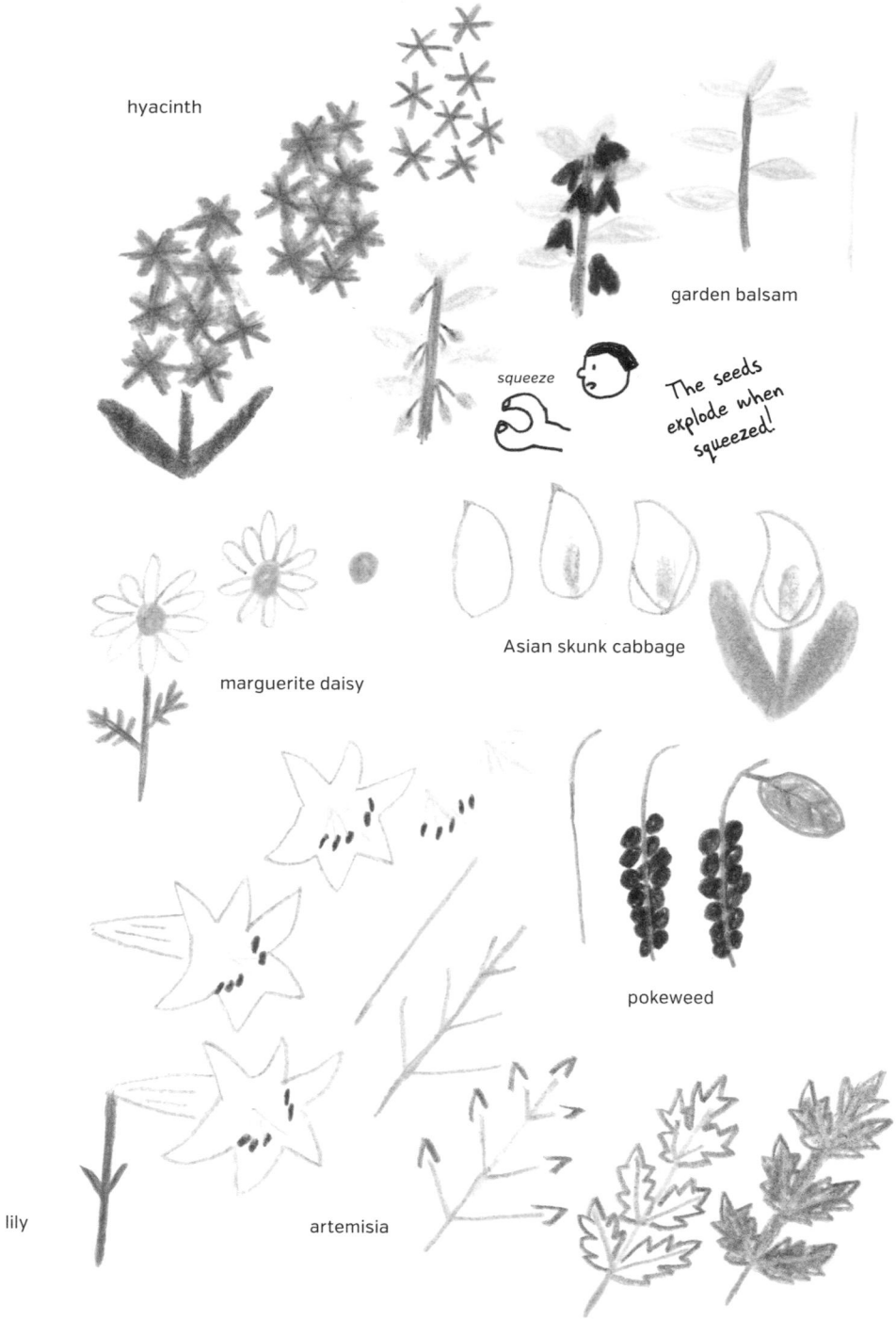
hyacinth
garden balsam
squeeze
The seeds explode when squeezed!
Asian skunk cabbage
marguerite daisy
pokeweed
lily
artemisia

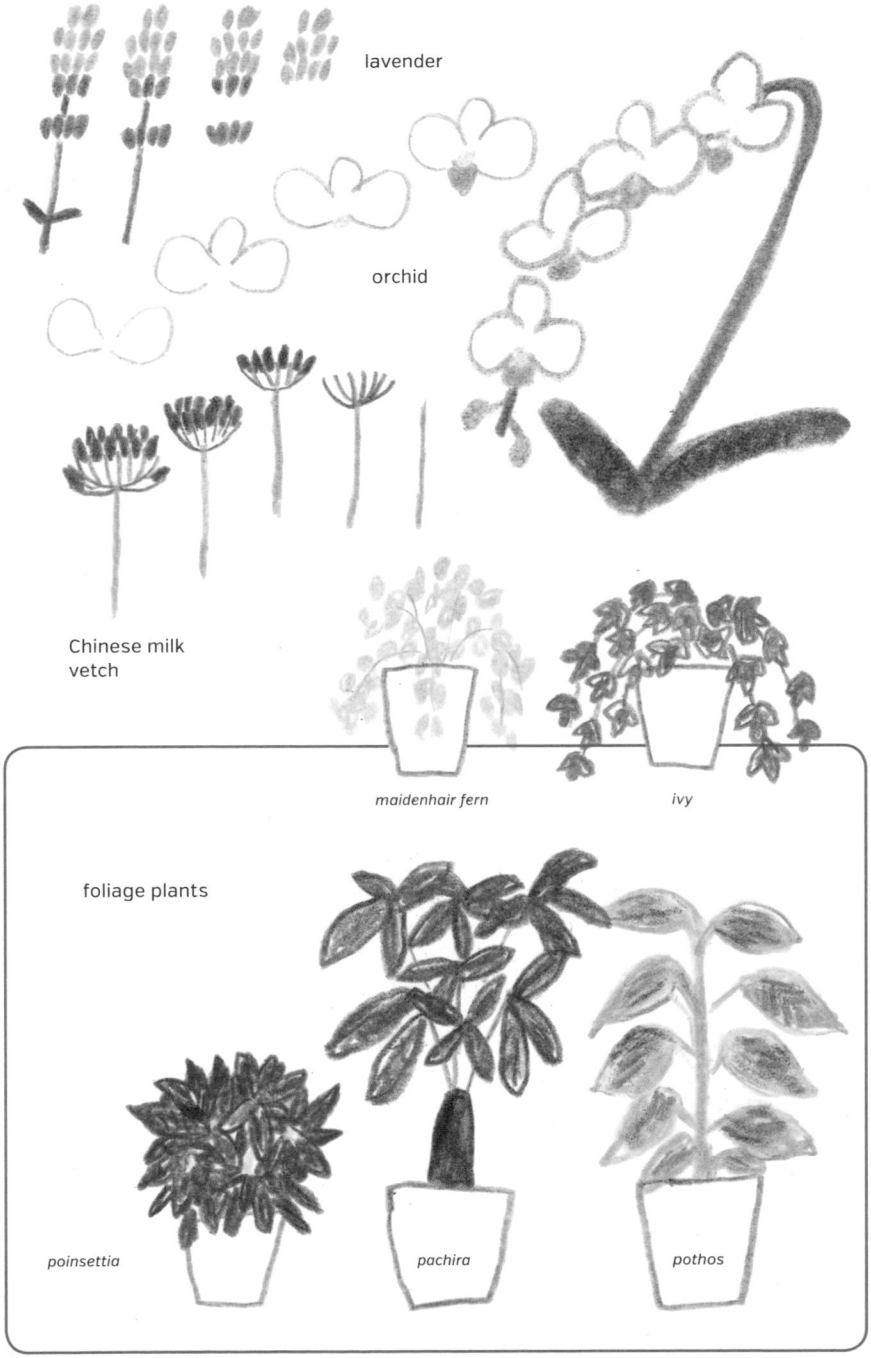
lavender
orchid
Chinese milk vetch
maidenhair fern
ivy
foliage plants
poinsettia
pachira
pothos

# Other Unique Plants

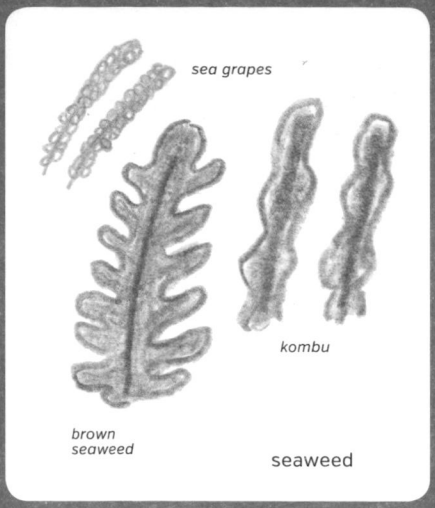


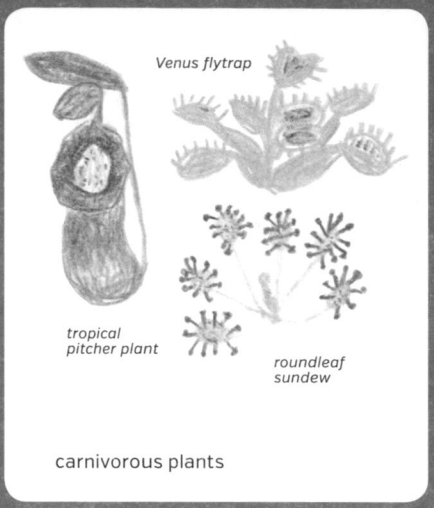


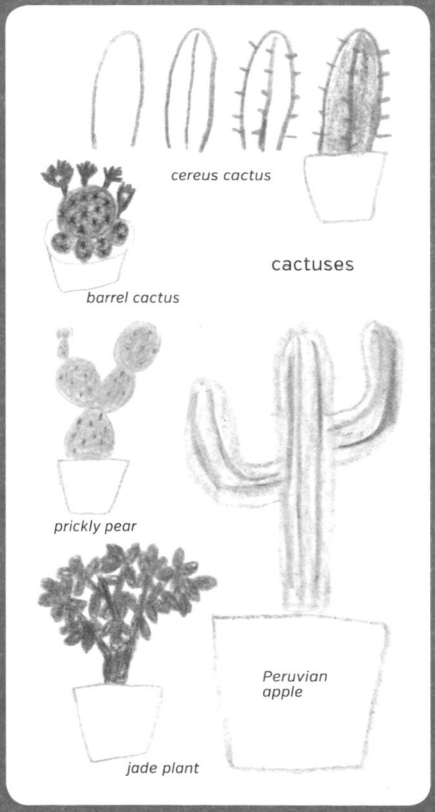


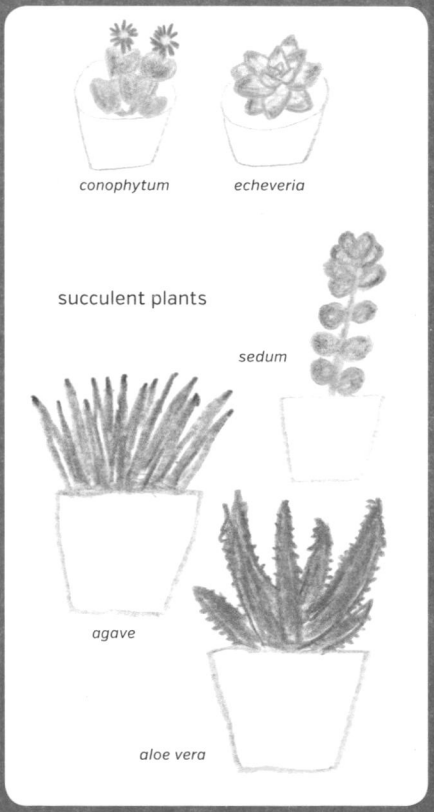

# Foods

Fruits

Vegetables

Main Dishes

Snacks

Drinks

Packaged Foods

## Fruits

Draw clean curves to keep your fruit looking fresh.

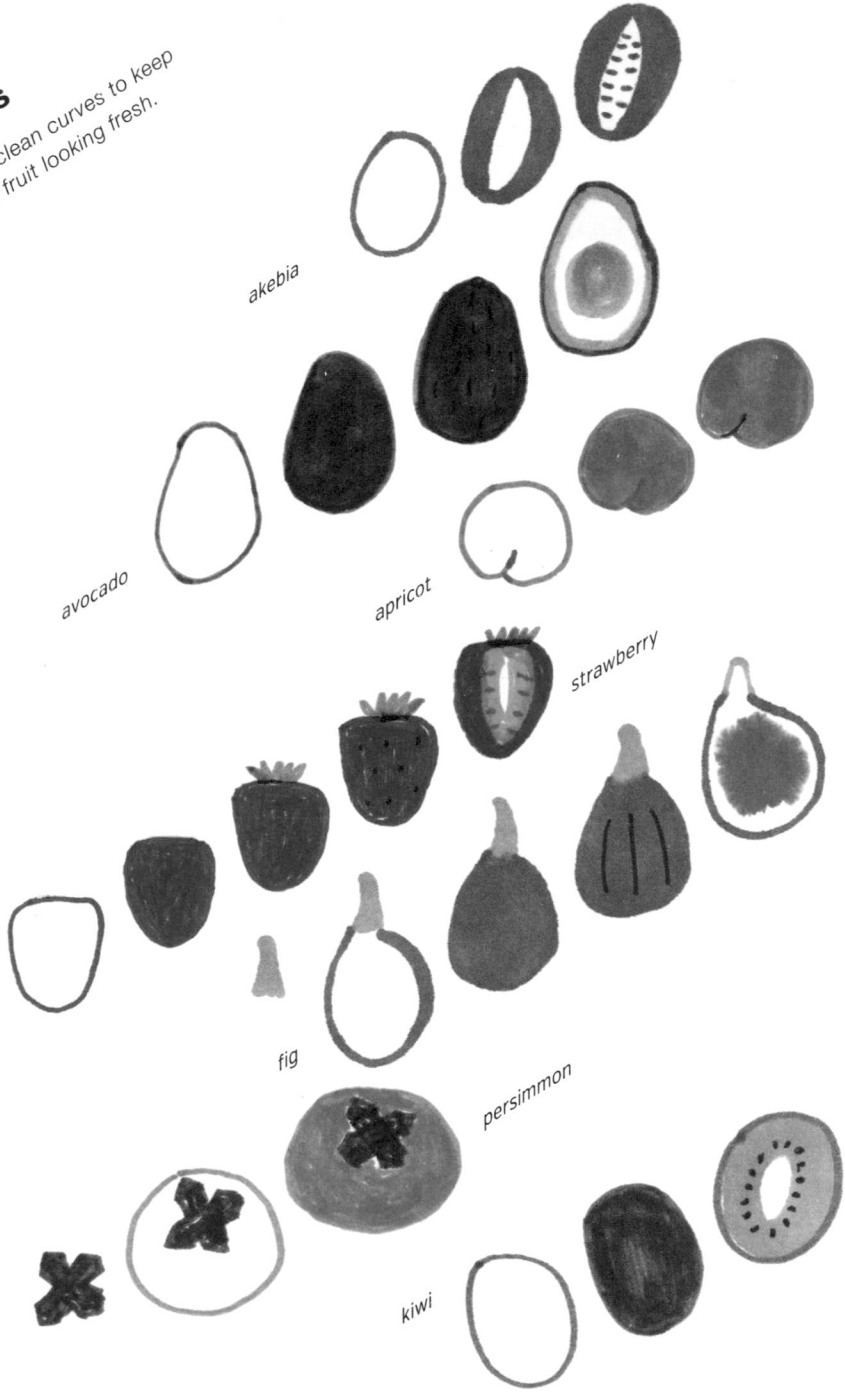

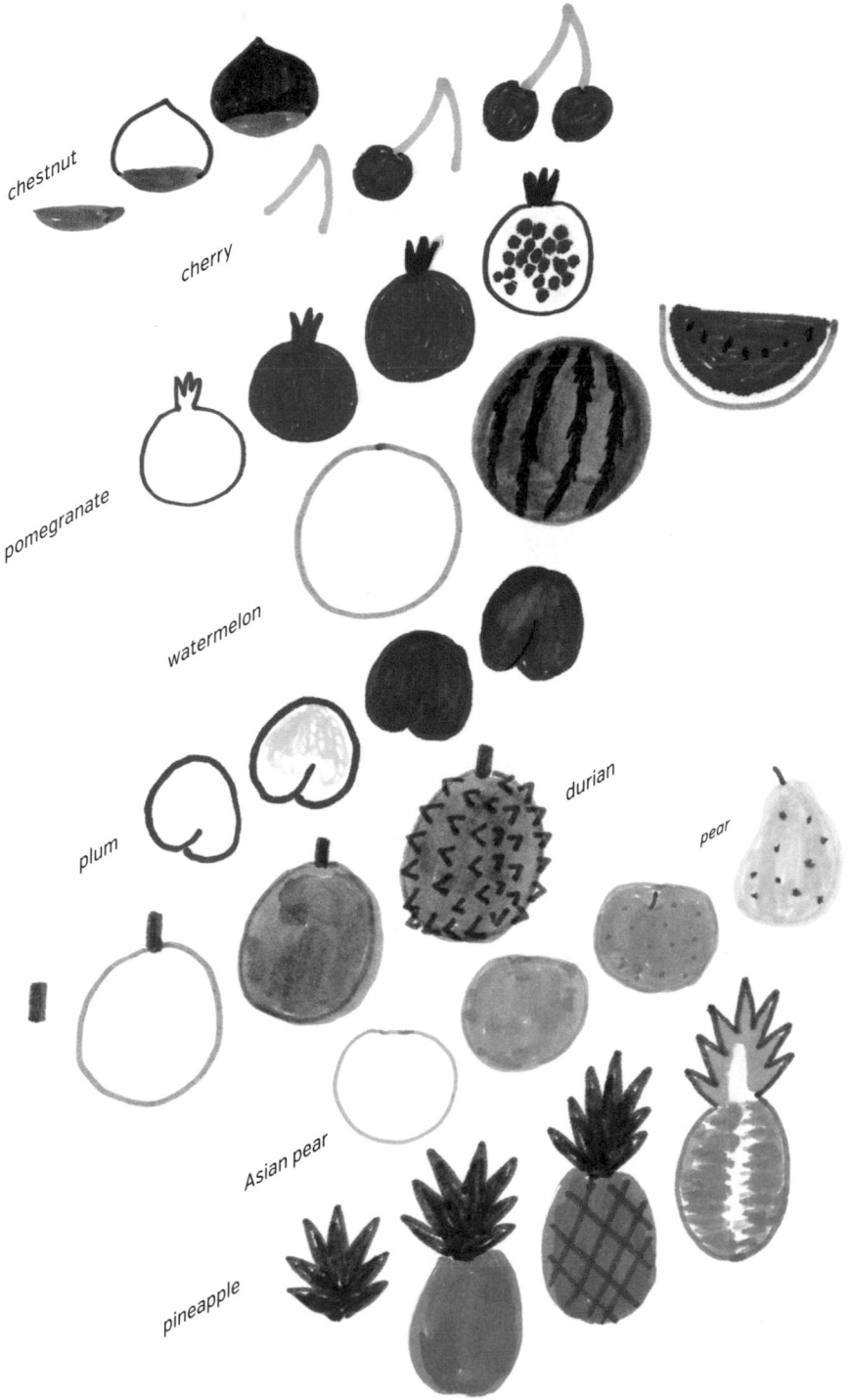
chestnut
cherry
pomegranate
watermelon
plum
durian
pear
Asian pear
pineapple

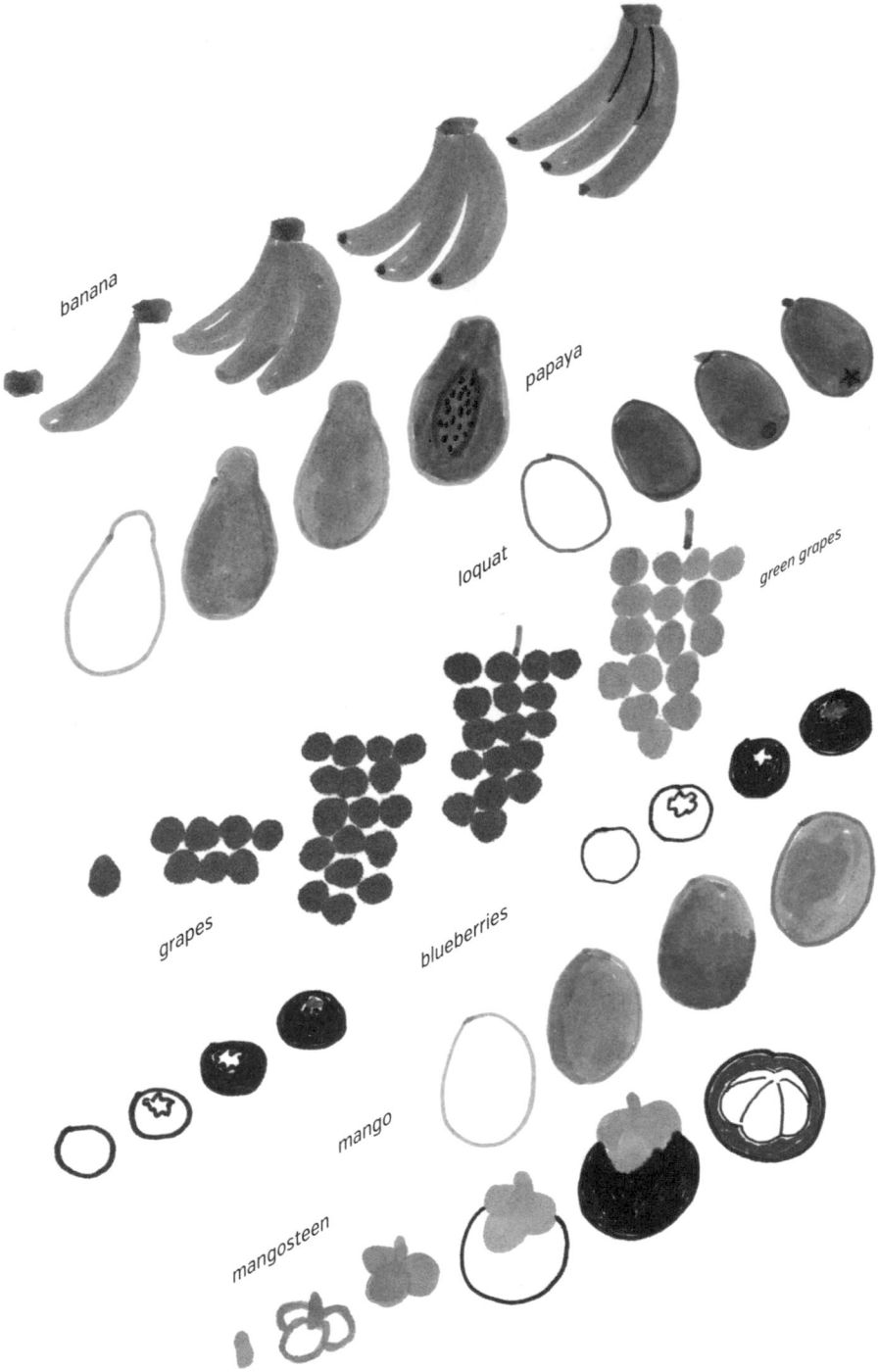
banana
papaya
loquat
green grapes
grapes
blueberries
mango
mangosteen

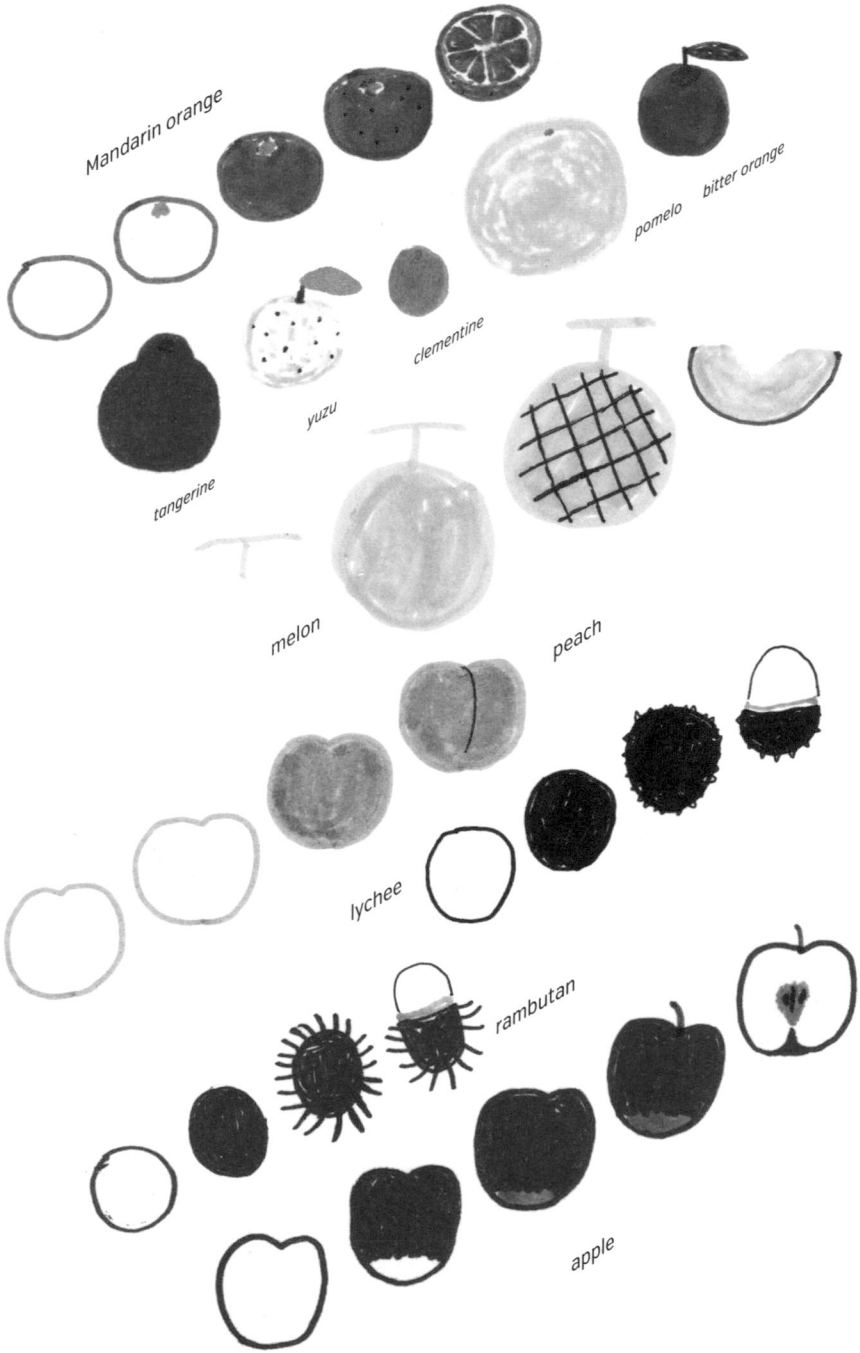
Mandarin orange
bitter orange
pomelo
clementine
yuzu
tangerine
melon
peach
lychee
rambutan
apple

## Vegetables

When coloring vegetables, use rough, streaky lines to add dimension and texture.

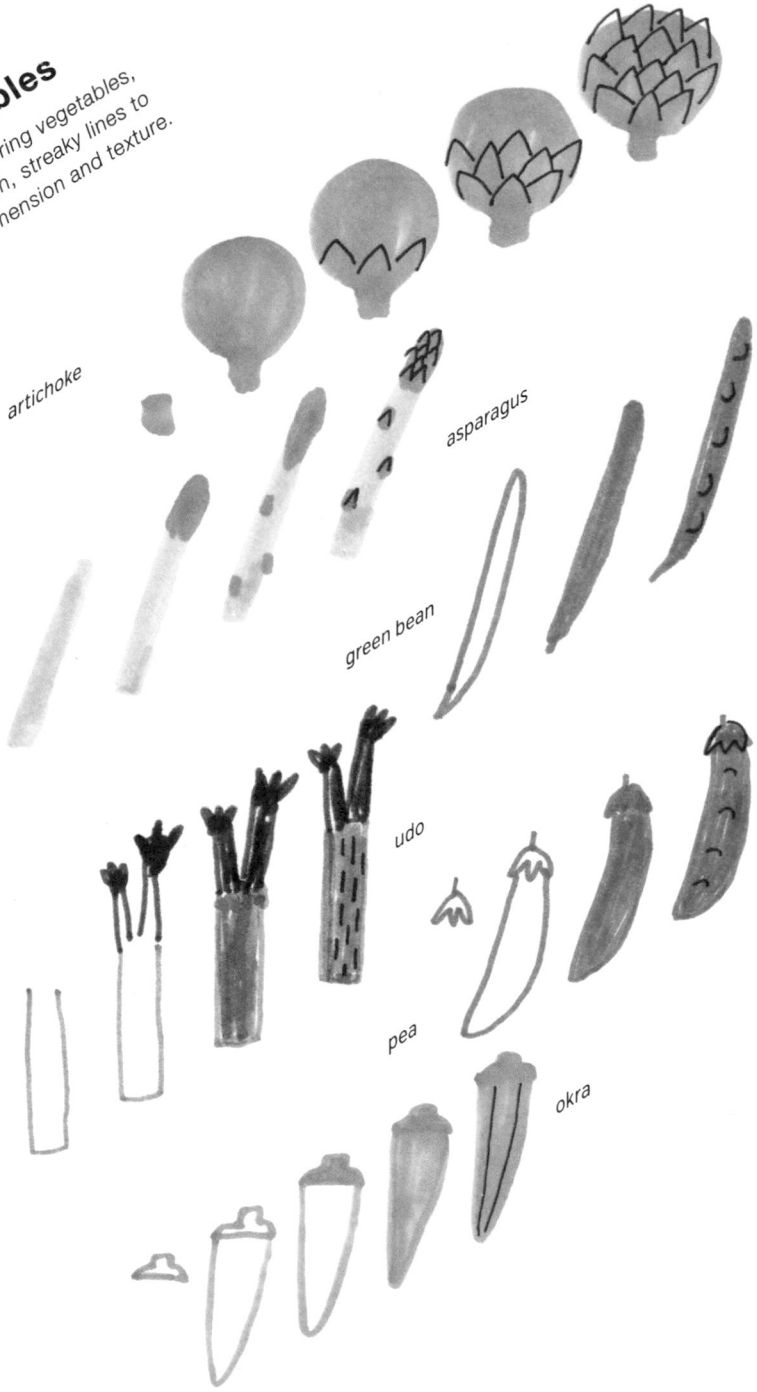

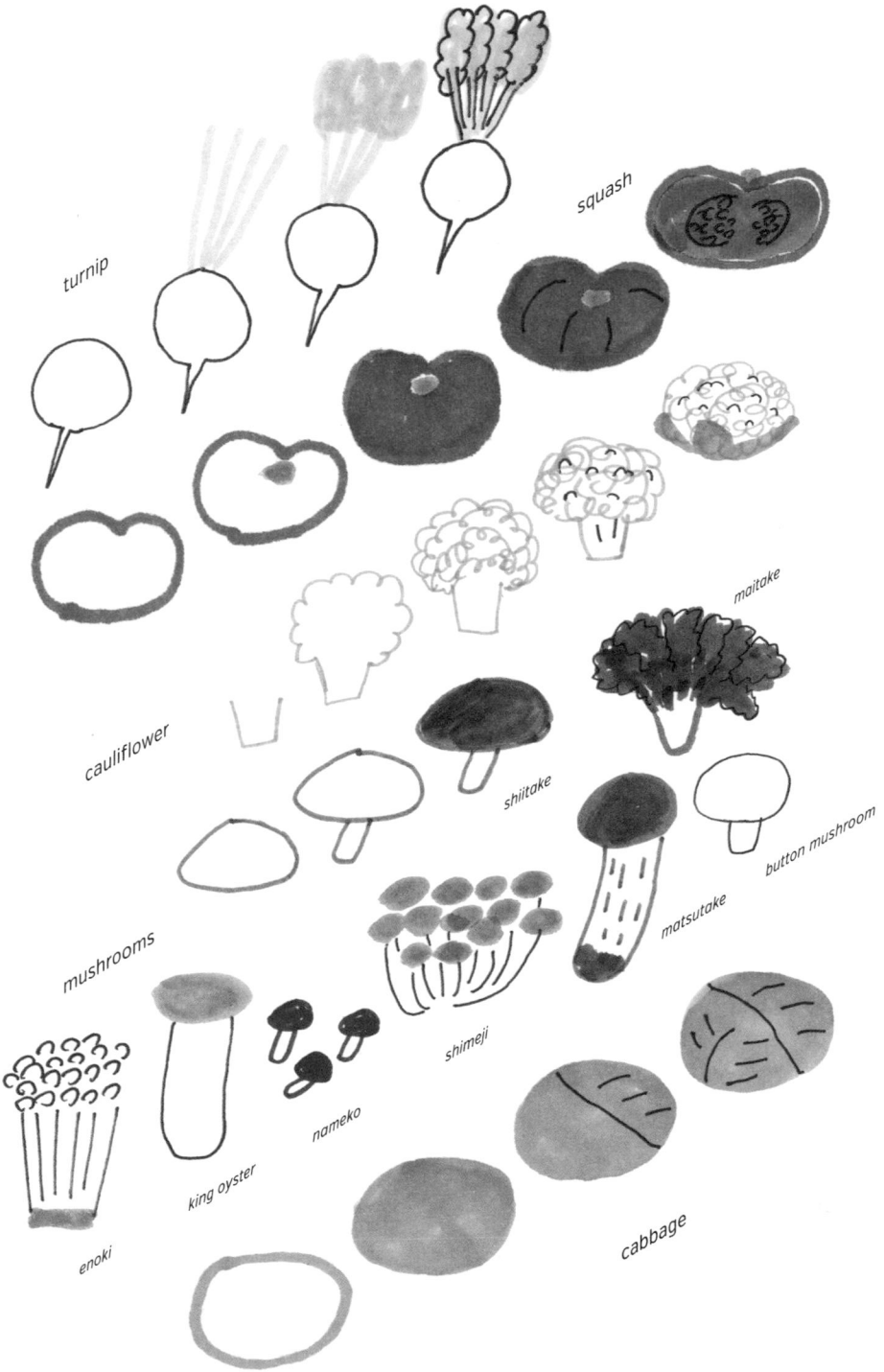
turnip
squash
cauliflower
maitake
shiitake
button mushroom
mushrooms
matsutake
shimeji
nameko
king oyster
enoki
cabbage

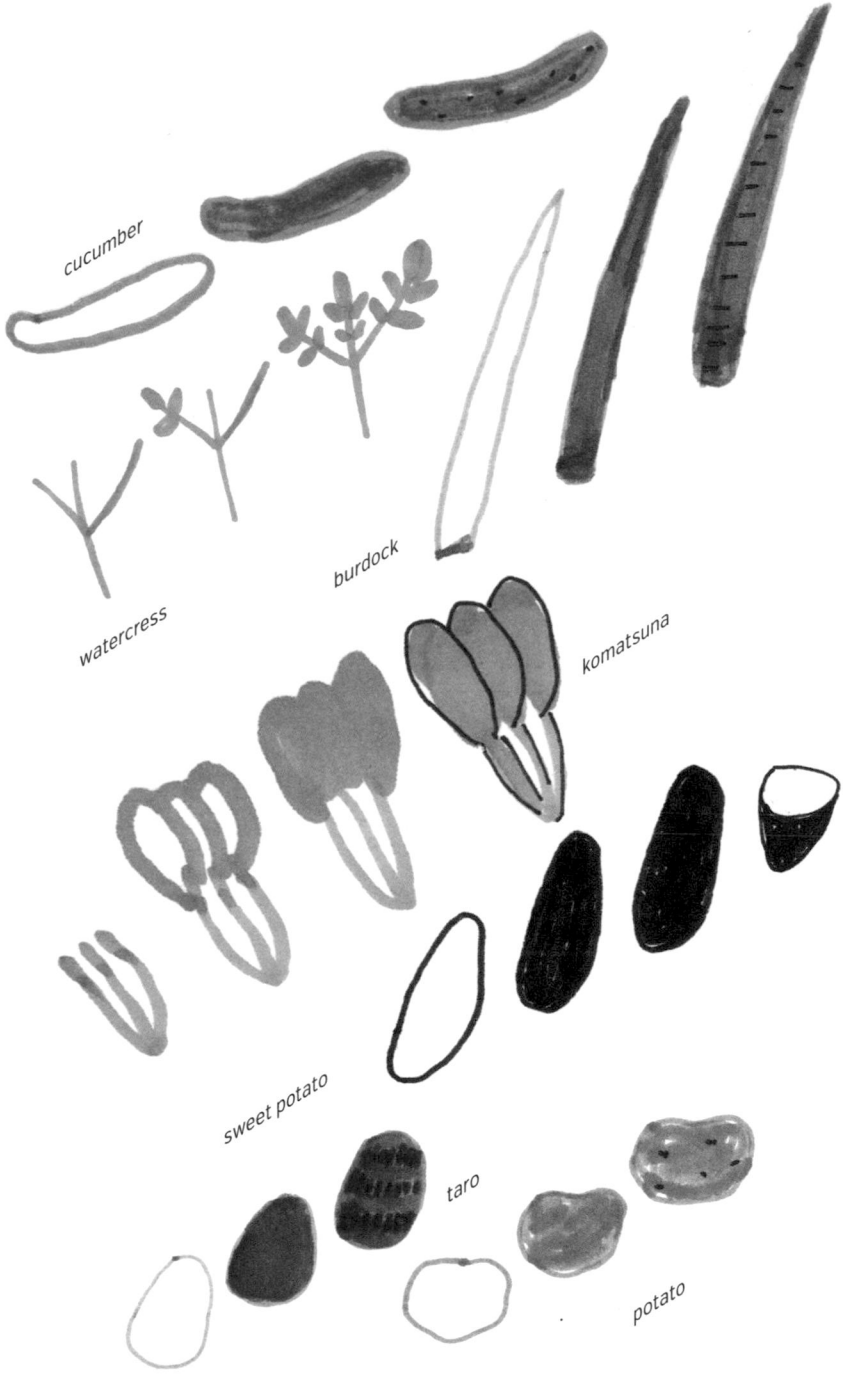
cucumber
watercress
burdock
komatsuna
sweet potato
taro
potato

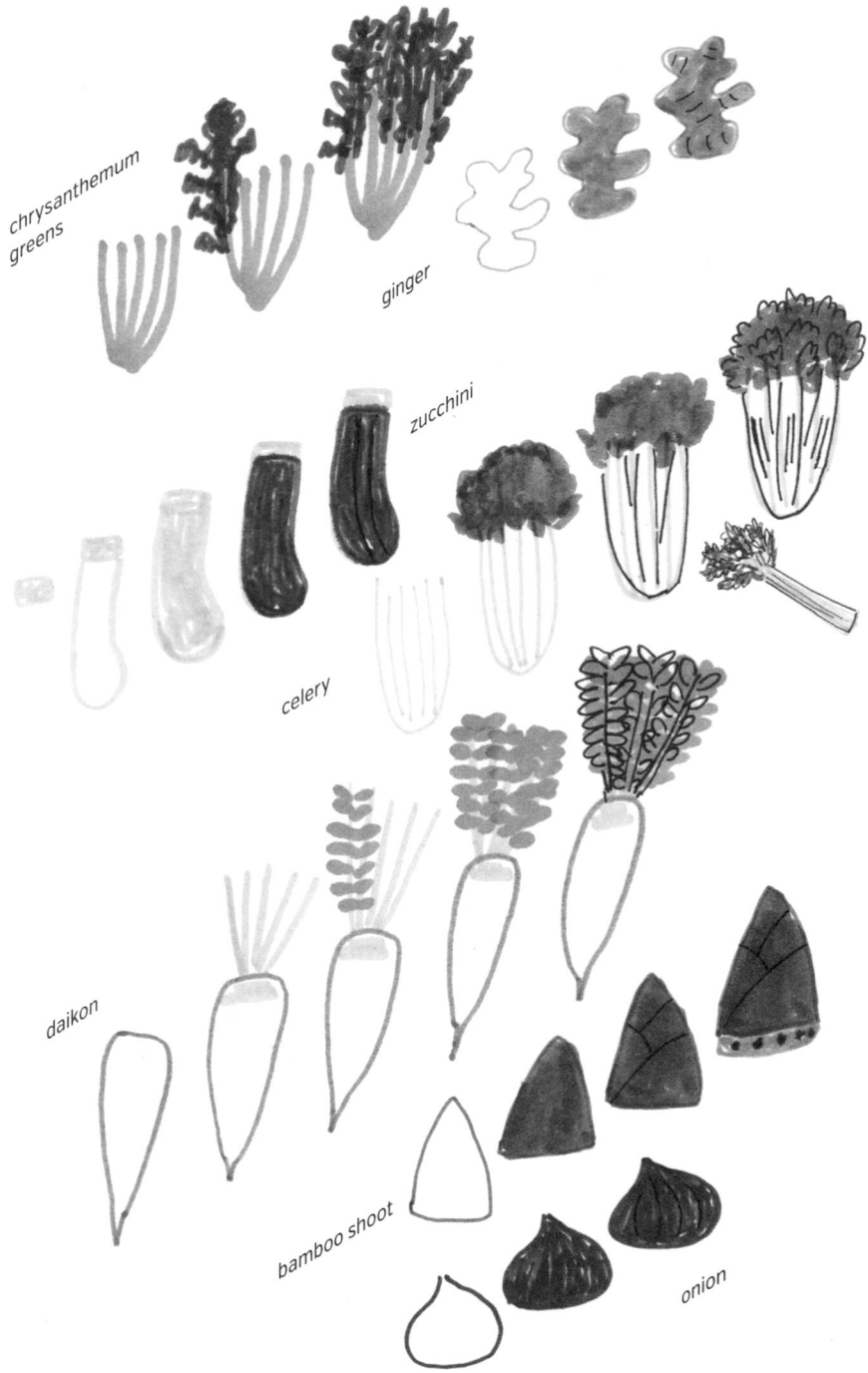
chrysanthemum greens
ginger
zucchini
celery
daikon
bamboo shoot
onion

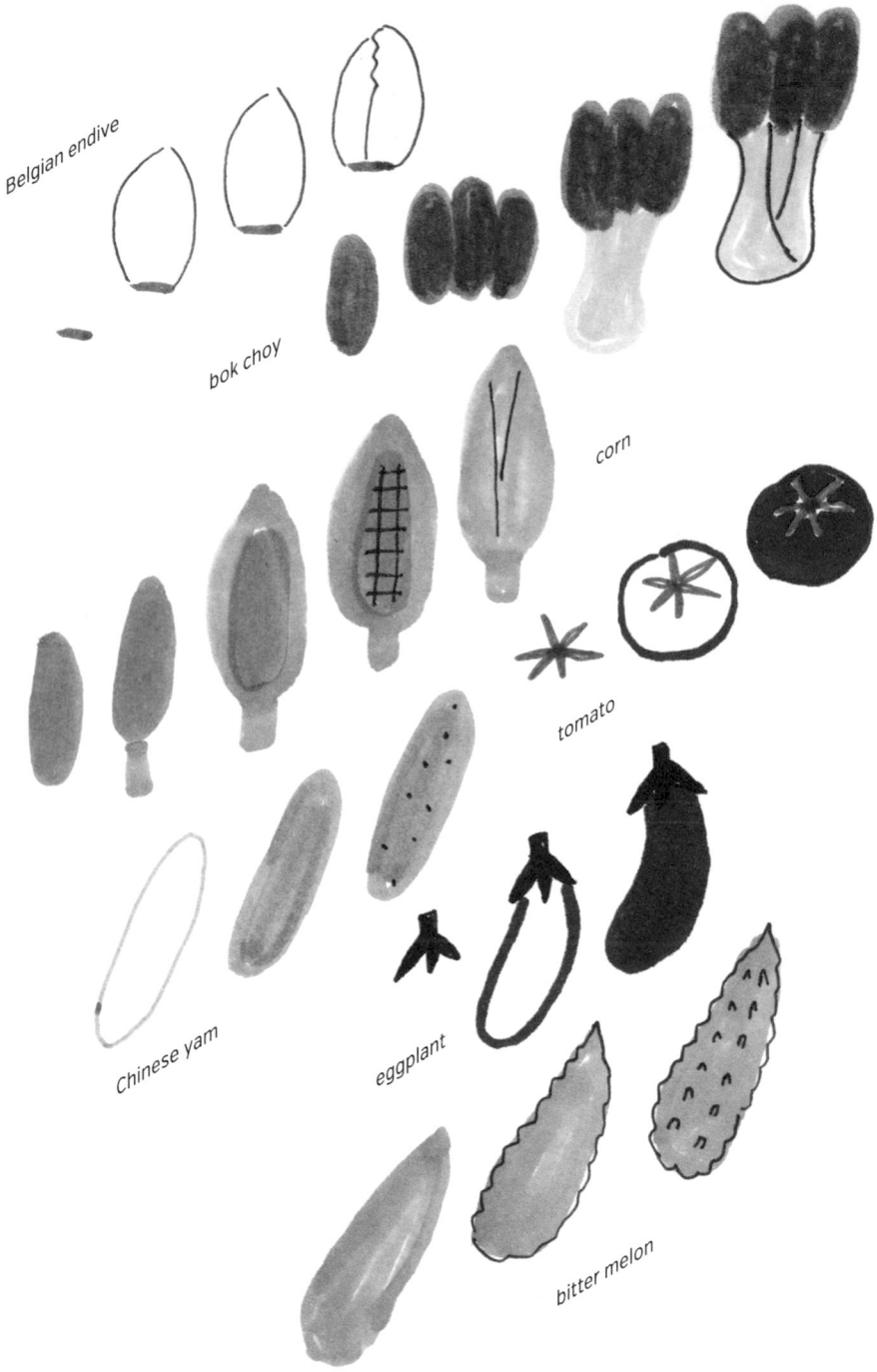
Belgian endive
bok choy
corn
tomato
Chinese yam
eggplant
bitter melon

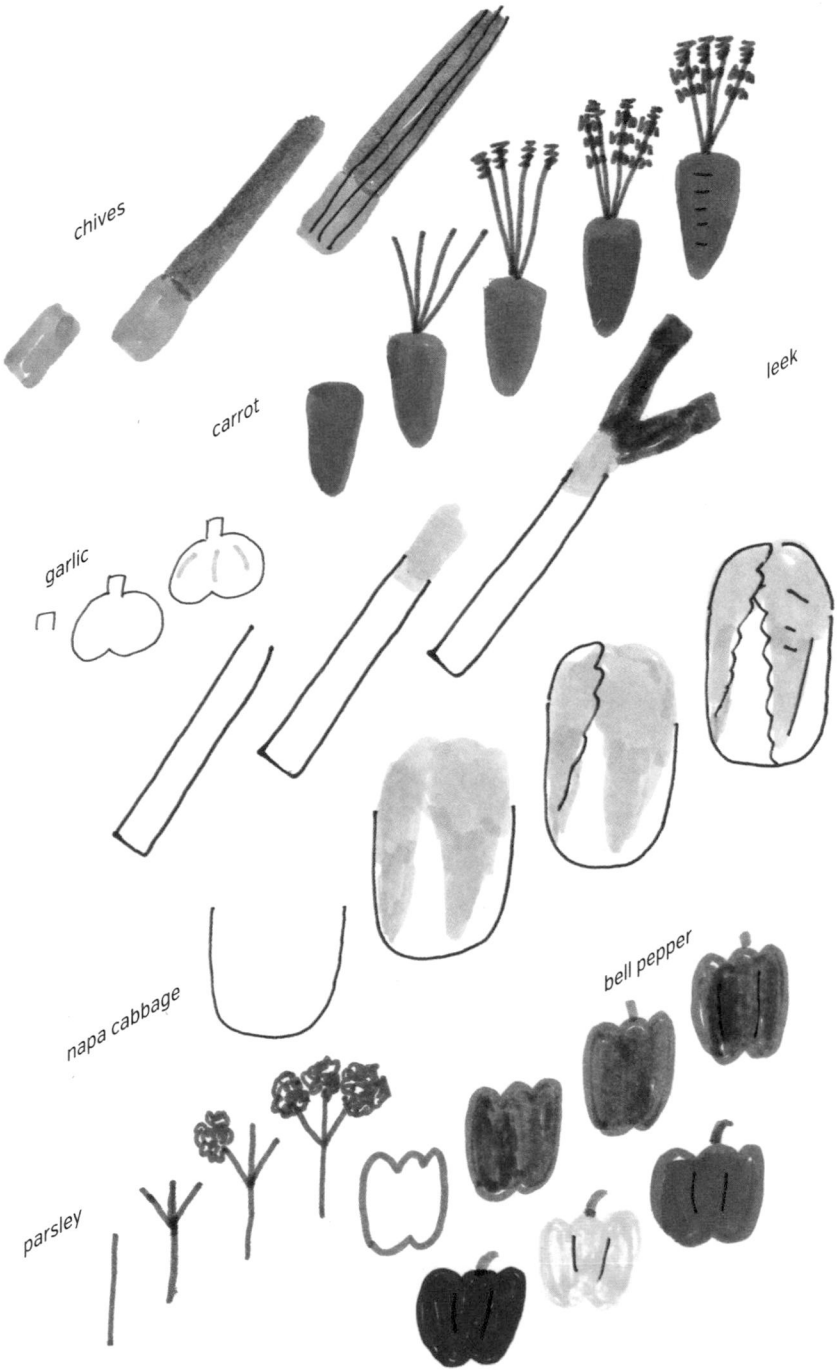
chives
carrot
leek
garlic
napa cabbage
bell pepper
parsley

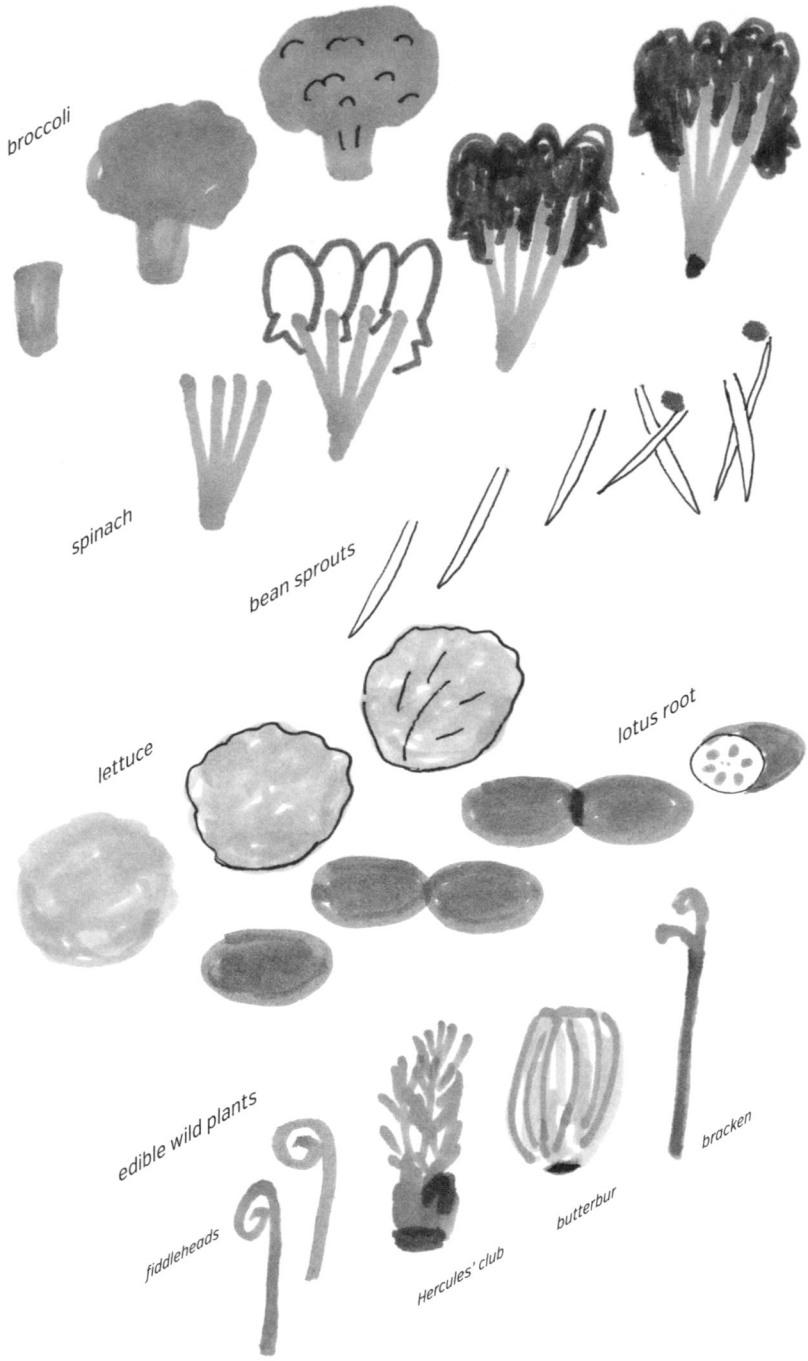
broccoli
spinach
bean sprouts
lettuce
lotus root
edible wild plants
fiddleheads
Hercules' club
butterbur
bracken

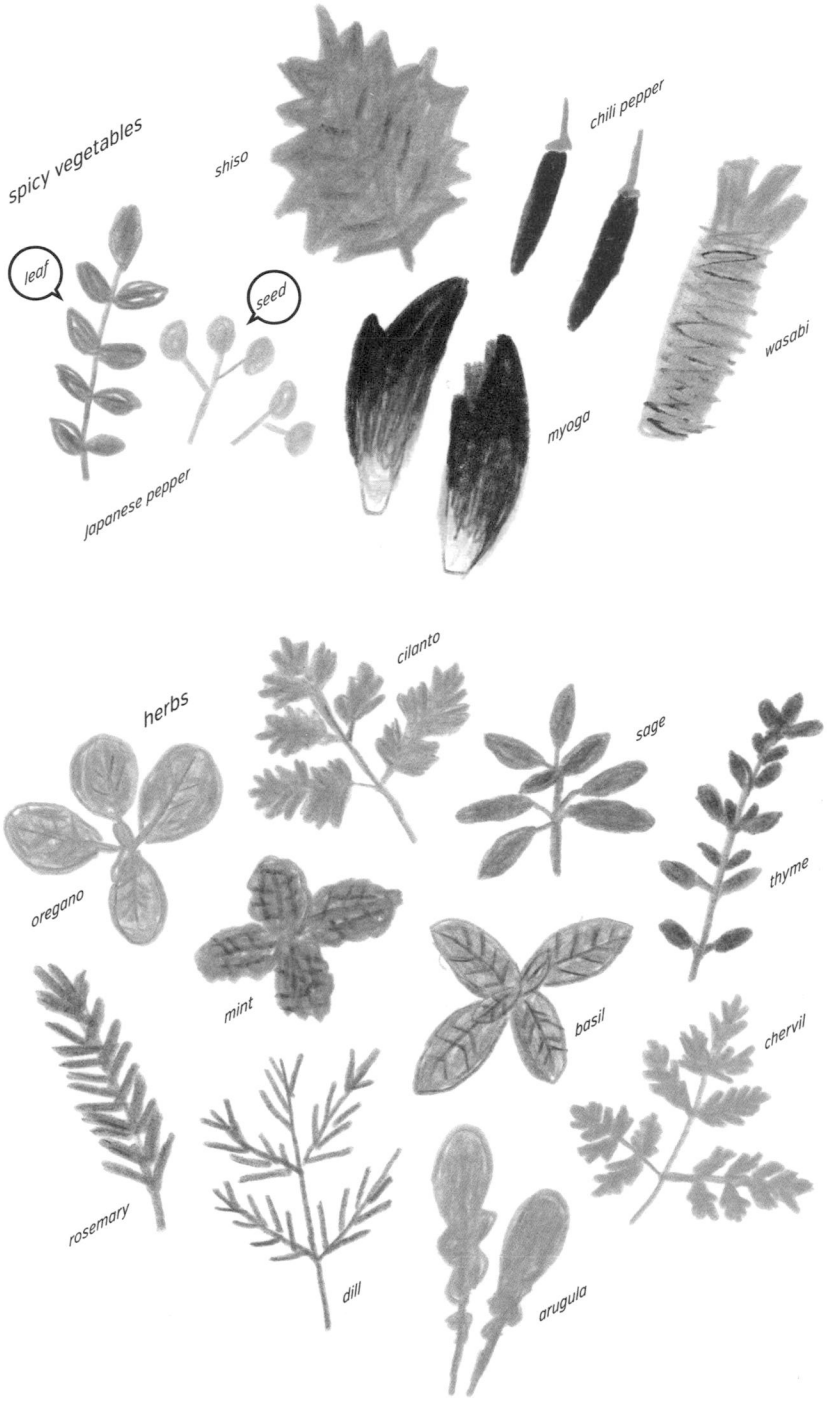
spicy vegetables
shiso
chili pepper
leaf
seed
wasabi
myoga
Japanese pepper
herbs
cilanto
sage
oregano
thyme
mint
basil
chervil
rosemary
dill
arugula

# Main Dishes

When drawing main dishes, it helps to think about the way you serve each meal. Which ingredients are visible when the dish is plated? Is the dish traditionally served with certain garnishes or condiments? These details help make an illustration more accurate.

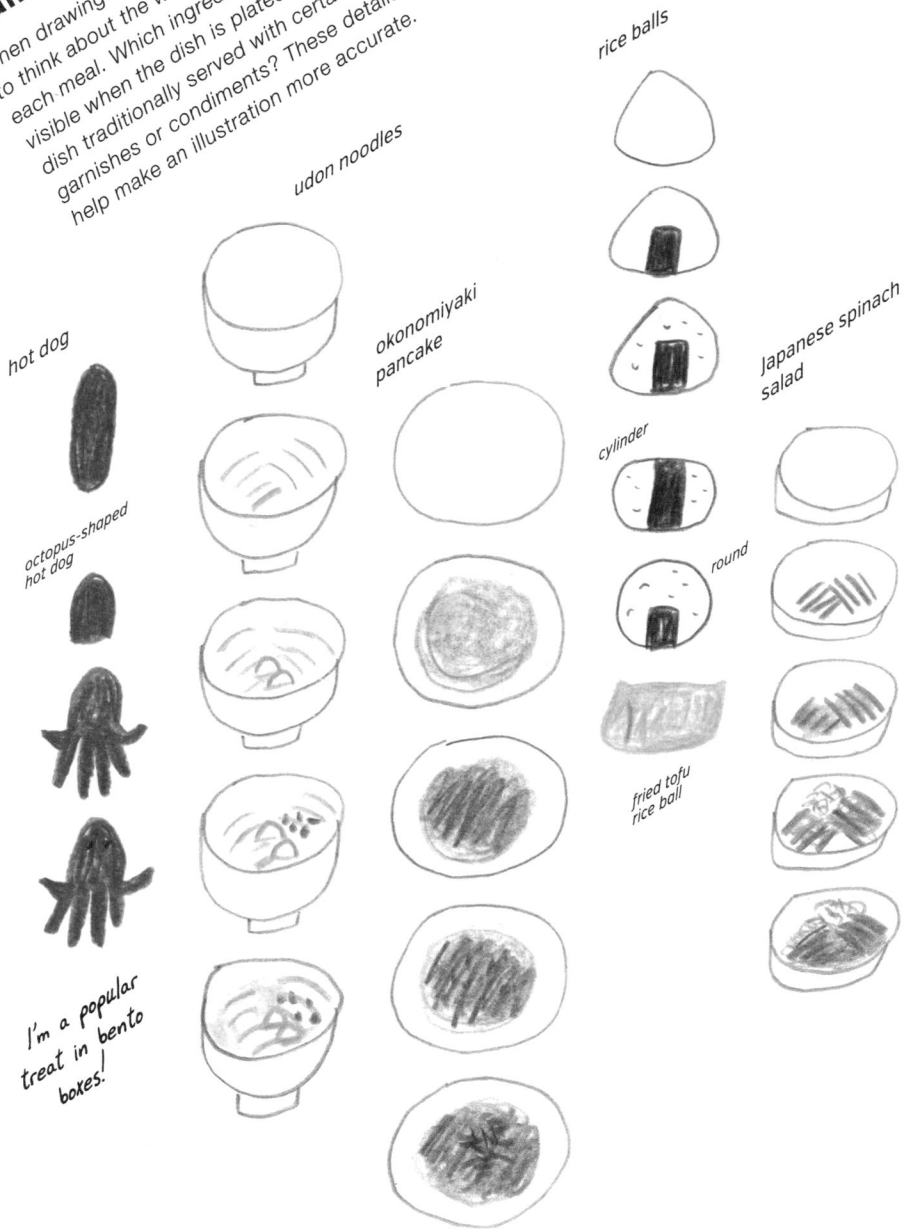

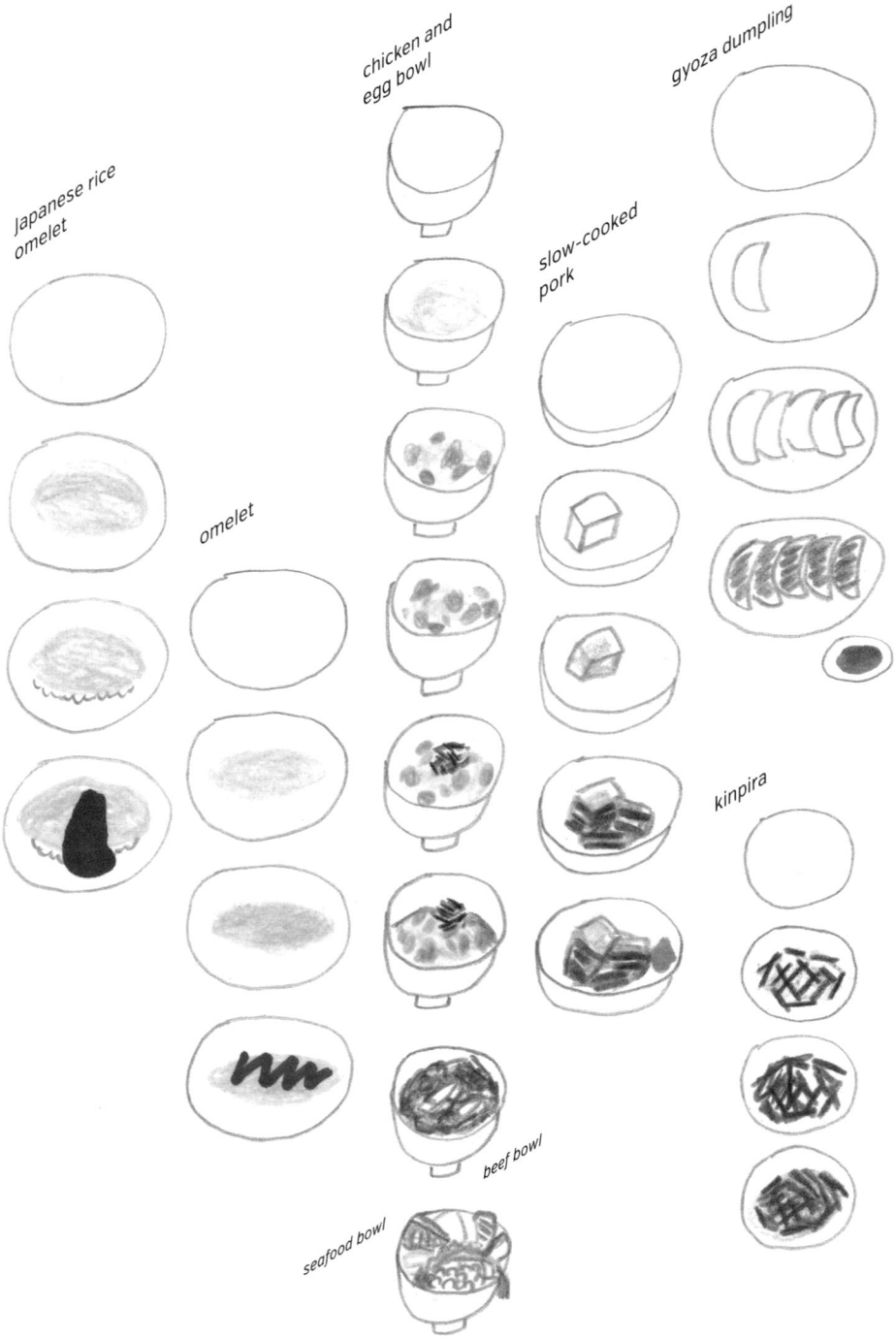
Japanese rice omelet
omelet
chicken and egg bowl
beef bowl
seafood bowl
slow-cooked pork
gyoza dumpling
kinpira

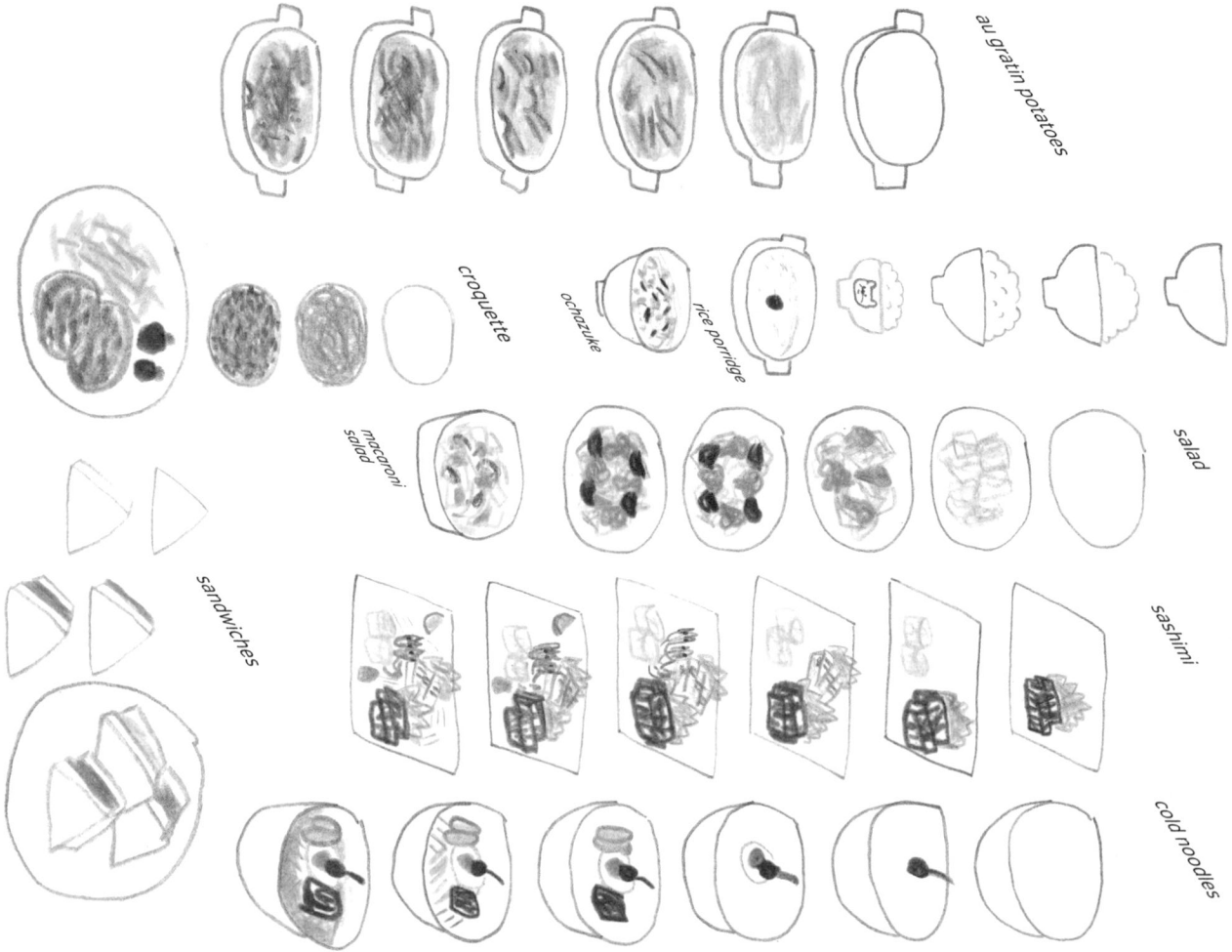
rice
salad
sashimi
cold noodles
au gratin potatoes
rice porridge
ochazuke
croquette
macaroni salad
sandwiches

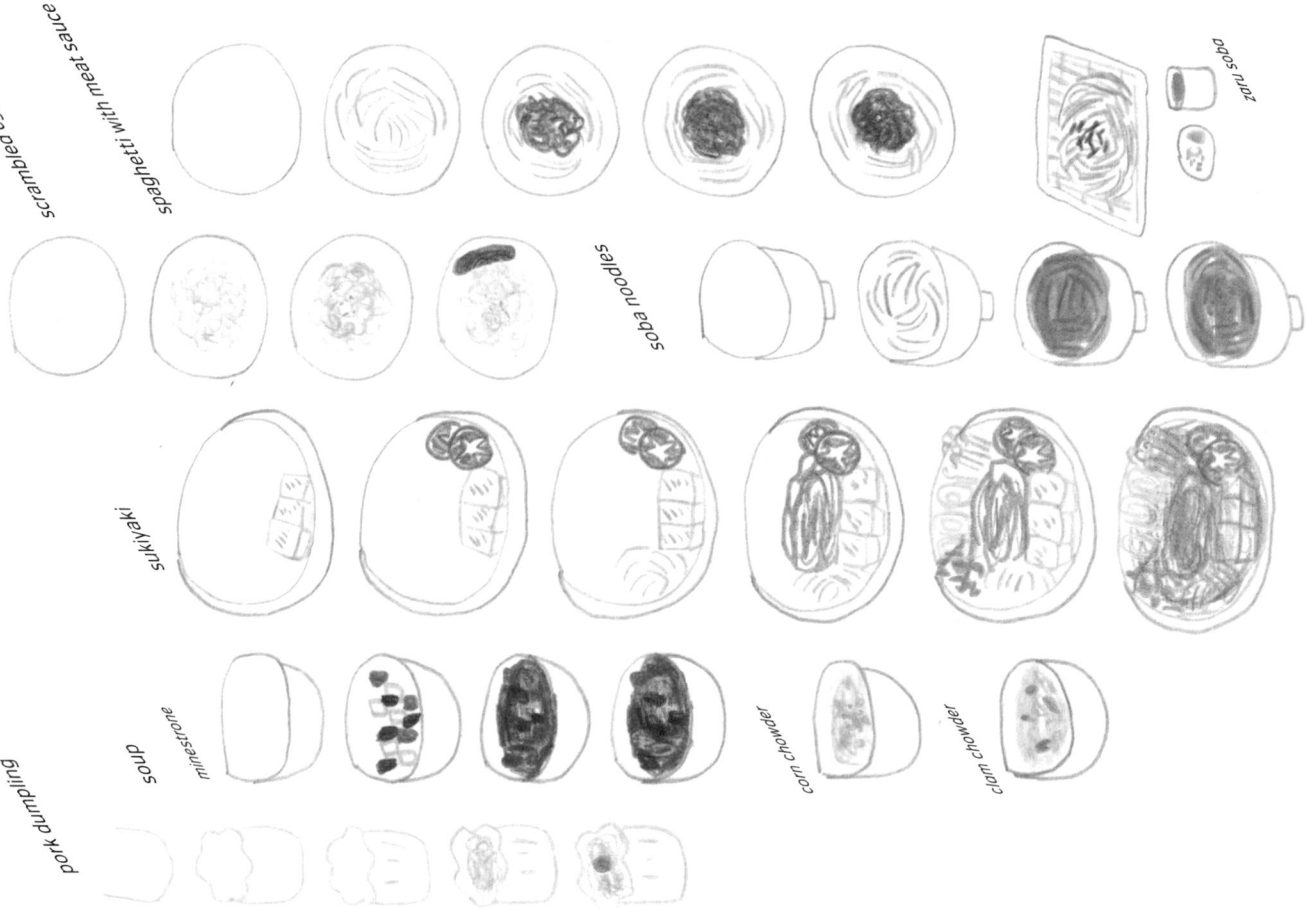
zuni soba
corn chowder
corn chowder
soba noodles
spaghetti with meat sauce
scrambled eggs
sukiyaki
minestrone
soup
pork dumpling

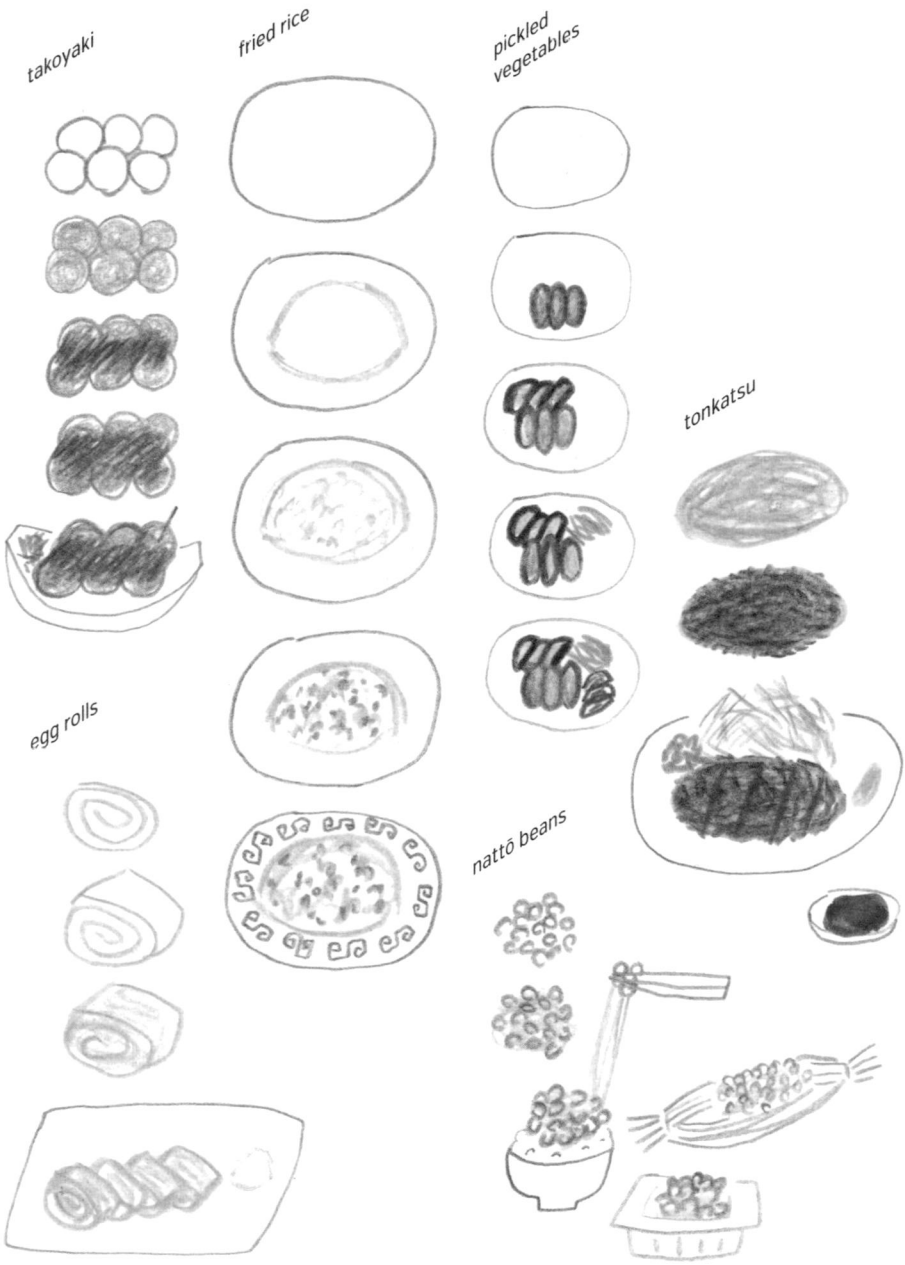
takoyaki
fried rice
pickled vegetables
tonkatsu
egg rolls
nattō beans

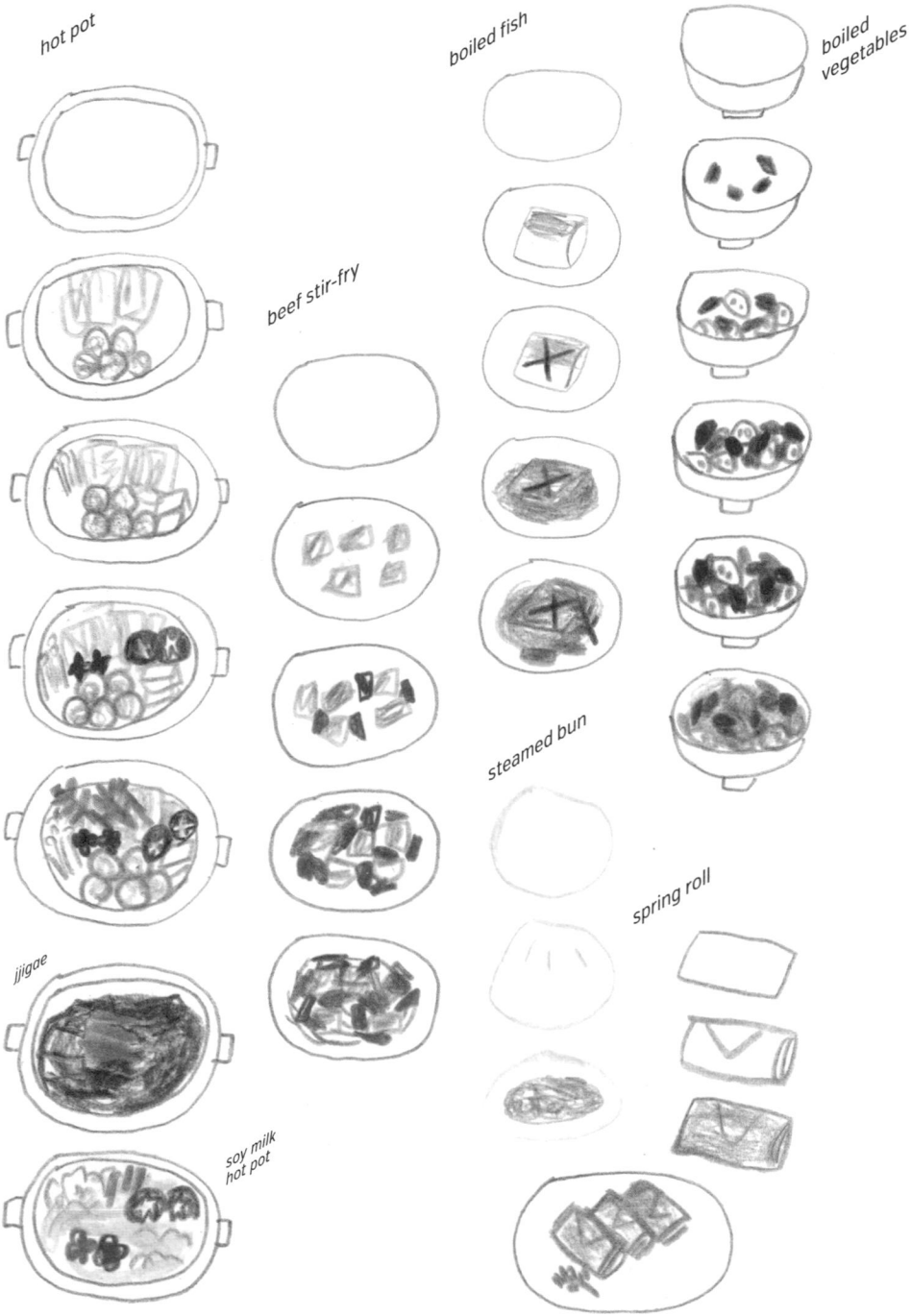
hot pot
beef stir-fry
boiled fish
boiled vegetables
steamed bun
spring roll
jjigae
soy milk hot pot

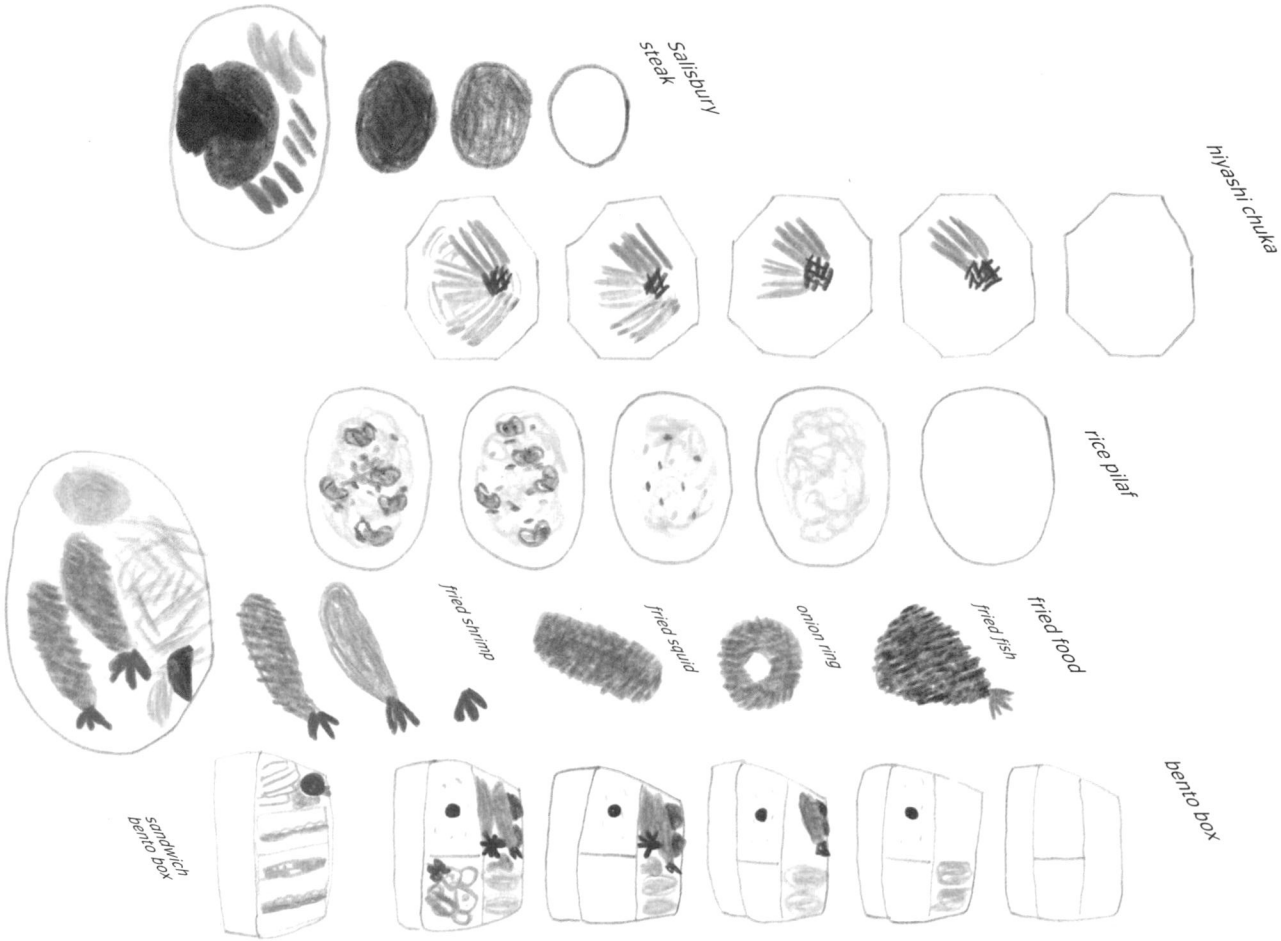
hiyashi chuka
rice pilaf
fried food
fried fish
onion ring
fried squid
fried shrimp
bento box
Salisbury steak
sandwich bento box

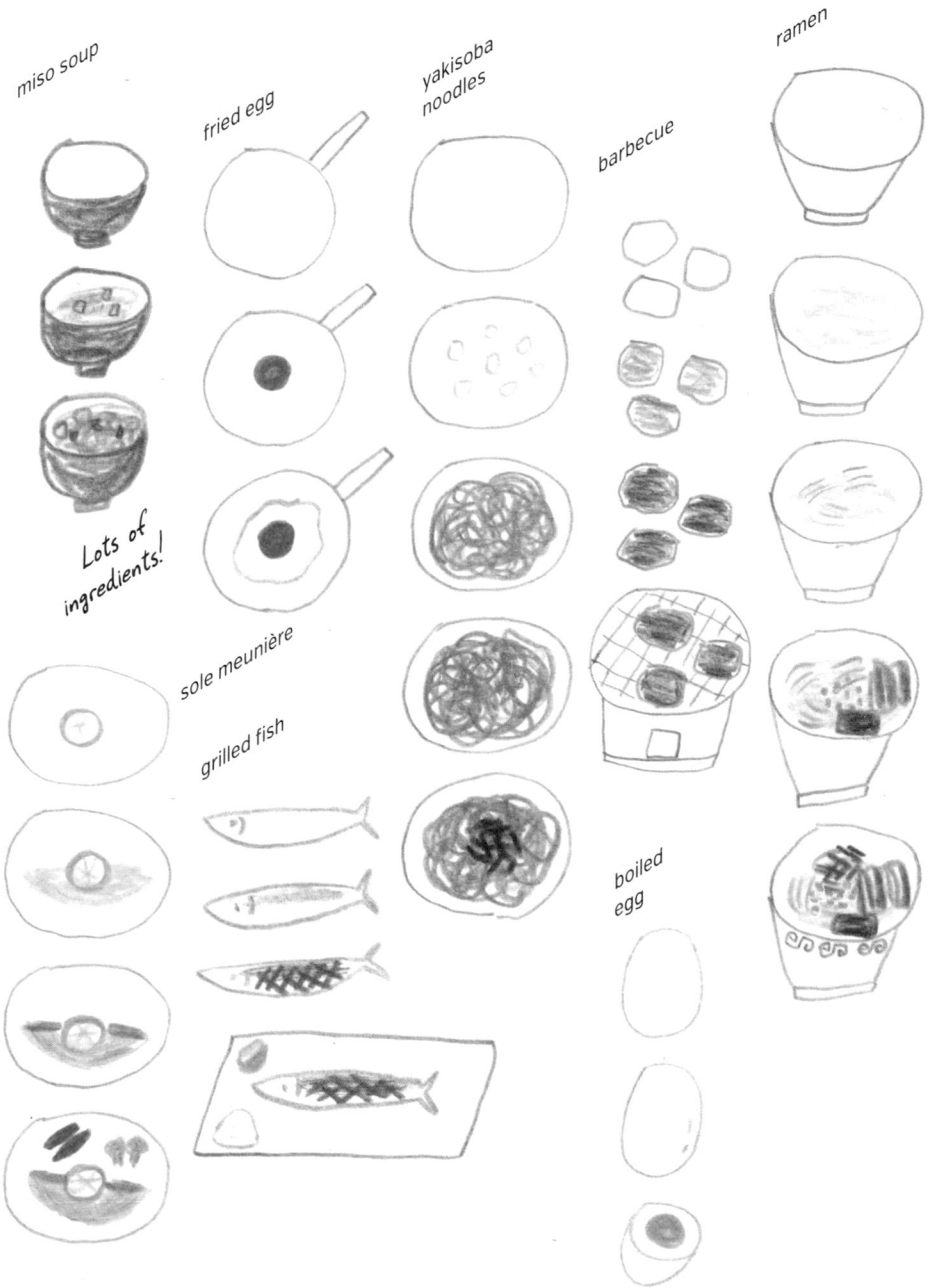
miso soup
fried egg
yakisoba noodles
barbecue
ramen
Lots of ingredients!
sole meunière
grilled fish
boiled egg

# Dishes of the World

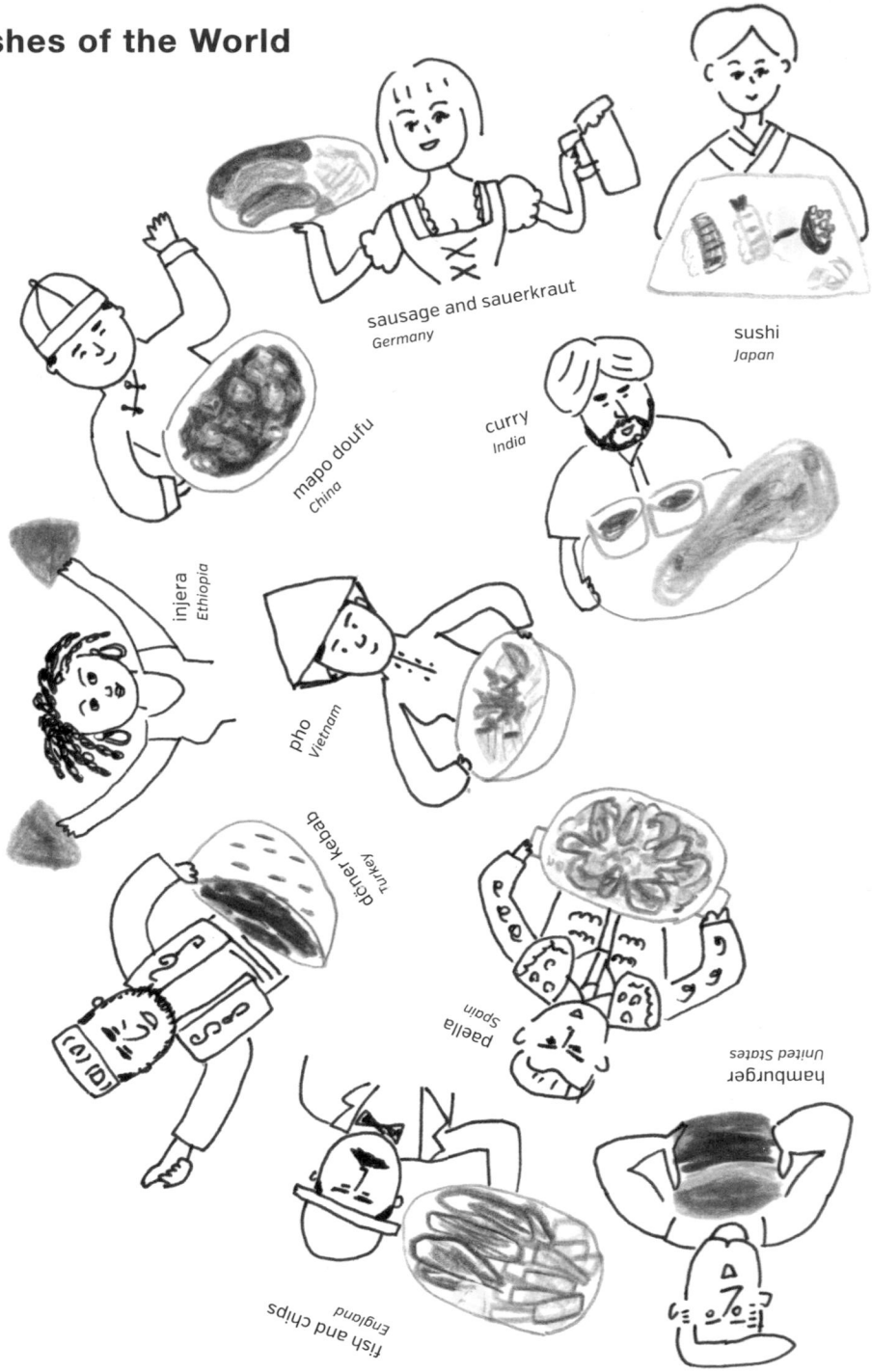

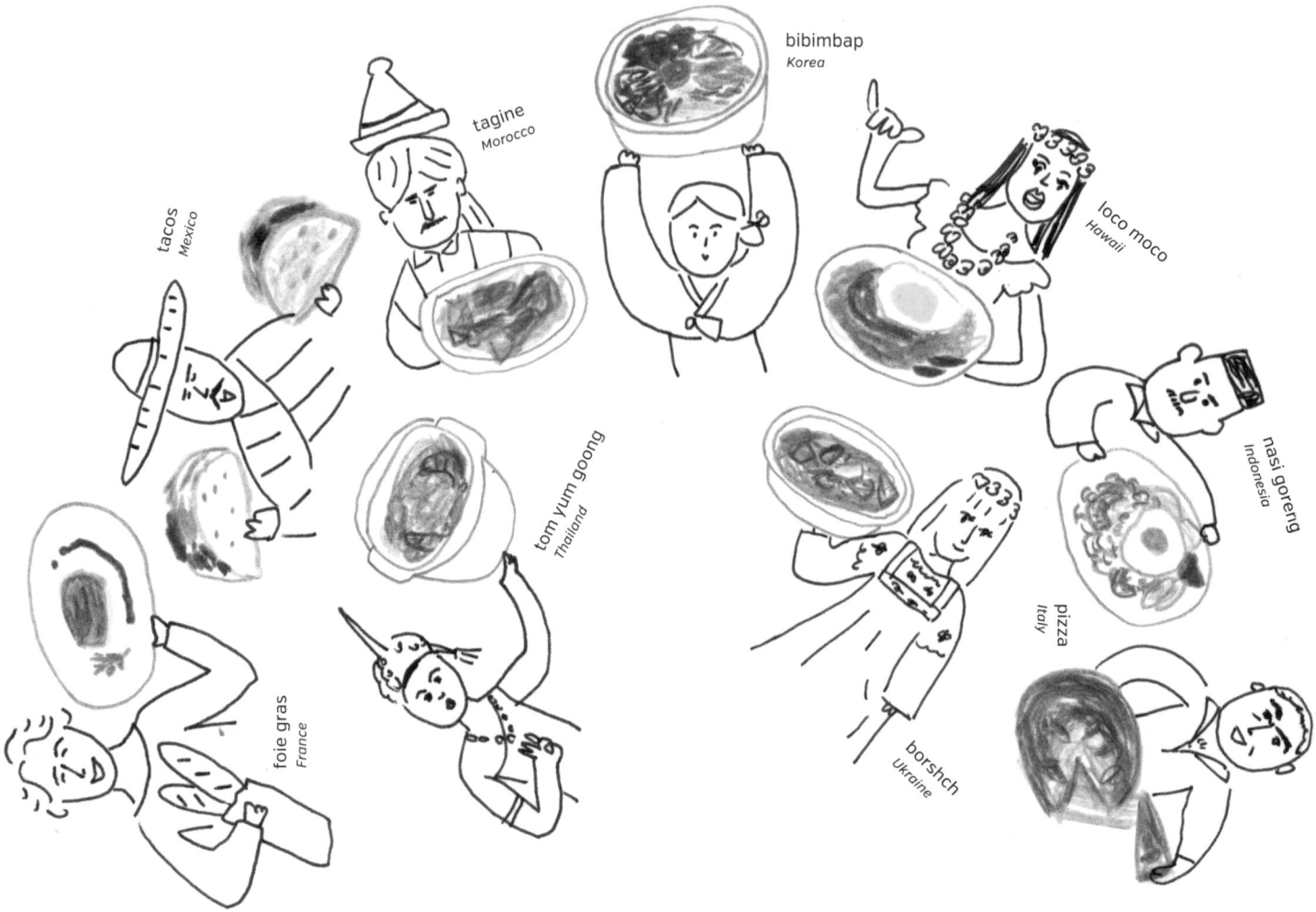
loco moco
Hawaii
bibimbap
Korea
nasi goreng
Indonesia
tagine
Morocco
pizza
Italy
tacos
Mexico
borshch
Ukraine
tom yum goong
Thailand
foie gras
France

## Snacks

Use a marker to replicate the smooth, shiny texture of frosting, ice cream, and other sweets.

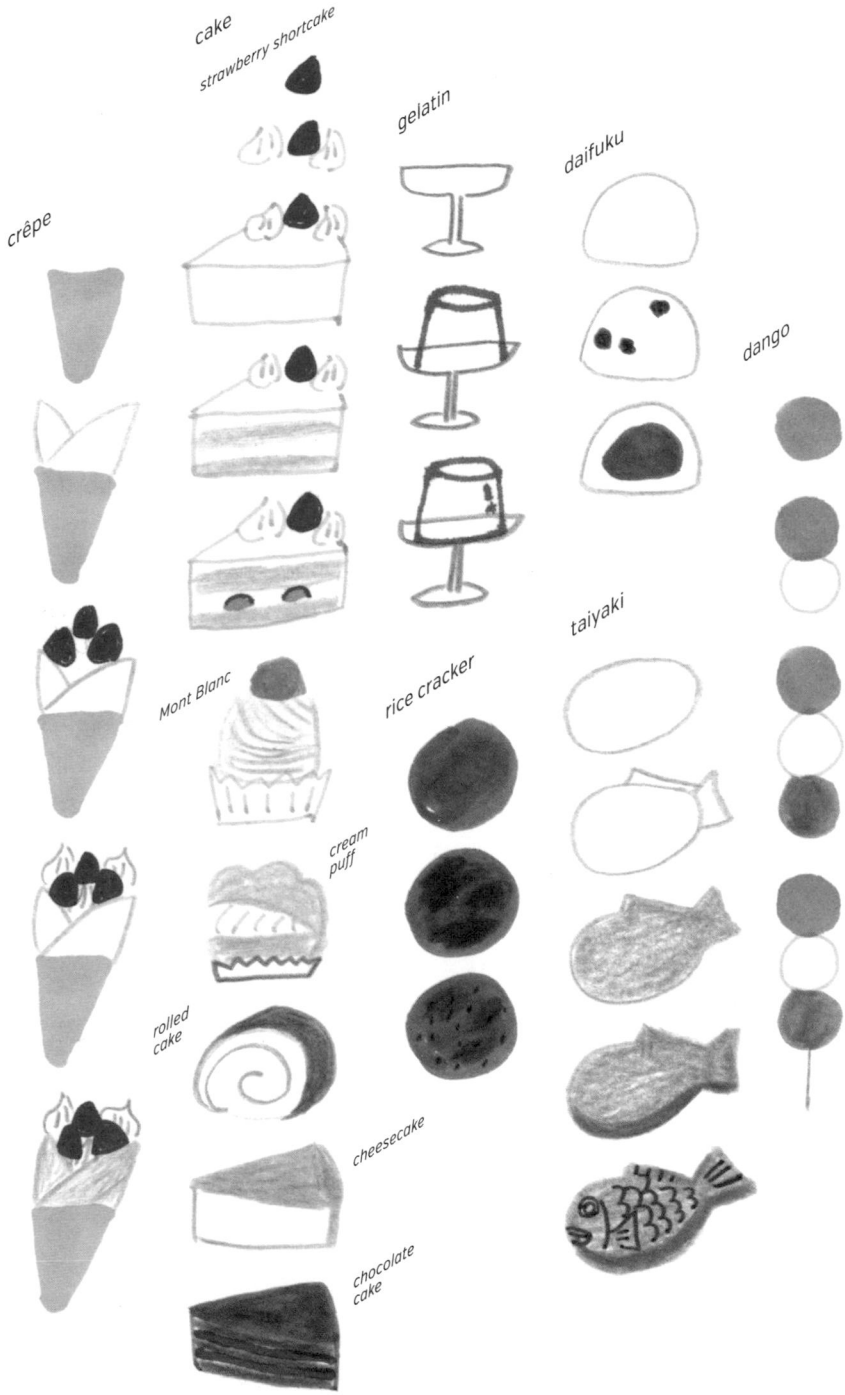
cake
strawberry shortcake
gelatin
daifuku
crêpe
dango
taiyaki
Mont Blanc
rice cracker
cream puff
rolled cake
cheesecake
chocolate cake

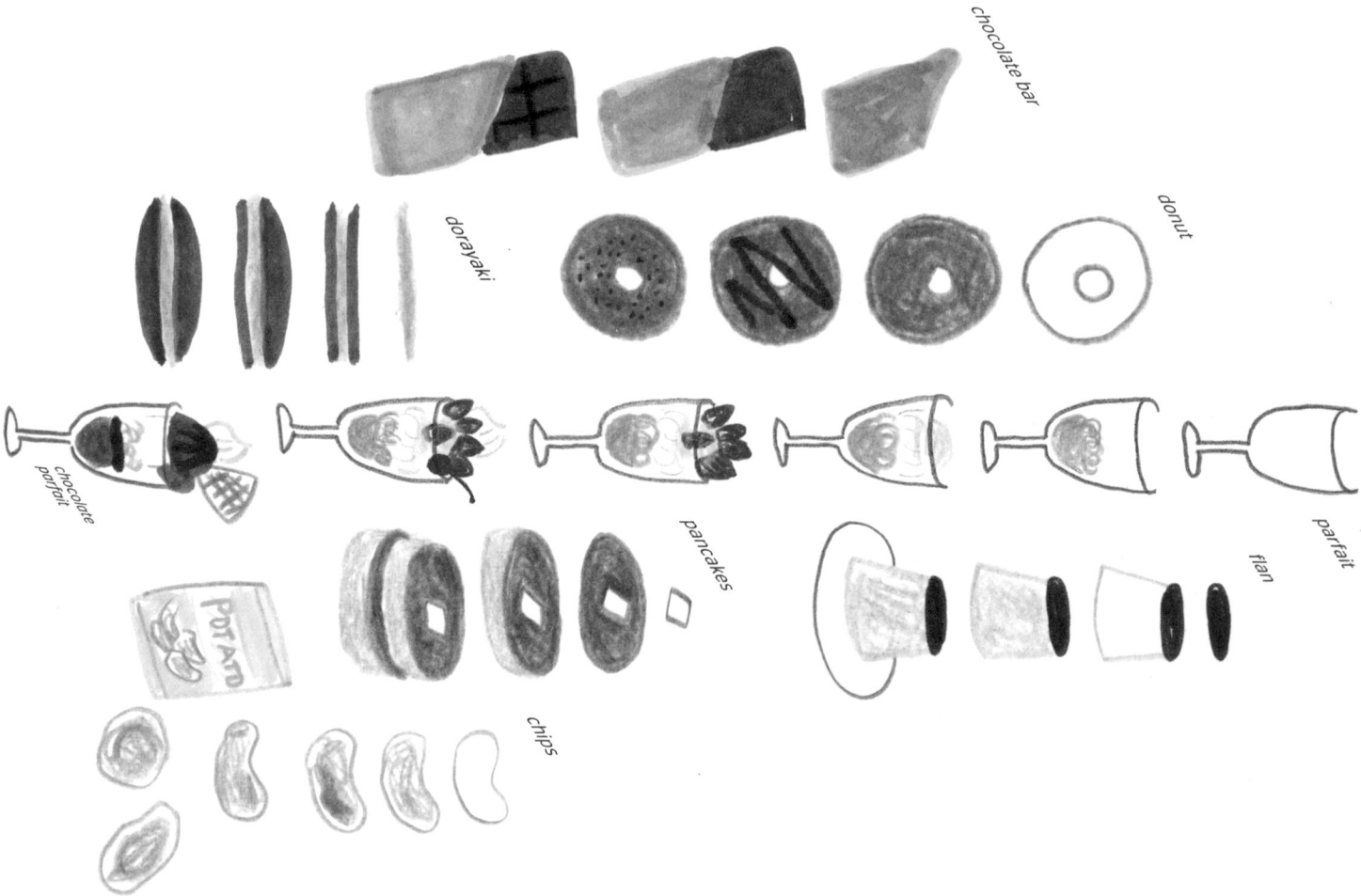
chocolate bar
donut
dorayaki
parfait
flan
pancakes
chocolate parfait
POTATO
chips

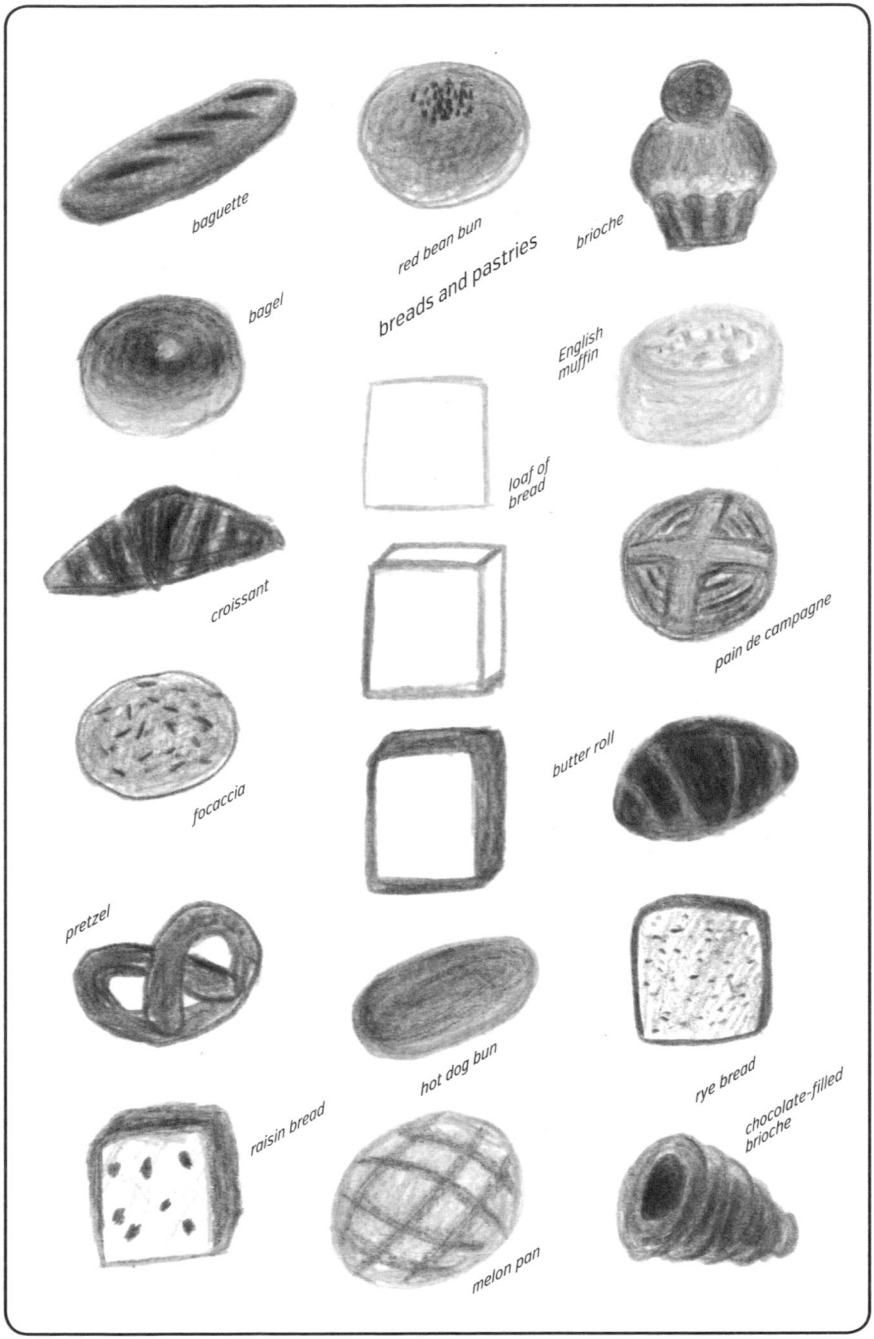
baguette
red bean bun
brioche
breads and pastries
bagel
English muffin
loaf of bread
croissant
pain de campagne
focaccia
butter roll
pretzel
hot dog bun
rye bread
raisin bread
chocolate-filled brioche
melon pan

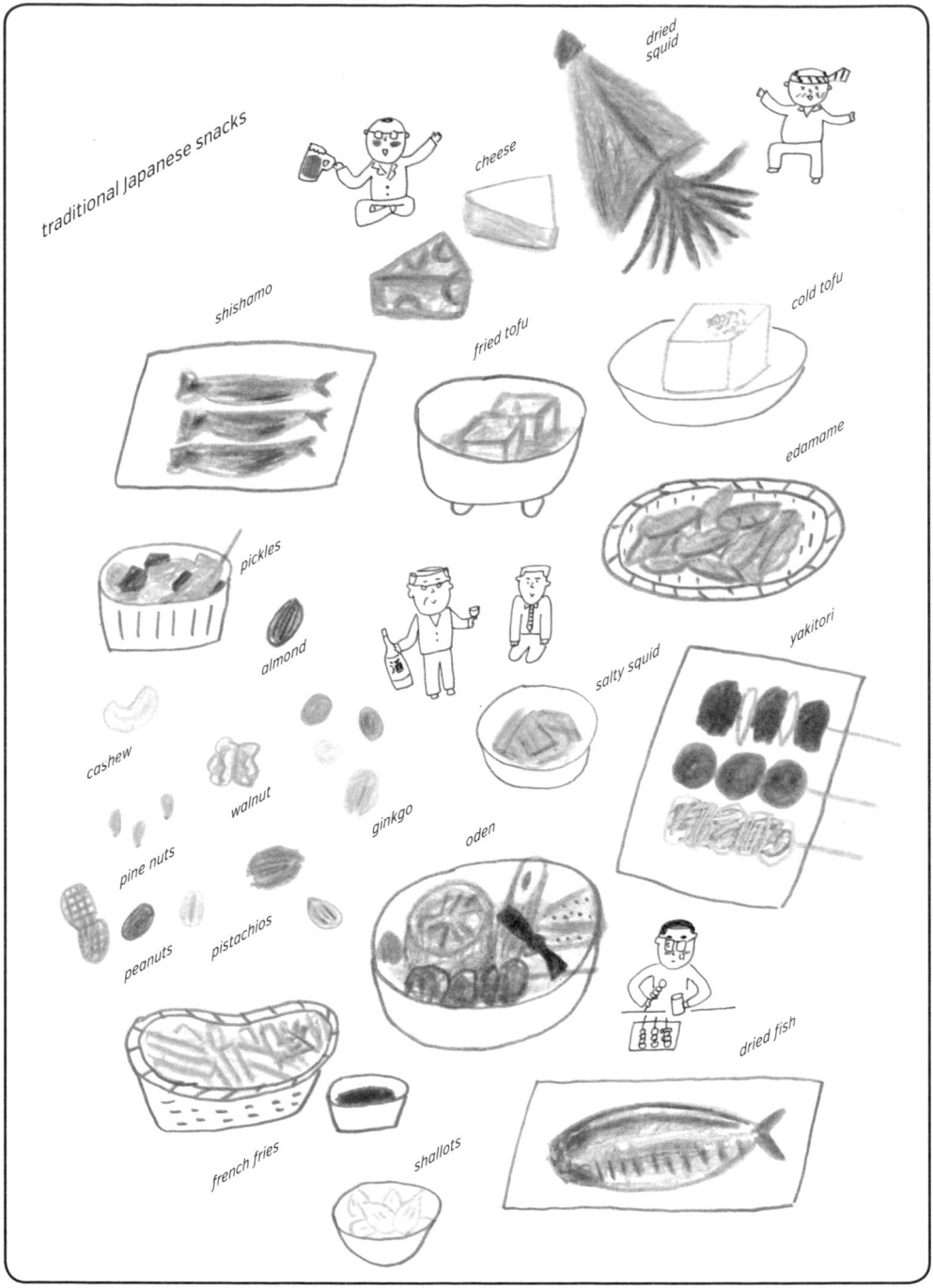
traditional Japanese snacks
dried squid
cheese
shishamo
fried tofu
cold tofu
edamame
pickles
almond
salty squid
yakitori
cashew
walnut
ginkgo
oden
pine nuts
pistachios
peanuts
dried fish
french fries
shallots

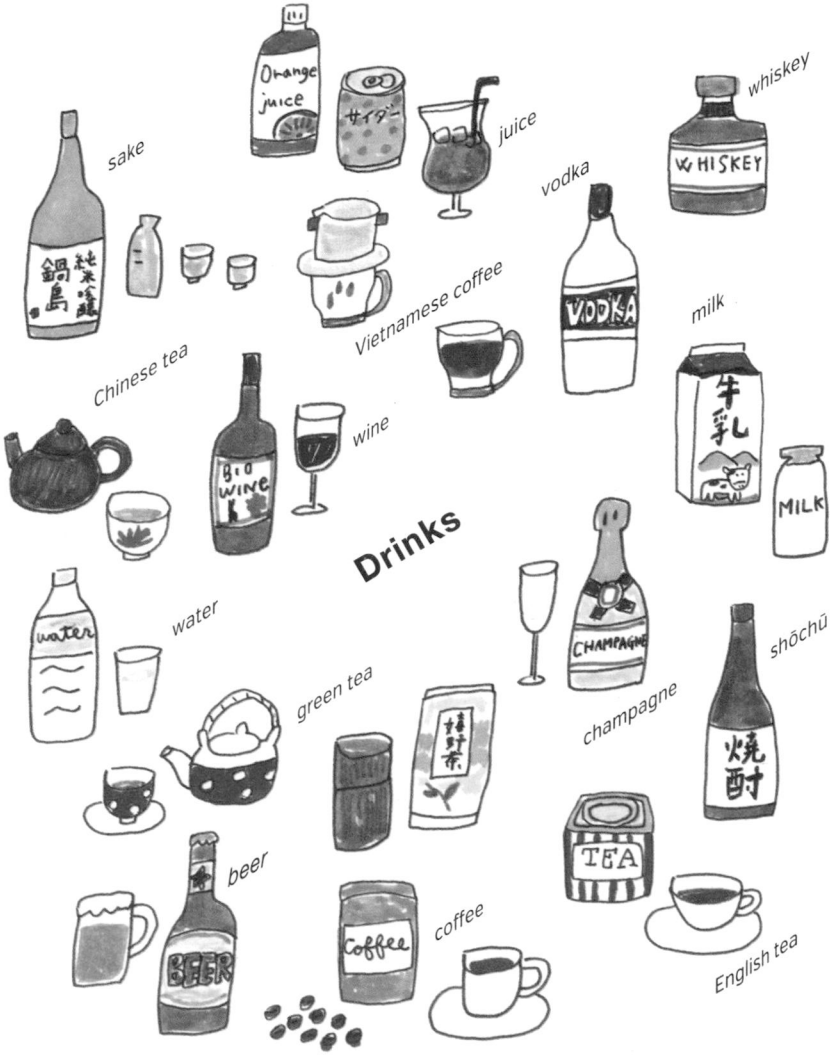


## CHALLENGE #2: Draw Bottles

I like to find bottles with unique shapes and interesting labels to use for drawing practice. These drawings often look best when done in black pen.

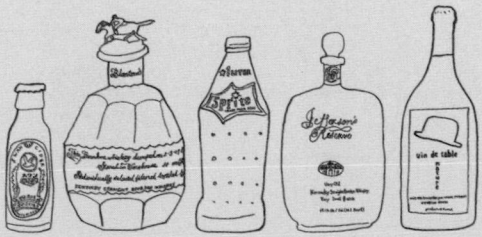

## Packaged Foods

When drawing packaged foods, think about the shapes of the bottles and jars, the colors of the logos, and the imagery used on the labels.

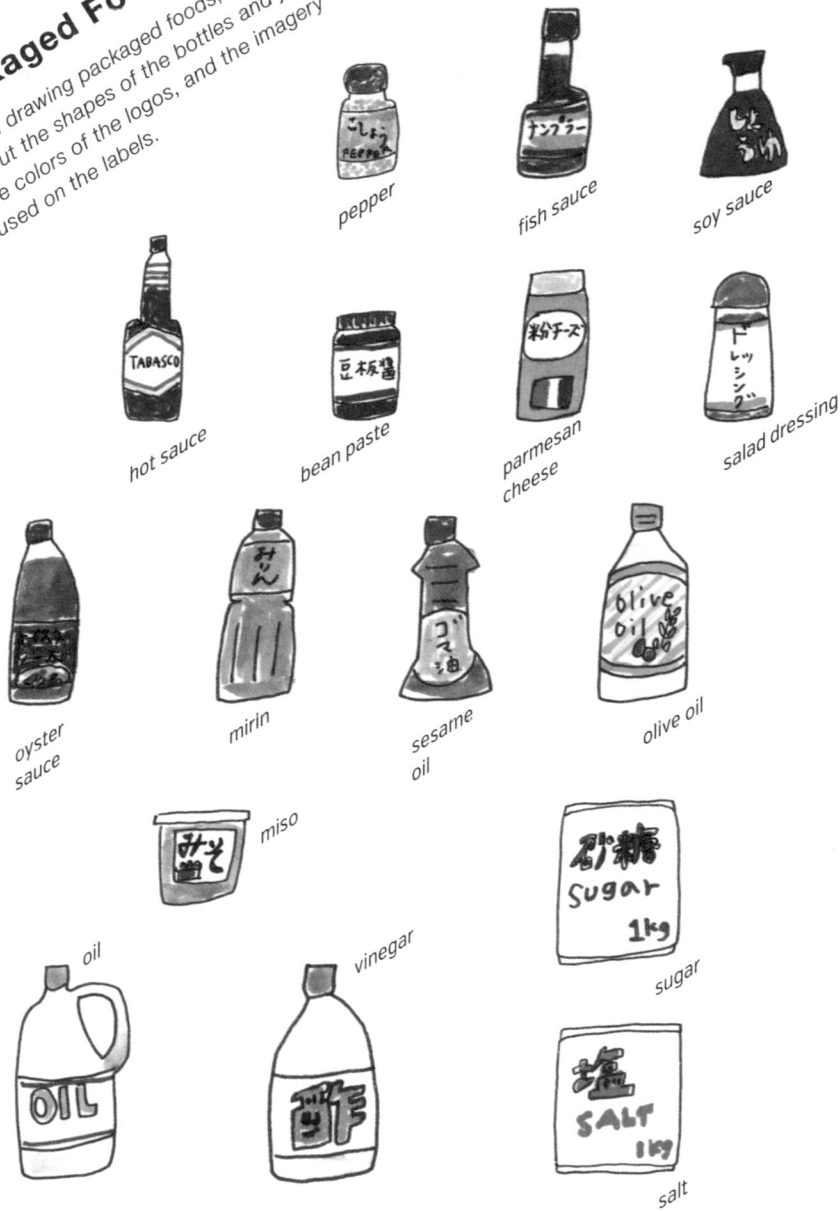


pepper

fish sauce

soy sauce

hot sauce

bean paste

parmesan cheese

salad dressing

oyster sauce

mirin

sesame oil

olive oil

miso

sugar

oil

vinegar

salt

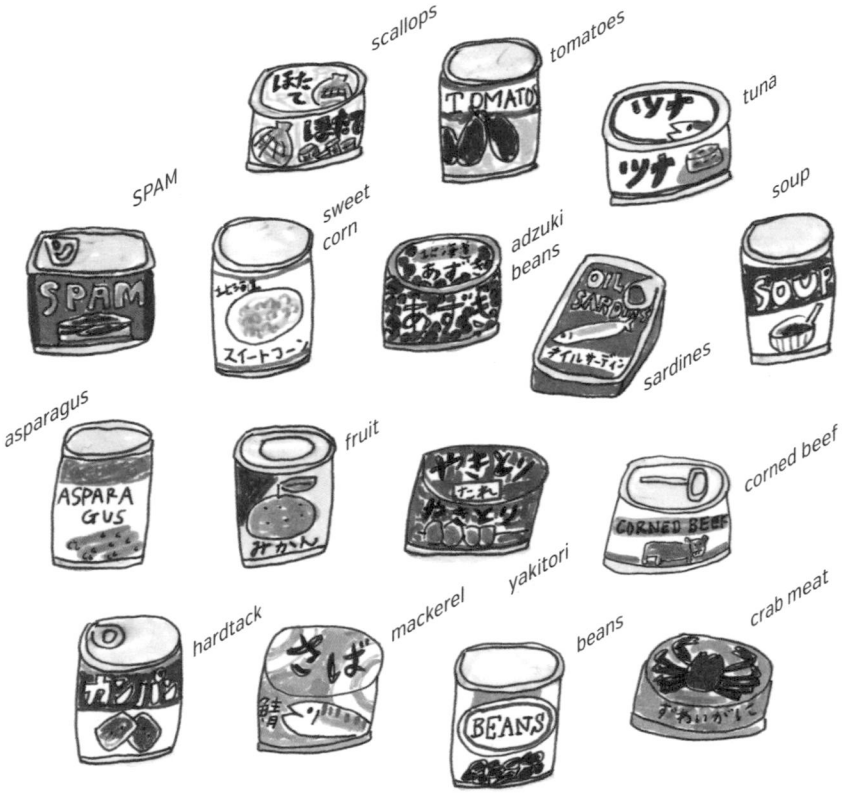


## CHALLENGE #3:

### Draw Food Packaging

Gather some of your favorite packaged foods and draw what you see. Don't worry about the details, like text. Instead, focus on capturing the correct colors and shapes since these elements make a package recognizable.

# CHALLENGE #4: Make a Food Journal

I love to create a visual food journal when I travel or visit restaurants. Just like a written diary, a visual diary will help you remember memorable trips and events. In addition to drawing what you ate, add details about the restaurant's atmosphere, service, and best dishes. Here's a tip: Draw first, then add text once the sketch is complete.

**Date: September 3**

Breakfast

Breakfast is the most important meal of the day!

orange juice

salad

jam

pancakes

yogurt

Lunch

I had udon noodles and seaweed. I topped this dish with some spicy yuzu pepper sauce made by my grandmother.

vegetables

seaweed

yuzu pepper sauce

Dinner

I went out to dinner with friends and we shared many different dishes.

squid served with miso vinegar sauce

We started with cocktails and appetizers

yakitori

miso soup

On the house!

rice balls

grilled eggplant

My favorite

fried chicken

# Around the House

- Entryway
- Kitchen
- Living Room
- Bedroom
- Study
- Bathroom
- Patio
- Home Maintenance

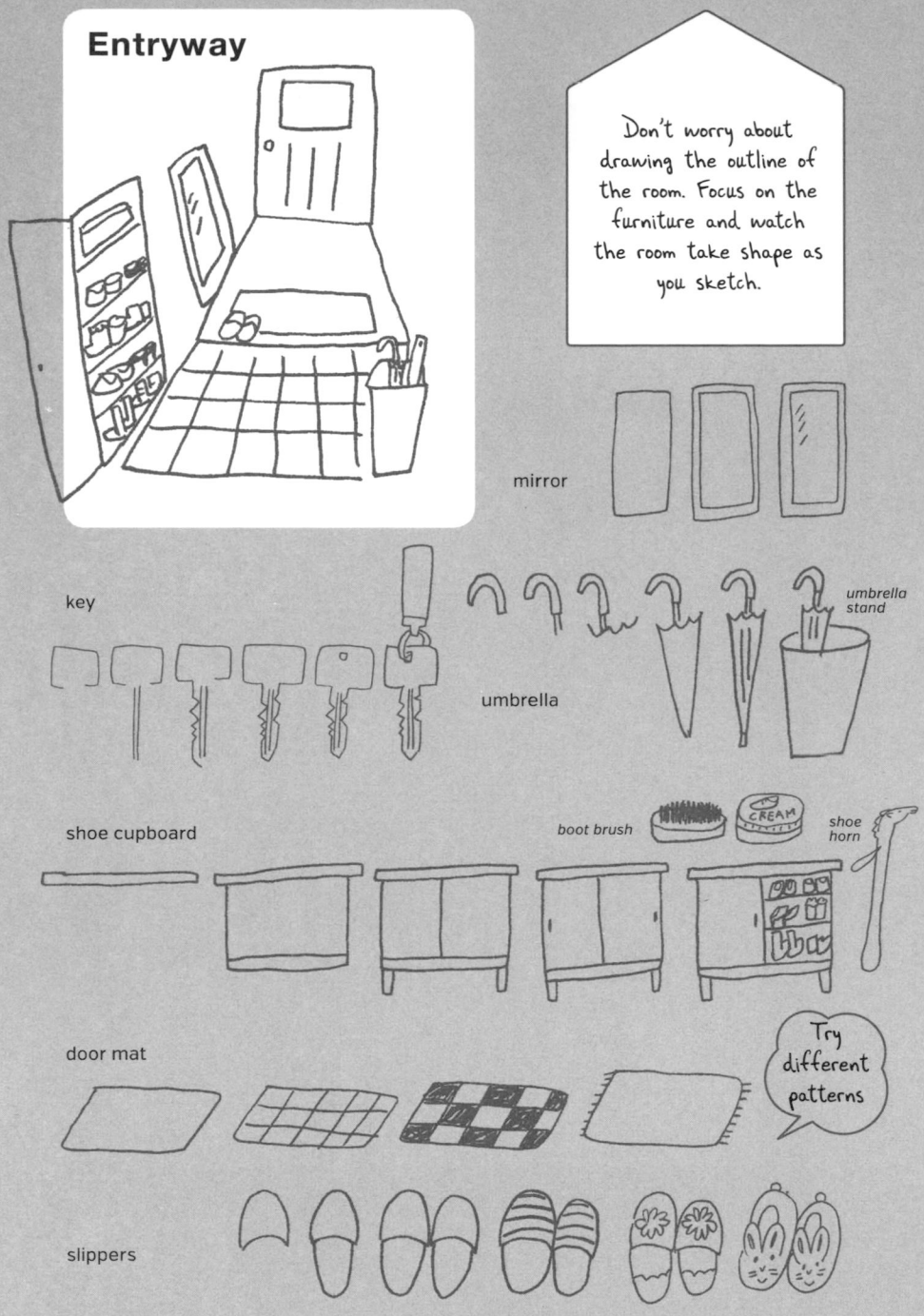
Entryway
Don't worry about drawing the outline of the room. Focus on the furniture and watch the room take shape as you sketch.
mirror
key
umbrella
umbrella stand
shoe cupboard
boot brush
CREAM
shoe horn
door mat
Try different patterns
slippers

# Kitchen

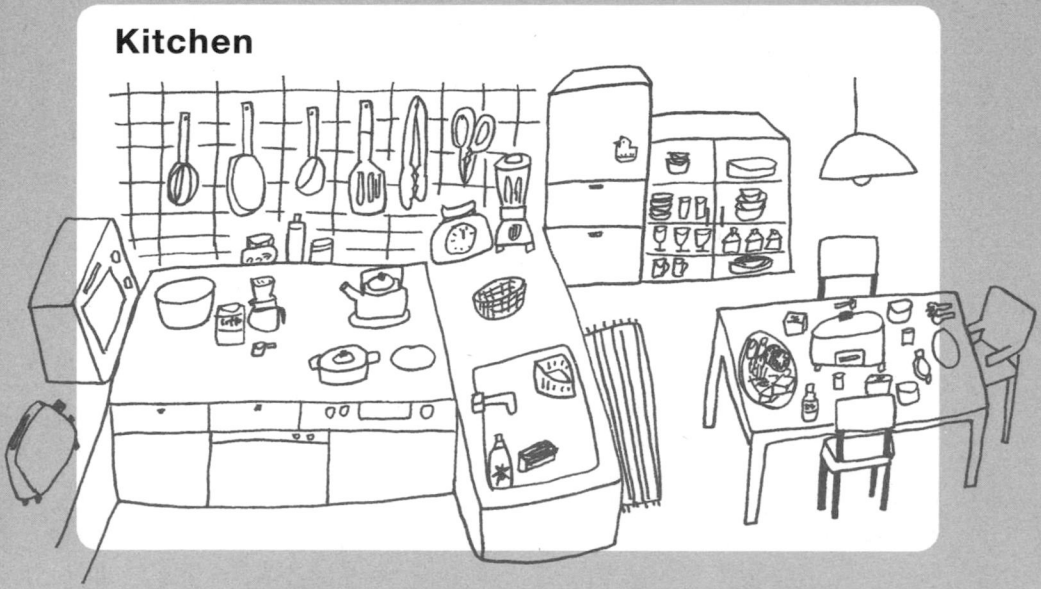

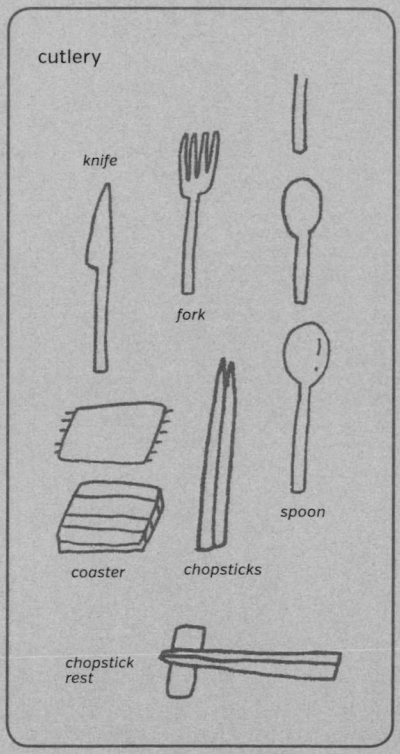
cutlery
knife
fork
spoon
coaster
chopsticks
chopstick rest

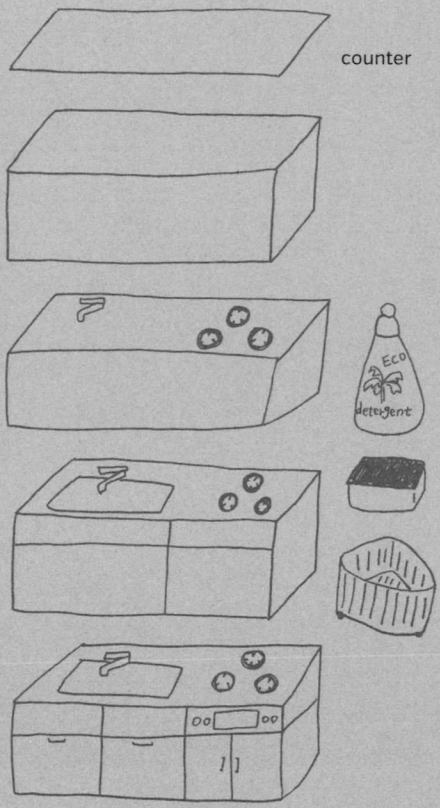
counter
Eco
detergent

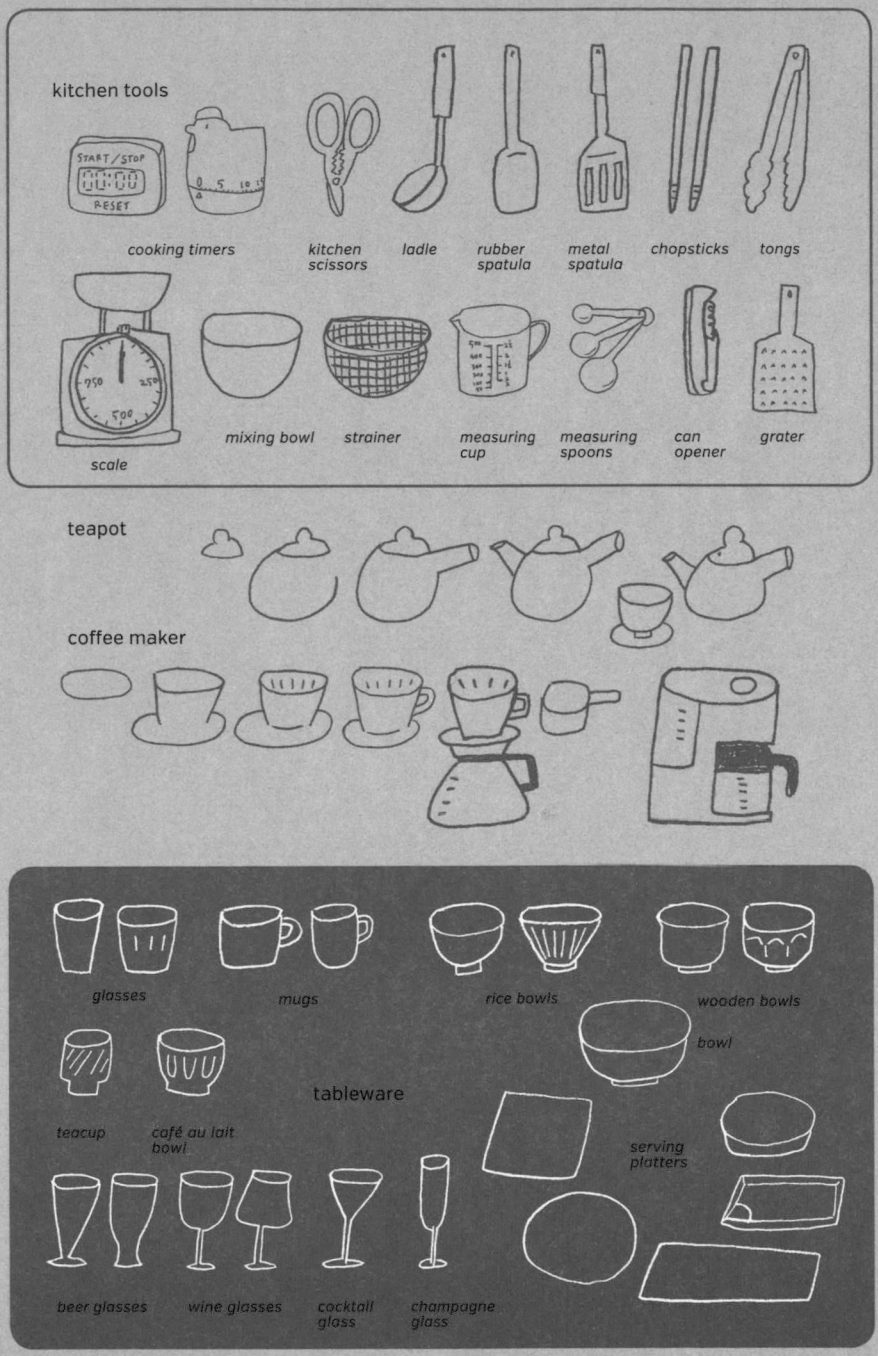
kitchen tools
START/STOP
RESET
cooking timers
kitchen scissors
ladle
rubber spatula
metal spatula
chopsticks
tongs
scale
mixing bowl
strainer
measuring cup
measuring spoons
can opener
grater
teapot
coffee maker
glasses
mugs
rice bowls
wooden bowls
bowl
tableware
teacup
café au lait bowl
serving platters
beer glasses
wine glasses
cocktail glass
champagne glass

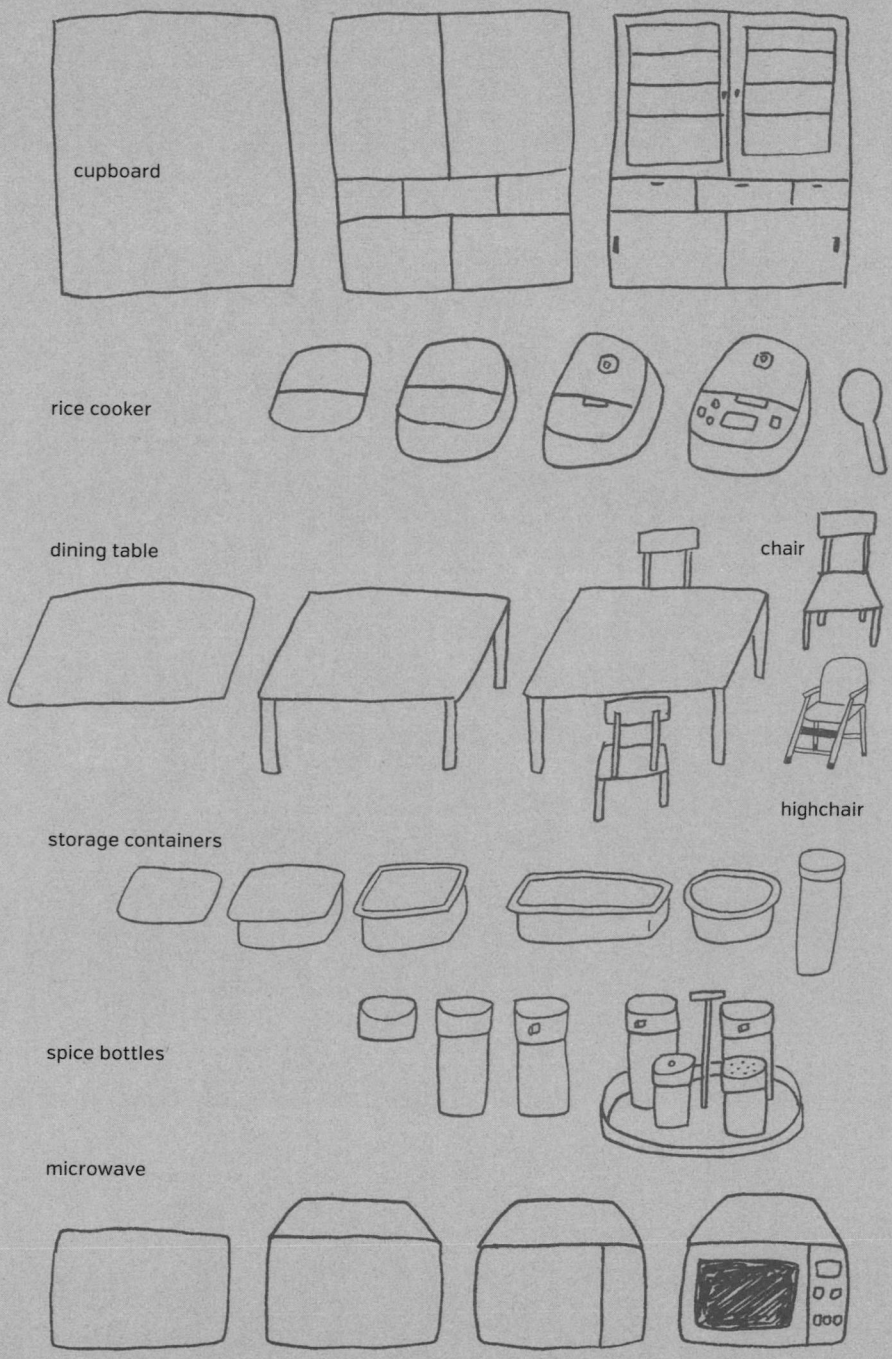
cupboard
rice cooker
dining table
chair
highchair
storage containers
spice bottles
microwave

toaster

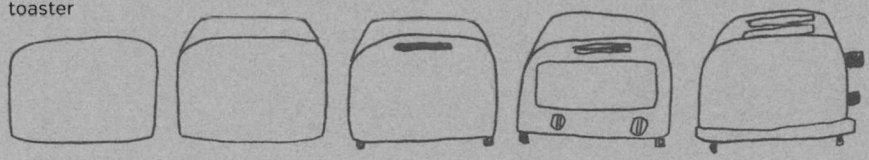

pots and pans

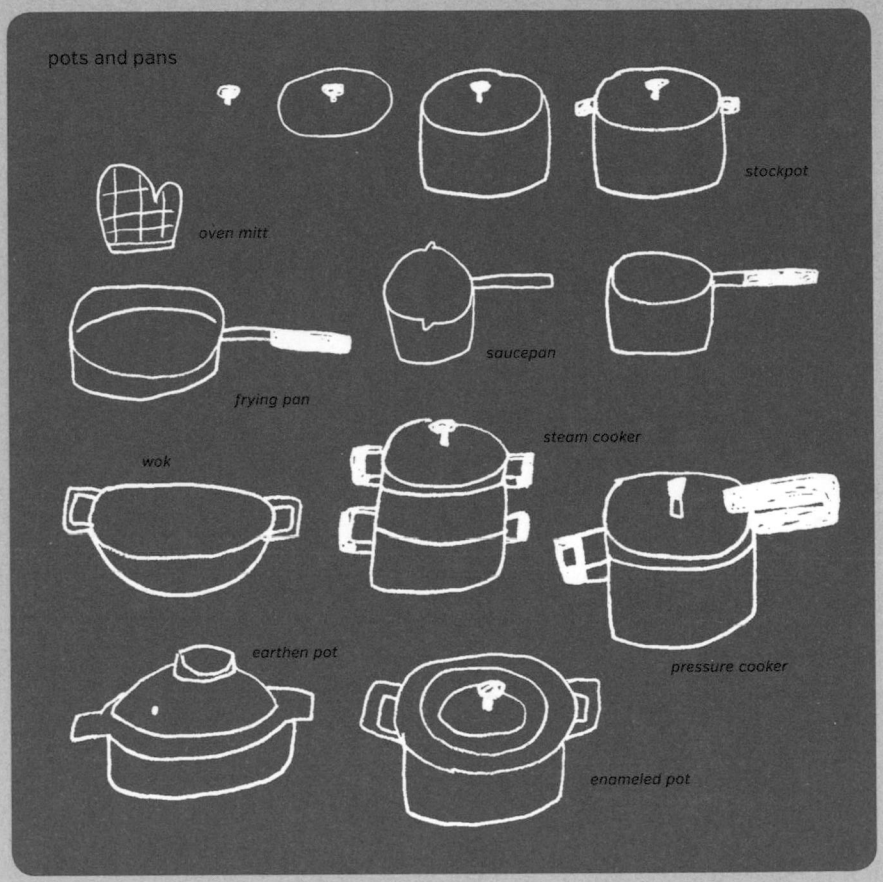


bread machine

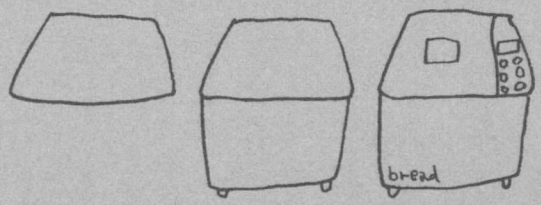

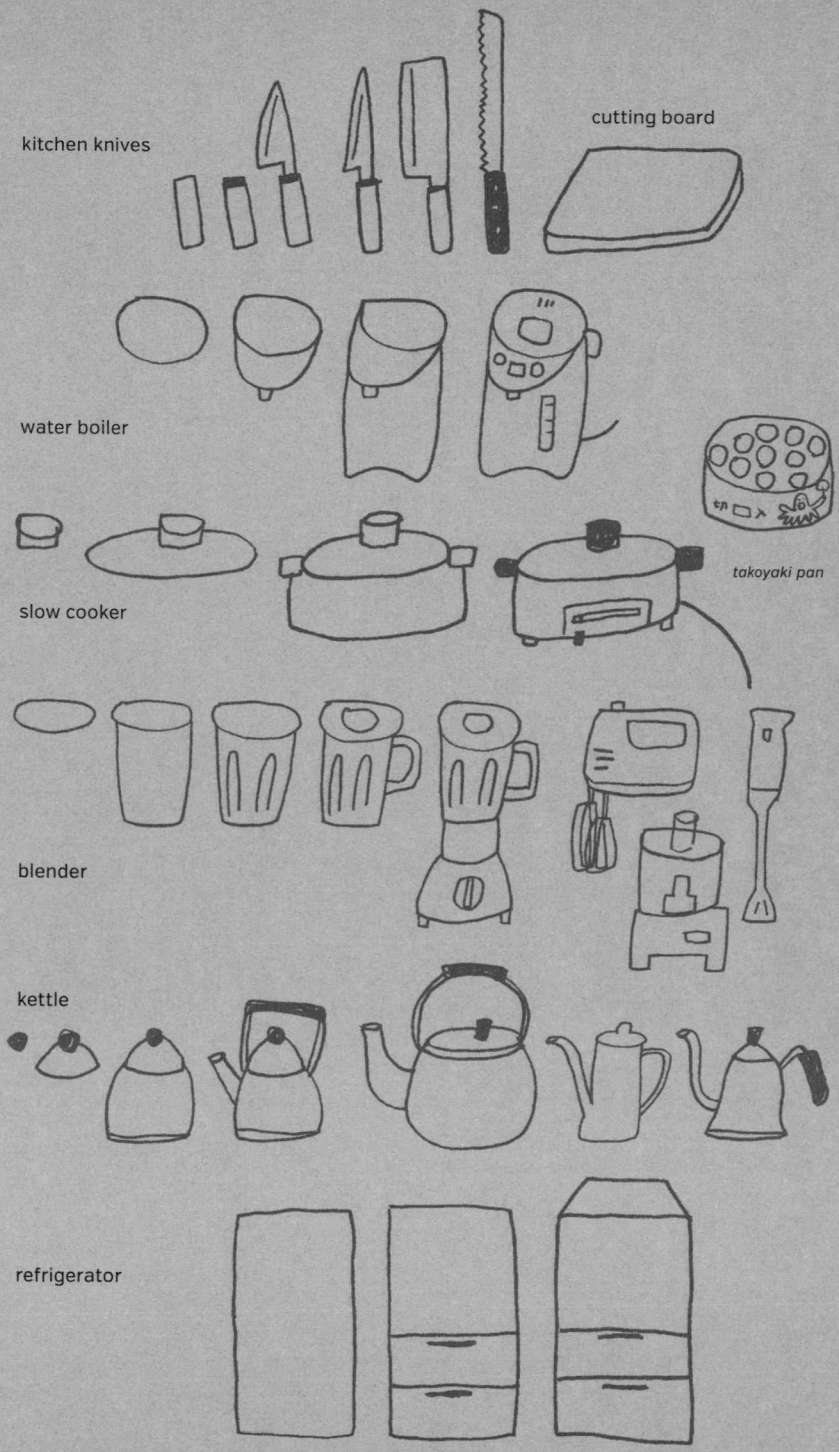
kitchen knives
cutting board
water boiler
takoyaki pan
slow cooker
blender
kettle
refrigerator

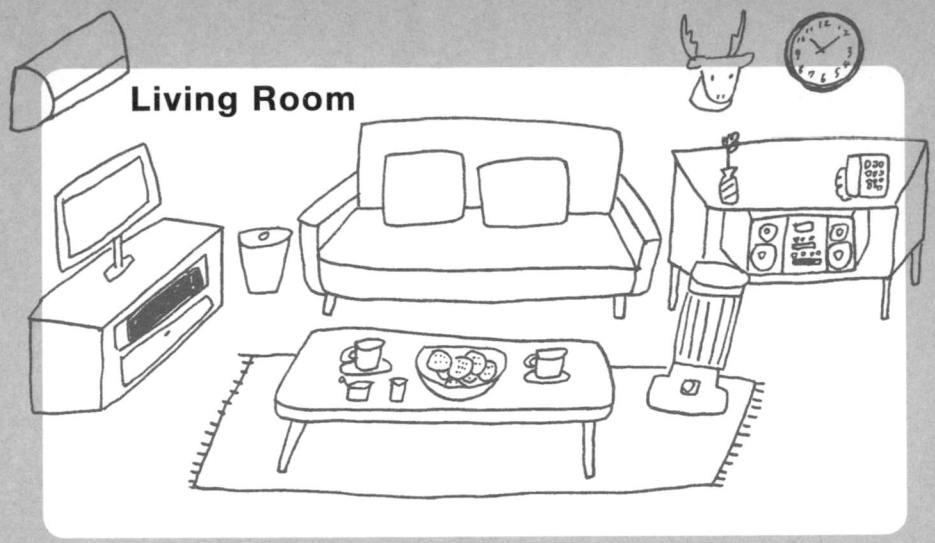
Living Room

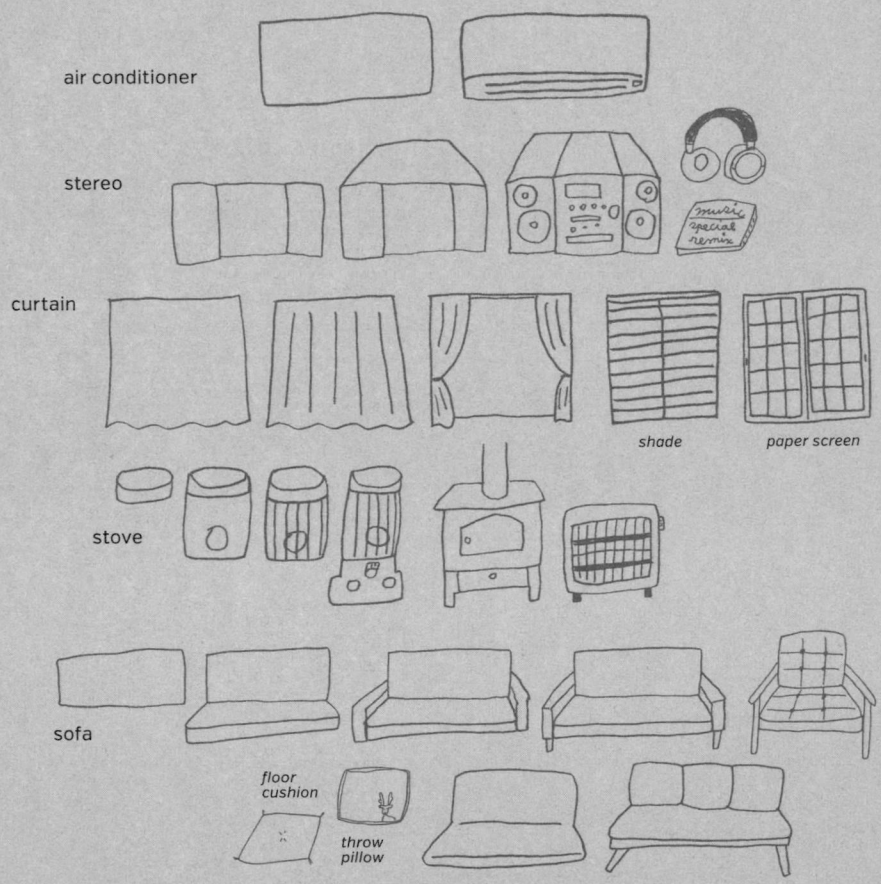
air conditioner
stereo
music special remix
curtain
shade
paper screen
stove
sofa
floor cushion
throw pillow

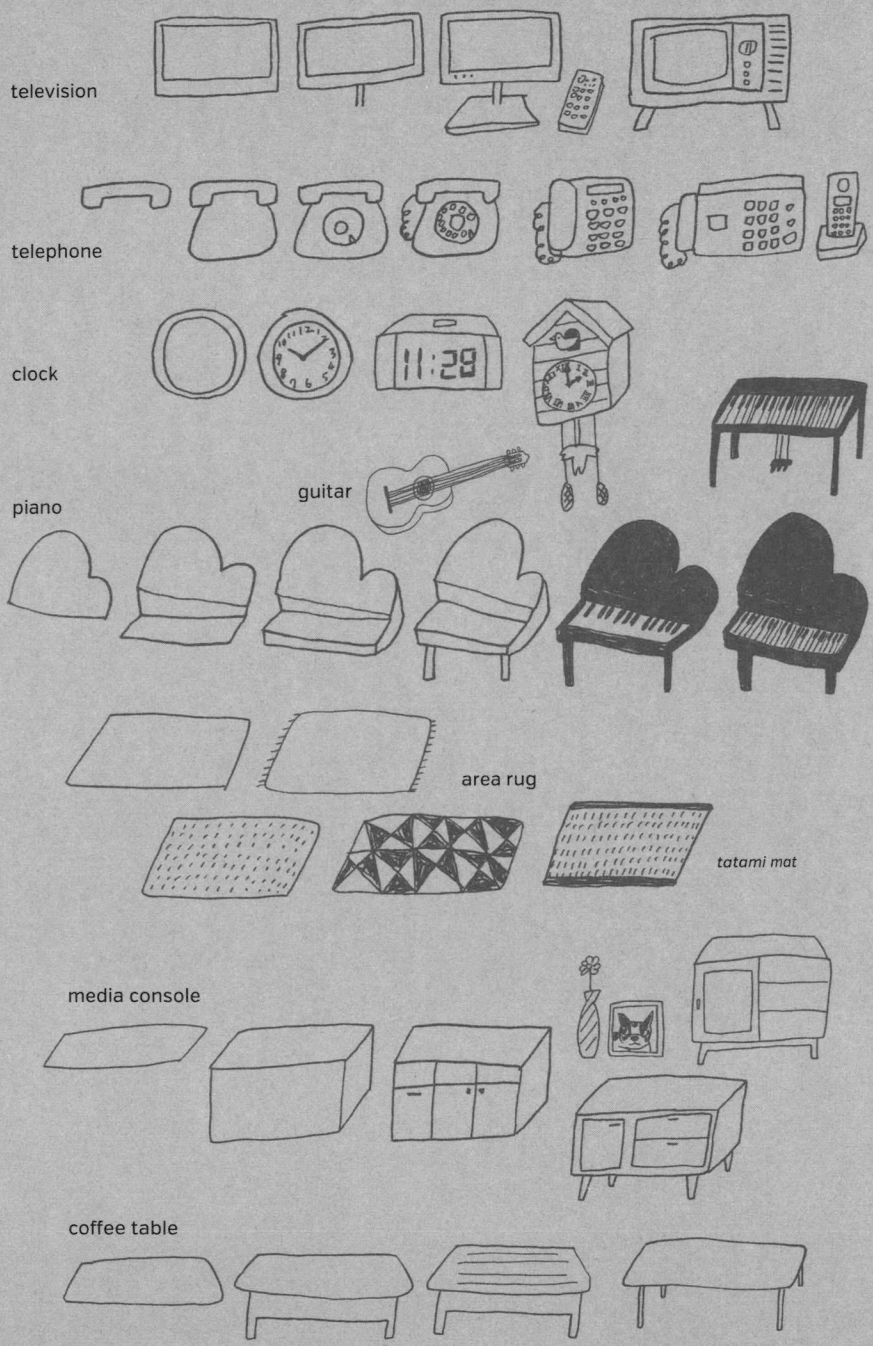
television
telephone
clock
11:29
piano
guitar
area rug
tatami mat
media console
coffee table

# Bedroom

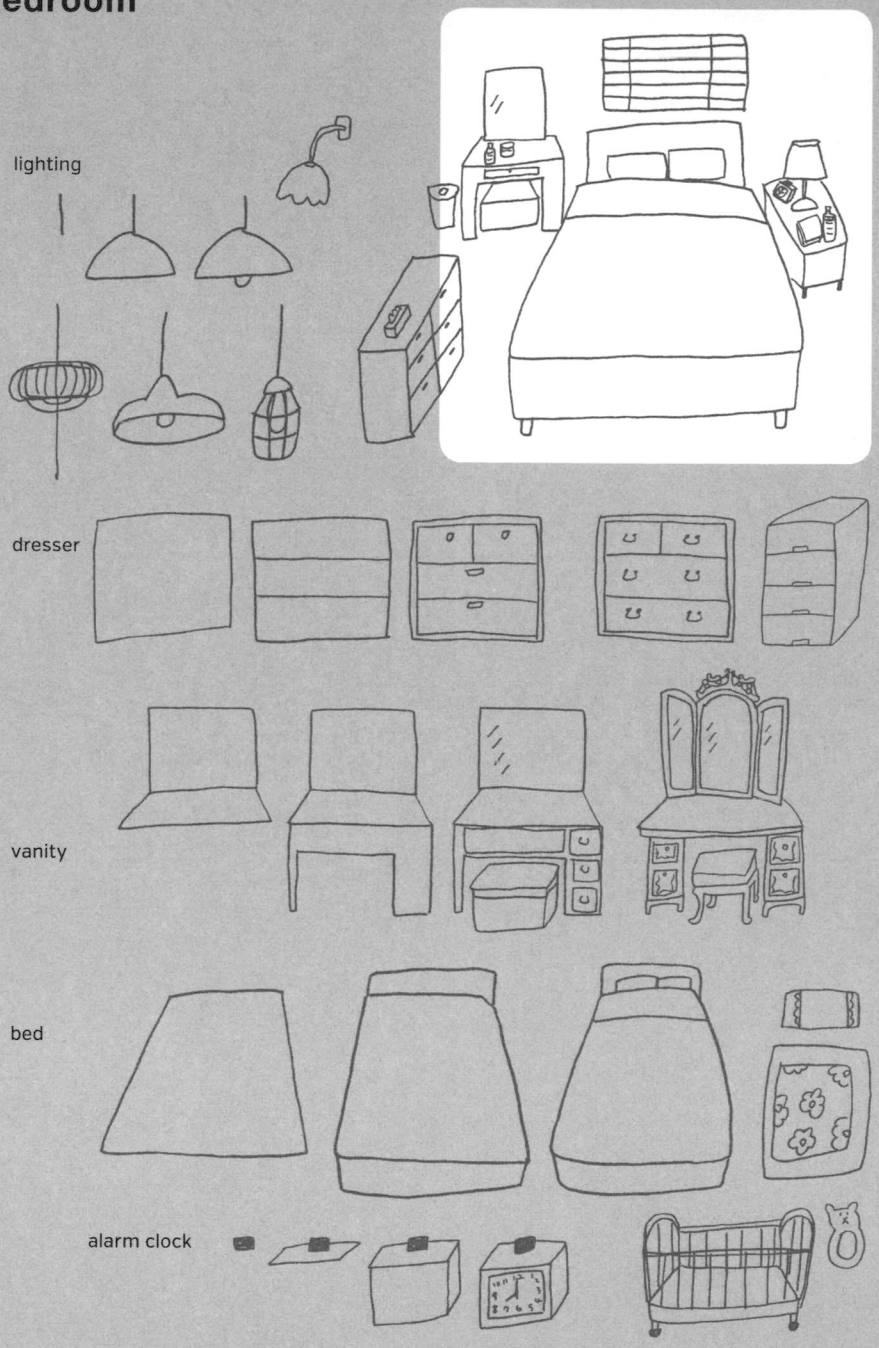

# Study

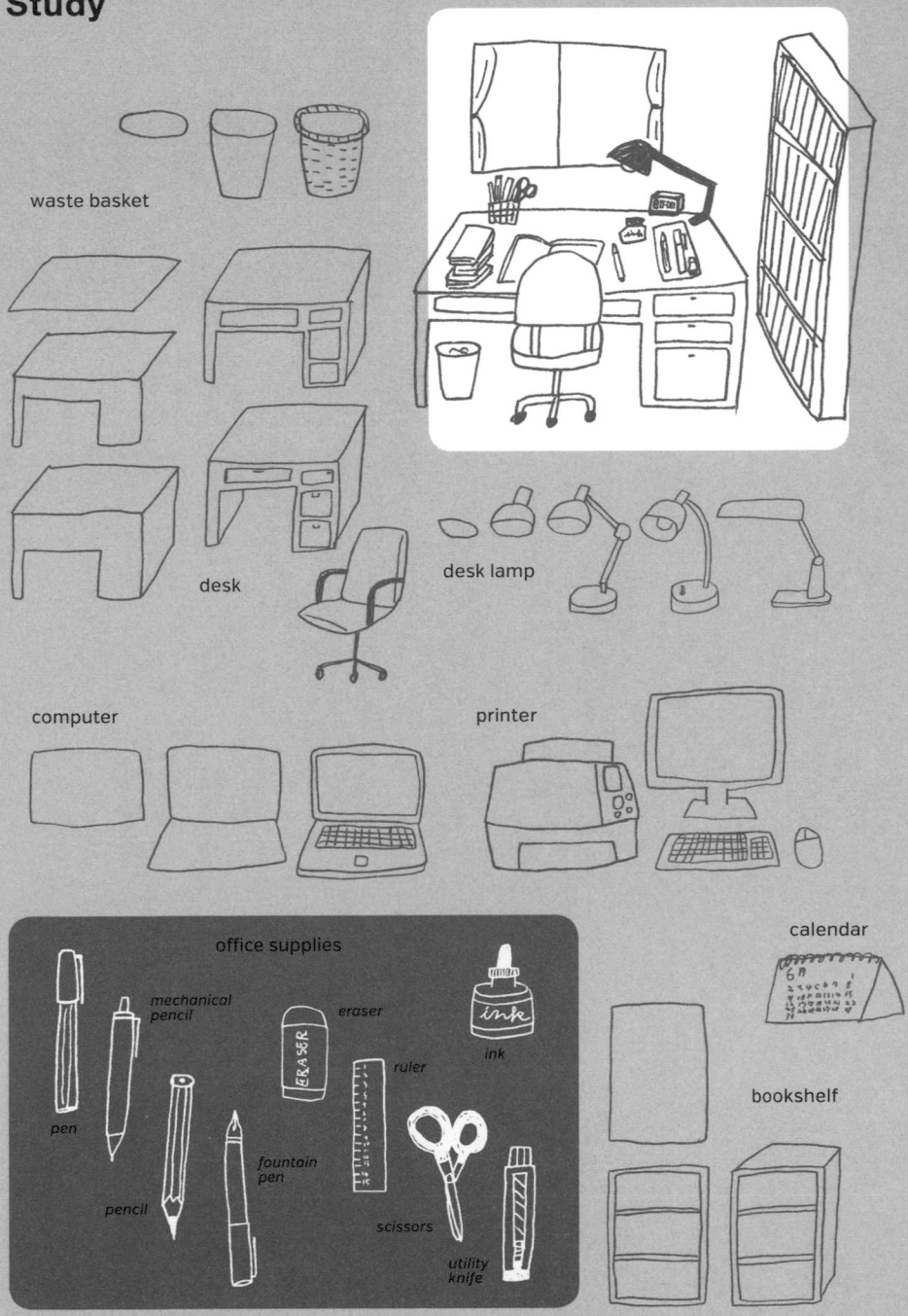
waste basket
desk
desk lamp
computer
printer
office supplies
pen
mechanical pencil
pencil
fountain pen
eraser
ERASER
ruler
ink
scissors
utility knife
calendar
bookshelf

# Bathroom

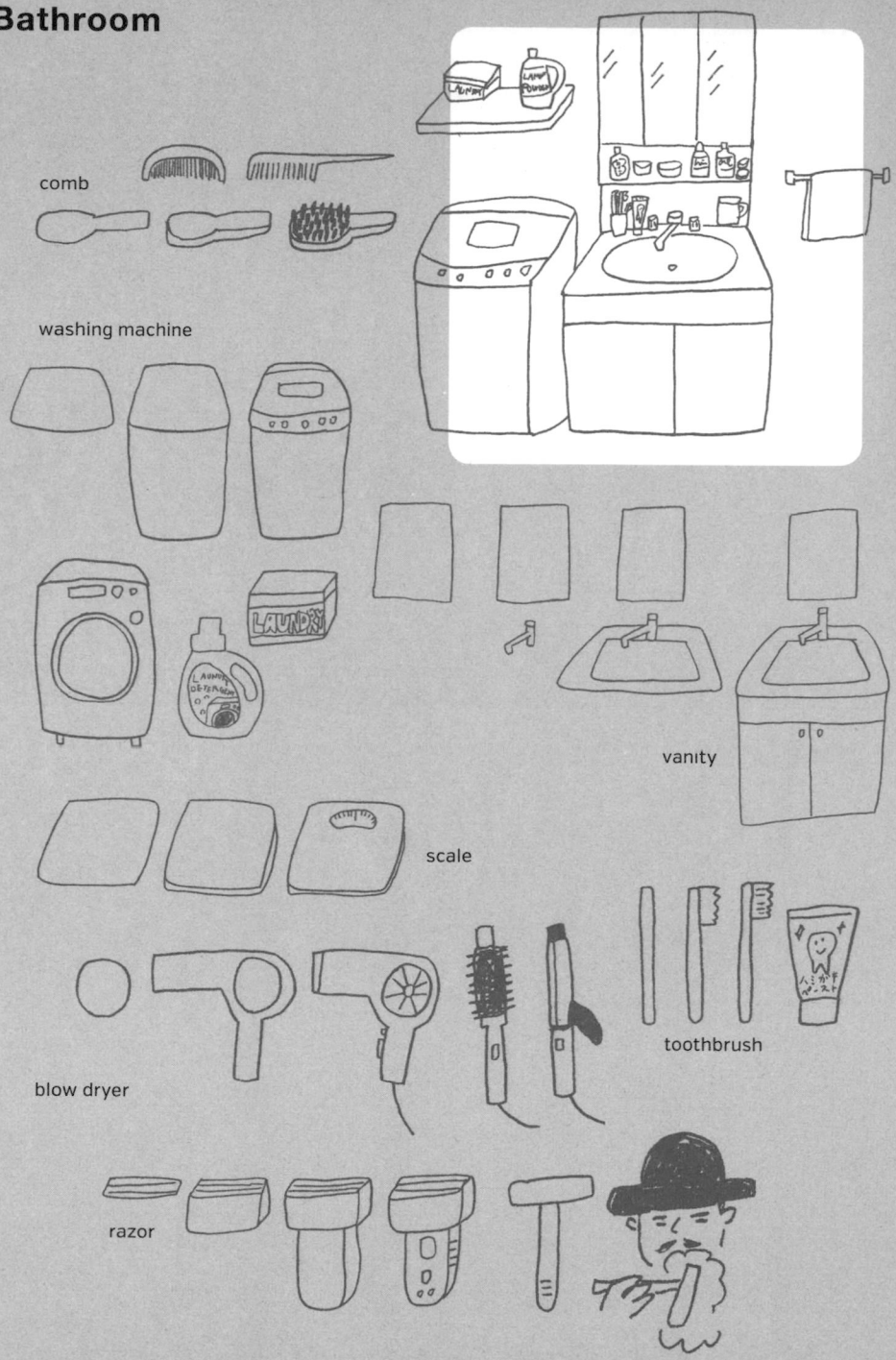
comb
washing machine
LAUNDRY
LAUNDRY
vanity
scale
toothbrush
blow dryer
razor

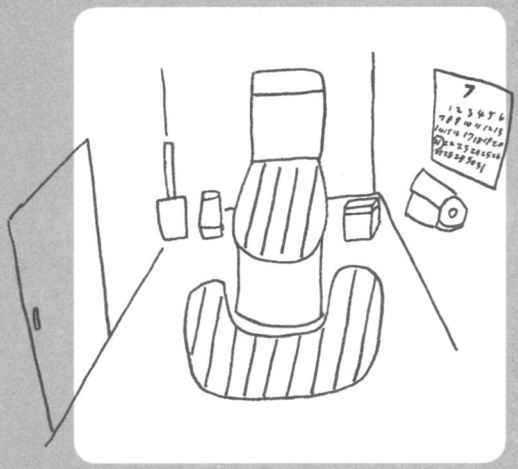

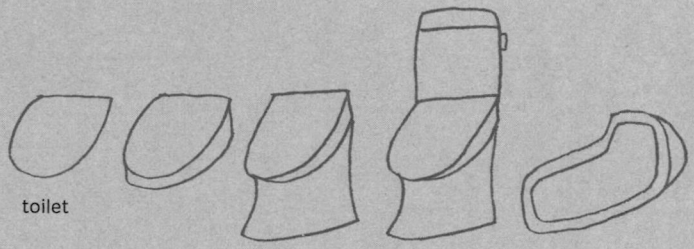

toilet

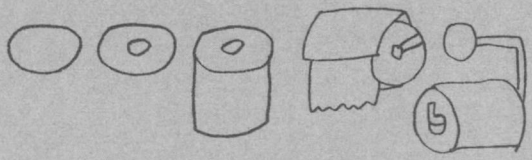

toilet paper

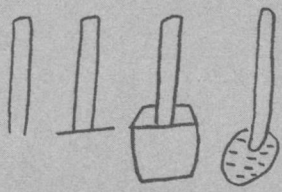

toilet brush

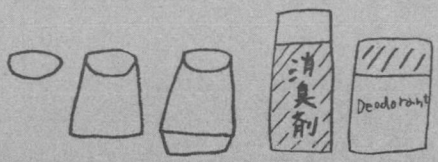


air freshener

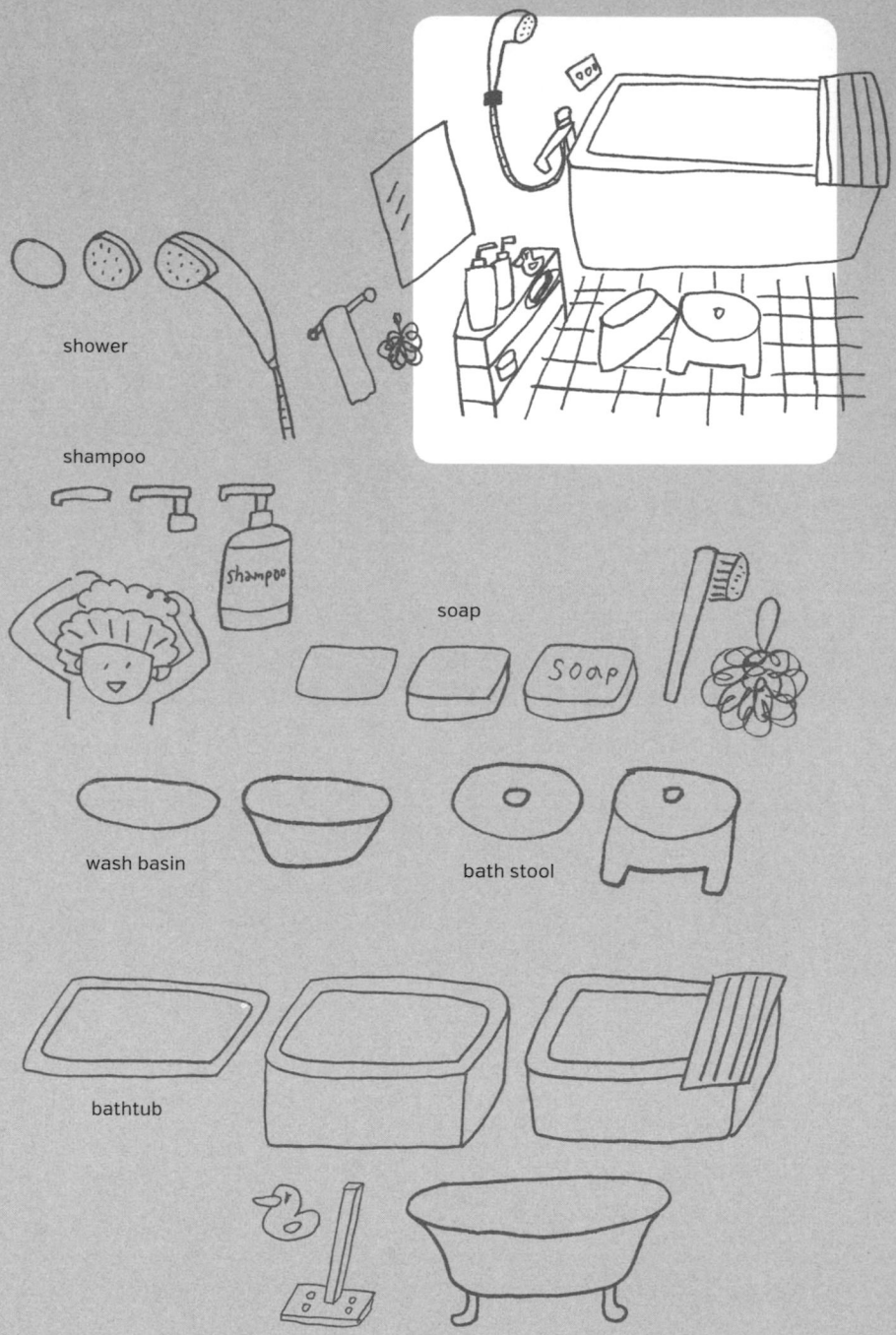
shower
shampoo
shampoo
soap
soap
wash basin
bath stool
bathtub

# Patio

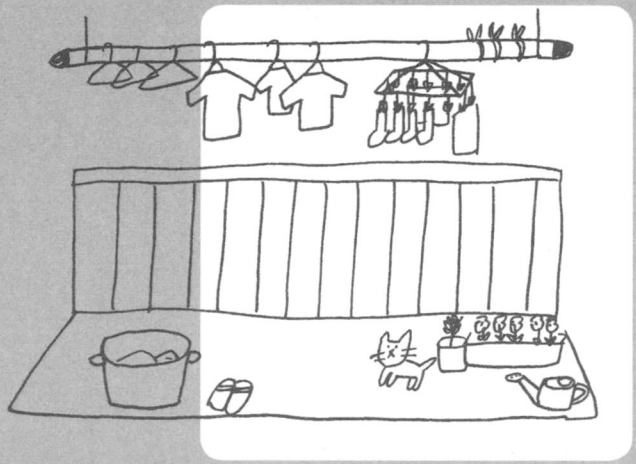

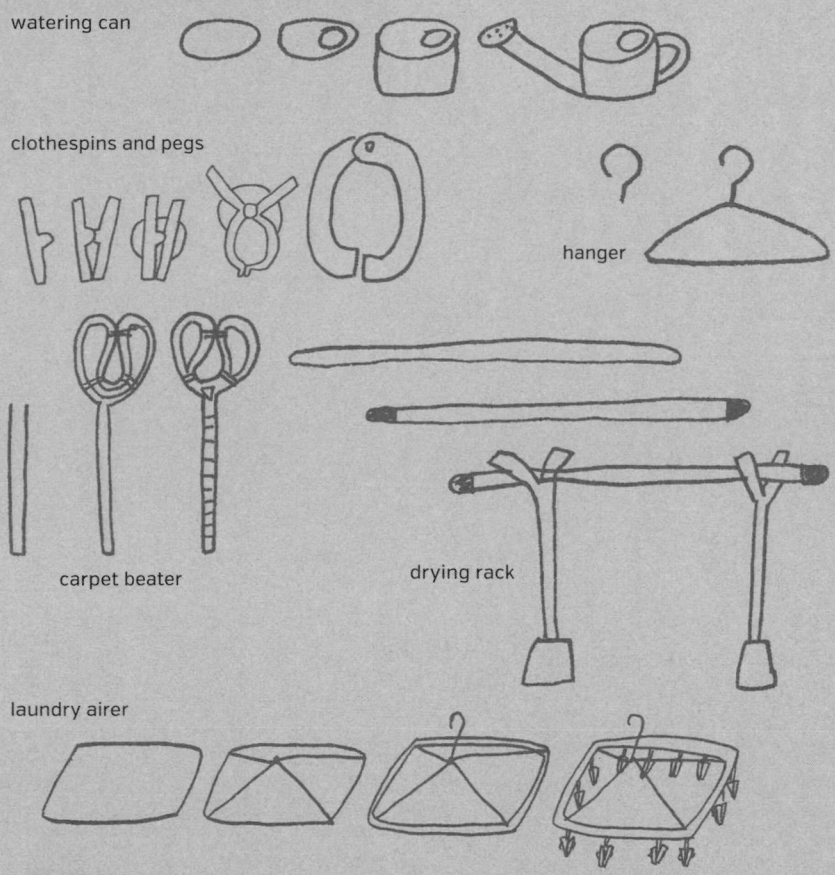
watering can
clothespins and pegs
hanger
carpet beater
drying rack
laundry airer

## Home Maintenance

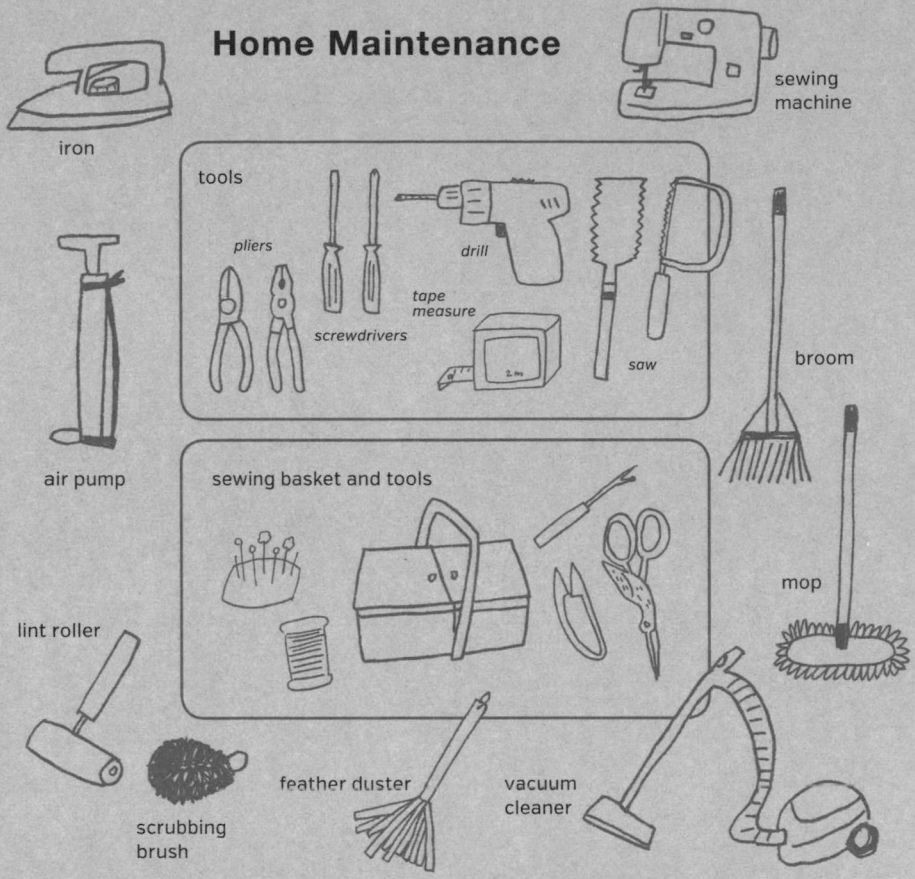


## CHALLENGE #5:

### Draw Windows and Doors

Practice drawing different styles of windows and doors, as these architectural elements can completely change the appearance of a room or house.

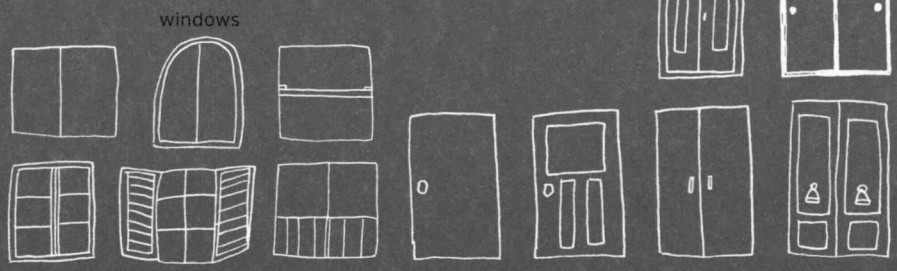

# Architectures and Sites

Around the Neighborhood

Famous Sites in Japan

Famous Sites Around the World

# Around the Neighborhood

*When drawing a building, start with a rough outline, then add features like windows, doors, and signs.*

apartment building

single-family house

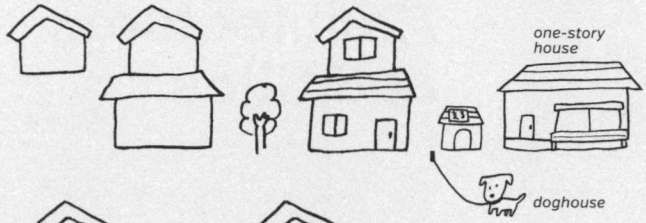


train station

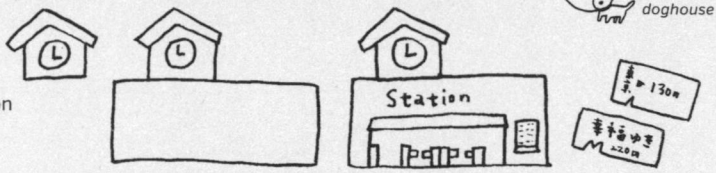


gas station

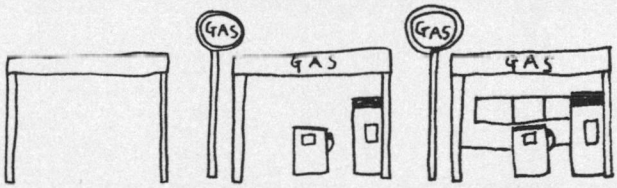


school

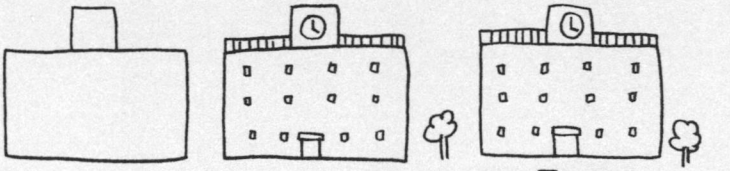

church

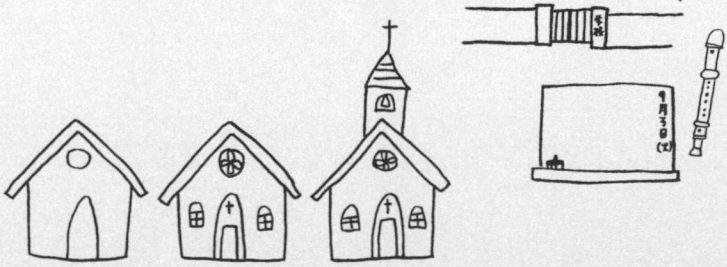

bank

athletic fields

*track* *soccer field* *baseball field*

playground

police station

convenience store

stores

*butcher* *café* *barbershop* *Japanese bath house*

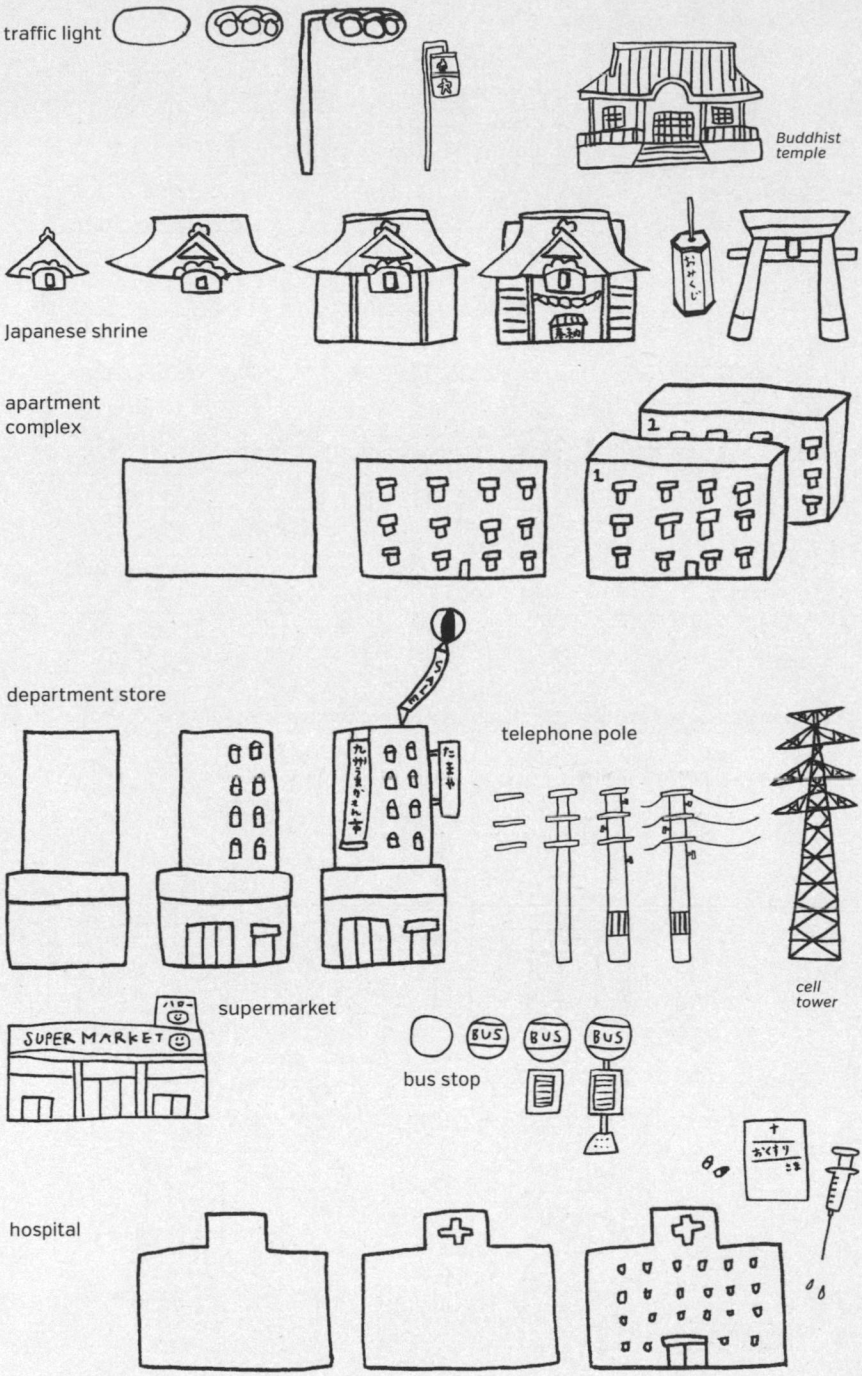
traffic light
Buddhist temple
Japanese shrine
apartment complex
department store
telephone pole
cell tower
supermarket
SUPER MARKET
bus stop
BUS
BUS
BUS
hospital

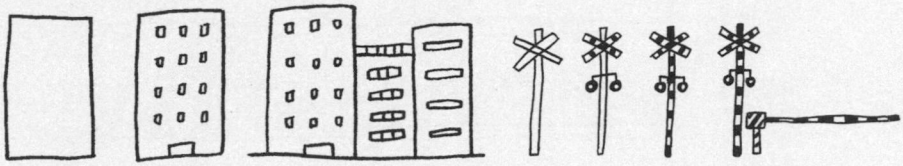

office building

railroad crossing

overpass

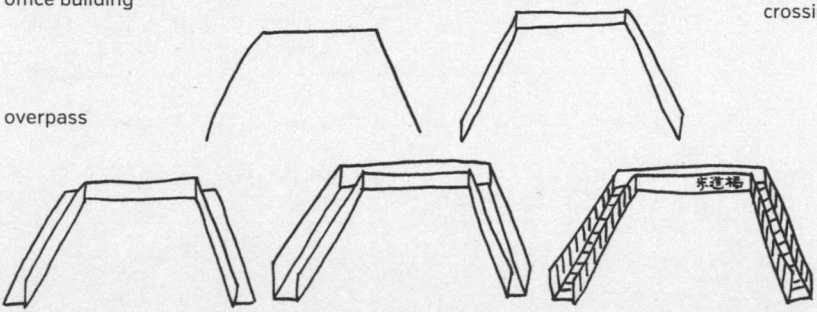


condominium building

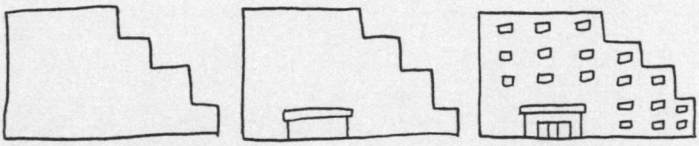

pharmacy

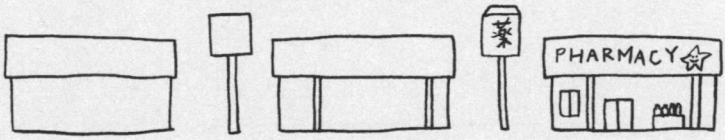


post office

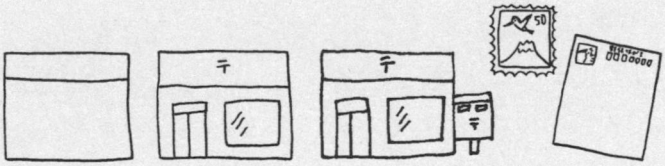

daycare center

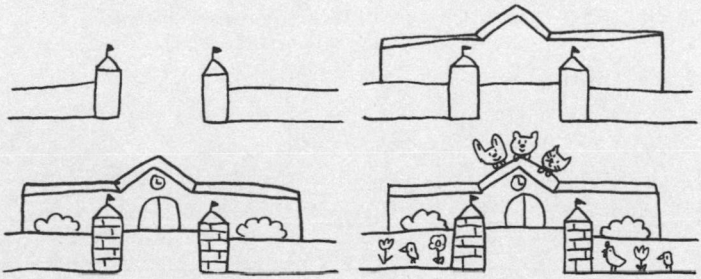

bridge

restaurant

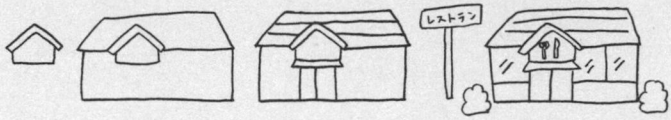


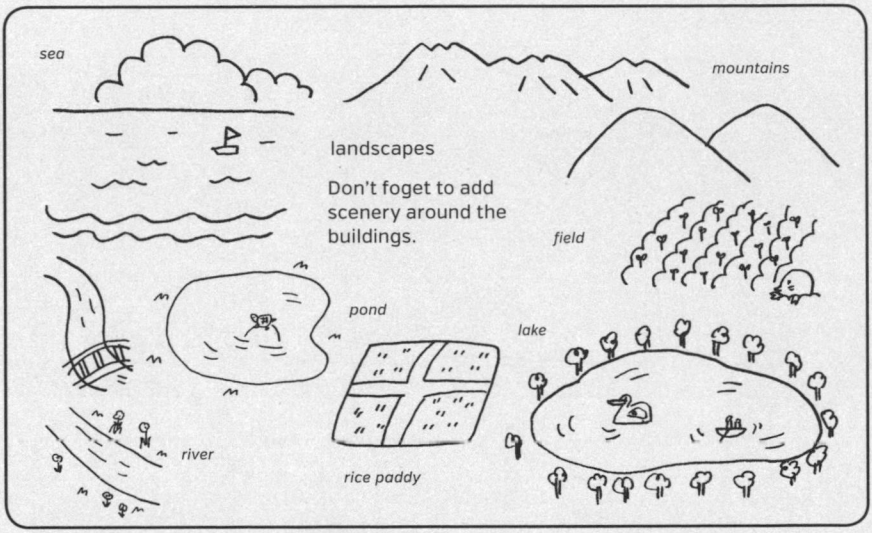


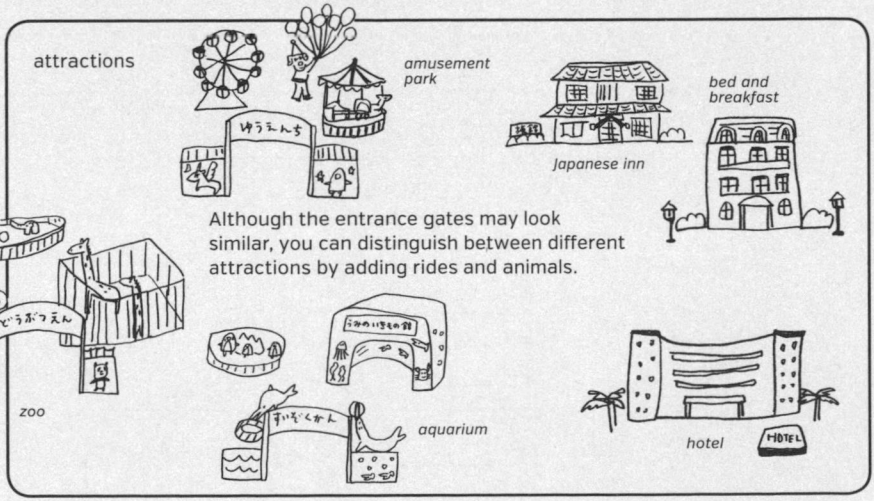

## CHALLENGE #6:

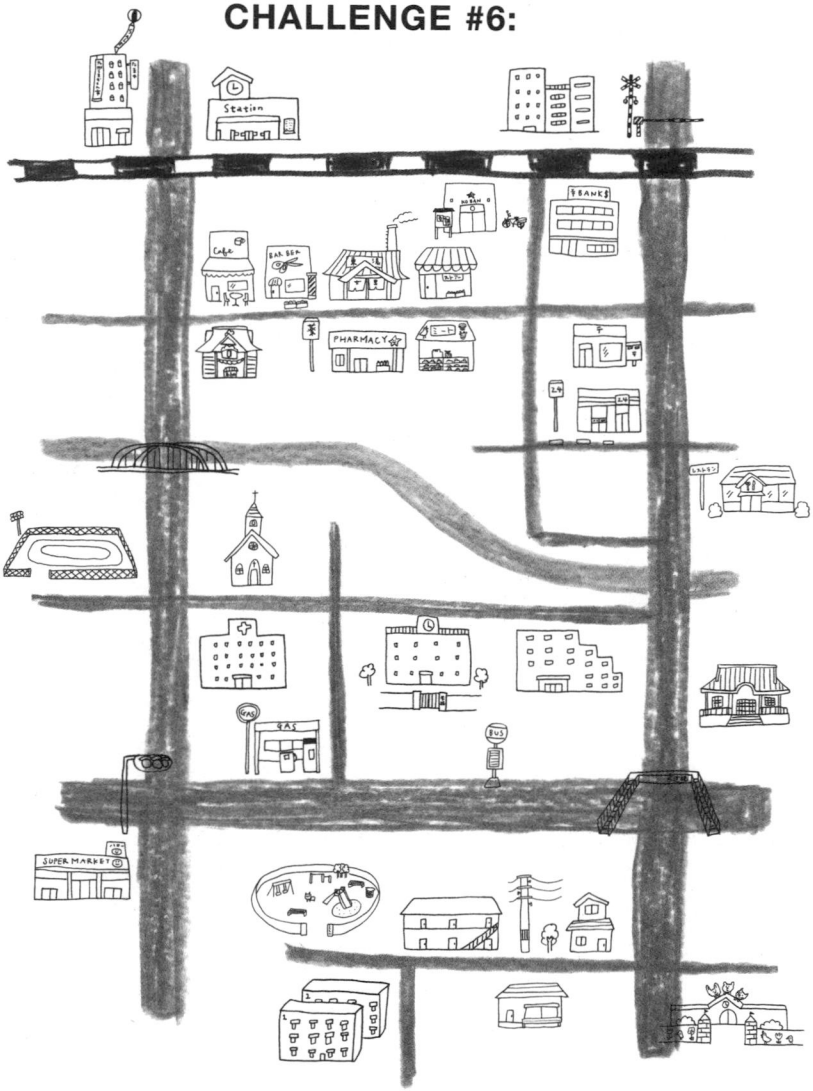


## Draw a Street Map

Creating a map is a perfect way to practice drawing buildings and other neighborhood sites. Start out by drawing major roads, side streets, railroad tracks, and rivers. Then add buildings and other important landmarks. Being able to incorporate illustrations into your maps is a great skill to possess—it will make your directions much easier to follow.

# Famous Sites in Japan

*When drawing a building or landmark, start with the largest components of the structure, such as the roof, columns, or beams.*

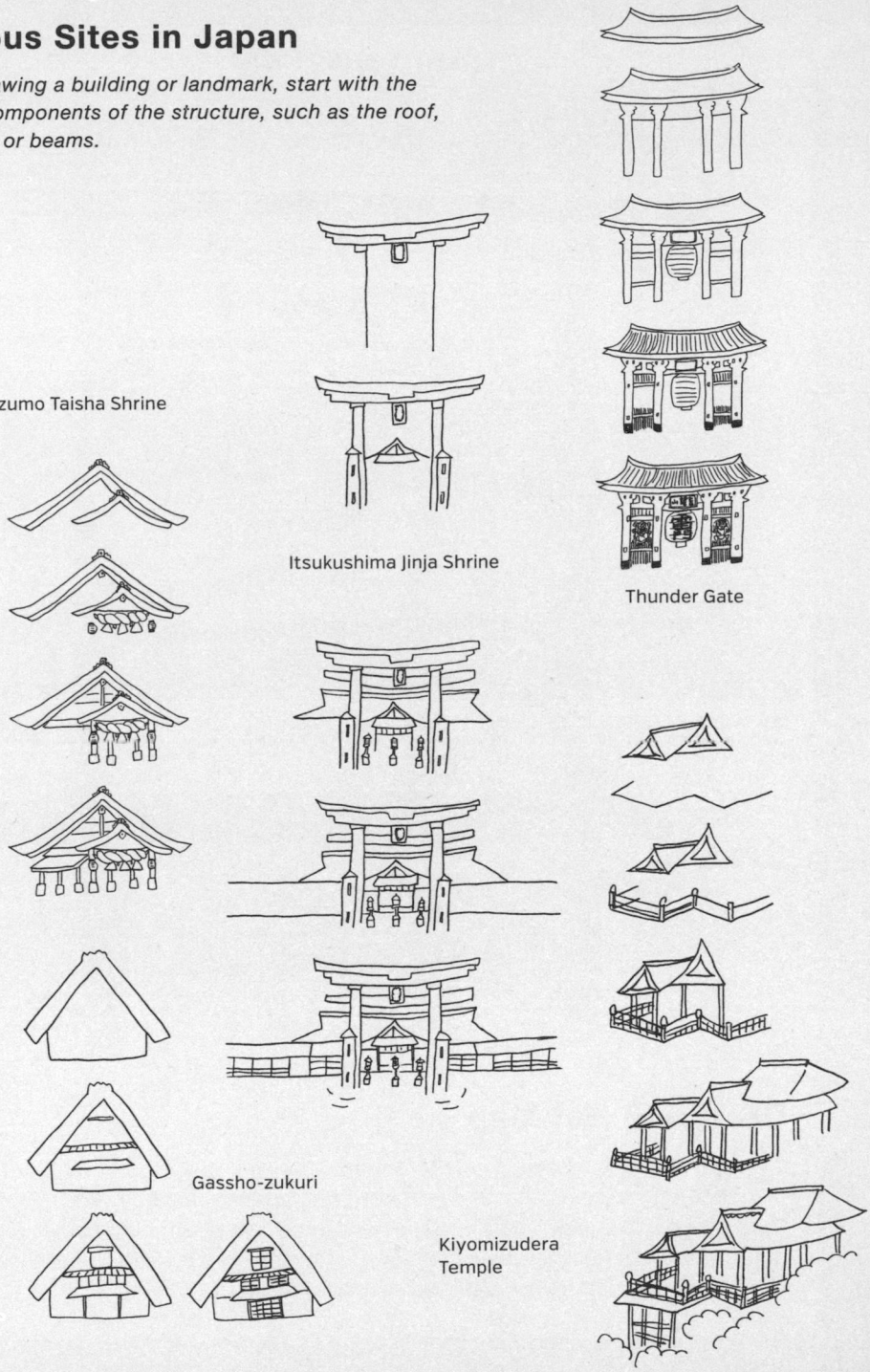

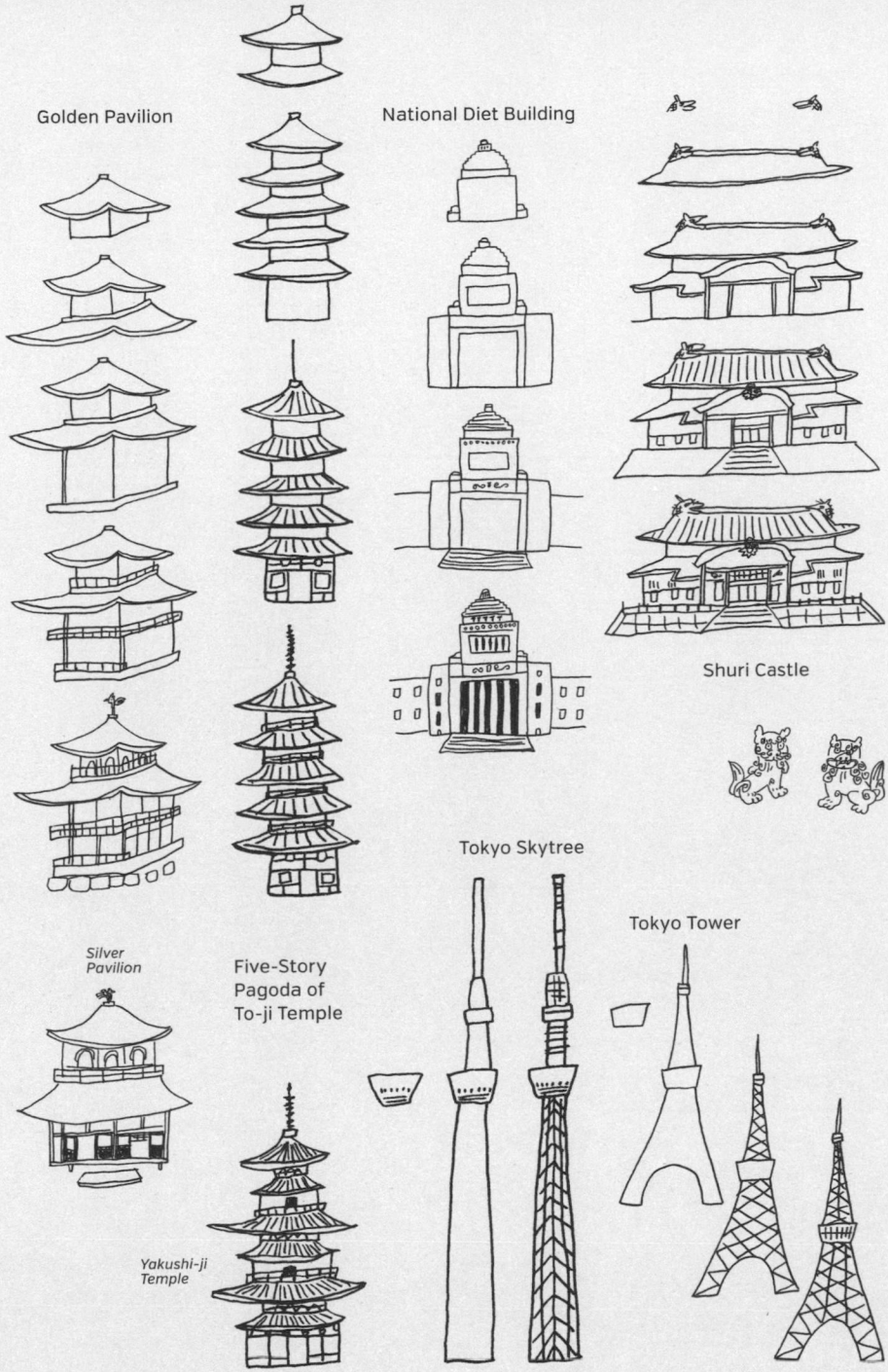
Golden Pavilion
National Diet Building
Shuri Castle
Tokyo Skytree
Tokyo Tower
Silver Pavilion
Five-Story Pagoda of To-ji Temple
Yakushi-ji Temple

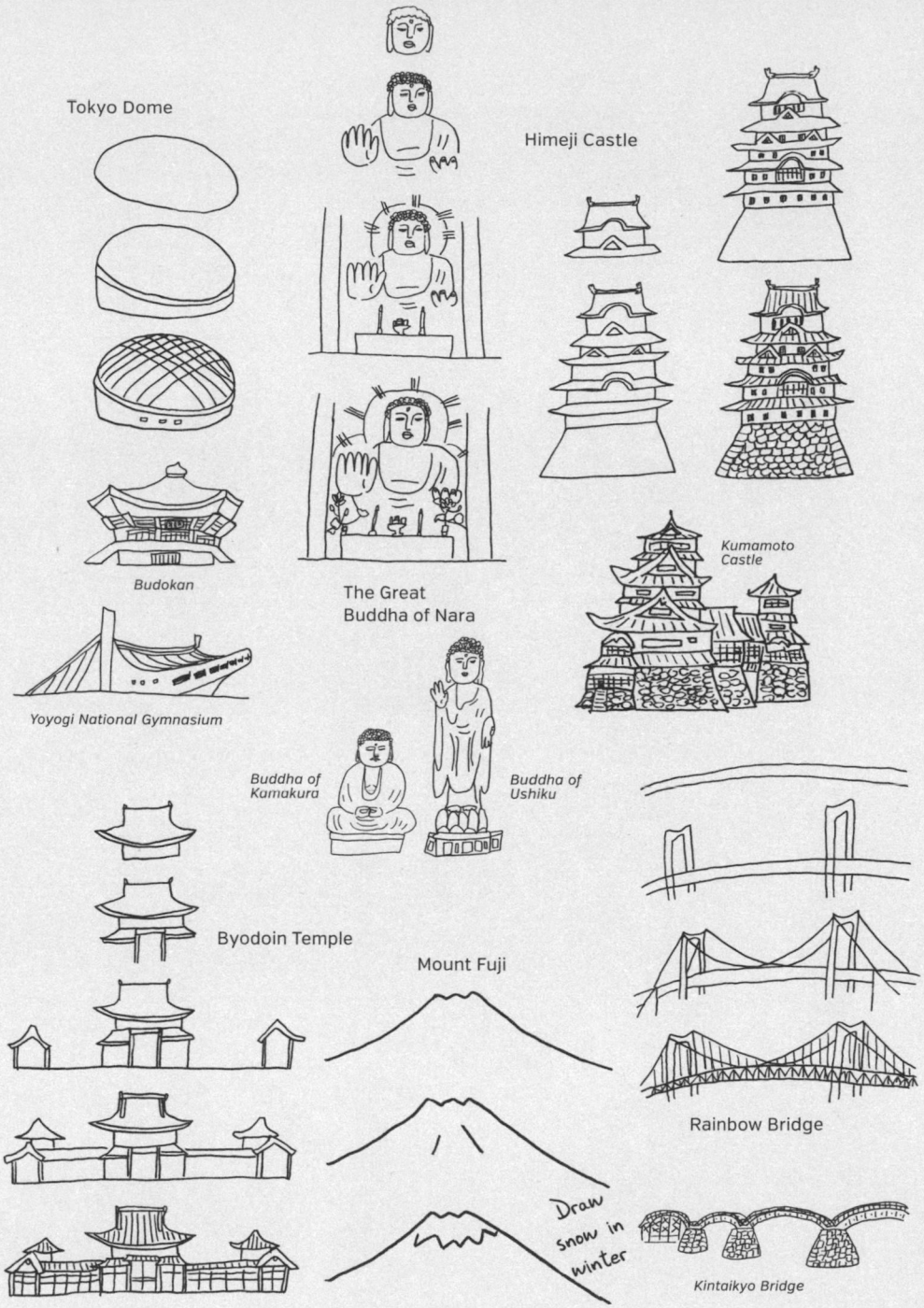
Tokyo Dome
Budokan
Yoyogi National Gymnasium
The Great Buddha of Nara
Himeji Castle
Kumamoto Castle
Buddha of Kamakura
Buddha of Ushiku
Byodoin Temple
Mount Fuji
Draw snow in winter
Rainbow Bridge
Kintaikyo Bridge

# Famous Sites Around the World

*Don't forget to add detail! Many of these famous landmarks are known for their elegant and elaborate decorations.*

Arc de Triomphe

Angkor Wat

Eiffel Tower

Empire State Building

*Chrysler Building*

Palais Garnier

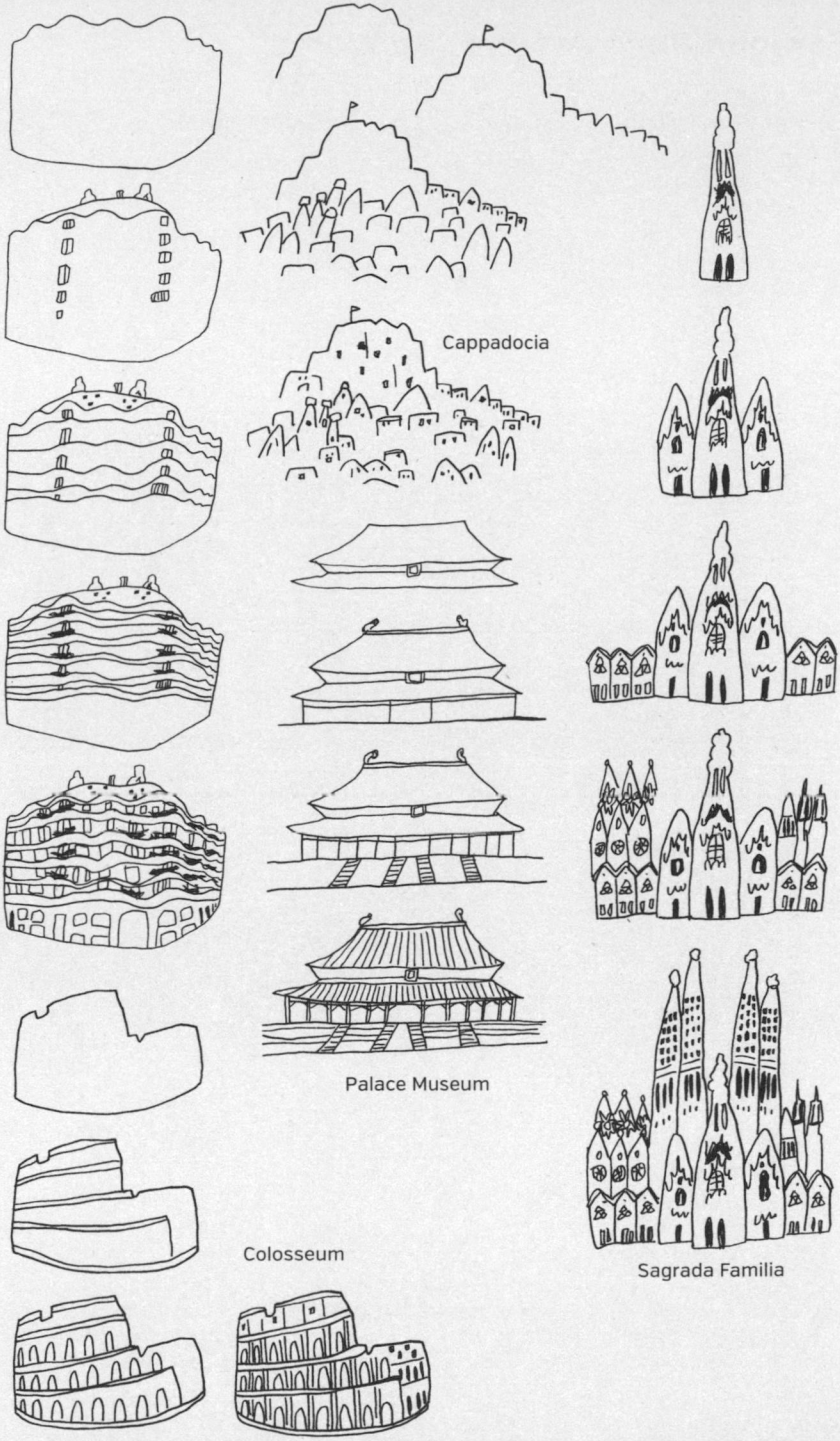
Casa Milà
Cappadocia
Palace Museum
Colosseum
Sagrada Familia

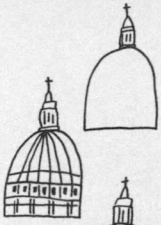

St. Peter's Basilica

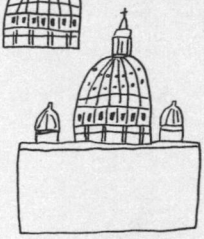

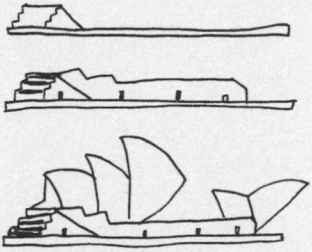

Sydney Opera House

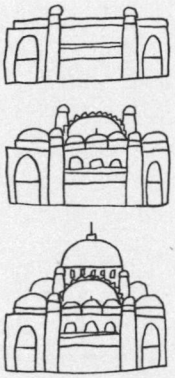

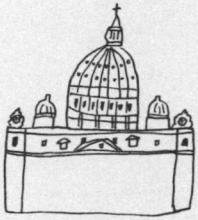

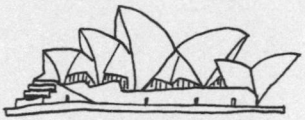

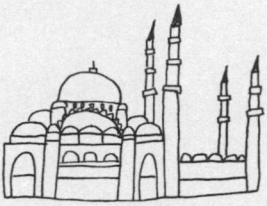

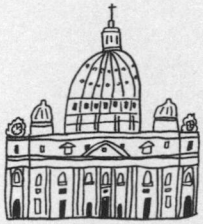

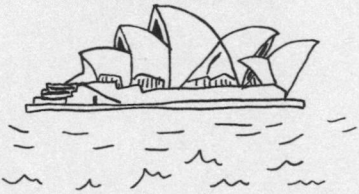

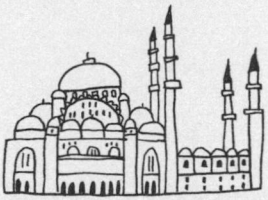

Süleymaniye Mosque

Statue of Liberty

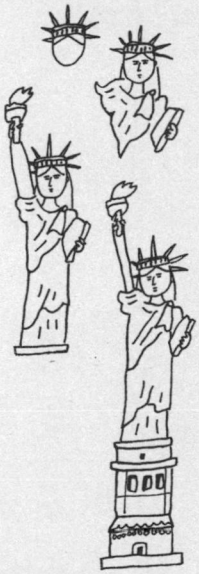

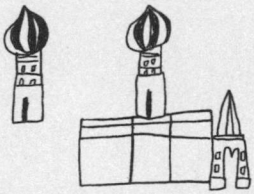

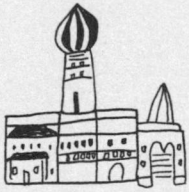

St. Basil's
Cathedral

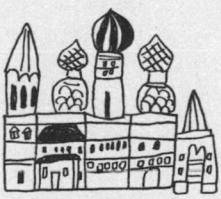

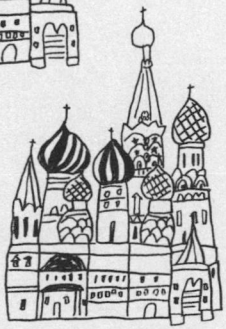

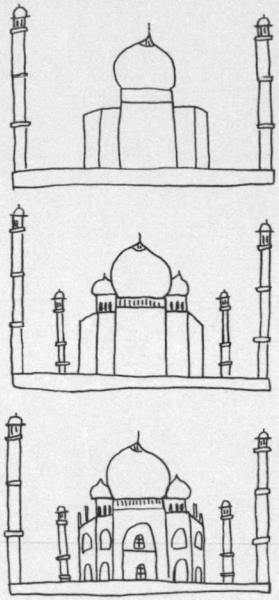

Taj Mahal

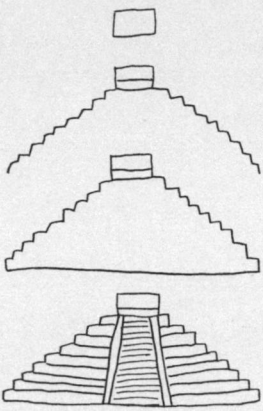

Chichen Itza

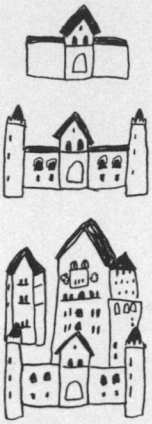

Neuschwanstein Castle

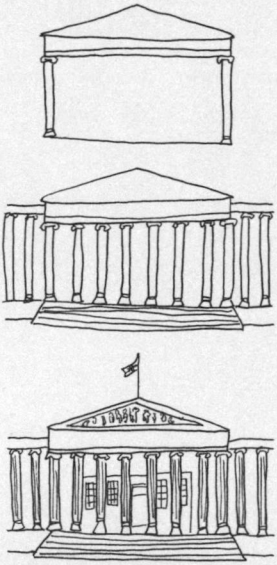

British Museum

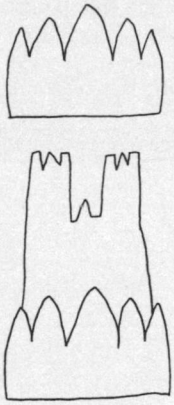

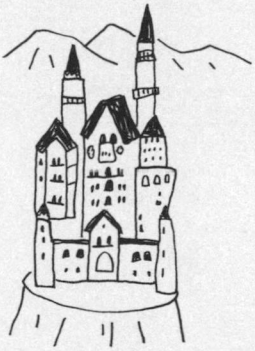

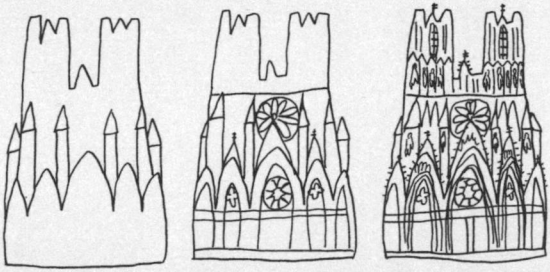

Notre-Dame Cathedral

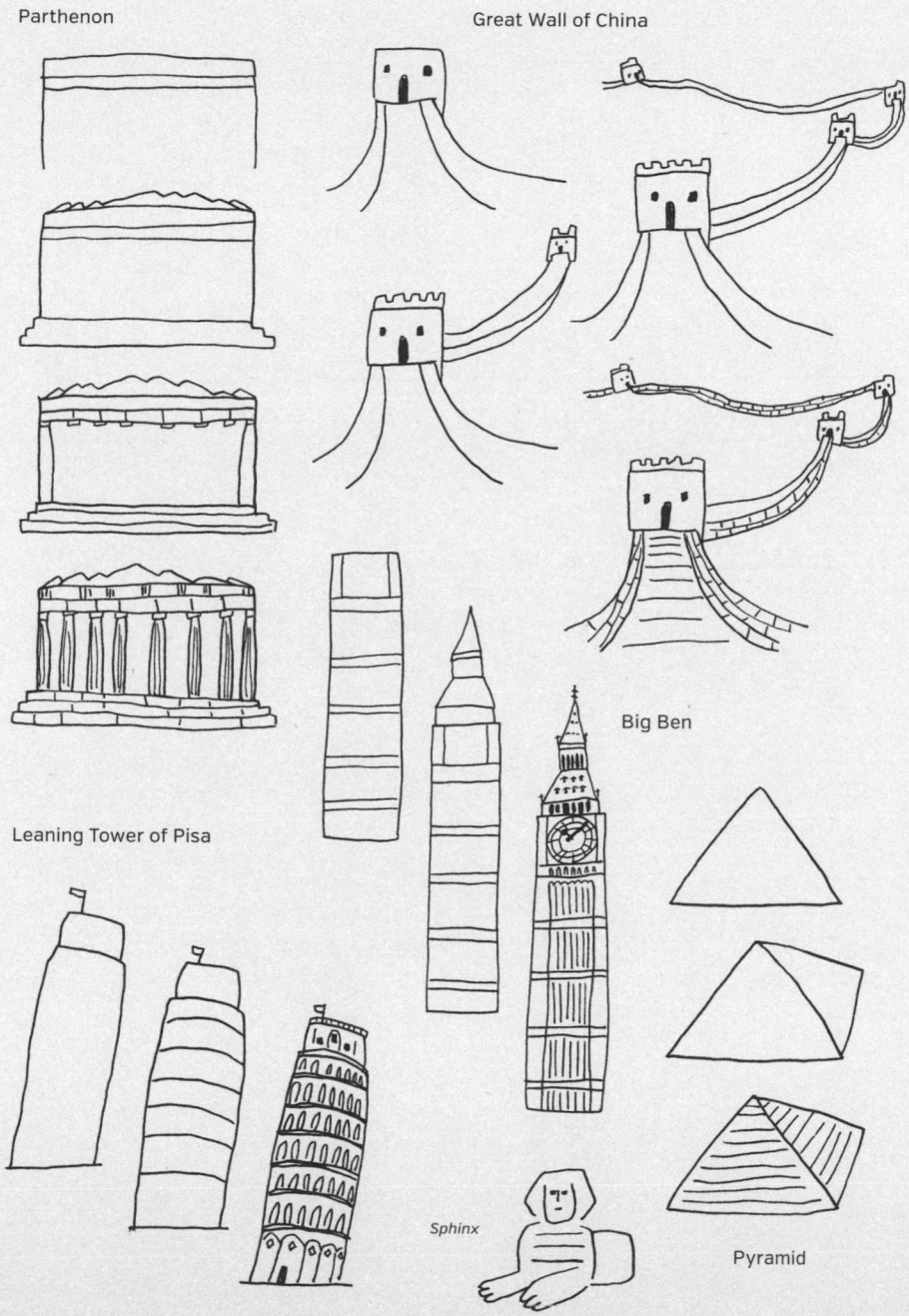
Parthenon
Great Wall of China
Big Ben
Leaning Tower of Pisa
Sphinx
Pyramid

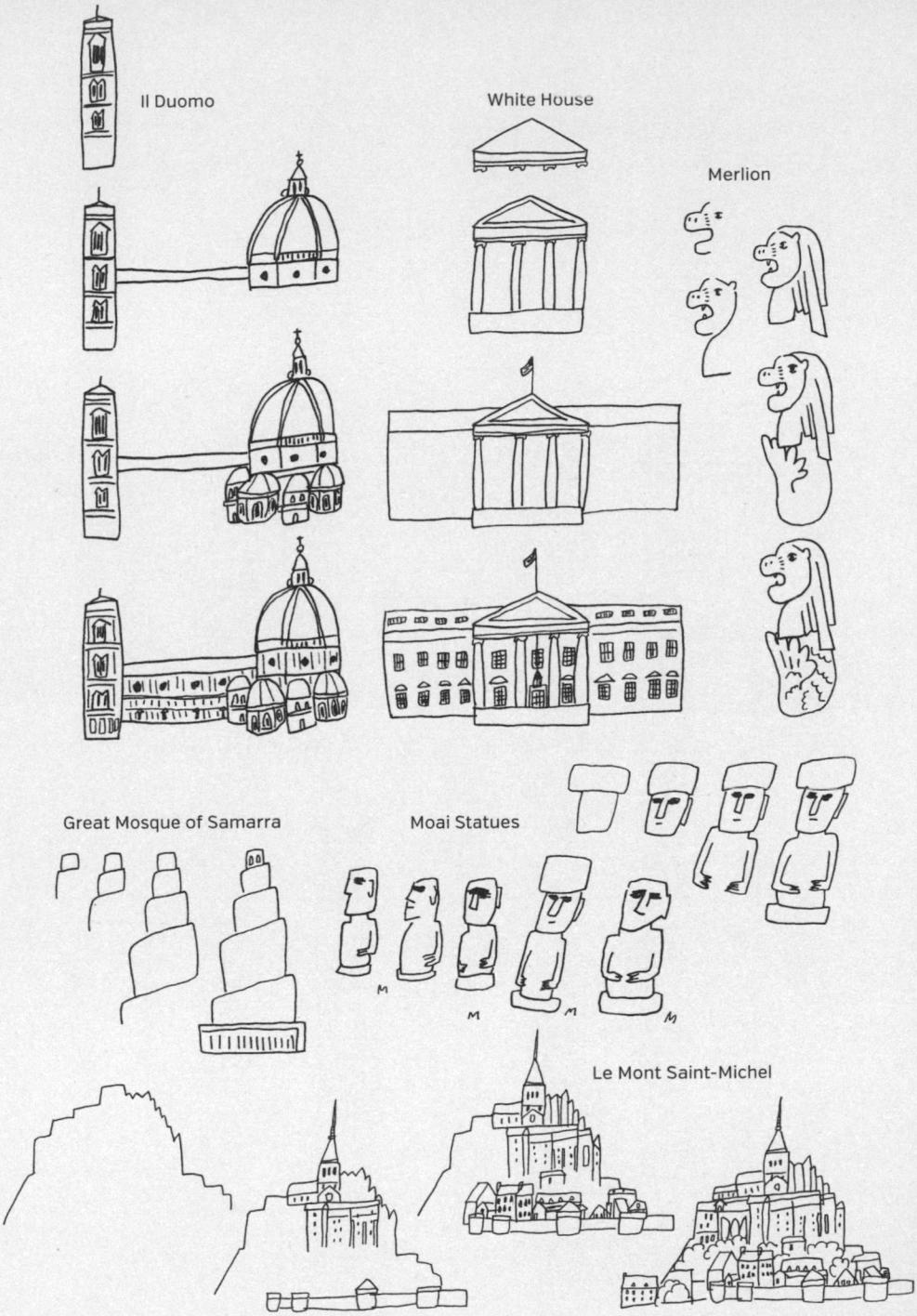
Il Duomo
White House
Merlion
Great Mosque of Samarra
Moai Statues
Le Mont Saint-Michel

# Vehicles


On the Road

On the Tracks

In the Air

On the Water

Other Vehicles

## On the Road

*Pay special attention to the wheels when drawing road vehicles. Notice how the position and size of the wheels changes for each vehicle.*

motorcycle

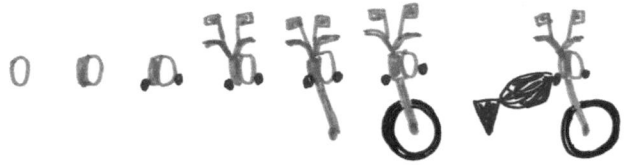

convertible

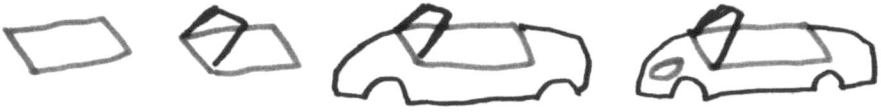

go-kart

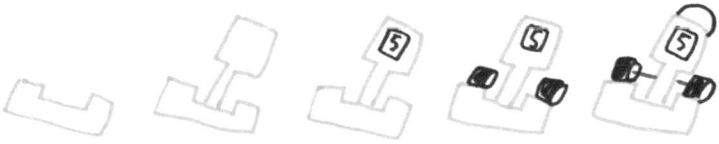

camper

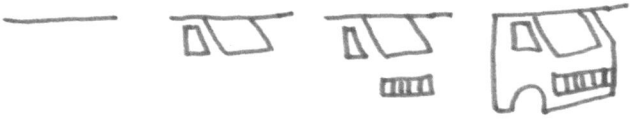

ambulance

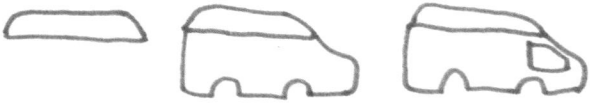

unicycle

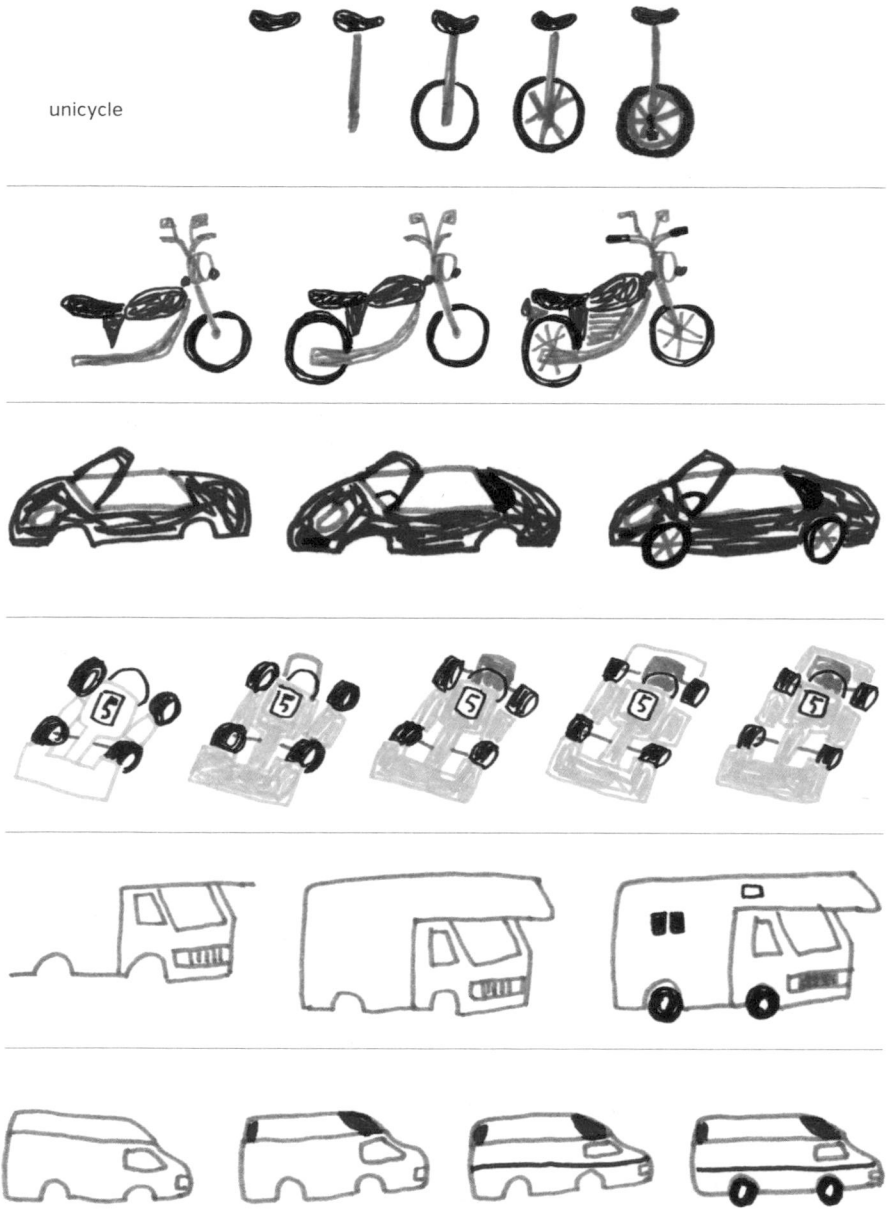

vintage car

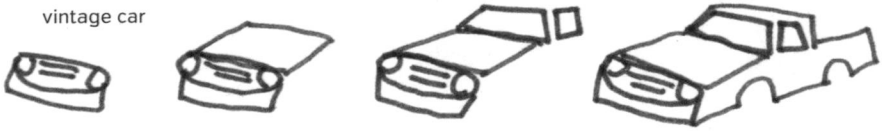

crane truck

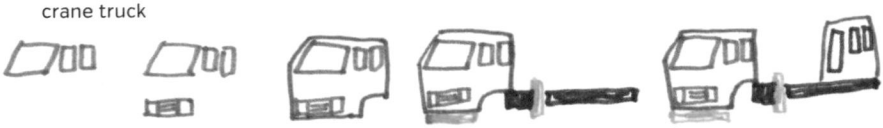

light commercial vehicle

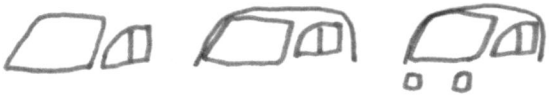

garbage truck

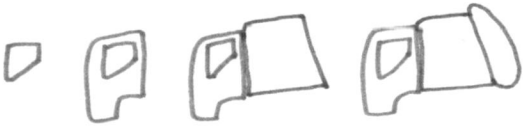

penny-farthing

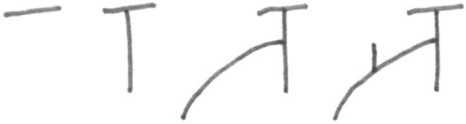

safari bus

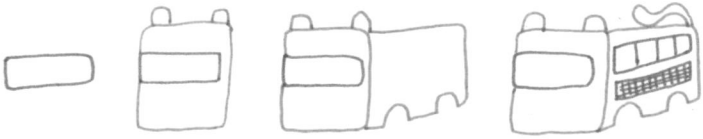

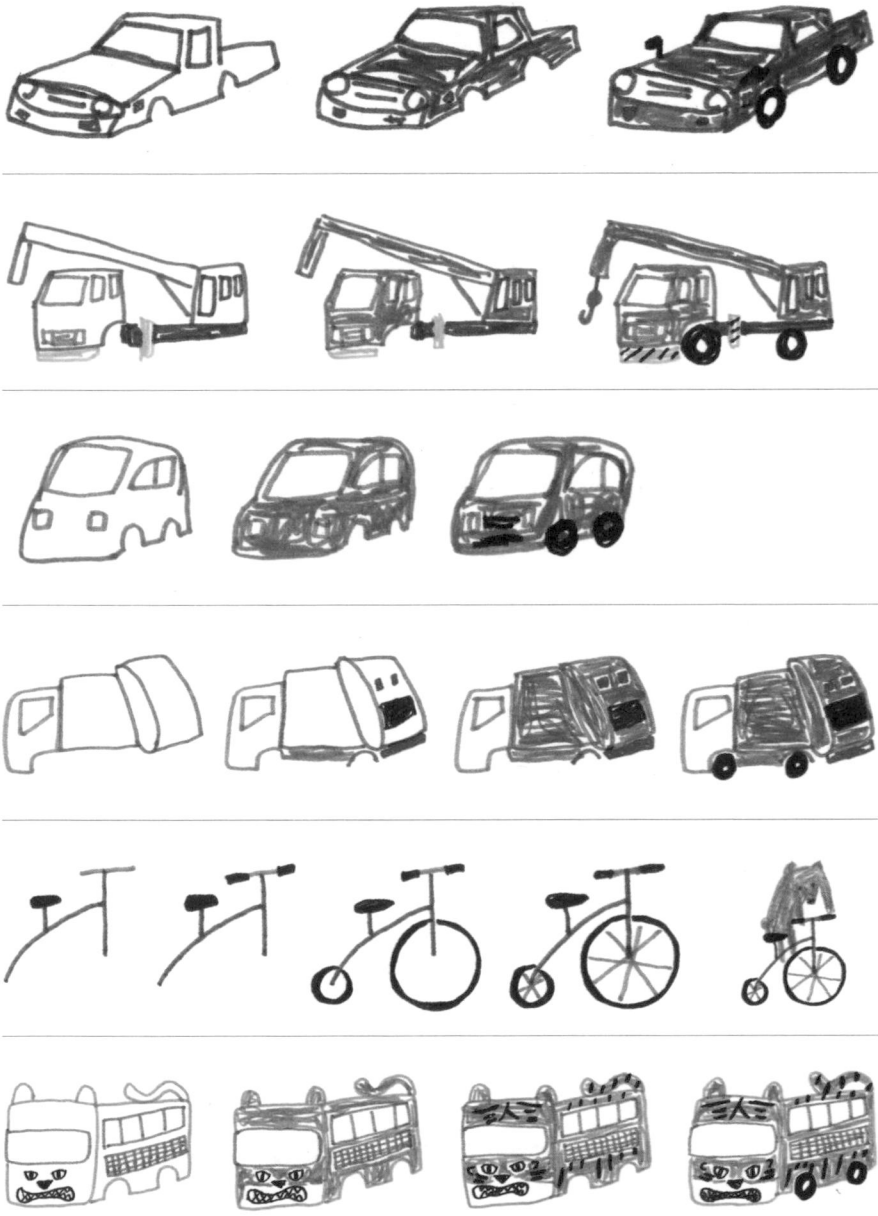

tricycle

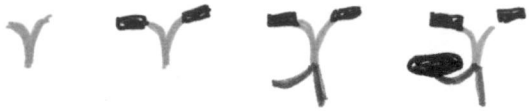

bicycle

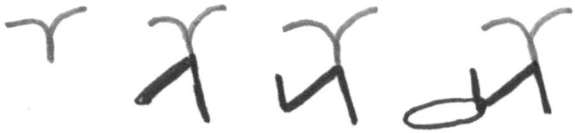

road bike

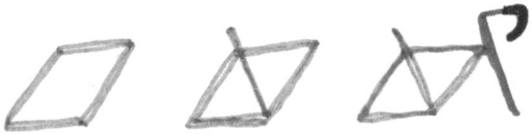

fire engines

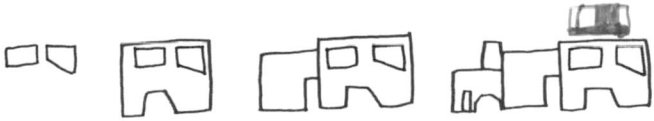

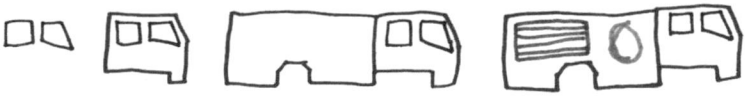

excavator

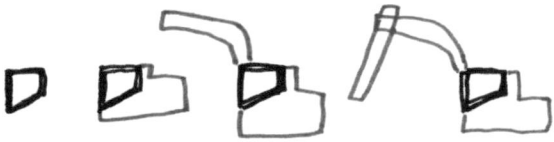

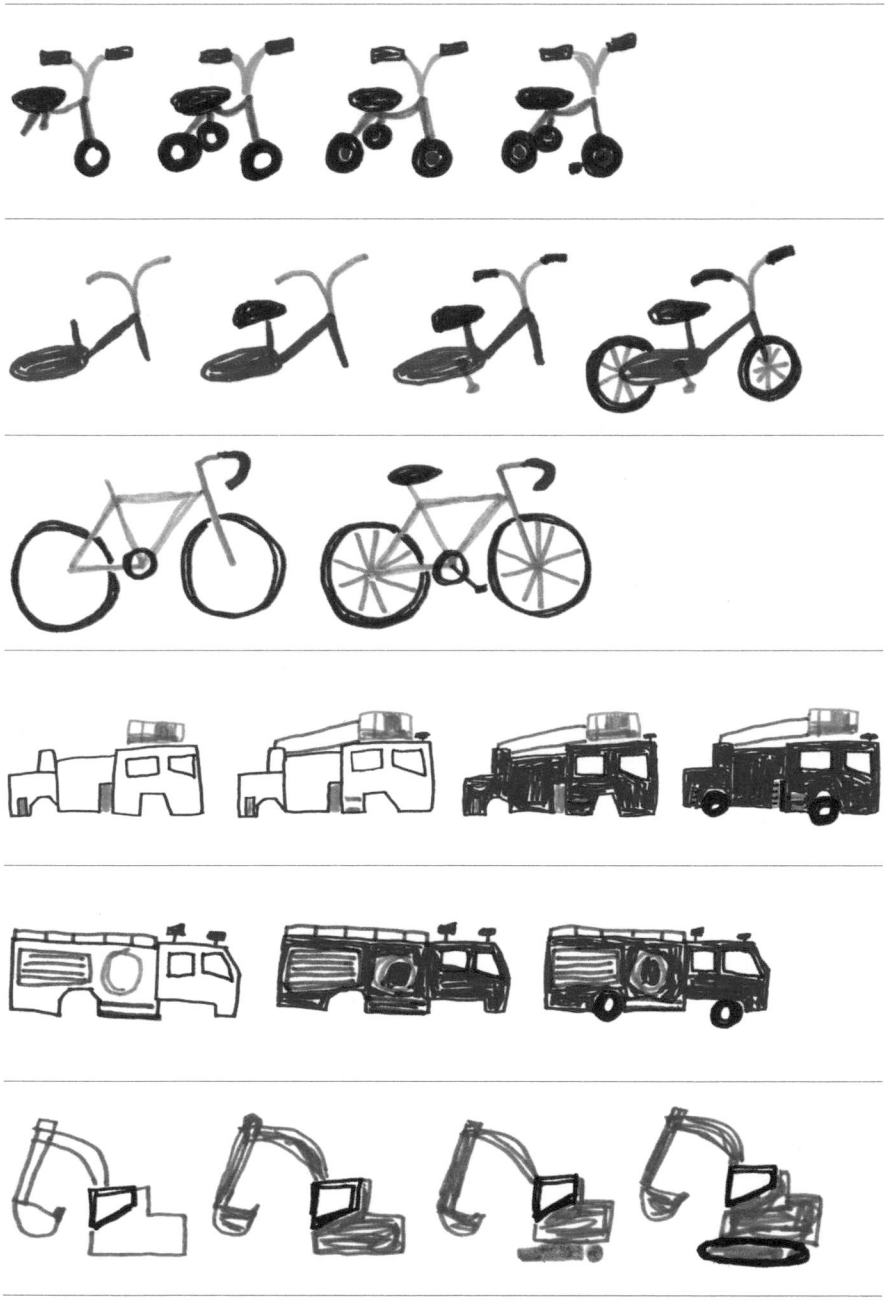

police motorcycle

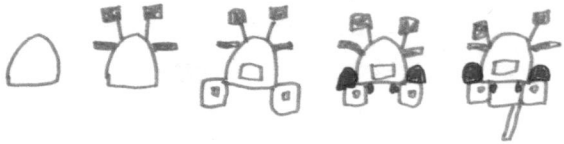

steamroller

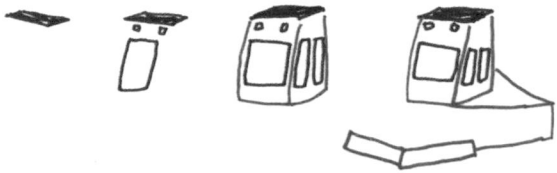

scooter

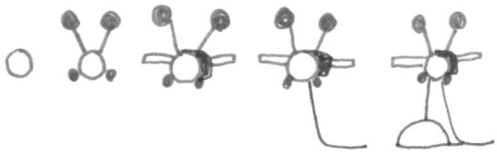

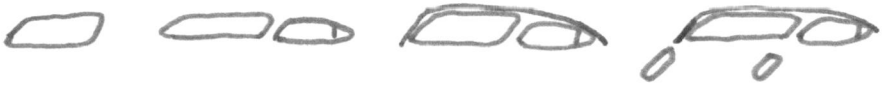

sports car

Segway scooter

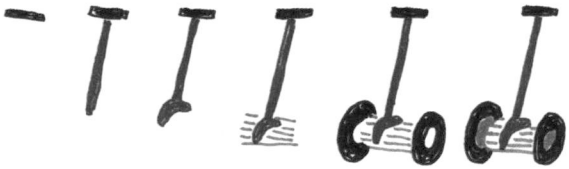

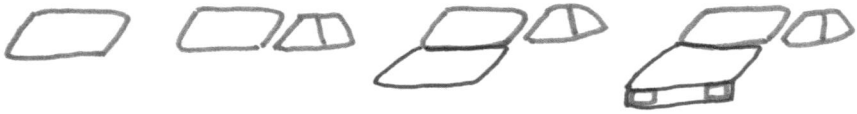

sedan

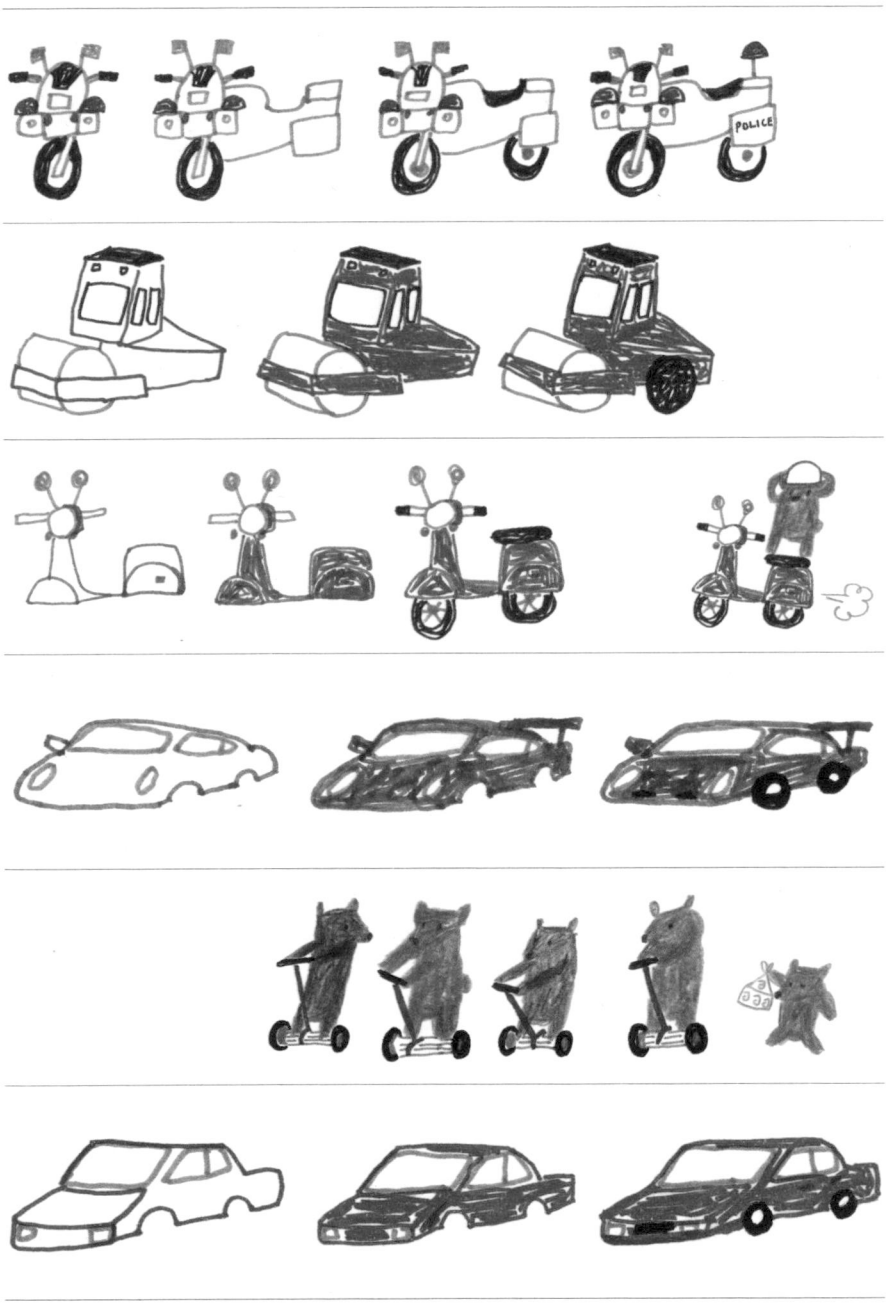
POLICE

taxi

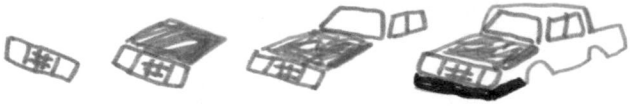

delivery truck

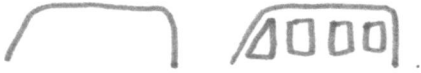

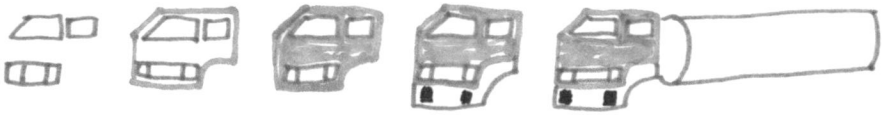

tanker truck

dump truck

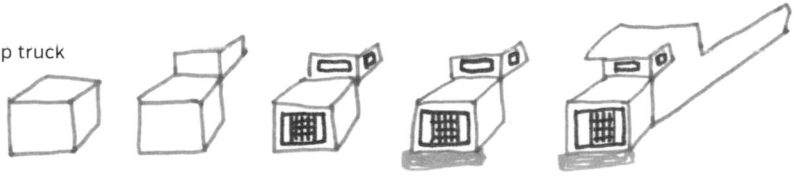

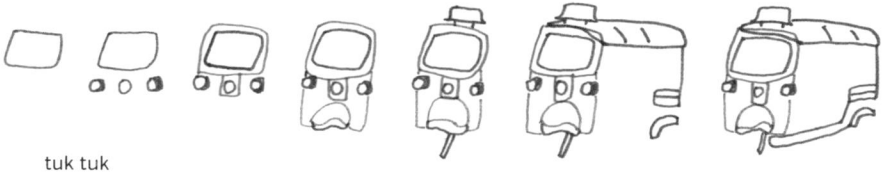

tuk tuk

truck

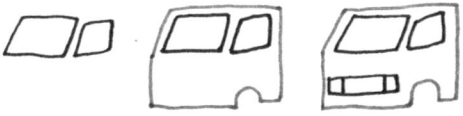

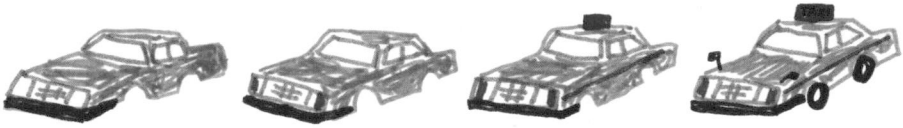

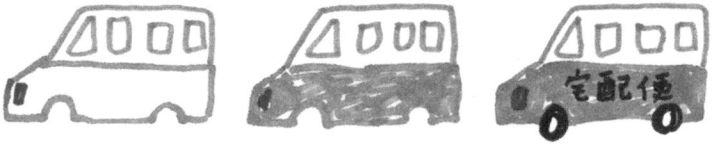
宅配便

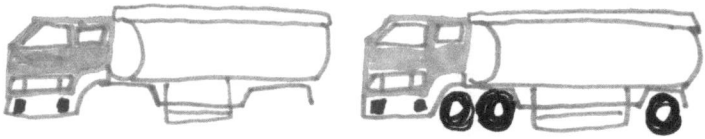

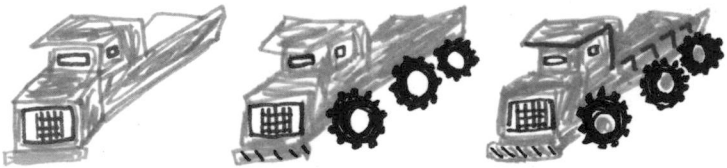

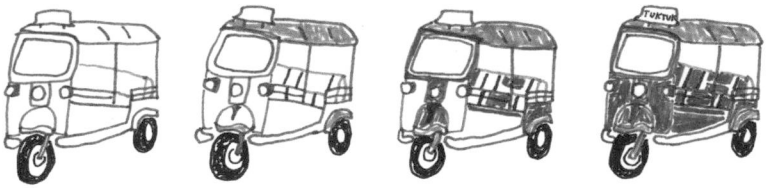
TUKTUK

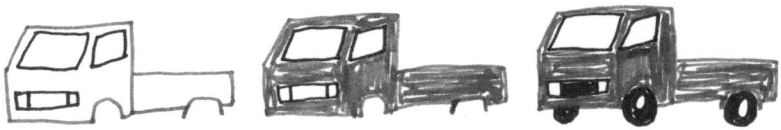

trolley

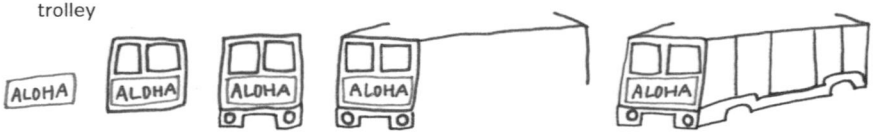


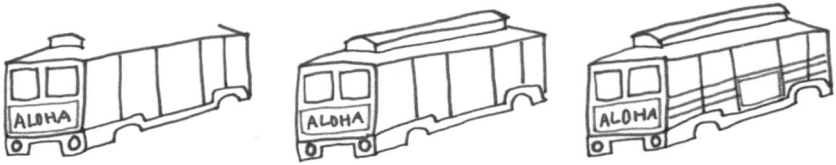


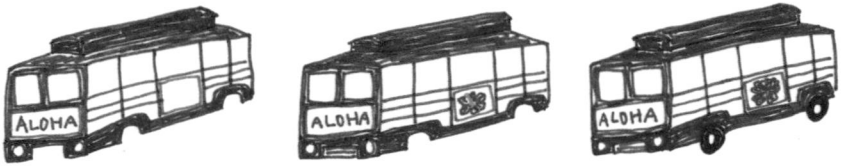


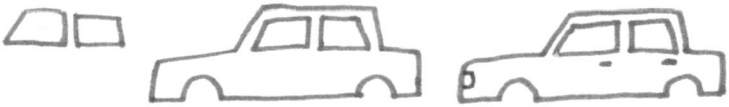

police car

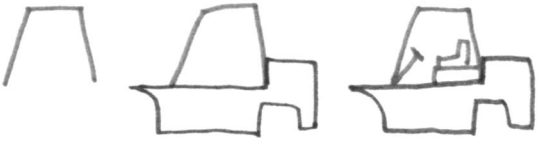

forklift

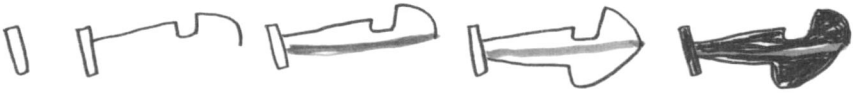

Formula One car

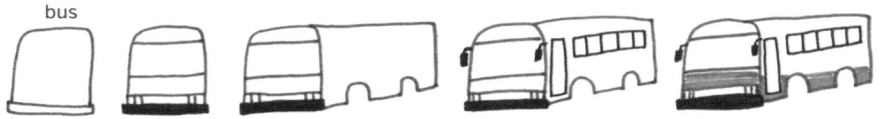
bus

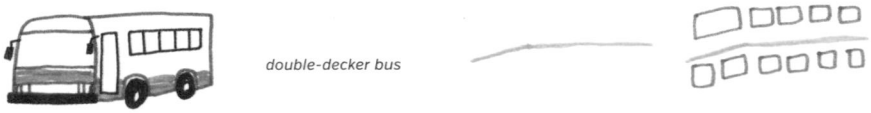
double-decker bus

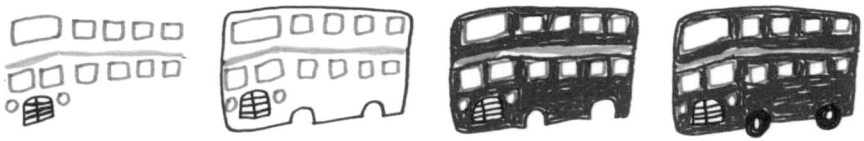

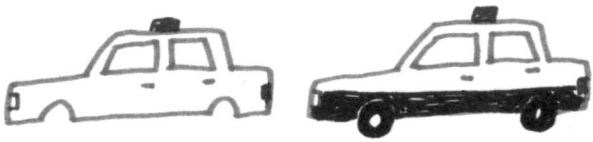

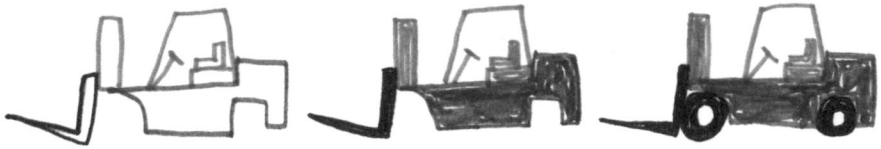

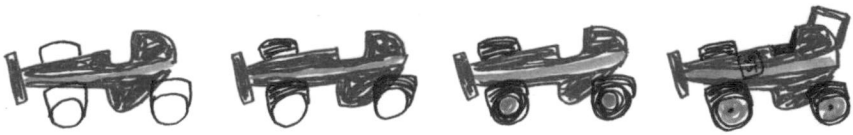

bulldozer

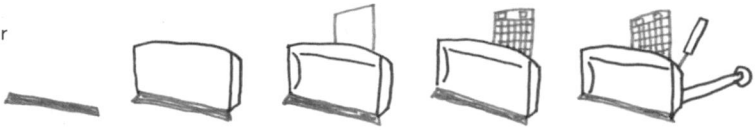

school bus

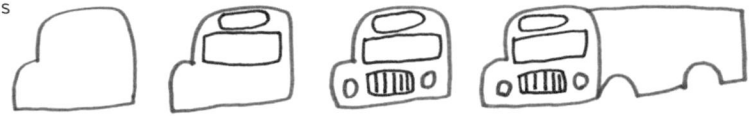

concrete mixer truck

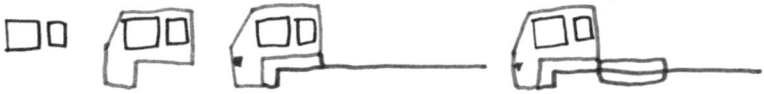

limousine

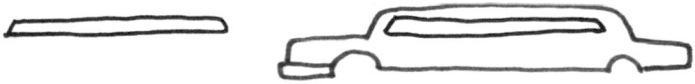

van

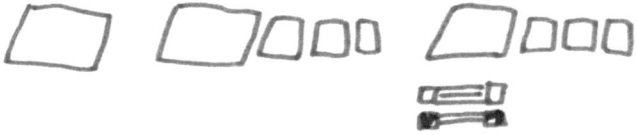

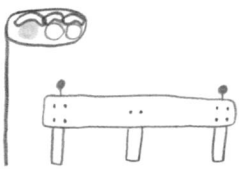

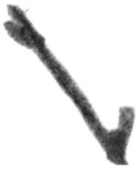

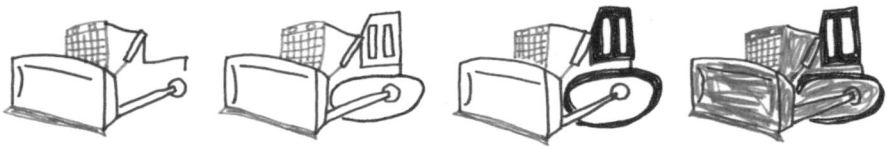

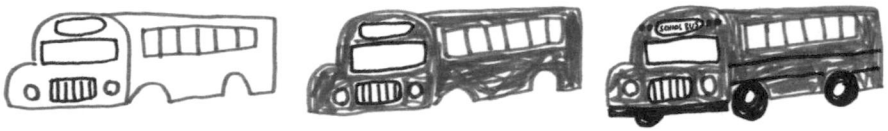

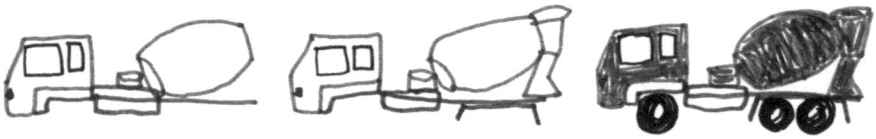

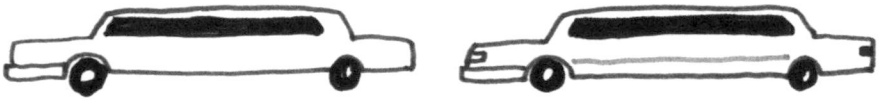

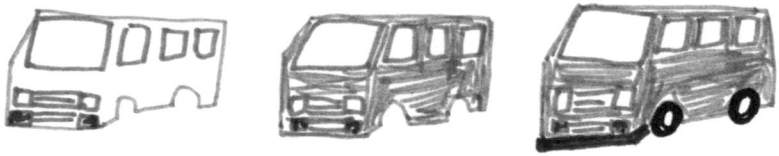

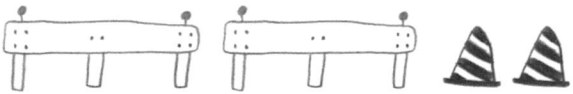

## On the Tracks

*When drawing a train, make the front larger and the back smaller to capture the correct perspective.*

freight train

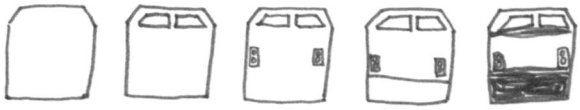

steam locomotive

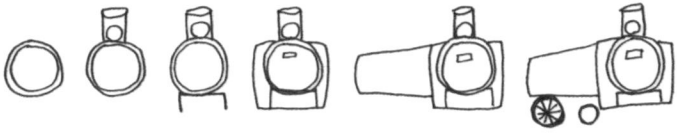

bullet train

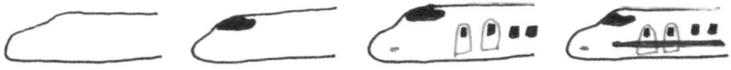

subway

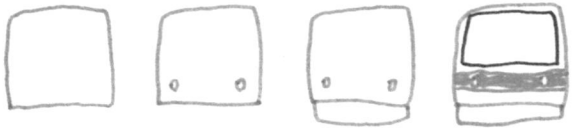

monorail

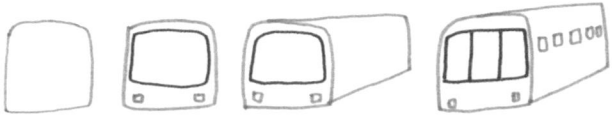

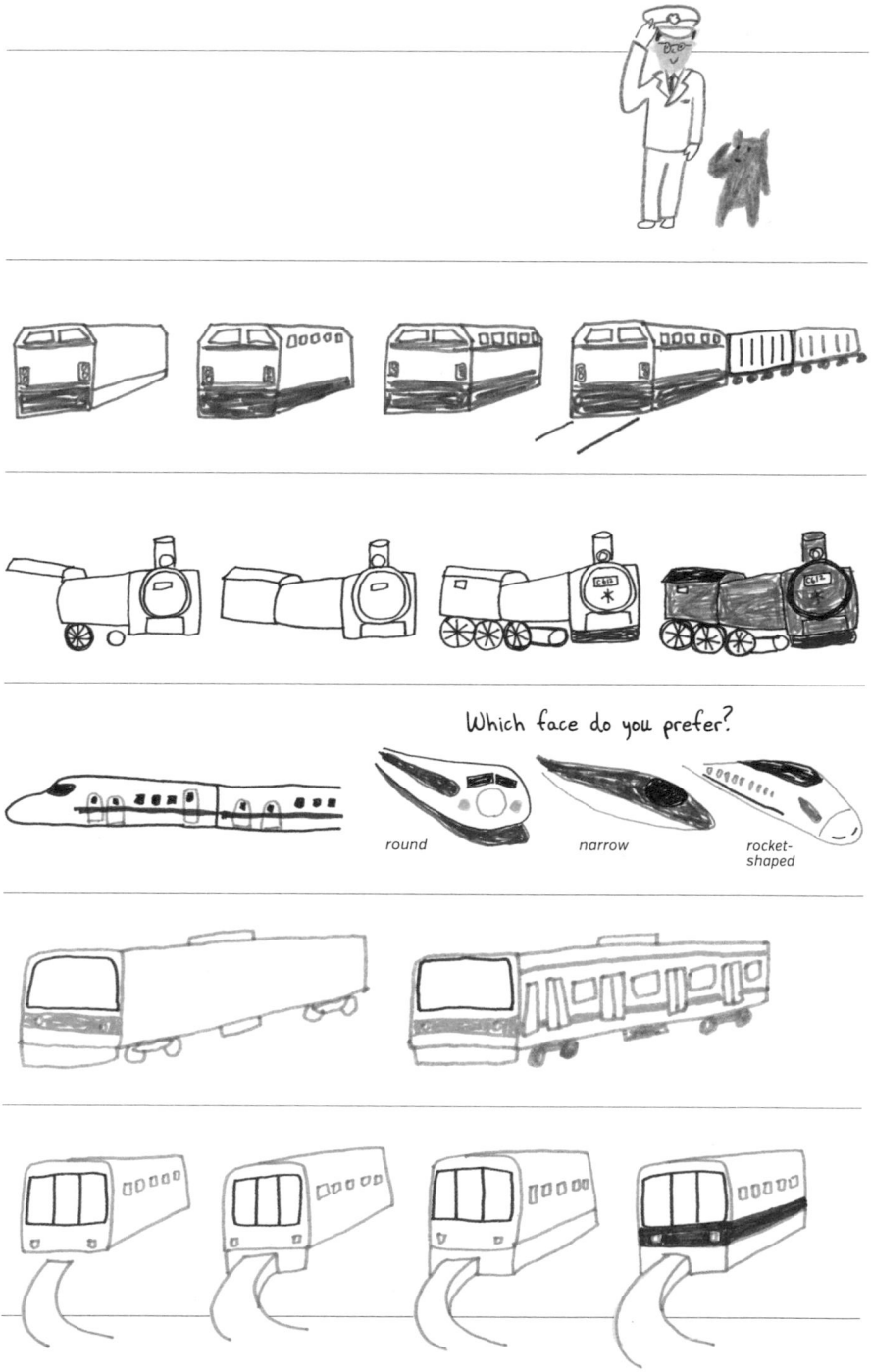
Which face do you prefer?
round
narrow
rocket-shaped

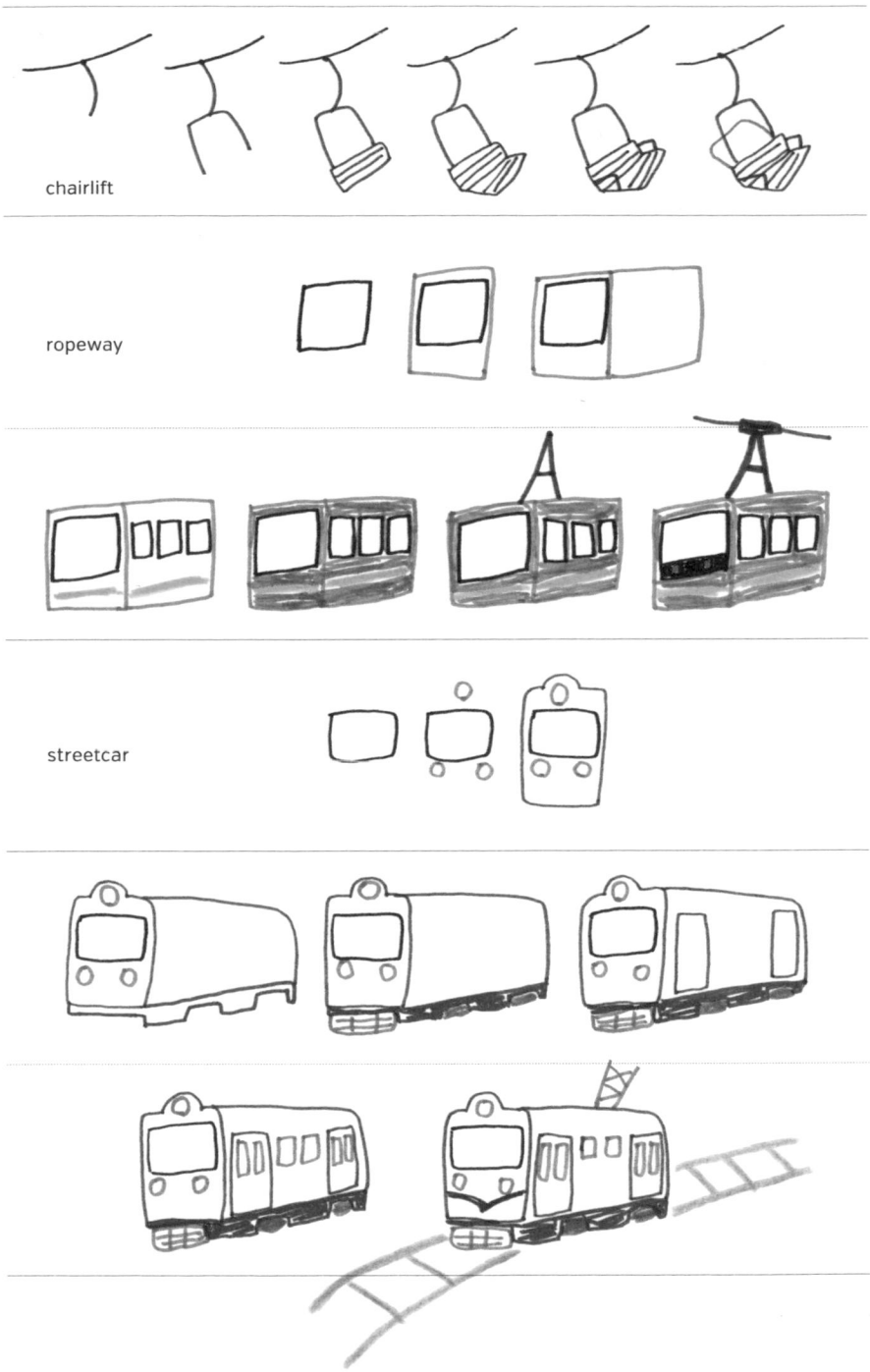
chairlift
ropeway
streetcar

## In the Air

*When drawing aircraft, remember that the sleeker the silhouette, the faster the aircraft can travel.*

International Space Station

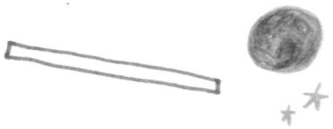

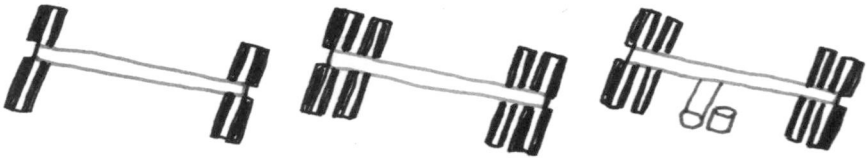

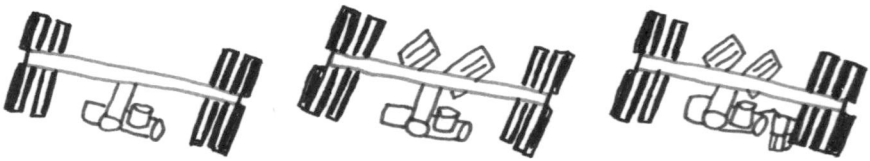

space shuttle

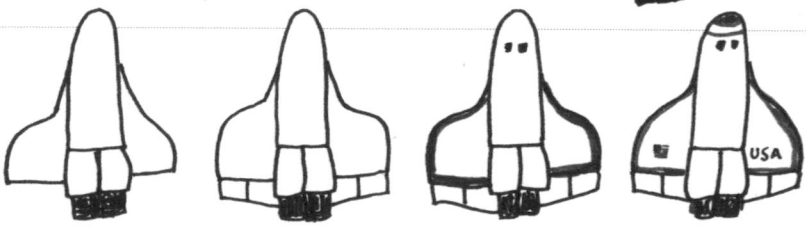

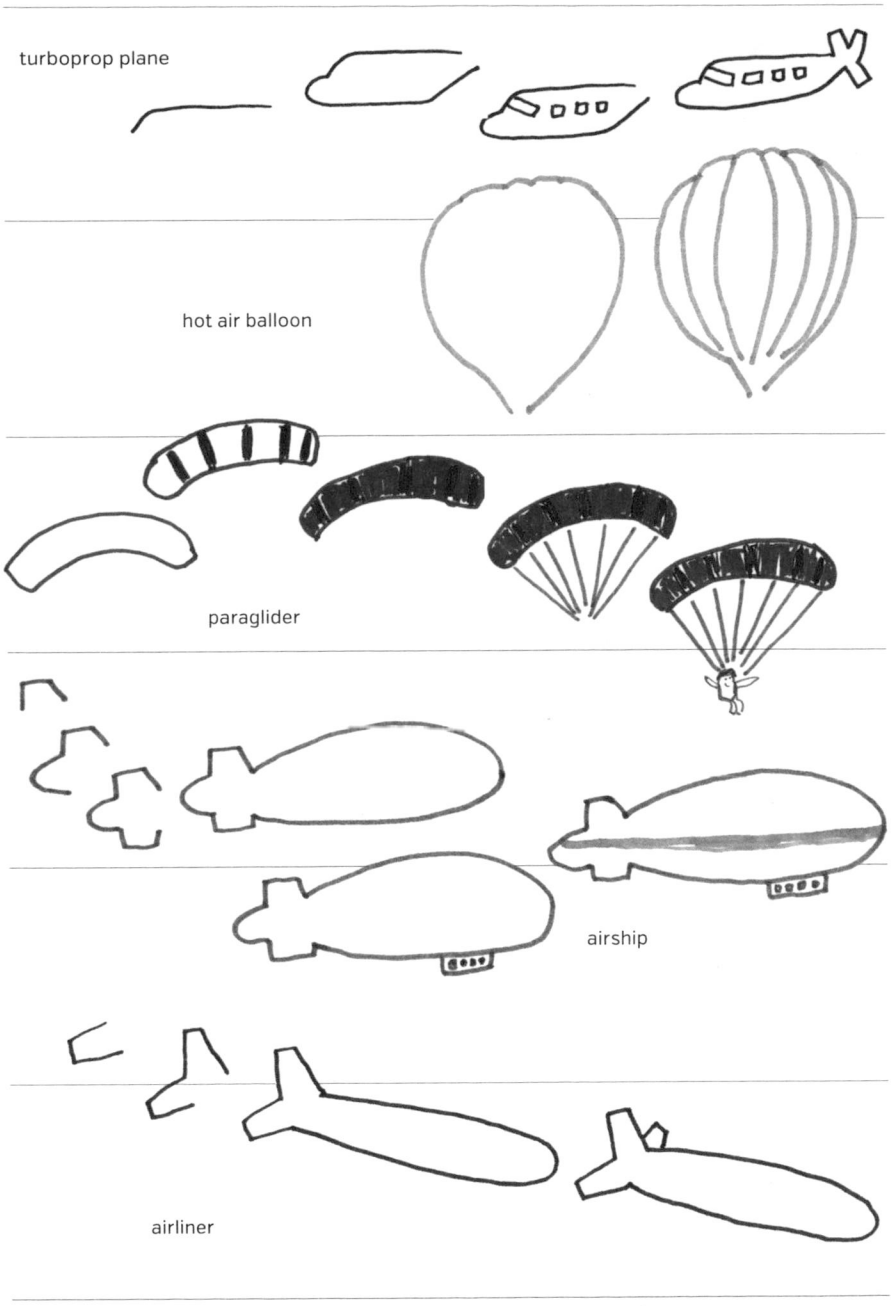
turboprop plane
hot air balloon
paraglider
airship
airliner

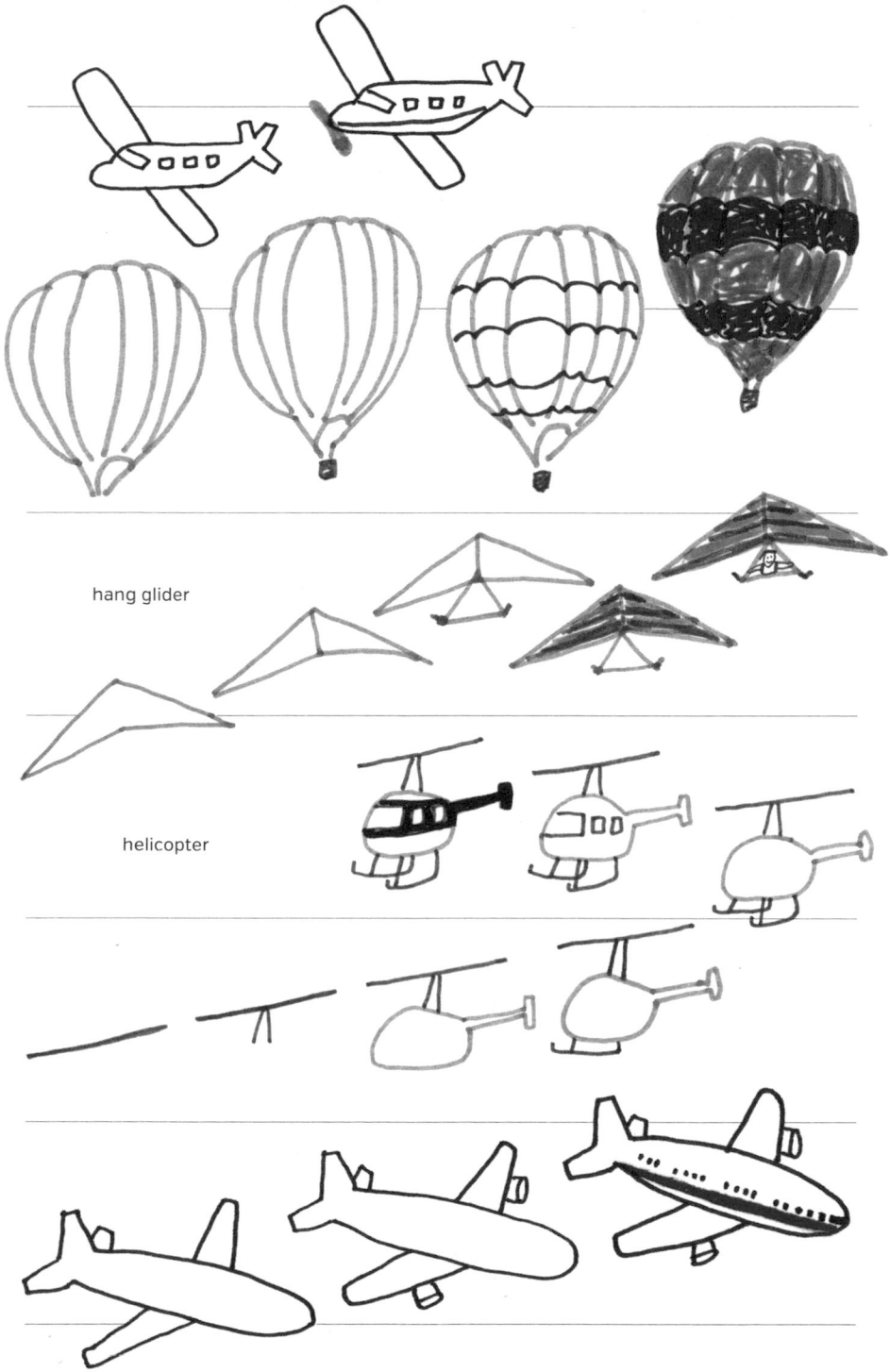
hang glider
helicopter

## CHALLENGE #7:

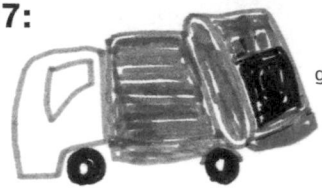

garbage truck at the dump

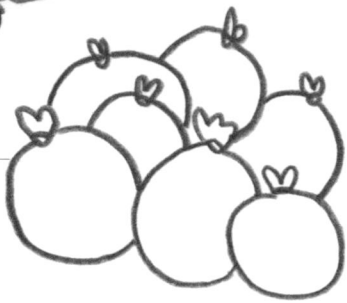

## Draw Vehicles and Landscapes

Although vehicles look cool on their own, they look even better in their working environments. Drawing a vehicle among its surrounding landscape also allows you to suggest motion. Use soft colors for the landscape so the vehicle will stand out.

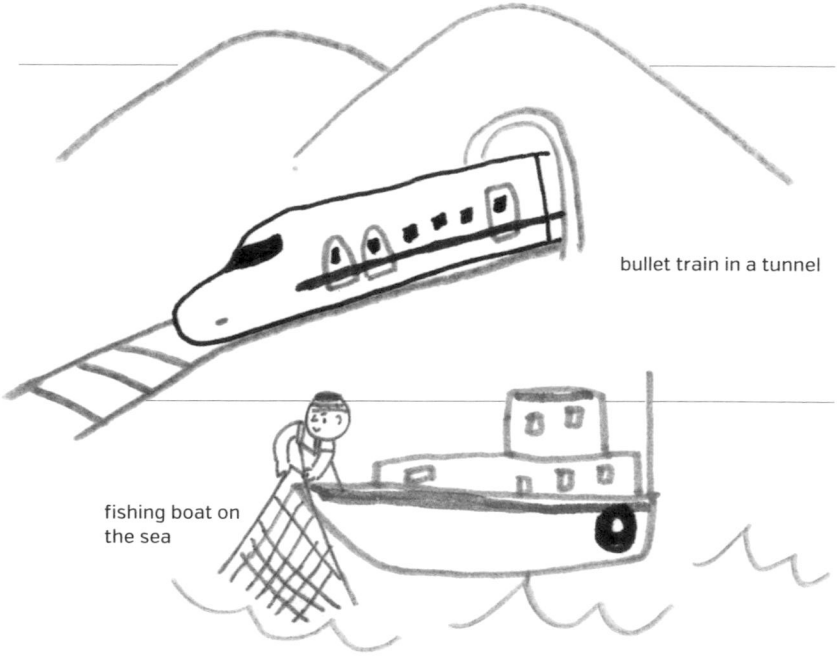

bullet train in a tunnel

fishing boat on the sea

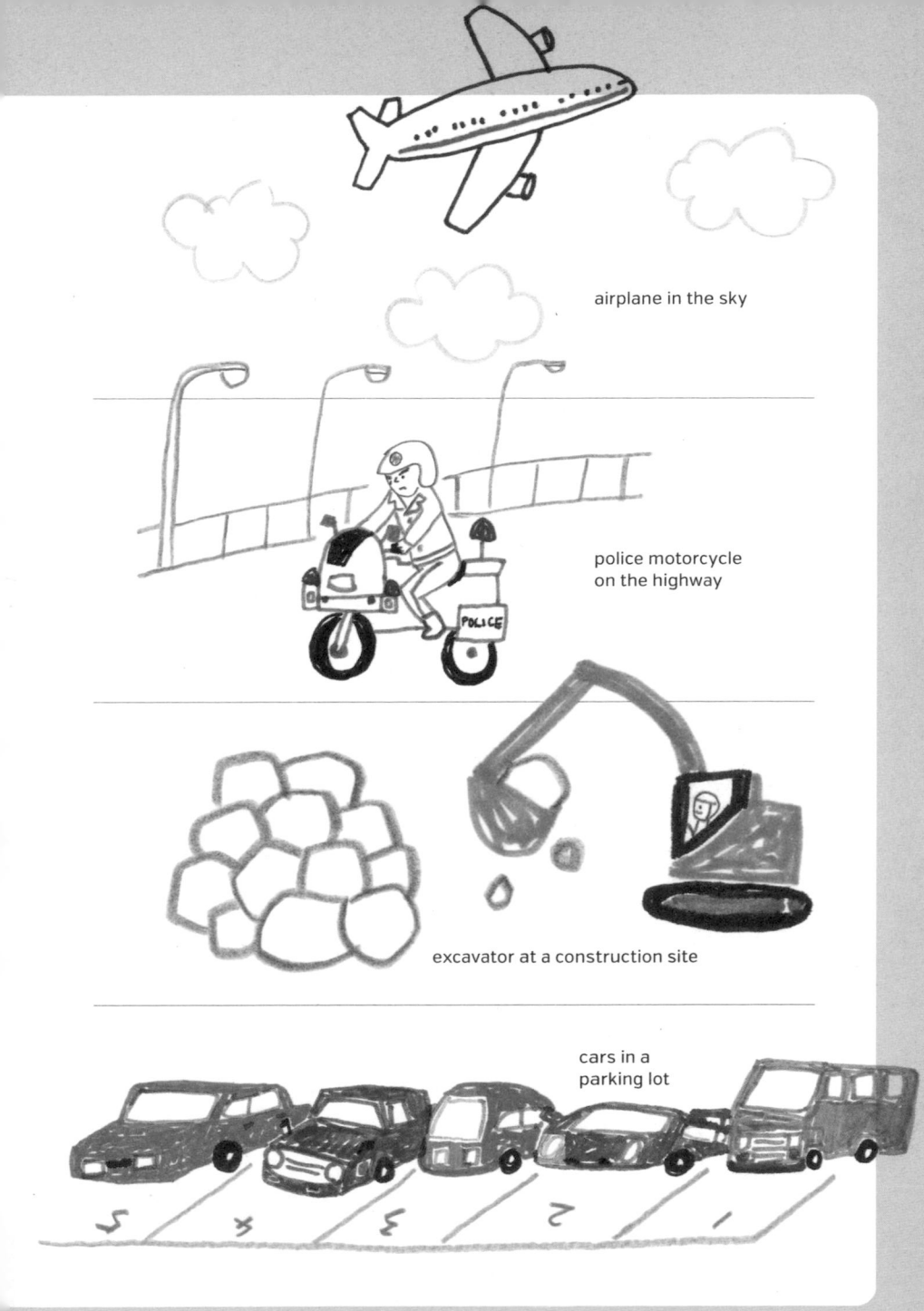


airplane in the sky

police motorcycle
on the highway

excavator at a construction site

cars in a
parking lot

## On the Water

*Draw sharply angled bows to suggest that the boat is moving through the water.*

raft

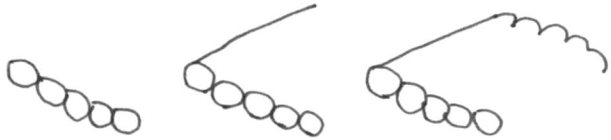

fishing vessel

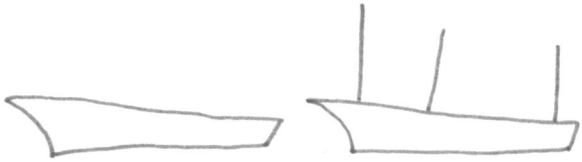

oil tanker

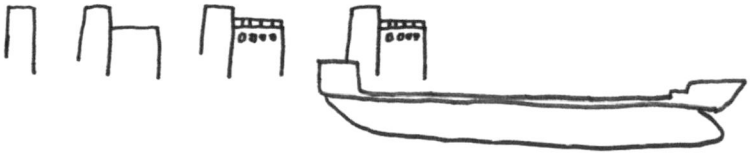

pirate ship

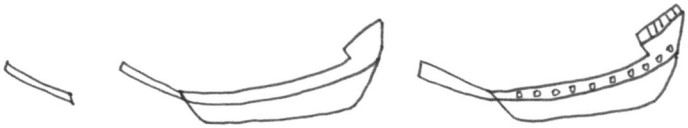

kayak

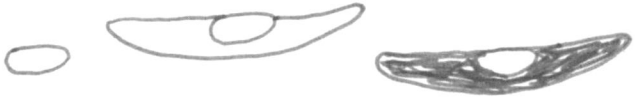

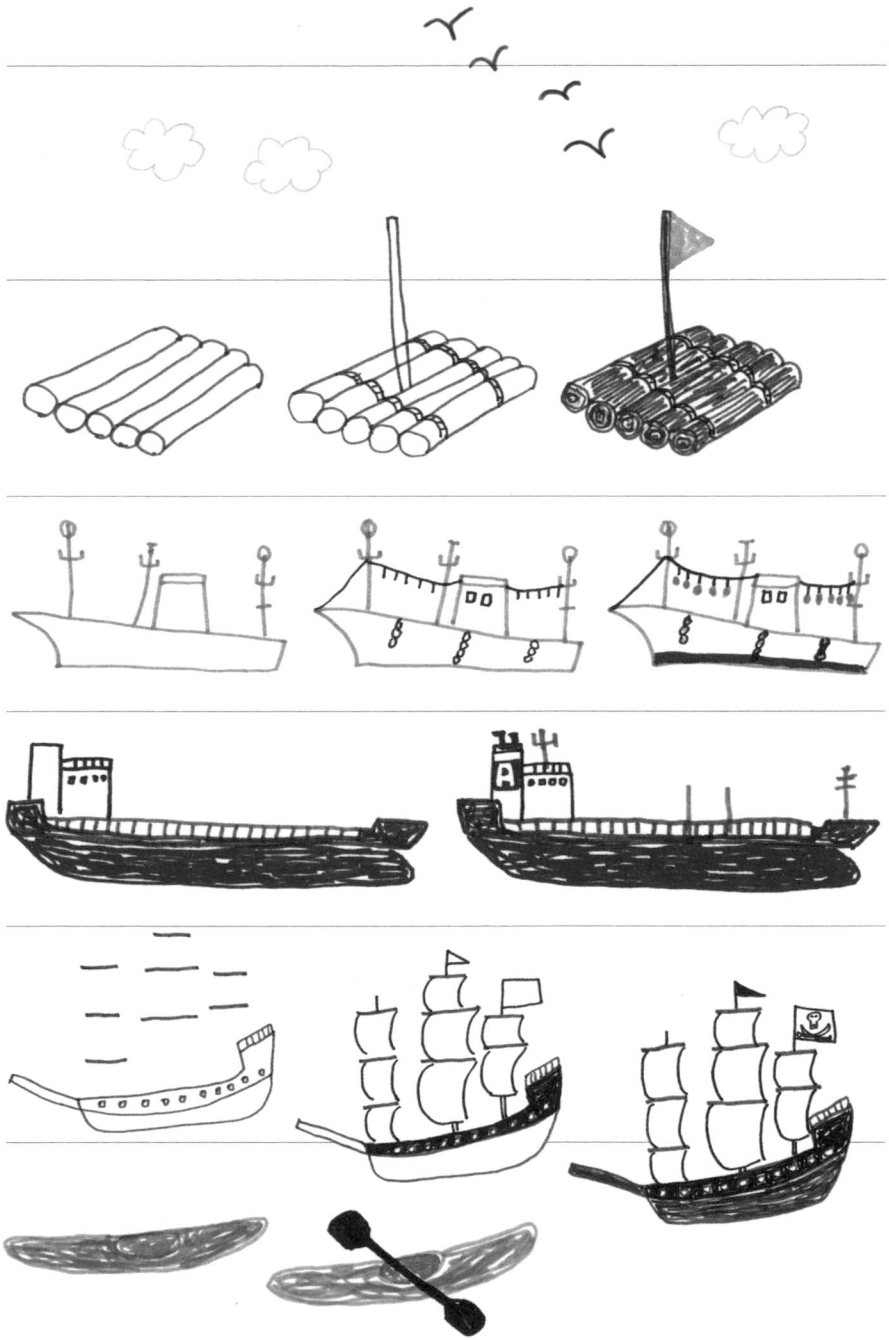

fishing boat

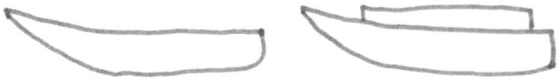

cruise ship

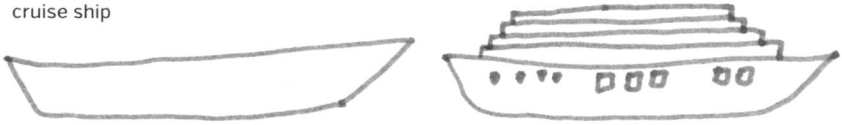

swan boat

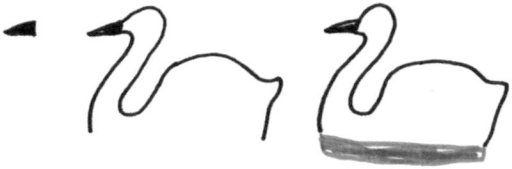

submarine

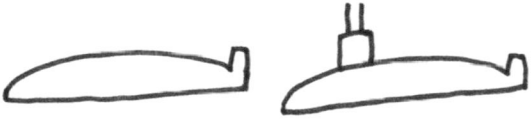

rowboat

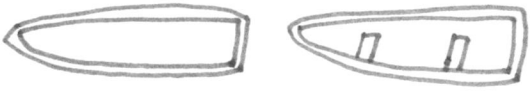

banana boat

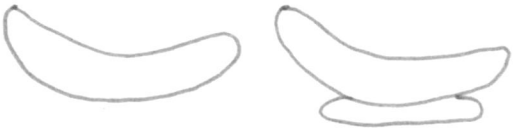

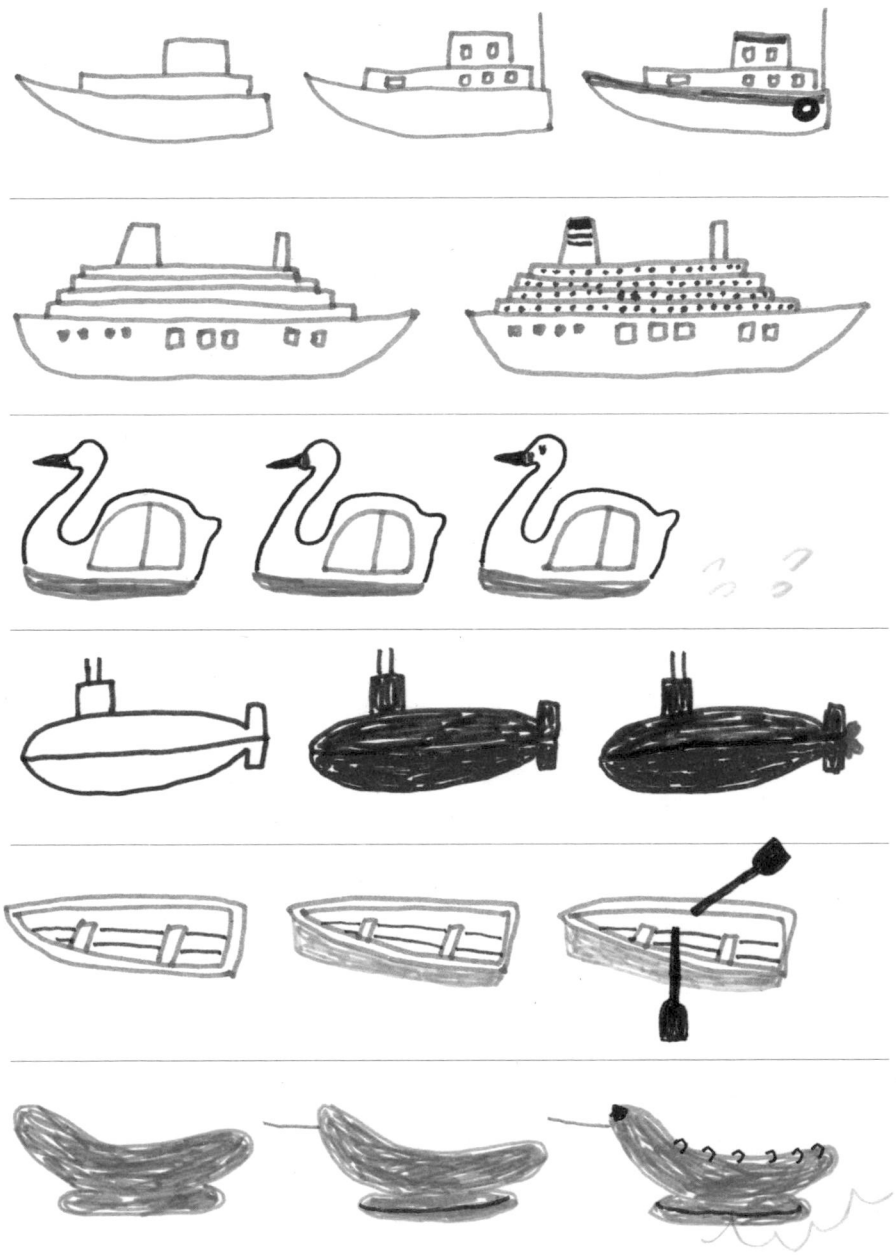

hovercraft

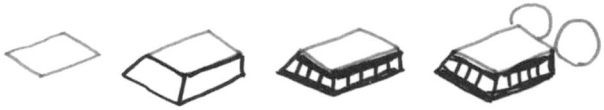

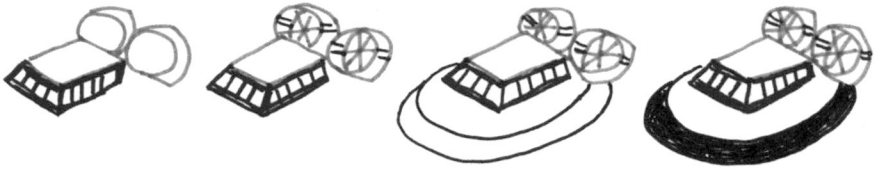

houseboat

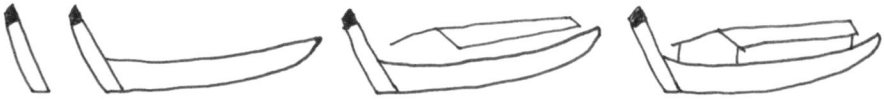

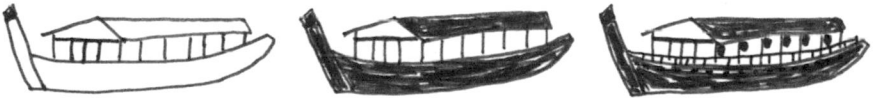

sailboat

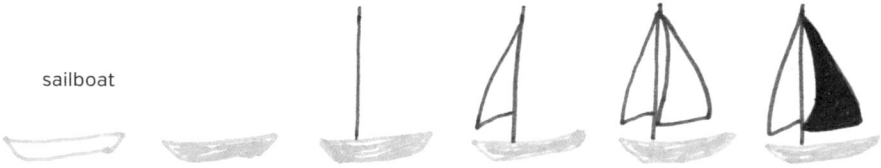

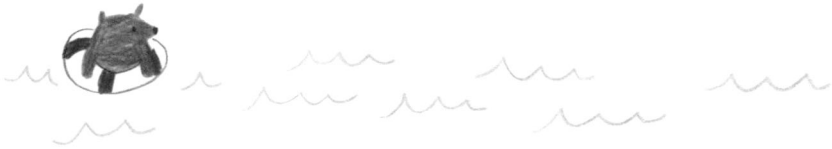

## Other Vehicles

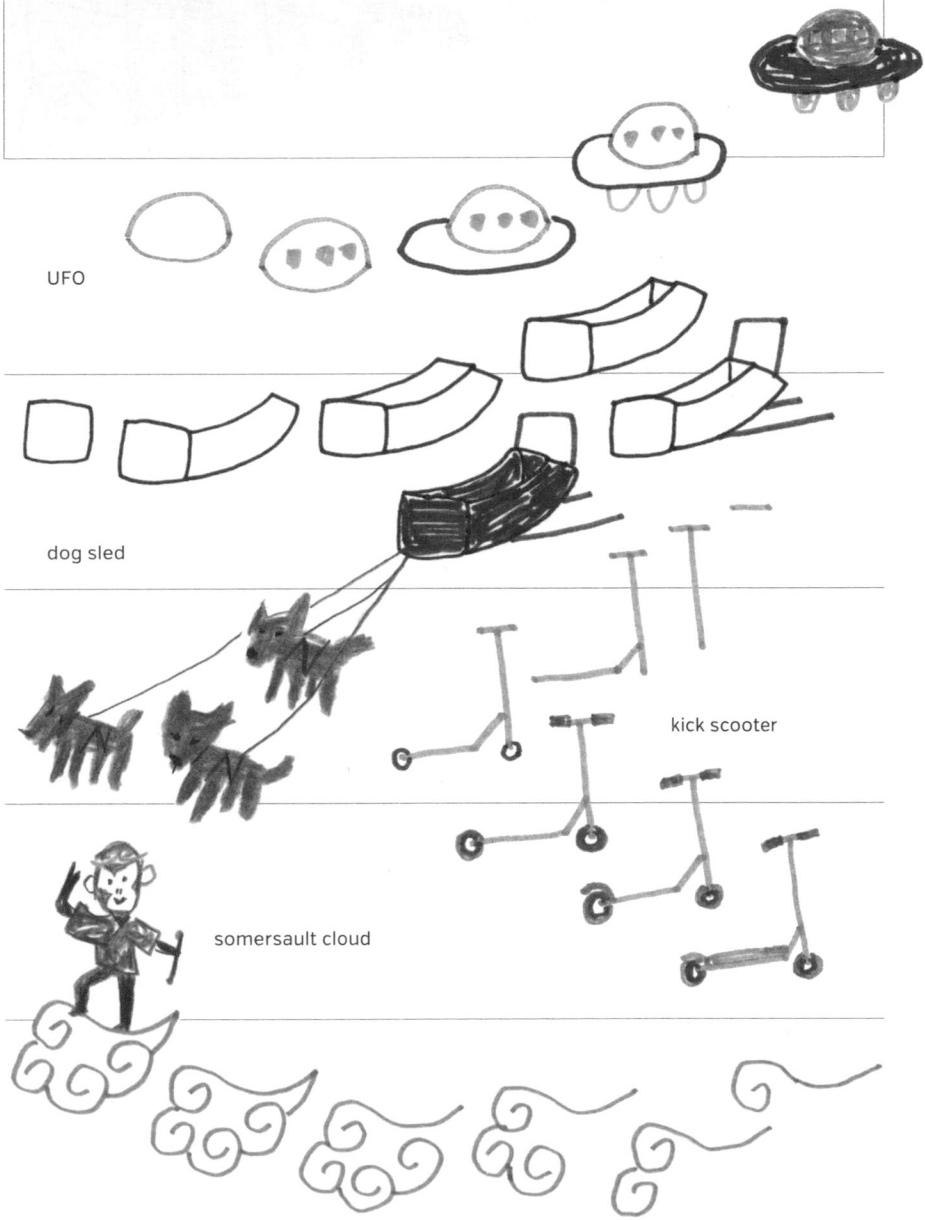

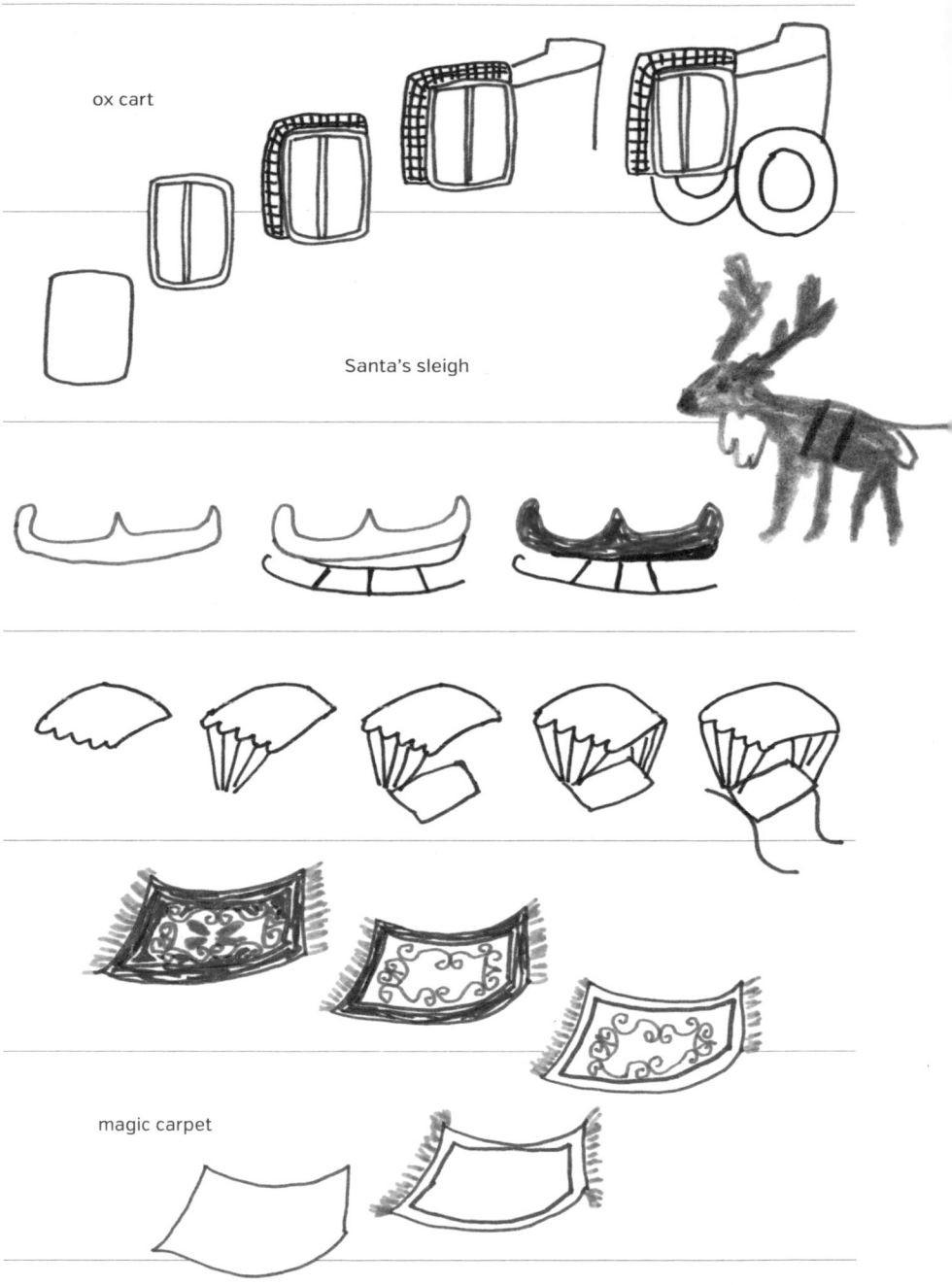
ox cart
Santa's sleigh
magic carpet

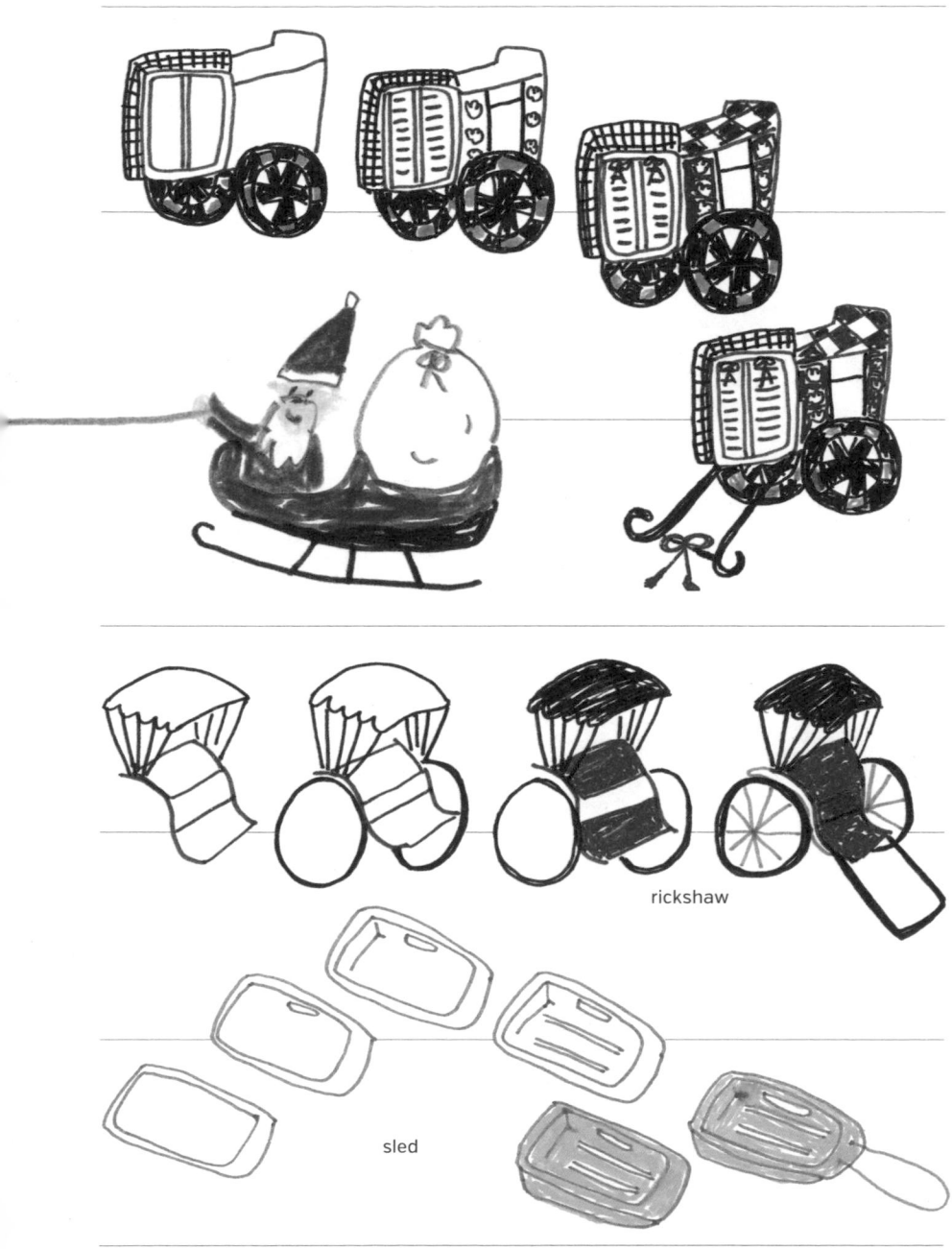
rickshaw
sled

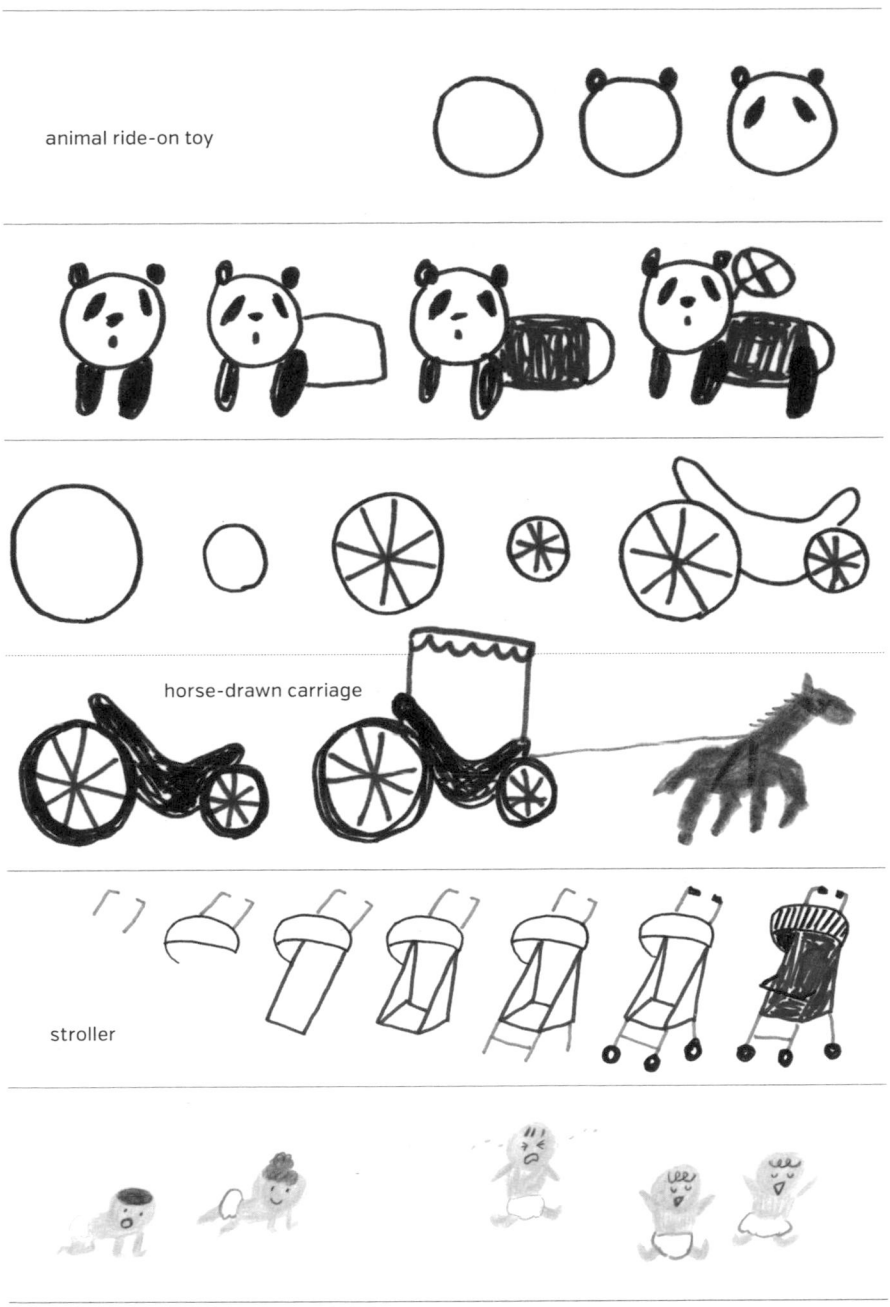
animal ride-on toy
horse-drawn carriage
stroller

# Seasons

- Everyday Events
- Holidays & Seasonal Events
- Weather
- Chinese Zodiac
- Astrological Signs

Use for your date book!

## Everyday Events

*Use simple lines to draw these icons which can be used to illustrate daily life.*

event

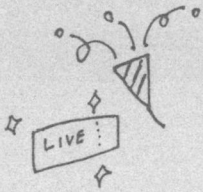


meeting

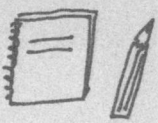

movie

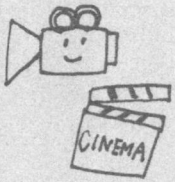


spa day

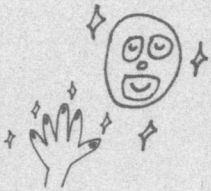

dining out

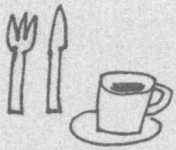

shopping

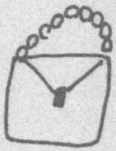

payday

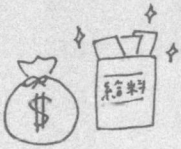


wedding

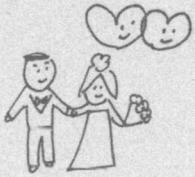

work/study date

travel

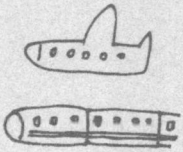

sports game

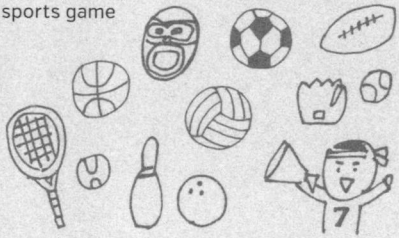

birthday

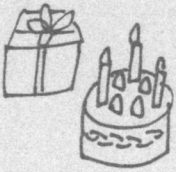

date

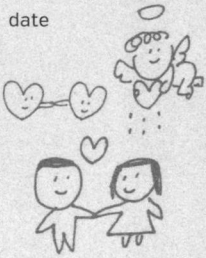

drinks

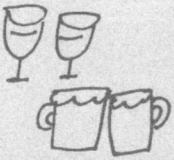

dentist appointment

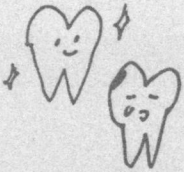

hairdresser appointment

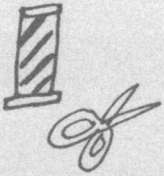

roadtrip

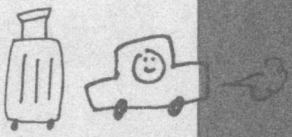

## CHALLENGE #8:

## Illustrate Your Date Book

Add images to your date book or calendar when recording appointments and events. These drawings should be rough, quick sketches rather than precise illustrations. Adding art to your date book makes scheduling your time into a fun activity!

| | |
|---|---|
| 1 mon. | Coffee date at 3:00 pm |
| 2 tue. | |
| 3 wed. | Date night! Take Fido to the dog park! |
| 4 thu. | Drinks at 8:00 pm |
| 5 fri. | Movies at 9:00 pm movie |
| 6 sat. | Dentist appointment at 1:00 pm |
| 7 sun. | Lunch 12:00 pm |
| 8 mon. | Trip to the zoo! |
| 9 tue. | |
| 10 wed. | 12:30 pm Haircut appointment |
| 11 thu. | Wedding at 3:00 pm |
| 12 fri. | Payday! |
| 13 sat. | Drinks at 7:30 pm |

# Holidays & Seasonal Events

*Use these festive illustrations to celebrate the holidays. These designs can be used for greeting cards, invitations, and decorations.*

Valentine's Day

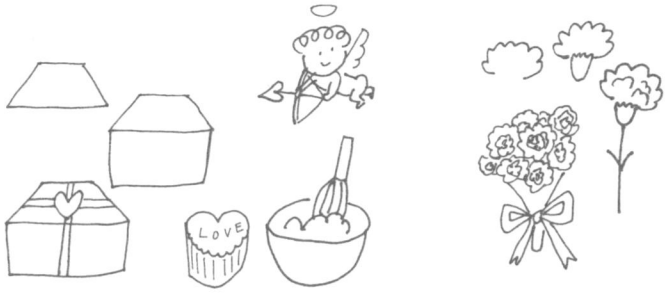


weddings

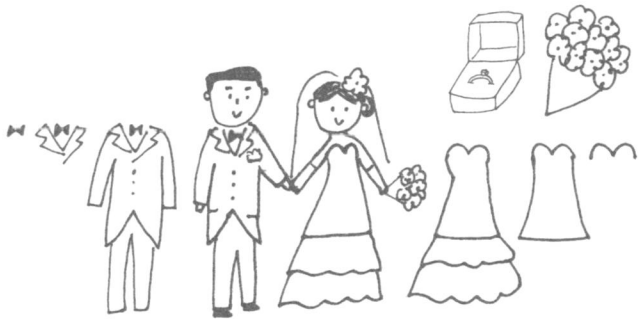

Mother's Day

Father's Day

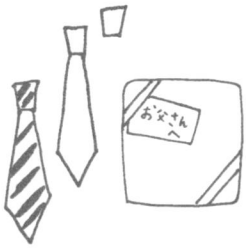

summer vacation

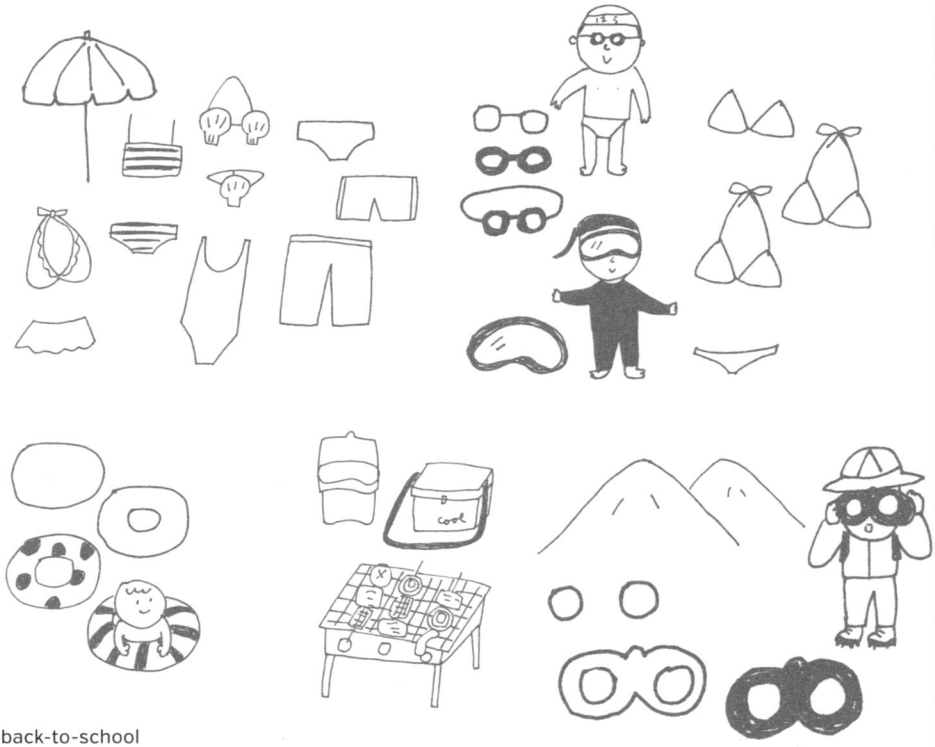


back-to-school

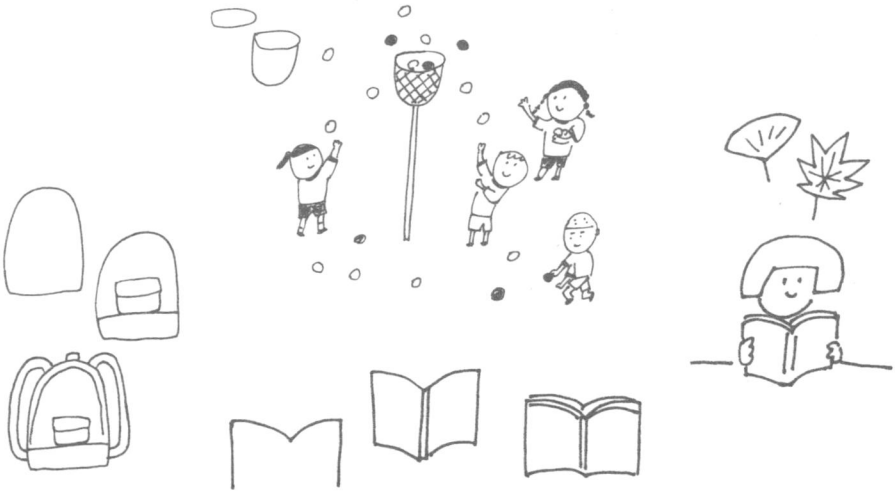

Halloween

Thanksgiving

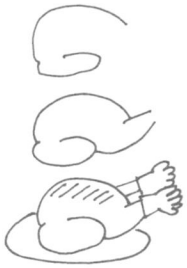

Christmas and winter

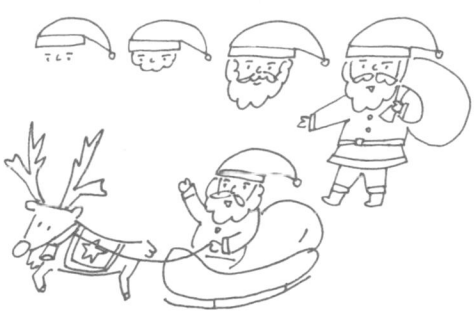

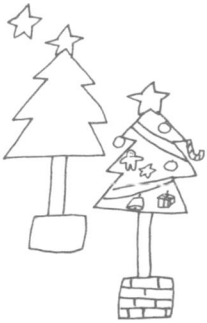

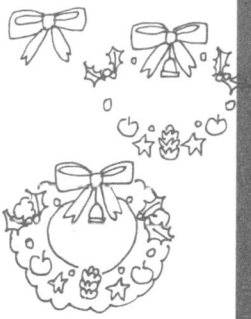

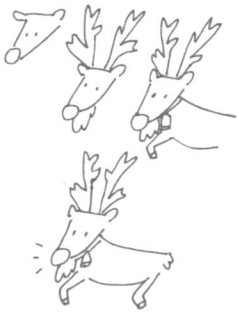

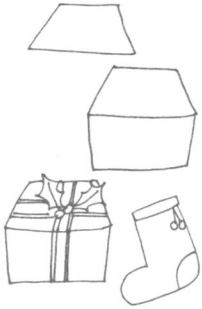

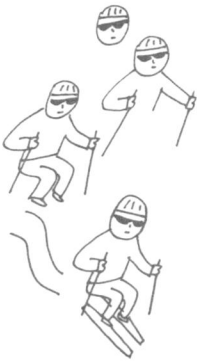

# Weather

*Feel free to mix and match elements from these illustrations to create different weather scenarios.*

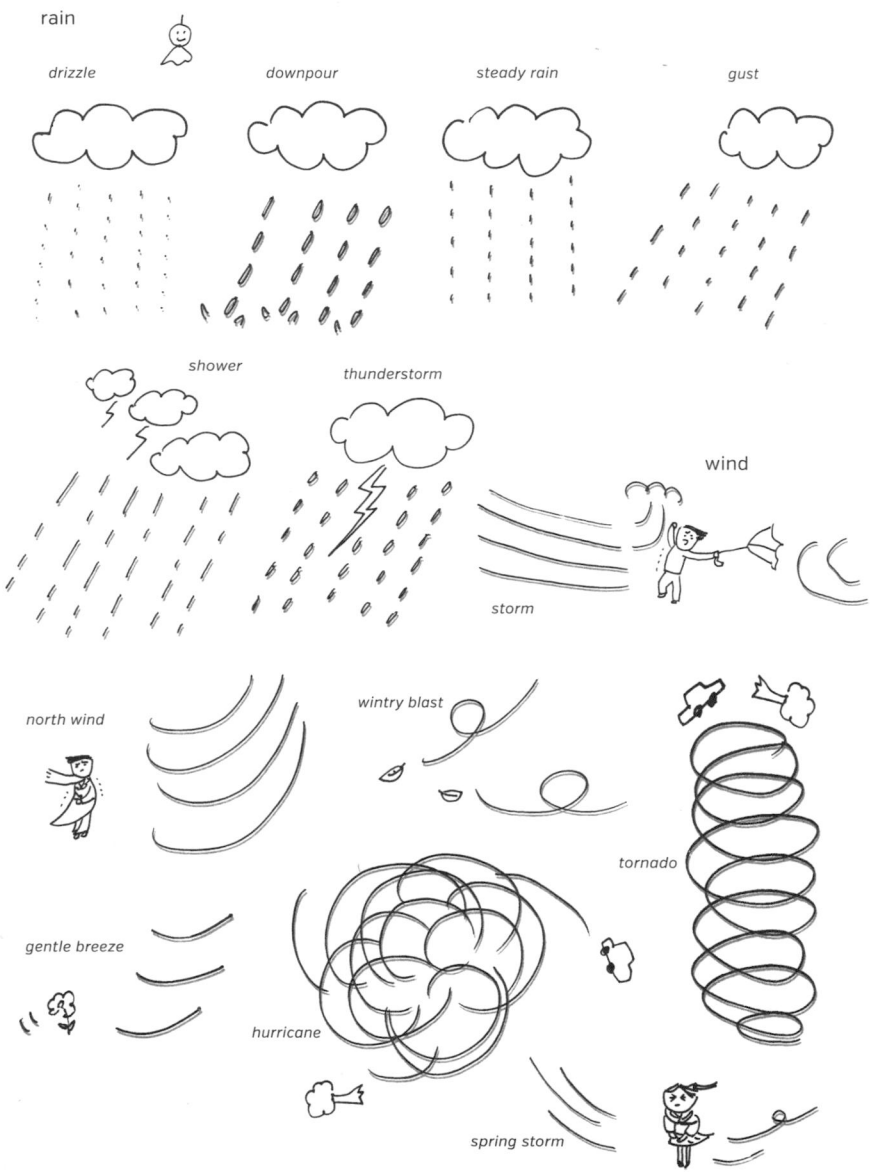

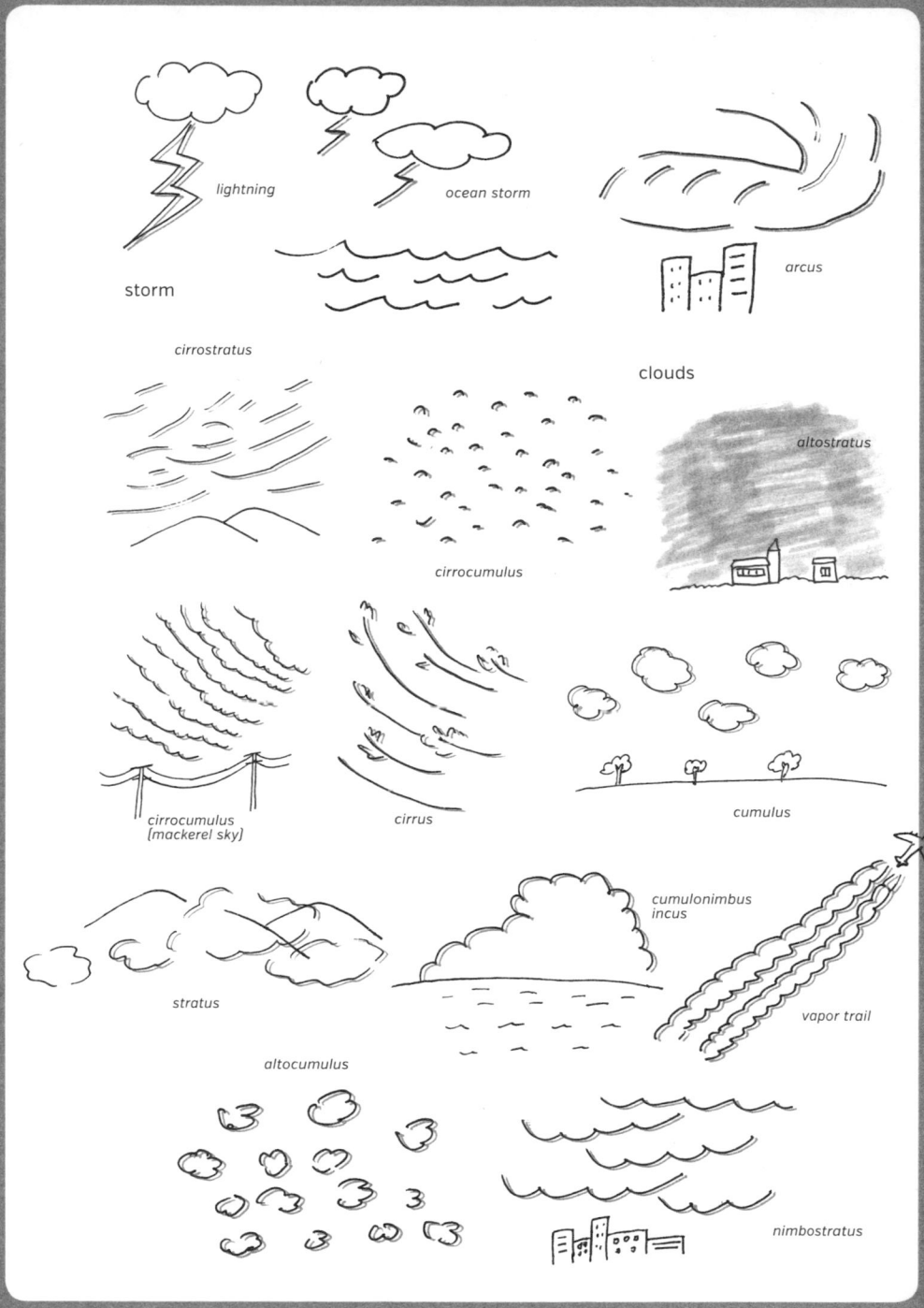
lightning
ocean storm
storm
arcus
cirrostratus
clouds
altostratus
cirrocumulus
cirrocumulus
(mackerel sky)
cirrus
cumulus
cumulonimbus
incus
stratus
vapor trail
altocumulus
nimbostratus

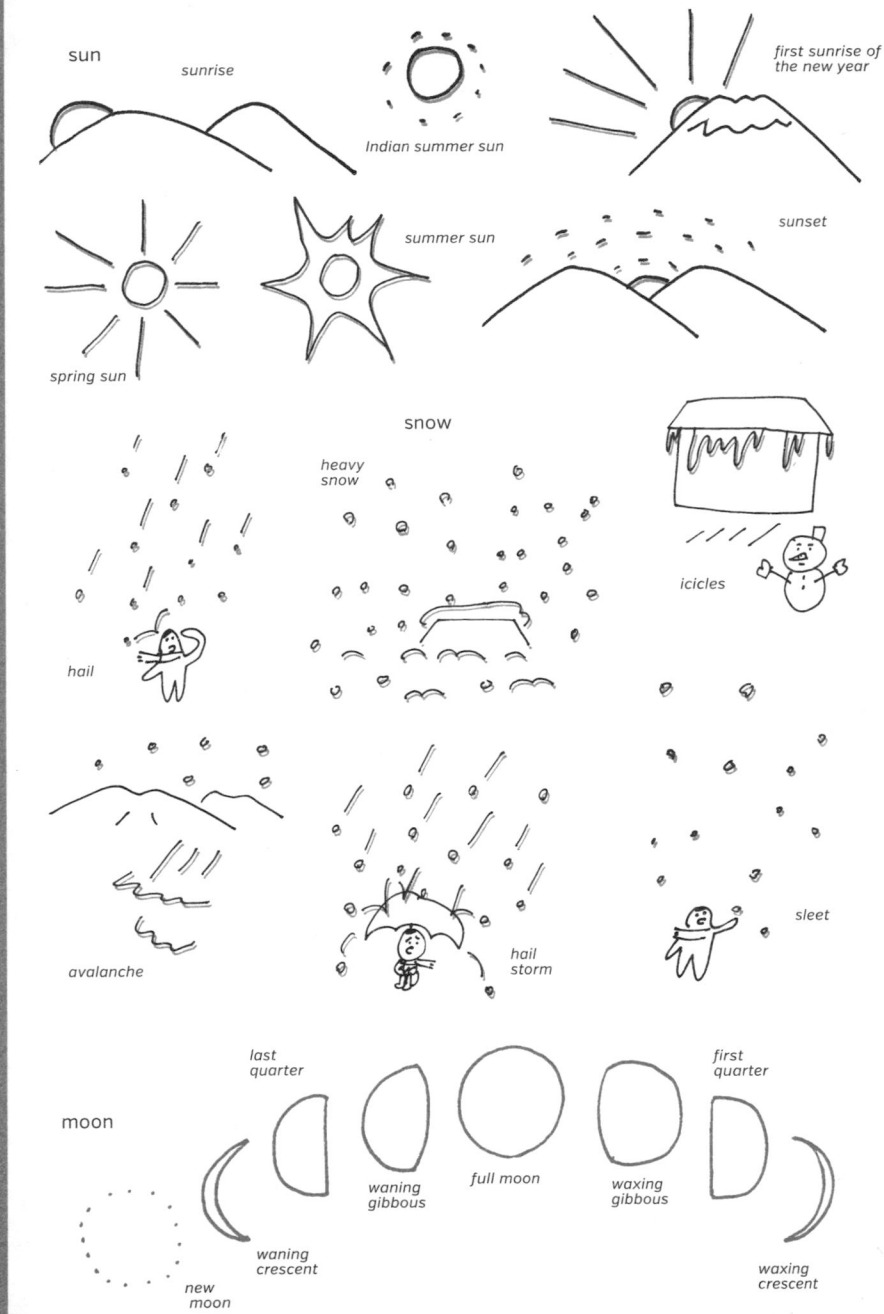
sun
sunrise
Indian summer sun
first sunrise of the new year
spring sun
summer sun
sunset
snow
heavy snow
icicles
hail
avalanche
hail storm
sleet
moon
last quarter
first quarter
waning gibbous
full moon
waxing gibbous
waning crescent
waxing crescent
new moon

## Chinese Zodiac

*Use a brush pen for a more traditional look.*

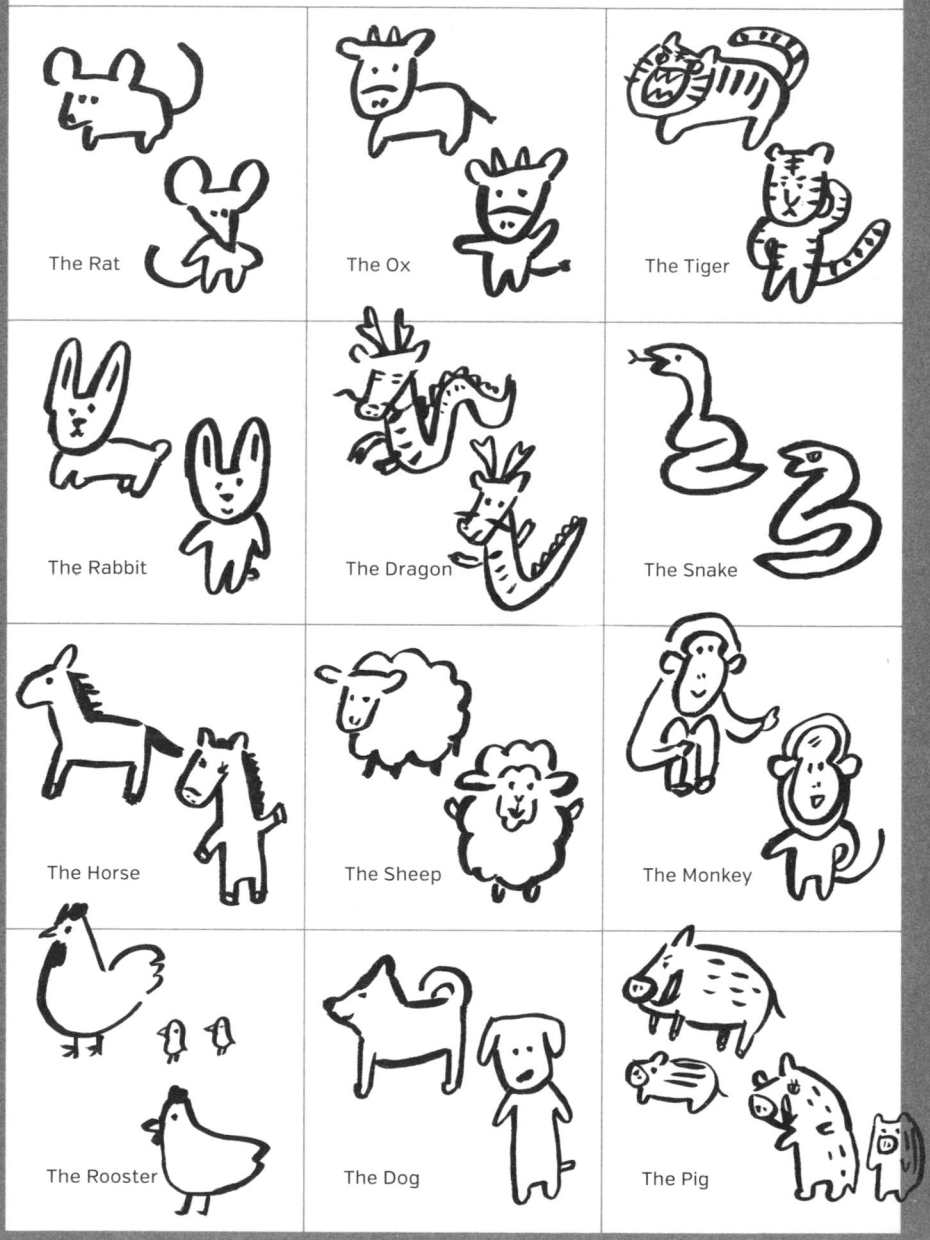

## Astrological Signs

*There's no right or wrong way to draw these astrological signs. Feel free to take artistic liberties, just as you would when illustrating characters in a story.*

Aries

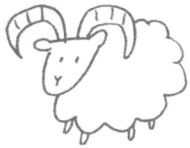

Taurus

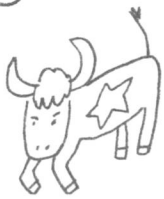

Gemini

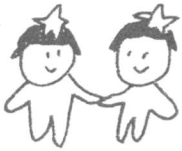

Cancer

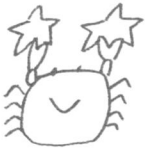

Leo

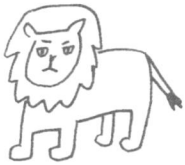

Virgo

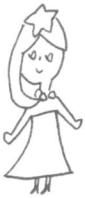

Libra

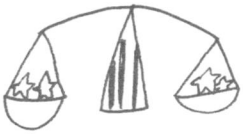

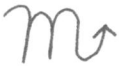
Scorpio

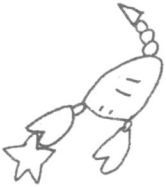

Sagittarius

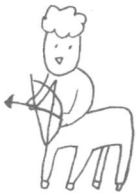

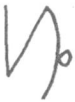
Capricorn

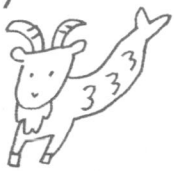

Aquarius

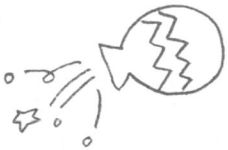

Pisces

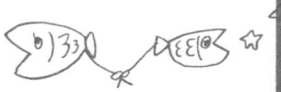

# CHALLENGE #9:

## Draw Scenes from Your Favorite Movies

I love drawing scenes from classic movies because the clothing, cars, and other props have such a unique style. Sketch scenes from your favorite movies. I've included a few of mine as inspiration.

The Godfather

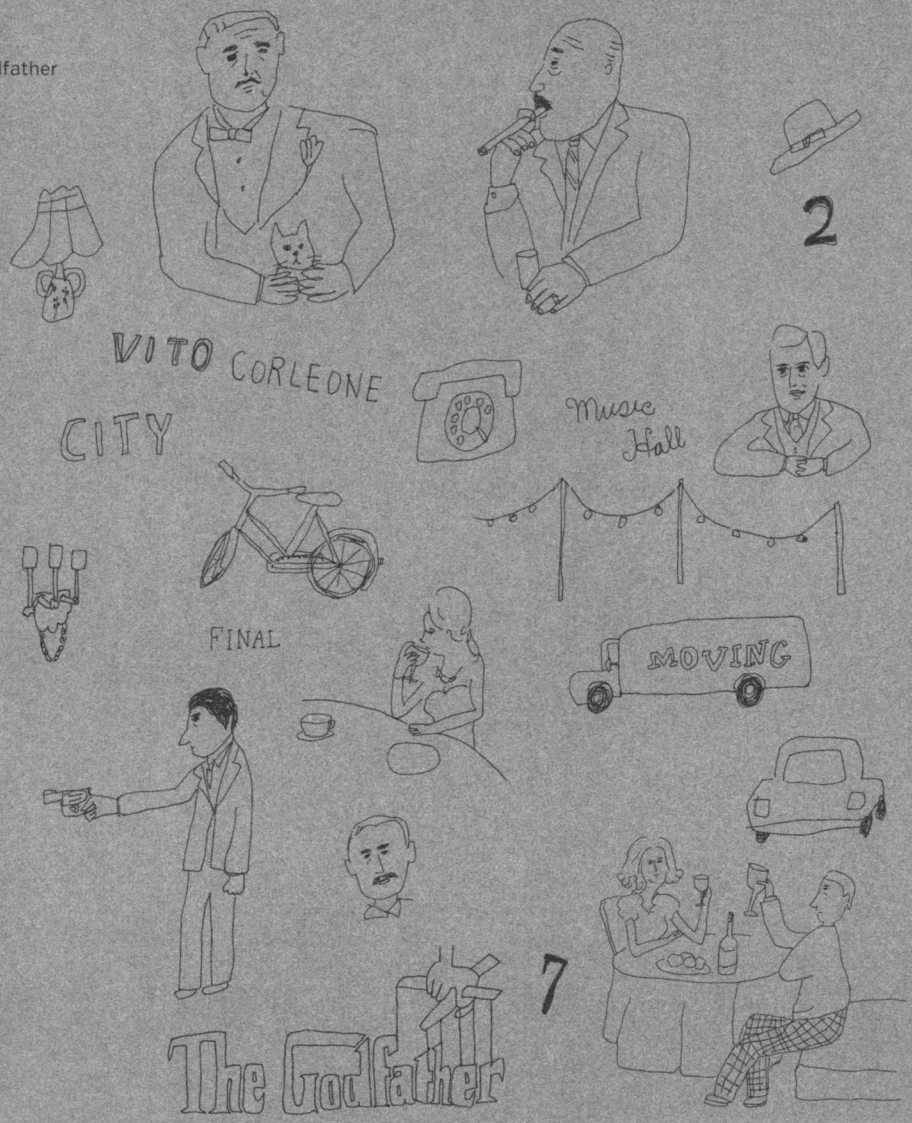

# CHALLENGE #10:

## Animal Alphabet

I enjoy incorporating artwork into text, so I designed this alphabet featuring animals. Feel free to use this alphabet, or have fun designing your own!

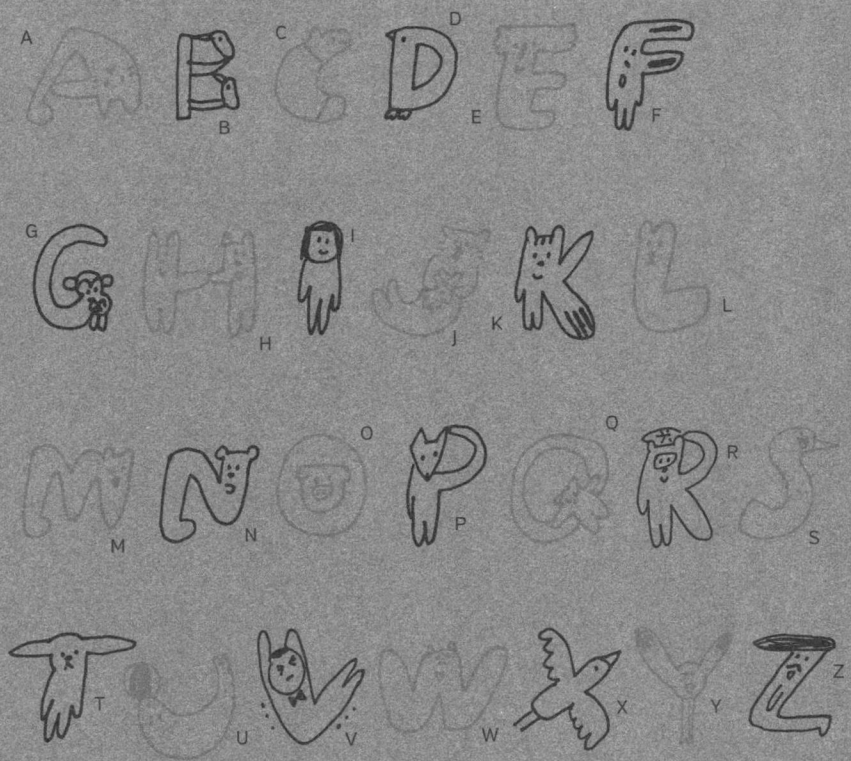

# Author's Note

When I was younger, I loved to visit Inokashira Nature and Culture Park, in Tokyo. The park includes a wonderful zoo that is home to many animals, including Hanako the elephant. Every time I visited the zoo, I would always see the same man outside Hanako's enclosure. Eventually, I began drawing Hanako and her friend.

When I look back at those drawings in my sketchbook, I am filled with happiness. No two drawings look alike—each sketch features different lines, angles, and colors. It is almost as if these drawings captured my emotions at the time. To me, that is the most interesting aspect of drawing.

Have fun sketching and don't worry about perfection. In my opinion, the most interesting drawings are the ones with crooked lines or the ones with lines that extend beyond the edge of the paper. I love children's artwork because they draw without following any rules.

I will be happy if at least one person who does not consider themselves to be a good artist picks up this book and says "drawing is not so hard after all. It is actually quite fun!"

—Chika Miyata

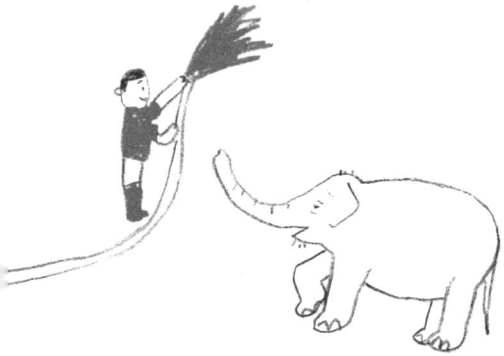